Understanding Cultural Diversity

Culture, Curriculum, and Community in Nursing

NLN PRESS SERIES

Understanding Cultural Diversity

Culture, Curriculum, and Community in Nursing

Mary Lebreck Kelley, MSN, MEd, RN
Virginia Macken Fitzsimons, EdD, RNC

JONES AND BARTLETT PUBLISHERS
Sudbury, Massachusetts
BOSTON   TORONTO   LONDON   SINGAPORE

World Headquarters
Jones and Bartlett Publishers
40 Tall Pine Drive
Sudbury, MA 01776
978-443-5000
info@jbpub.com
www.jbpub.com

Jones and Bartlett Publishers Canada
2100 Bloor Street West
Suite 6-272
Toronto, ON M6S 5A5
CANADA

Jones and Bartlett Publishers International
Barb House, Barb Mews
London W6 7PA
UK

PRODUCTION CREDITS
SENIOR ACQUISITIONS EDITOR   Greg Vis
PRODUCTION EDITOR   Linda S. DeBruyn
MANUFACTURING BUYER   Kristen Guevara
TEXT DESIGN   Argosy
EDITORIAL PRODUCTION SERVICE   Argosy
TYPESETTING   Argosy
COVER DESIGN   Anne Spencer
PRINTING AND BINDING   Braun-Brumfield

Library of Congress Cataloging-in-Publication Data
Understanding cultural diversity : culture, curriculum, and community
  in nursing / [edited by] Mary Lebreck Kelley, Virginia Macken
  Fitzsimons.
       p.   cm.
    At head of title: NLN Press.
    Includes bibliographical references and index.
    ISBN 0-7637-1106-3 (pbk.)
    1. Medical education—Philosophy.   2. Medical personnel—Study and
  teaching.   3. Interdisciplinary approach in education.   I. Kelley,
  Mary Lebreck.   II. Fitzsimons, Virginia Macken, 1943–   .
  R737.U55   2000
  610.71'1—DC21   99-29470
                                                                        CIP

Printed in the United States of America
02 01 00 99   10 9 8 7 6 5 4 3 2 1

Contents

PART ONE: CULTURE

PART FOUR: ADMINISTRATIVE METAPHORS: TUGBOATS REVISITED

This book is dedicated to

Todd and Michael Kelley

and

Neil and Christine Fitzsimons

ONE

Let your culture live
   and let live

Give us your stories
   and songs of ago

We'll swirl and dance
   in the radiance

With hearts and souls
   painted rainbow

Let your history learn
   and let tell

The tales and trials of
   peoples proud

Love and live free in
   hope and harmony

The voices of many made one
   and raised loud.

Daniel R. Collins

Acknowledgments

Projects with the scope and complexity of the Transcultural Leadership Continuum (TLC) project were impossible without extensive conceptual and financial support. We continue to be grateful to the Robert Wood Johnson Foundation, Inc. for its generosity and its recognition of minority nurse access, retention, and mobility as essential to building a dynamic and effective health care system.

The BARD Foundation, Inc., provided early seed money as our master's program in clinical administration with a transcultural nursing perspective was being developed. While the grants themselves have been over for some time, the concepts and inquiry they supported have been institutionalized in our agencies.

Special thanks to the students, faculty, administration, and staff of Kean University for their support and participation in this project from the very beginning of our plans for our graduate program.

Special thanks also to the students, faculty, administration, and staff of the Cooperative Nursing program at the Elizabeth General Medical Center School of Nursing and Union County College for their initiative and commitment to improving the health status of their community.

And a very special thank-you to the authors who have contributed to this book. It was our privilege to work with you on this project. Your time, research, expertise, and commitment to students are very much appreciated.

MK & VF

Foreword

DAVID M. GIBSON

Education should be dispensed and acquired through a multiplicity of means. All kinds of existing institutions, whether designed for teaching or not, and many forms of social and economic activity, must be used for educational purposes. The important thing is not the path an individual has followed, but what he has learned or acquired.

—*Faure, E. et al.* (1972). Learning to Be: The World of Education Today and Tomorrow. *New York: Unipub, p. 185.*

Although much of this book is dedicated to health professions education, it is not an exaggeration to note that many of the chapters, if not all of them, pertain in the deepest sense to teaching and learning in our pluralistic society regardless of the disciplines. Even such issues as managed care or men's health-care have a major impact on how we teach, what we teach, to whom we teach, and surely where we teach. Faure's observation quoted above has an even more riveting imperative today than it did some twenty-five years ago. The classroom is not by any means fixed by walls and chalkboards: It is in small and large communities, in the basements of churches, recreation centers, public housing units, hospitals, and hospices. In effect, the world is the classroom.

The authors in this work seek to uncover the cultural and philosophical underpinnings of the teaching-learning experience and the dynamics of curricular responses to changes within our society. They recognize the central role of faculty in delivering instruction in ways that are most understandable to culturally, gender-, and age-mixed groups of students. They suggest ways in which the faculty members themselves, too, are learners as they seek to understand and implement teaching styles and techniques that will best provide their students with a rich and challenging education. The authors also embrace the moral imperative for integrity, competency, and compassion to be seeded in the curriculum and imbedded in the very souls of students who will one day practice the healing arts. It is no mean challenge.

The tripartite mission of education, research, and service dear to almost every college and university needs to be made incarnate and whole. It is rendered the former through the daily interactions of faculty and students side by side learning and teaching and touching our neighbors in the community. It is made whole by the serious study of what we do, how well we do what we say we wish to accomplish, and by the honest evaluation of our efforts and outcomes. The authors attempt to show ways in which we as educators and our students together may best learn of the differences and similarities of our shared human nature as we seek to understand the cultural underpinnings of the mosaic of American pluralism. Whether through direct community involvement or through the marvels of technology that seem to transcend time and space, a new culture of learning is gradually evolving.

What is a community? It is a term used so frequently and loosely that one may easily forget its most pristine meaning: a group held together by common beliefs, mores, and values. Perhaps we have used the term too tritely. We speak, for example, of various and sundry communities, such as the "community of scholars" who all too often—to outsiders, at least—resemble a group of individual exegetes squabbling over textual minutiae. In this section, the authors select groups with common concerns or interests in well-defined contexts. The authors correctly assume that a community also has a broader meaning than that which is only tied together by common beliefs, mores, and values. They do not, however, fail to see that this larger community is constituted of smaller, more closely knotted, and value-sharing communities. The term "community" may be extended to mean a geographic region such as a city or neighborhood, which may envelope multiple cultures, various lifestyles, corporations, service agencies, and a host of ethnic and racial groups. In general, however, the authors' underlying assumption about community is that it can sustain differences in cultural views, styles, beliefs, values, and mores. The authors provide the readers with riveting examples of cultural differences and nuances of further understanding and appreciation of the constituents in our communities and in the workforce. Although it would be virtually impossible to fix every culture into one opus, these pages are intended to ease our intellectual and moral appetites for increased knowledge and appreciation of cultural and social heterogeneity. Most important, it is the authors' collective hope that teachers, students, and members of our communities will be enriched by these reflections and that all engaged in higher education will view the classroom much more from the outside than from within.

Editorial Review Board

Contributors

xvi ❖❖❖ *Understanding Cultural Diversity*

Dennis R. Finger, EdD
Associate Professor
Department of Psychology
Kean University of New Jersey
Union, New Jersey

David Anthony Forrester, PhD, RN
Professor, School of Nursing
University of Medicine and
  Dentistry of New Jersey
Newark, New Jersey

David M. Gibson, EdD
Dean
School of Health Related Professions
University of Medicine and
  Dentistry of New Jersey
Newark, New Jersey

George J. Hebert, MA, RN, ANP, C
Associate Director
Christ Hospital School of Nursing
Jersey City, New Jersey

Karen A. Joho, MS, RN
Clinical Assistant Professor
Cooperative Nursing Program
Elizabeth General Medical Center
  School of Nursing
Union County College
Elizabeth, New Jersey

Henry L. Kaplowitz, PhD
Professor, Department of
  Psychology
Kean University of New Jersey
Union, New Jersey

Anunciacion S. Lipat, MA, RN
Clinical Assistant Professor
Cooperative Nursing Program
Elizabeth General Medical Center
  School of Nursing
Union County College, Elizabeth,
  New Jersey

Katherine Macken, BA
Educational Consultant
Atlanta, Georgia

Sandra Seals McQueen, MSN, RN
Staff Development
Essex Valley VNA
East Orange, New Jersey

Karen Verni-Moosvi, MSN, RN, CS
Clinical Instructor
Christ Hospital School of Nursing
Jersey City, New Jersey

Patricia L. Munhall, AARON, EdD,
  PsyA, FAAN
Professor and Associate Dean for
  Graduate Studies
University of South Carolina
Columbia, South Carolina

Frank Naughton, PhD
Professor and Chairperson
Department of Sociology
Kean University of New Jersey

Kathleen Neville, PhD, RN
Associate Professor
Department of Nursing
Kean University of New Jersey
Union, New Jersey

Anne Ormsby, MSN, RNC
Clinical Assistant Professor
Cooperative Nursing Program
Elizabeth General Medical Center
  School of Nursing
Union County College, Elizabeth,
New Jersey

Dula F. Pacquiao, EdD, RN, CTN
Associate Professor & Graduate
    Program Coordinator
Department of Nursing
Kean University of New Jersey
Union, New Jersey

Fran Quinless, PhD, RN
Dean
School of Nursing
University of Medicine and
    Dentistry of New Jersey,
Newark, New Jersey

Susan W. Salmond, EdD, RNC
Professor & Chairperson
Department of Nursing
Kean University of New Jersey
Union, New Jersey

Ellen E. Shelley, MSN, RNC
Case Manager
Visiting Nurse Affiliate
Cranford, New Jersey

Florence G. Sitelman, MA
Consultant
New York, New York

Robert Sitelman, PhD
Professor
Department of Philosophy-Religion
Kean University of New Jersey
Union, New Jersey

Fred C. Smith, Jr., BS, FACMPE
Fellow, American College Medical
    Practice Executives
Healthcare Consultant
South Orange, New Jersey

Rose Thering, OP, PhD
Professor Emerita
Seton Hall University
South Orange, New Jersey

Robert T. Tobin
Short Hills, New Jersey

Paula Dunn Tropello, MSN, RNC
Chairperson
Department of Nursing
Wagner College
Staten Island, New York

Virginia Villanueva, MEd, RN
Clinical Assistant Professor
Cooperative Nursing Program
Elizabeth General Medical Center
    School of Nursing, Union County
    College
Elizabeth, New Jersey

Leland J. White, JD, PhD
Editor
Biblical Theology Bulletin
Associate Counsel
New Jersey Law Revision
    Commission

Introduction

MARY L. KELLEY AND
VIRGINIA M. FITZSIMONS

The major social issue facing the U.S. is whether this nation can embrace a new generation of Americans and build a renewed sense of national unity while rejoicing in diversity. . . . Our response to this urgent and persistent challenge will have an impact far beyond the classroom and will reach into the future as far as anyone can see.

Ernest Boyer (1983)

AND SO IT CONTINUES

What is past is prologue and serves as our introduction to this book. The year is 1991. "There is so much to be done for students. Let's do a project together." With that statement, a four-year project, the Transcultural Leadership Continuum **(TLC)** for the Robert Wood Johnson Foundation, Inc., was begun at a group of nursing programs in New Jersey. The project changed the educational culture, and so the nature of the relationships, curricula, student population, learning outcomes, and understanding of the learning process in the schools. *The Culture of Learning* (Fitzsimons & Kelley, 1996) described the processes of the activities, as well as the personal changes within the faculty and students who participated in that **TLC** project. *Understanding Cultural Diversity: Culture, Curriculum, and Community in Nursing* continues the story of the evolution of these nursing programs that were committed to change, increased diversity, and innovative curricula.

The Santovec (1994) quote that began our first Prologue remains as an authentic beacon for our ongoing educational endeavors.

Why should higher education be concerned with diversity? If the goals of higher education include teaching people to think critically, to be socially responsible, to communicate effectively, and to value differences, diversity becomes a necessity. Diversity is the spice that adds to the quality of life and culture. And if we are to effectively cope with rapid social, political, and economic changes, we must be able to appreciate and include people who are different from us (Santovec, 1994).

A NEW AGE DAWNS

The new century is imminent. The persistent health issues such as sexually transmitted diseases, perinatal mortality, childhood diseases, tuberculosis, and family violence that raged as this century began, continue to drive up morbidity and mortality rates throughout this nation. Our populations across the country are widely diverse in every measure, yet our health professionals, including nurses, remain largely white middle-class individuals. If these seemingly intractable health problems are to be addressed and solved, it is imperative that sufficiently larger numbers of minority nurses, prepared at advanced practice levels, be educated. Our diploma/associate degree, baccalaureate, and graduate-level programs are charged with this responsibility: to prepare pools of minority nurses with a broad range and depth of competencies in order that new solutions for our diverse communities at risk are developed. The dawning millennium demands creativity and innovation if the goals of a uniformly high-level wellness are to be actualized nationally.

TRENDS IN THE NATIONAL PICTURE BASIC NURSING PROGRAMS MINORITY ENROLLMENT AND GRADUATION 1990–1995

Enrollment trends in all basic nursing programs for minority students for the years 1990–1995 show African American students comprising 10.4% of the student population in 1990 and 9.4% in 1995; Hispanic students 3.0% in 1990 and 3.5% in 1995; and Asian students 3.0% in 1990 and 4.0% in 1995. Graduation trends show African American students comprising 6.8% of the graduating students from all basic nursing programs in 1990 and 7.0% in 1995; Hispanic students 3.1% in 1990 and 3.1% in 1995; and Asian students 2.4% in 1990 and 3.0% in 1995 (NLN, Datasource, 1996).

MASTERS PROGRAMS MINORITY STUDENT GRADUATION 1991–1994

Graduations of minority students from master's programs showed a slight increase from 1991–1994. African American student graduations increased from 4.9% in 1991 to 6.0% in 1994; Hispanic students 2.1% in 1991 to 3.3% in

1994; and Asian students 2.2% in 1991 to 3.2% in 1994 (NLN, Nursing Data Review, 1996).

LICENSED PRACTICAL NURSE PROGRAMS MINORITY ENROLLMENT AND GRADUATION 1989–1994

The highest percentages of minority students are enrolled and graduate from practical nurse level programs. Five-year trends showed that enrollment of African American students held at 17.6% for the years 1989–1994; Hispanic student enrollment ranged from 4.5% in 1989 to 5.7% in 1994; and Asian students 2.5% in 1989 to 3.1% in 1994. Graduations from Licensed Practical Nurse programs showed that 14.8% of the graduates in 1990, and 14.3% in 1994, were African American; 4.5% in 1990 and 4.3% in 1994 were Hispanic; and 2.1% in 1990 and 3.5% in 1994 were Asian students (NLN, Nursing Data Review, 1996).

WHAT TLC DEMONSTRATED TO US

The Transcultural Leadership Continuum project lasted four years and involved the teamwork of four programs of nursing from a community college/diploma school cooperative unit and an upper division baccalaureate/master's university department of nursing. Four major areas of activities were addressed:

1. Increasing retention rates of minority students through:

    a. Improving success rates in early preclinical courses
    b. Addressing student life needs

3. Educating the faculty regarding the concept of "Educational Biculturalism"
4. Developing various modes and approaches for economic support during the progression through the programs
5. Increasing minority representation in nursing at the administrative, clinical practice, and faculty levels through mobility to BSN and MSN clinical administrative levels

Measuring the outcomes of the project after four years was a complex task because of the many variables put into place: an academic support and learning center; minority nurse mentors; new studying methods; economic and mobility strategies; AD to BSN to MSN progression efforts; and extensive faculty development. It was best to use both standard quantitative measures, as well as innovative qualitative designs.

It was not too surprising, but without question, that our students' lives were complex. Self-reports by the students related personal stories of grinding poverty, exhausting days working at minimum level wages, waiting in the rain and cold for city buses that didn't come, and trips to clinics with sick and feverish children. Heart wrenching were the revelations of beatings by jealous husbands when successful grades were earned on microbiology exams, and the emotional pain of misunderstanding what behaviors were expected in stressful clinical practice situations. Through it all, the students wrote of their dreams to move from the desperation of the underclass and the blue-collar worker's struggle out of poverty to a comfortable level of affluence. They identified these nursing degrees as being the vehicles to a middle-class life for themselves and their families.

RETENTION TO GRADUATION

Increasingly successful retention at each level of the programs, achievement of the associate's degree, graduation, licensure, and then progressive mobility to the BSN then MSN levels were monitored. As high as a 50 percent attrition rate at each intermittent level had been our previous experience. The intensive integration of Learning to Learn studying techniques, minority nurse mentoring and role-modeling, the Nursing Academic Support Center, and insights into culturally sensitive learner and teacher situations all factored into our retention and mobility success.

The steady progressive improvement in the retention, mobility, and graduation of minority students at the baccalaureate and master's level is heartening (Table I–1). Such a level of success acknowledges that an open, multifaceted and in-depth approach to supporting minority nursing majors' achievement is an entirely possible, and a most desirable, educational outcome. The data gives testimony to the efforts of a faculty that is willing to explore new instructional

TABLE I–1
Kean University Department of Nursing Enrollment and Graduation

	1992		1994		1997	
	Enrollment	Graduation	Enrollment	Graduation	Enrollment	Graduation
African American	27 13.3%	5 13.8%	40 20.7%	10 23%	48 17.9%	14 25.4%
Hispanic	14 6.8%	1 2.7%	11 5.6%	3 6.9%	12 4.4%	5 9%
Caucasian	155 76.3%	27 75%	142 73.5%	29 67.4%	208 77.6%	36 65.4%
Other	7 3.4%	3 8.3%	0	1		
Total	203	36	193	43	268	55

methods and curricula and illustrates that it can effect impressive increases in the pool of diverse, well-educated nurse leaders.

THE BOTTOM LINE

What did we learn? Without question, we would recommend that faculty desiring more successful graduation rates for minority students on all levels should:

- Include intensive learning strategies early in the program
- Encourage friendship and academic relationships as important even in the presence of time constraints; a sense of connectiveness/bonding to others in the program is essential
- Include minority mentor/role models the among the faculty and senior students
- Have scheduling and course credit loads flexible to accommodate heavy family and work responsibilities
- Raise career goals; introduce information regarding the AD/BSN/MSN access tracks early in the programs

CULTURE

Because, indeed, what is past is prologue, we began this book by striving for an added depth of understanding of the concept of culture. Our first unit, Culture, presents a cross-section of discussions of the development, theory base, and literature of the concept of culture held by a selection of liberal arts disciplines. We realize that some of the discussions reflect particular points of view and that the discussions certainly, in no way, are addressing *the* only single point of view or school of thought on the topic. The nature of scholarly discourse is the exploration of topics from varied perspectives. And so each chapter develops "culture" in particularly defined ways.

In Culture, we hear from philosophers, psychologists, an attorney, a sociologist, a librarian, health care administrator, adult nurse practitioner, and a nurse-psychoanalyst.

The philosophers argue that contemporary multiculturalism need not and should not entail ethical relativism. Ethical values, they maintain, can be distinguished from cultural norms and can provide a critique of those norms. It does not follow from the claim that ethics is culturally dependent that all cultural practices have the same ethical value or that such practices cannot be criticized from a moral perspective. Nor does it follow, claim the authors, from the fact that all values are ultimately arbitrary, ultimately human, that all values are of equal ethical worth.

A nurse and two psychologists discuss the development of psychological theories that have been influenced by the exposure of some well-known psychologists to differing cultural experiences. Exploration of cultural implications deepened self-understanding in each of the behavioral scientists and enriched the scope of the perspective of the theoretical framework.

An attorney and professor of religion and culture address how a civic ethic is used as a basis for public discussion of pressing contemporary issues. The discussion of methods of teaching pluralism by using the notion of values to move across cultural barriers is presented through the experience of a sociologist.

Teaching pluralism, a crucial theme in today's educational context, offers a mechanism to move values across cultural barriers. The discussion highlights the major advances in social progress made in the twentieth century and addresses the additional efforts that must be made for social justice in the new century.

A presentation of contemporary health care is incomplete without a pause to consider the dramatic changes causing shift and restructuring of the basic organizational network of wellness and illness care delivery. Two chapters addressing managed care and reengineering explore the changes wrought by managed care and the unsettling phenomenon of downsizing. These chapters are written using the perspective of persons within the system itself.

Scholars are charged with the responsibility to immerse themselves in and add to the literature of their discipline. Historically, that literature has been housed is the physical plant of the library collection. Failure to include the technological revolution of our contemporary library would be to overlook the single most essential cultural change that has occurred in this century and the major thrust of the new century. The library in cyberspace speaks to the decisive change that has singularly transformed the storage and retrieval of information since the hammer and chisel first were used to express concepts and forms on stone walls and tablets.

The Culture unit is completed with an excerpt from a classic journal article on existentialism and phenomenology. The work laid a cornerstone for nursing to describe its practice, and therefore its culture, in a scholarly and qualitative manner. This nurse-scholar has given us an indispensable classic for the development of professional practice standards grounded in a philosophical understanding of the essence of the human experience.

And so it is on this liberal arts foundation that we explore the crucial, yet sensitive, topic of culture. Such a posture frees us to know others not merely from our single perspective, but rather moves us into the light of a lucid, reflective, and researched-base understanding of our world.

CURRICULUM

When we have an understanding of our education goals, it is the curriculum that offers us the vehicle to reach that end. Unit Two presents a cross-section of educational plans that move students, from many levels, to a better understanding of the concept and integration of diversity principles.

The first two chapters offer culture in an international framework and on the graduate level of a nursing administration program. They point out the advances, frustrations, successes, and limitations of using culture as an imperative focus of an educational program.

Four subsequent pieces discuss student responses to cultural themes in course work. Because learning is commonly defined as a change in behavior more or less consistent over time, hearing the students' perspective on the lived experience of this change offers us insight and added understanding of the reality of learning about cultural diversity.

Because we define "culture" as a group of persons sharing common beliefs, behaviors, and values, and not merely in terms of ethnicity, a subgroup often neglected in the health literature is men. Therefore, inclusion of a piece regarding men's health in the curriculum fills a critical gap. Also included are chapters viewing the freshmen college experience and minority students' experience in a work-study setting.

COMMUNITY

Reading and talking about culture are one thing. However, the reality of culture as a human experience can be achieved only in the actualization of the community. Our final unit moves theory and concept into practice. The community is the ultimate laboratory and assessor. It is organized to present the multifaceted definition of culture.

The American Indian, the Filipino American, the Puerto Rican, the Asian Indian American, and the African American experiences are played out in the rich texture of their ethnic histories and traditions. Woven in are the human issues and concerns of their communities and the descriptions of problems identified and problems solved in the context of their individual cultural traditions and understandings. The richness of these historical cultures is manifested in the strengths and innovation of their people.

Homelessness, home health care, and the challenge of a group's response to AIDS are issues that rage in all communities. As humans struggle in the face of lost health, lost employment, and lost hope, all seek humanistic answers grounded in cultural responses to the human beings faced with the problems. These challenges are met in the final chapters of Community—new solutions for persistent problems, new hope for courageous people.

AND SO

We, as a group of nursing education programs, move together into a new century. As a leadership team, we are challenged to know more about cultural diversity, to understand more fully how we can organize to change ourselves and to improve the standards of nursing services in the geographical region we serve and to grow ourselves in the light of self-understanding. The chapters that follow are the unfolding of that self-understanding.

REFERENCES

Boyer, E. (1983). A nation at risk: The imperative for educational reform. Washington, DC, U.S. Department of Education.

Center for Research in Nursing Education and Community Health. (1996). *Nursing data review.* New York: NLN Press. Publ.19-6851.

Center for Research in Nursing Education and Community Health. (1996). *Nursing datasource—volume 1—Trends in contemporary nursing education.* New York: NLN Press. Publ.19-6932.

Dewey, J. (1969). *Pedagogical creed in education today.* Westport, CN: Greenwood Press.

Essex and Union Advisory Board for Health Planning, Ind. (1993). Needs assessment for Region III. Essex and Union Counties, *Planning report No. 3,* South Orange, NJ.

Fitzsimons, V. & Kelley, M. (1996). *The culture of learning.* New York: NLN Press.

Gronland, N. (1976). *Measurement and evaluation in teaching.* New York: Macmillan.

Munhall, P. L. (1994). *Qualitative research proposals and reports:* A guide. New York: NLN Press.

Santovec, M. (1994). *Recruitment and retention in higher education.* Madison, WI: Magna Publications.

Part One

CULTURE

Chapter 1

Ethics and Culture:
From the Claim That God Is Dead,
It Does Not Follow
That Everything Is Permitted

FLORENCE G. SITELMAN
AND ROBERT SITELMAN

CULTURE VERSUS ETHICS

Culture had to recede in order that ethics might emerge. Culture is an open-textured concept that isolates its instances by reference to a highly varied mixture of overlapping characteristics; by allusion to a certain common history and shared sense of destiny, to a distinctive language often featured by an idiosyncratic vocabulary and a highly particularized body of distinctions, to a value order that is often embedded in a particular cosmic design, religion, or mythology, to a distinct system of traditions and rituals, to a set of narratives that give expression to norms and models of behavior which are favored or reviled. It might include reference to foods, dress, household arrangements, and even furniture of a special type or character; it may incorporate reference to a unique art and/or a singular social structure, namely, a certain, distinctive kind of caste or class system; it may be defined by ethnic or racial differences. There are among cultures, of course, subcultures and interconnected cultures, cultures of greater or lesser distinctiveness. Thus, we may speak very broadly of Western culture as opposed to African culture or Eastern culture or even Buddhist culture, and then distinguish Irish culture from Southern Italian and Slavic cultures, as we distinguish Twi from Nubian. There is, or used to be, a Middle-European Jewish culture as well as a Hopi tribal culture, which could be distinguished from ancient Greek culture, and these separated from Iranian or Tutsi culture, and so on. A culture, needless to say, like all else, is noted by its distinctiveness—in this case, from other cultures.

Culture defines the individual in terms of a particular group distinct from other peoples. Insofar as individuals are defined in cultural terms, they are distinguished from individuals of other cultures and their worth is measured relative to their distinctive culture. In this case, the individual is measured and receives value through his or her relationship to the group in terms of the norms that distinguish and help to define the collectivity. Contribution to the group helps both to define the group, the culture, and to distinguish the norms and values that constitute the distinctive features of the group. Conversely, noncontribution to the group in terms of the special values and norms that constitute the distinctive character of the group is a mark of diminished value at least with respect to that group. When cultures attempt to depict themselves as in some respects superior or special, when they compete and become cultures in conflict, to the extent that a culture attempts to assert itself against other cultures, demands conversion, tries to hold onto its own in the face of what it perceives as cultural invasion and internal dissolution, or, to the extent that, for some reason, the culture attempts to induce heightened militancy and increased unity, there ethics as we understand it is threatened if not submerged.

The study of culture reveals a story of slanted vision and cruel presumption. Each culture will embody bias. Who can read the Bible and walk away with a positive attitude toward the Philistines? The attitude of Aristotle toward slaves is notorious. The prevalence of religious intolerance, racism, caste, and gender preference, of idiosyncrasy, dogma, and accident raised to metaphysical significance, of superstition and local values, of particular habits and customs expressed as eternal verities and unremitting absolutes is the history of culture. Every assertion presupposes unquestioned implications, and the unquestioned presumptions in the assertions of a culture will be perceived by members of those cultures that follow as the prejudices of that earlier culture. A culture might not know itself as a culture, but culture is local as well as historical and can only be known as such—as a culture—in contrast to other cultures.

Ethics evolved with the birth of the person. The person is an individual subjectivity both free and responsible to and for itself. According to seventeenth and eighteenth century European thought—first English, then French—personhood began as a political concept, though already implicit in Protestant declarations and its seedlings traceable back to biblical injunctions. Personhood, the idea of the free and responsible subject, formed the basis of the notion of a universal ethics that, among other things, declared all men equal. Each individual is sovereign over his or her own life and actions, allowing that one's free doings not inhibit or curtail the freedom of others.

In the discussion that follows, we shall speak of "the ethical perspective." The ethical perspective, here, is characterized by a universalism that regards human beings as persons; indeed, proposes autonomous personhood, namely, the fully realized, autonomous, ethical subject, as an ideal for all human beings; that contemplates and promotes, moreover, what from the ethical perspective may be characterized as well-being, forms of being, that is, which support emergent personhood; and that takes all other distinctions with respect to human beings as relative and secondary to, as special cases of personhood, intended to give shape to personhood; it does not make personhood second to race, ethnic group, religion, class, caste, or gender. Obviously, as we here use the term, the ethical perspective is broadly conceived and will, in fact, incorporate significant differences as that perspective is embodied in distinctive value orders within specific social, cultural contexts.

It is not coincident that the early assertions of personhood were accompanied with an explosion of atheism. Personhood is also the assertion of the primacy of the individual conscience. Each individual is a measure of itself on the basis of values and norms each chooses for itself. That is, the person is measured not simply on the basis of behavior relative to the values and norms to which that behavior is subject, the values and norms are themselves subjectivized, and the individual is measured now both by his or her norms as well as the behavior relative to those norms. Subjectivity dominant is coincident with a God irrelevant. In this respect, Nietzsche's announcement that God is dead was but to make explicit what was already lurking in the social contract theory of Thomas Hobbes: Individuals must make their own arrangements. The acknowledgment of personhood and the primacy of the individual conscience was the basis for the concept of mutual respect and provided the foundation for a universal ethic that declared the value of the subject on the grounds of his or her very humanity. The Age of Enlightenment brought all these themes together.

ETHICS VERSUS CULTURE

The emergence of the person and with it the autonomy of ethics came at a high, perhaps insufferable, cost. With freedom and individual responsibility, the person is no longer culture-bound. When the individual is defined in terms of a collective, and receives worth relative to the norms of that collective, then that individual is expected to suffer the fate of the collective as that collective defines itself. If, for example, that collective is defined by the voice of a certain acknowledged leadership or by certain distinctive actions, activities, or achievements, then responsibility is shared, and the fate of the community is also the rightfully considered fate of the individual. In such circumstances, one shares in the success and accomplishments but also assumes the responsibilities and obligations for what is done in the name of the collective. Collective responsibility, as depicted, for example, in the Bible when Moses brings a plague on a city, killing what we would regard as innocent Egyptian babies because of the decisions of the Pharaoh, or in *Oedipus Rex* when responsibility for the king's actions is borne by his subjects, entails what from an ethical perspective would be regarded as an unacceptable and unjust condition, namely, that individuals be held responsible for and, indeed, be punished because of actions they did not perform nor particularly know of or endorse. Should a Jew, living in the twentieth century, be held accountable for the role certain Jews may have played in the death of Jesus? Should a contemporary Bosnian Muslim be punished because of the behavior of some Bosnians in the Second World War, let alone in the seventeenth century? With the emergence of the ethical perspective, based on the principle of respect for the individual and the idea of personal freedom, the notion of individual responsibility and personal choice, comes an assault on the concept of collective responsibility. With the acknowledgment of the rights of the individual and the full realization of the notion of personhood as an ethical proposition comes the dissolution of guilt by mere virtue of membership in a group, the decline of guilt by association.

What are the costs for the ethical perspective? There are at least two, each of which may have unacceptable implications. The first involves the notion of meaningless suffering, that is, pain that is not punishment. With the idea of individual responsibility, and the correlative decline of adherence to the principles of collective responsibility, pain and suffering may more readily appear where punishment, let alone commensurate punishment, is not called for. When it is equated with what a person as such may reasonably, from an ethical perspective, be held responsible for, then punishment will be rapidly disentangled from what individuals suffer. That is, innocent people will suffer unjustly. But when suffering is no longer punishment meant for purposes of rehabilitation or salvation, then it may well be perceived as suffering without purpose. And if suffering is bad, suffering that is without purpose is often deemed intolerable. The subject is complex, for when people suffer ailments of various sorts, they will often feel further burdened by the thought that their affliction is a punishment, and that they are in some respect responsible for their misfortunes.

The dismissal of guilt insofar as it functions as a source of added distress, a secondary affliction compounding the original misery, may in many cases alleviate suffering, but the residue is pain without purpose, and the latter may well require a new and different state of mind to accommodate such a reality—a reality in which suffering may be unjustified, arbitrary, and pointless. But these issues call for another discussion, different from the purposes of this paper.

A second cost of the ethical perspective and the concomitant respect for personhood is the assumed weight of individual responsibility for one's own destiny, the loss of identity defined previously in terms of the collective, and the relative isolation consequent upon the disintegration of cultural bonds. Here community is no longer given, but must be won. In our time of personhood, community and culture has to be chosen, sought, and actively preserved. Moreover, in our time of mingled communities and multiple, overlapping cultures, the choices can be difficult and success is not assured. The freedom to choose entails by its very nature a certain distance from the objects of one's choice. It arrives adorned by the knowledge that one could have chosen otherwise. It denies necessity and renders tentative all decisions at the same time that it makes one's life the consequence of one's behavior, and the consequences of one's behavior the responsibility of the individual. Personhood can deny any and even all relationships (e.g., Bartleby the Scrivener). Any association with a culture in modern times, in an age of personhood, bears the corrosive marks of the freedom to choose. In this respect, it defeats culture even when it subscribes to it. Personhood leaves the individual isolated from his or her associations.

The ascendance of subjectivity—the subject who makes subjective his or her norms and values, his or her goals and purposes—comes with the recession of the binding necessities and unchallenged determinants of a dominating and irresistible culture. The subject, therefore, runs the risks of isolation. Isolation can induce a deadening of the spirit, a sense of purposelessness and loss of direction. Moving about in such a state can denude us of the ability to take action insofar as actions entail goals, and can leave the individual in a condition of oppression, hopelessness, and despair. There is nothing to be done and nothing can be done. Work insofar as it can be performed is joyless. Adrift, one cannot find oneself. Isolation can, ultimately, turn on itself.

From the perspective of personhood, the decline of culturally derived values and norms can leave ethics in an overly abstract and insubstantial condition. Ethics without values is disembodied, overly abstract, and incapable of providing direction for action. So isolated from values to a great measure culturally determined, pure ethics is formal and limited to issues of universalization and equality stripped of those descriptive and evaluative elements which provide the basis for the application of ethical principle in a manner specific enough to determine appropriate distinctions. For example, ethical principle would require us to treat equal things in an equal fashion, but culture will often determine what is, in fact, to be regarded as equal in the respects pertinent to the determination of the treatment (e.g., in what respects are women to be regarded as equal to men, Africans to Europeans, Jews to Christians; in what respects are nationality, caste differences, breeding, intellect to be regarded as decisive, and so on). How we describe things cannot ultimately be distinguished from how we use them, and how we describe things is to a great measure culturally determined.

One danger that lies in drawing a distinction between culture and ethics is that ethics, in itself highly abstract and general, perceived in itself as vacuous, as too frail or attenuated to sustain itself in an independent fashion, is collapsed into culture and is overly relativized, delegitimized, despised, or simply ignored, leaving the field open to a cultural arbitrariness that rejects all intersubjective standards and treats all values as equal, including those which would violate norms of reasonableness, and even morality itself. Such a situation courts the bizarre and is vulnerable to the destructive—Nazism and racism are good examples. It does not follow that all cultural values are of equal ethical status because ethical distinctions are culturally dependent. If morality thrives on values and characterizations that emerge from cultural life, culture, conversely, lacking the critique and discipline provided by ethics, is vulnerable to arbitrariness and tribalism of the most destructive nature.

Thus, culture in one form or another always reasserts itself—as it did, for example, in the nineteenth century in response to the failures of the Enlightenment, as it has in recent years in response to splintering hegemonies, to the fall of international communism and to the ebbing of Western imperialism and the values of democratic liberalism. Rational norms divorced from cultural values cannot be sustained. From the perspective of ethics, however, the reassertion of culture is, as suggested earlier, but another expression of personhood, the latter once articulated, like the loss of innocence, being irrevocable. Hereafter, any effort to submerge personhood is itself an act of personhood, subjectivity, once gained, never to be lost. (The man who chooses to be an animal will be a man acting like an animal, but never an animal, e.g., *Animal House*.) Cultural reassertion from the perspective of personhood is only the affirmation of new forms of self-legitimization, that is, of personhood.

CULTURE AND ETHICS

The reemergence of culturalism as an expression of personhood operates as a unifying force which asserts a system of arrangements and promotes a set of customs that permit individuals to define themselves in contrast to those the culture would exclude. It provides norms and values for those otherwise displaced, lost, or adrift. It can have special appeal for the powerless. In this regard, culture can be liberating as well as empowering. Moreover, employed as an organizing force which is also exclusive, it can function as an expression of the pursuit of power—as culture, indeed, did before the emergence of ethics. So asserted, it would submerge ethics. K. Anthony Appiah recently argued that, "The growing salience of race and gender as social irritants, which may seem to reflect the call of collective identities, is a reflection, as much as anything else, of the individual's concern for dignity and respect." And, we may add, the legitimate demand for dignity and respect often translates into the pursuit of power. Thus, cultural difference may be employed for political purpose. But, Appiah goes on: "The trouble with appeal to cultural difference is that it obscures rather than illuminates this situation. It is not black culture that the racist disdains, but blacks. There is no conflict of visions between black and white cultures that is the source of racial discord. . . . Culture is not the problem, and it is not the solution." Indeed, we would insist, the appeal to cultural difference by those who seek dignity and respect only aggravates the problem because it rejects an immoral conclusion, that is, X deserves no respect because he is Y (black, Muslim, Jewish, Hispanic, etc.), but accedes to an unethical premise—since it bases its claim to dignity on a cultural affiliation, that is, X deserves respect because he is a member of a great culture. (While we disagree with Appiah's claim that the racist disdains blacks but not black culture—he disdains both—we agree with Appiah that the pursuit of dignity and respect should be based on ethical and social considerations that reflect on the individual in his or her humanity and on his or her works and character.) "So maybe," Appiah writes, "we should conduct our discussions of education and citizenship, toleration and social peace, without the talk of cultures" (Appiah, 1997).

Cultural assertion in the context of cultural struggles is often a struggle over forms while struggle over forms is often a struggle for power. On a certain level, cultural difference may be nothing more than formal. By cultural forms we mean symbolism, imagery, ceremony, and ritual as opposed to the underlying and deeper values which the forms are meant to embody, express, convey, and encourage. Those deeper values can be local but are often human and give voice to the fundamentals of universal human experience. Yet every culture will exhibit its biases. Each culture will be qualified by what it leaves unquestioned, by what it assumes, by its noisiness. As a general matter, all answers are engulfed in what remains unanswered. It is no coincidence that the reemergence of culture is often accompanied by an assault on reason and a resurgence of religion. Moreover, the unchallenged prejudices and short-fallings that help to define and delimit a culture can often function to constitute the unique forms, the very imagery, which identify and help to isolate that culture; its peculiarities and oddities, its nonsublimated irrationalities defining what is most "quaint" and most interesting in that culture. In fact, arbitrariness can be appealing by virtue of its very arbitrariness. And, in fact, what is particular and even idiosyncratic can sometimes provide imagery which is especially refreshing, resonating, and differently revealing.

However, a sympathetic and close reading of cultural forms seen in the context of an appreciation of the limitations and presumptions that the social milieu generates will often expose those aspects of culture that bespeak the human condition, address universal issues, and emerge as expressions of virtue that celebrate human dignity and voice its struggles. Western literature is rife with misogyny, and densely limned with racial and ethnic stereotypes. Anti-Semitism sprinkles the writings of Shakespeare, Dickens, Walter Scott, and Tolstoy. Joseph Conrad's *The Heart of Darkness* has been noted for its racism. These writers each express the prejudices of their age and culture. Their achievements remain extraordinary notwithstanding. This point in our age needs emphasis. One can look beyond the stereotype to what the symbolism is meant to convey in order to grasp the humanity that is beneath the image—if the work is, indeed, a work of significant expression. And significance of expression and depth of vision can be assessed. What Conrad is speaking about is a febrile heat, a boisterous, unrestrained foliage and tropical decay, a cruel and savage ritualism that underlies Western civilities. If the imagery taken literally can be offensive, clearly, Africa, as is understood by the author, metaphorically as a certain kind of state of being functions as a powerful expressive device. Similarly, Shakespeare's use of physical deformity or of bastardy is notorious. To perceive the significance in the form, however, can often defuse what is obnoxious and perverse about the form itself, the latter often the accretion of historical circumstance, limited information, poor science, superstition, and prejudice. History and circumstance may generate associations that we may wish to disavow. Since such associations form the basis for the imagery by which those within a culture speak and express themselves, we can, if we take the expression as imagery, that is, as symbol and not as literal, recognize the association and grasp the meaning—which can be profound, beautiful, worthwhile, and true—we can even appreciate the vividness, even voluptuousness of the image, while rejecting the associations as a general state of affairs. Of course, there is the danger of those who are literal-minded or perhaps inclined in a certain kind of direction already to take old and false associations at face value.

Culture is afloat in its accumulated view of things. It describes and characterizes what it apprehends. It is against the backdrop of these cultural givens that ethics must operate. Culture helps to distinguish the virtues, gives substance to the terms of the discourse, defines courage, generosity, strength, moderation, and equality. Without culture, the concept of justice has no application. Having recognized the point, there are those who would collapse ethics into culture, who would insist that culture is everything, and that it does, will, and, in fact, should determine all values as it determines all truth. But to recognize that ethics without culture is nothing is not to grant that ethics is nothing but culture. There are values embedded in ethics which are noncultural even though they get application through culture. That is, culture provides values, but value and ethics are not the same. Values taken up in ethics become ethical values, and ethical values are not the same as cultural values.

Philosophers commonly speak of the Fallacy of Nothing-but-ism. From the recognition that X is Y, it may be a fallacy to infer that X is nothing but Y. From the fact that knowledge is power, it would be a mistake to infer that knowledge is nothing but power. Those guilty of what we may refer to as cultural Nothing-but-ism are often expressing the anger and arrogance of those with a special ax to grind. Ethical discourse commands a logic and argues for an approach that the articulation of values as such does not entail. Reductionism in these matters fails not simply to do justice to ethics; it ultimately demeans and diminishes culture insofar as culture supports and gives expression to ethics.

ETHICS AND CULTURE

We have now come a long way. From the fact that values are cultural deriva-
tives, from the meta-ethical argument that all values are ultimately arbitrary, it
does not follow that all values, all standards of judgment, all actions, attitudes,
works of art, and so on, are equally meritorious or deserving or equal in value.
It does not follow that anything goes. It does not follow from the claim that
God is dead that everything is permitted. For us, it may mean that the standards which we employ to make judgments of particulars are themselves open
to critique and analysis. And this is a lot, because such acknowledgments can
make us more self-conscious, more specific, more explicit, clearer in what we
mean by calling this good and that bad. It can lead to a more refined judgment. It can induce a greater modesty in our claims and more flexibility in our
assertions. It should lead to a diminished not a heightened arbitrariness. It
should lead to a sharpening of values, not to a diminution or to anarchy and
certainly not to the dislodgment of what some may perceive as one tyranny—
the tyranny of Western, white male culture—in favor of the enthronement of
other tyrannies.

Ethics now emergent, we return to the matter of culture from a new perspective. The imperatives of ethics and the point of view of a realized personhood provide the basis for an examination of culture from the perspective of a
responsible subjectivity. The truths that riddle and define cultures, that are given
in the descriptions and characterizations embedded in diverse cultures, are now
subject to the critique that ethics would offer to truth as persons understand it.
The racism, anti-Semitism, misogyny, the local cruelties and barbarisms which
often deny humanity to humans, the very degradations and slander that are
often hallmarks of a culture, are no longer without responsibility to an external
set of norms. From the claim that facts are value-laden, it does not follow that
anyone's truth is as good as anyone else's, or that there is no truth; it follows
instead that our truths are subject to ethical consideration. That is, racism is subject both to a factual as well as an ethical evaluation. As culture gives substance
to ethics, so ethics would inform and discipline culture. From the point of view
of realized subjectivity, we embrace culture, culture no longer engulfs us. Thus,
as we return to culture to find our historical place, to locate our roots, to establish or reestablish bonds, to give substance to norms, both ethical and nonethical, we can do so in a manner that heightens our sense of ourselves, that
augments personhood, that gives body to who and what we are and how we see
ourselves, that makes us matter in respects that help to define us.

Unfortunately, however, the restoration of a culture, for too many individuals, represents the resurrection of a past denuded of what came in between. It sig-
nals a submersion of responsible personhood into a collective consciousness that
would obliterate the subject and demean ethical values. Reconstituted in the pursuit of power, it can function as an organizing tool which knows itself through
its separation from others, through an exclusivity that proclaims superiority
by virtue of its association with the culture, and, more important, its radical

disassociation from other cultures (e.g., Blacks should only vote for Blacks; Jews should only vote for Jews; Irish should only vote for Irish; women for women) one should always support and defend any member of one's own racial, ethnic group against anyone not in one's group, no matter the issue or circumstance. All literary values reflect cultural biases, and, therefore, there is no reasonable ground for arguing that Tolstoy and Dostoevsky are better writers than Q; thus, time is better spent for blacks, Jews, Irish, or women to read Q, who is black, Jewish, Irish, or a woman than to read Tolstoy, Thomas Mann, or Victor Hugo. Aristotle and Shakespeare are not for blacks or Jews or women. All whites are X; all Italians are Y; all blacks are Z. Those not in your culture are your enemy, etc. Similarly, because ethics champions human value over specific cultural, racial, ethnic, or gender values, ethical norms may be cast aside as simply different forms of cultural prejudice, completely arbitrary because ultimately subjective. All such moves fail in the sense that they are unethical, just as parallel moves to deny ascertainable literary values in literature and to denounce merit in art are nonliterary and extra-aesthetic. All such moves fail, as suggested earlier, because they are the doings of an articulated and responsible subjectivity, and there is no going back from that. Ancient tribalism is not the moral equivalent of twentieth-century tribalism. Today, if one grows up in a Nazi household and adopts the values of that household, then one will be regarded as a Nazi and be held morally accountable. In that respect at least, there is no going back to the past.

Having so argued, we do not mean to maintain that the forces of cultural absolutism which denigrates personhood and the ethical subject in the name of collectivist politics cannot win out from time to time or even, in some respect, ultimately. Culture has the capacity to collapse ethics, dissolve the concept of responsible subjectivity and personhood, and splinter human society. Cultural absolutism can no longer make us be what we can no longer be, but it can make us act as if we are what we can no longer be. Men can no longer be nonethical but they can be unethical; they can suppress their subjectivity, deny themselves and their humanity; they can adopt old characterizations; they can resurrect ancient grievances and turn away from the concept of individual justice. Insofar as the pursuit of power at a cost to others remains a driving force in human affairs, culture seen as a tool to such ends will continue to threaten ethical values and rational standards. Insofar as politics is constituted by a pursuit of power, culture politicized, that is, culture politically employed, will be contentious culture at war with ethics and humanity.

REFERENCES

Appiah, K. Anthony. (1997, October 9) The multicultural misunderstanding. *The New York Review of Books*, XLIV, pp. 30–36.

Bernstein, R. (Ed.) (1985). *Habermas and morality*. Cambridge, MA: MIT Press.

Bromwich, D. (1992). *Politics by other means: Higher education and group thinking*. New Haven: Yale University Press.

Danto, A. (1987). *Nietzsche as philosopher.* New York: Columbia University Press.

Harris, E. (1966). Respect for persons in R. T. De George (Ed.), *Ethics and society* (pp. 111–132). Garden City, New York: Doubleday Anchor.

Megill, A. (1985). *Prophets of extremity.* Berkeley: University of California Press.

Rosen, S. (1969). Nihilism. In J.M. Edie (Ed.), *New essays in phenomenology* (pp. 151–158). Chicago: Quadrangle Books.

Chapter 2

Psychology and Culture

L UCY W. B ENNETT
AND D ENNIS R. F INGER

This chapter looks at the relationship of psychology and culture by taking a journey with three prominent mental health professionals who have made significant contributions to psychology. Carl Jung, Erik Erikson, and Alan Roland all experienced encounters with a variety of cultures. Our journey begins with Carl Gustav Jung and his travels to North Africa, India, and other places and peoples, followed by Erik Erikson and Alan Roland.

CARL GUSTAV JUNG: GEOGRAPHY

Carl Gustav Jung, the founder of analytic psychology, was a Swiss psychiatrist who lived all of his life in Switzerland, a small country in the very heart of Europe. It is relevant to note that Switzerland is a country whose boundaries were defined slowly over the thirteenth through nineteenth centuries, and it consists now of cantons (similar to our states) that originally belonged to what we now know as France, Italy, Germany, and Austria. A democratic republic, Switzerland has worked to maintain ethnic diversity, a task not achieved easily, and resulting from a conscious policy of maintaining cultural, linguistic, and religious differences. Jung's writings about his psychological theories and beliefs contain some references to his own Swiss cultural background and numerous references to the important role other cultures can play in helping one to understand ones own culture. He discusses the perils of living without the ability to see ourselves as others see us.

> We always require an outside point to stand on, in order to apply the lever of criticism. . . . How, for example, can we become conscious of national peculiarities if we have never had the opportunity to regard our own nation from outside? Regarding it from outside means regarding it from the standpoint of another nation. . . . Through my acquaintance with many Americans, and my trips to and in America, I have obtained an enormous amount of insight into the European character; it has always seemed to me that there can be nothing more useful for a European than some time or other to look out at Europe from the top of a skyscraper (Jung, 1961, pp. 246–247).

JUNG'S ANALYTIC PSYCHOLOGY

A brief review of Jung's theory of psychology, sometimes referred to as depth psychology or analytic psychology (to differentiate it from Freudian psychoanalytic theory), will begin with his belief in the existence of a collective unconscious or archetypal psyche. After years of work and study, and in disagreement with Freud, Jung proposed that in addition to the existence of a person's own or personal unconscious, there was in each human being a deeper layer of the unconscious that included images and affects buried from time immemorial; images and affects from our human ancestors which have helped to shape our common psychic heritage. Jung referred to those particular images in the unconscious that seemed to stimulate common affects in different cultures as archetypes. According to one

Jung biographer, "Thus, on appropriate occasions, archetypes give rise to similar thoughts, images, mythologems, feelings, and ideas in people, irrespective of their class, creed, race, geographical location, or historical epoch" (Stevens, p. 33).

Based on his belief in the presence of common affects and concerns across cultures, albeit affects buried deep in the collective unconscious, it might be said of Jung that he believed all of humanity to have a common psychic heritage. However, because of personal life experiences in different countries, cultures, families, etc., one's personal individuation process (psychological development) must always be understood within the context of a search for one's self . . . a self deeply embedded in both a personal and a collective unconscious.

Jung further believed that those parts of ourselves that we have the most trouble seeing or believing are those that hide in our "shadow." These are the parts of ourselves that we deny, that we project onto others, and that he believed must be recognized and assimilated in our adult lives if we are to grow into the self (or selves) we are meant to be.

There are other parts of Jung's theories or work that might be discussed: His theory that people are either of the introverted or extroverted orientation; that each person has a typology that is either thinking or feeling and sensing or intuiting. However, these parts of his theory are not as relevant to the study of culture as Jung experienced it as are the concepts mentioned earlier.

Jung's belief in the importance of dreams and the understanding of one's dreams as an excellent and psychologically objective guide to one's own individuation process is very relevant to the study of culture and psyche. It was through dreams that Jung discovered the existence of the collective unconscious, the archetypes, and the importance these have in the individuation process.

It should be said here that critics of Jung have questioned the significance he attributed to images or symbols buried in dreams (unconscious), and his propositions that these images are often impersonal and therefore representative of the collective and not the personal unconscious.

For the purpose of this paper, the authors are assuming that Jung's viewpoint is worthy of consideration and that his reactions to his experiences with other-than-Swiss cultures and the dreams and unconscious processes that these stimulated are relevant to this discussion.

If one is to explore Jung's opinions about the role of culture in the development of the individual and his quest toward psychological wholeness, one must acknowledge the fact that Jung was interested in the cultures of religion, of Europe, of Switzerland, of non-European countries, of the emerging field of psychoanalysis, of the mentally ill, and numerous other so-called "cultures." Jung dedicated his life's professional work to the understanding of the human psyche. He was always more interested in and present to those persons and situations that could teach him more about how the soul or psyche seeks its wholeness, incorporating always the opposites (good/bad, pretty/ugly, man/woman, black/white, primitive/civilized . . .). Part of his quest involved purposeful visits to other cultures in order to understand himself and his own culture better. Some of those travels and their impacts on Jung will now be reviewed.

TRAVELS

In his quest to better understand himself by experiencing the reactions of other cultures to his "European white man" identity (and to indulge his interest in travel!), Jung traveled to several countries over his lifetime: North Africa, America, tropical Africa, and India. The following discussion will present some of his reactions to these travels, especially as they help us understand how Jung viewed these cultures vis-à-vis his own psychological theory and personal self development.

NORTH AFRICA

In 1920, at the age of 45, Jung was invited to accompany a friend on a trip to the North African areas of Algiers, Tunis, Sousse, and on into the Sahara. It was on this trip that Jung wrote of experiencing an alteration in the sense of time, becoming acutely aware of the importance Europeans attach to watches (especially Swiss watches) and all things mechanical, to the point of forgetting the more natural ways.

> The deeper we penetrated into the Sahara, the more time slowed down for me; it even threatened to move backward. . . . As we approached the oasis, a single rider, wholly swathed in white, came toward us. With proud bearing he rode by without offering us any greeting, mounted on a black mule whose harness was banded and studded with silver. He made an impressive, elegant figure. Here was a man who certainly possessed no pocket watch, let alone a wrist watch; for he was obviously and unself-consciously the person he had always been. He lacked that faint note of foolishness which clings to the European. The European is, to be sure, convinced that he is no longer what he was ages ago; but he does no know what he has since become (Jung, 1961, p. 240).

Jung was deeply affected by the apparent emotional nature of these people whom he described as unreflective but so much closer to life and vitality than Europeans. His dreams as he left North Africa cautioned him to not be overwhelmed by his experiences, but to try to integrate into his conscious life those parts of himself buried in his collective unconscious that were like the ancient, timeless, close-to-the-earth peoples of the culture of North Africa.

> In traveling to Africa to find a psychic observation post outside the sphere of the European, I unconsciously wanted to find that part of my personality which had become invisible under the influence and pressure of being European. This part stands in unconscious opposition to myself, and indeed I attempt to suppress it (Jung, 1961, p. 244).

Jung had begun in North Africa an experiential discovery process that would lead to his growing conviction that other cultures can offer vital reflections of our own personal and collective buried, hidden, or unconscious human qualities. Indeed, the admitting of these "forgotten" human qualities into consciousness can be an overwhelming process, perhaps even dangerous if one completely identifies with the emerging images, but to deny the importance of these buried aspects of ourselves is to deny to process of individuation.

AMERICA: PUEBLO INDIANS

Jung visited America to lecture and present professional papers many times during his life, but it was his visit with the Pueblo Indians of New Mexico that touched him most deeply and gave him the most insight into that part of the white European male's ethnic shadow where the archetype of the "predator" lies hidden. Specifically, an Indian chief shared with Jung his view of the white man:

> See how cruel the whites look. Their lips are thin, their noses are sharp, their faces furrowed and distorted by folds. Their eyes have a staring expression; they are always seeking something. . . . We do not understand them. . . . They think with their heads. . . . We think with our hearts. . . . (Jung, 1961, p. 248).

Jung believed the Indian chief had spoken a truth; that "white" men over the centuries past had occupied themselves with the task of spreading civilization, spreading Christianity, etc., to the point of treating quite cruelly peoples of cultures deemed "in the way" of progress. Again, as in North Africa, Jung experienced the one-sidedness of the rational European/white way of being in the world.

The other noteworthy discovery Jung made during his visit with the Pueblos was one ritual that exemplified the depth of their religious convictions. These Pueblos, living on the top of a mountain plateau, were greeted daily with the brilliant rise of the sun and they believed they helped that sun to go across the sky all day until it disappeared into the night sky. They believed themselves vital to the world in that they saw their place in the world as that of sons to Father Sun . . . and that if they stopped practicing their religious attention to the Sun, the world would be plunged into darkness forever. Jung noted after this realization that although European rationalism could explain away the need for this form of Pueblo worship, we would do so at risk of increasing the distance between ourselves and our mythic heritage. And in fact, thought Jung, the notion that a ritual act or religious practice can affect the path of the sun is not unlike the Christian notion of using prayer or moral behavior to influence God. In summary, the Pueblos taught Jung the importance of believing one's existence meaningful in the world and in the presence of one's god . . . "Such a man is in the fullest sense of the word in his proper place" (Jung, 1961, p. 253).

AMERICA: "NEGROES"

As much as Jung believed the culture of the American Indian was vital in understanding the psyche of the white/European/American, he also believed the

American Negro culture played a vital role in the American psychology (American Negro is a term used by Jung and others in the time . . . surely Jung would be interested to know that today these persons are afforded a title that acknowledges their cultural heritage). His visit to a village of Negro foresters near New Orleans gave him the opportunity to observe behaviors he thought were indigenous to the Negroes and replicated, albeit unwittingly, in the American white community. These behaviors included specific types of music and dancing, a habit of leaving doors unlocked (as in Negro villages), a sociability and social life that was much more warm and friendly than that of the traditional European culture. One must remember that Jung studied and wrote about these issues decades before citizens of the United States began to bring into consciousness the need to recognize the cultural heritage of the peoples it had brought from Africa to be enslaved in this developing country (Jung, 1930, pp. 502–514).

TROPICAL AFRICA AND INDIA

Jung took lengthy trips to both tropical Africa (then, Kenya and Uganda), and India in 1925 and 1938, respectively. However, unlike his previous travels, he undertook these journeys to deepen his understanding of his personal psychology, not to expand his understanding of the role culture can play in the psychological development or individuation of all persons.

A major contribution to the field of analytic psychology that Jung discovered or articulated based on his tropical African trip was the age-old human quest for light and fear of darkness . . . symbolic (he believed) of man's quest for enlightenment or consciousness (Jung, 1961, pp. 253–274). India offered very different experiences . . . a highly developed religious system that embraces the opposites . . . the good and the evil, the mind and the body (Jung, 1939, pp. 515–524).

Frankly, reading Jung's descriptions of tropical African and Indian cultures in this day and age, one is required to hold in check our current-day sensitivity to the minimizing or outright intolerance of other peoples. In fact, many of Jung's writings about other cultures can seem exceedingly insensitive if judged by today's standards. However, Jung was looking for the differences, hoping to use those differences to complement his one-sided European experience.

APPLICATION OF JUNG'S IDEAS TO CULTURE, CURRICULUM, AND COMMUNITY

Carl Jung valued individuation over almost everything else, psychologically speaking. This process of individuation involves being open to "otherness," whether in our dreams or our waking lives. From the authors' personal experiences, this is probably one of the most difficult and potentially rewarding challenges facing human beings. Whether we are attempting this in our personal lives or in our public lives, it is perhaps relevant to consider the notion that we can experience how difficult and rewarding the process is from examining our day-to-day interactions with peoples from other cultures. As much as we might wish to embrace persons of all creeds, races, and religions, they and we are "other" and to some extent, therefore, frightening. To recognize, value, and even treasure this otherness can lead to the possibility of psychological growth and development, or individuation, to use Jung's terminology.

Finally, one interesting quote from Jung about the need to educate educators might be relevant:

> The educational method, then, that will best meet the needs of adults must not be a direct one, but indirect; that is, it must put him in possession of that psychological knowledge which will permit him to educate himself. Such an effort could not, and must not be expected from a child, but we must expect it from an adult, especially if he be a teacher. A teacher cannot be a passive sustainer of culture, he must also actively further culture through his own self-education [self-knowledge]. His education must never remain at a standstill, otherwise he will begin to correct in the children those faults which he has left untouched in himself. This is manifestly the opposite of education (Jung, 1928, pp. 322–333).

ERIK ERIKSON: GEOGRAPHY

Erik Homburger Erikson, a prominent author and child psychotherapist, was born in 1902 near Frankfurt, Germany. He never knew his Danish father, who left his mother before Erik was born. At age three, Erik became ill, and his mother took him to see Dr. Homburger, a pediatrician. Dr. Homburger married Erik's mother and they all lived in Germany. Erik's stepfather wanted him to be a physician but he became an artist instead, specializing in portraits of children. After finishing high school, Erik traveled across Europe sketching and reading. Little did Erikson, the young adult, realize that his drawings of children's outer appearance would one day change to a career focusing on children's inner psychological portraits and the development of self-identity throughout the life cycle. Erikson first came face to face with children in a small American school in Vienna and he continued his lifelong work with children as a psychotherapist. Erikson married an American artist, who had a Canadian background. They came to the United States in 1933. Erikson practiced psychotherapy in Boston and taught at Harvard and other universities. His first major book, *Childhood and Society,* appeared in 1950. In *Childhood and Society,* Erikson acknowledged the importance of his long talks with anthropologists "primarily Gregory Bateson, Ruth Benedict, Martin Loeb, and Margaret Mead." He recognized the value of understanding the role of culture in child training and development.

ERIKSON'S PSYCHOSOCIAL THEORY

A brief overview of Erikson's work includes major contributions in two areas: the psychosocial stages of development and the formation of one's self-identity.

These are eight psychosocial stages in which the individual has to establish new basic orientations to himself and his social world. Erikson believed that personality development continues throughout the life cycle, that each stage has a positive as well as a negative component, and that each stage builds upon the last—a process known as epigenetic development. According to Erikson, each stage of the life cycle emerges, and is profoundly shaped by, all earlier stages. Each of the eight stages has a unique developmental task that confronts individuals with a crisis that must be faced. This crisis is not a catastrophe but a turning point. The more an individual resolves the crisis successfully, the healthier development will be.

The first stage, extending through the first year of life, involves Basic Trust at one extreme and Mistrust at the other. Stage two, spanning the second and third year of life, emphasizes the emergence of Autonomy versus Shame and Doubt. Toddlers begin to assert their independence. The next stage occurs during the preschool years and includes Initiative at one pole versus Guilt at the other. Preschool children begin active, purposeful behavior in their widening social world and with new challenges with which to cope. The fourth stage, which spans the elementary years, focuses on the child's enthusiasm toward learning and gaining knowledge. At one end is Industry and at the other end is Inferiority. The child can develop feelings of incompetence during this stage. The adolescent years is the stage for the fifth developmental phase with Identity versus Identity Confusion as the challenge. Does the adolescent, through role-taking and various experiences, develop a positive identity or is the development of identity hindered by parents and significant others? In the sixth stage, young adults are confronted with Intimacy versus Isolation. Individuals face the task of forming close relationships with others or becoming socially isolated. During middle adulthood the developmental challenge is Generativity versus Stagnation. In this seventh stage, does the middle-aged person assist young people in developing and leading useful lives or does the person stagnate? In Erikson's final eighth stage the issue is Integrity versus Despair. Upon reflection and life review does the older person feel a sense of satisfaction in life or does the person feel doubt or gloom about how life was lived?

Cross-cultural psychologists may criticize Erikson's eight psychosocial stages as being too Westernized and not inclusive of other cultural emphases (Roland, 1997).

Erikson's second main contribution was in the development of self-identity. This developmental challenge is especially emphasized during the adolescent years. Teenagers are searching for who they are, what is their purpose, and where are they going in life. Erikson believed adolescents pass through a period of "psychological moratorium" during which they explore different roles available in their culture. Adolescents who develop identity confusion may withdraw and isolate themselves or seek to bury their individual identity in an identification with a group. Erikson emphasized that identity development involves relationships with people, community, and society.

In a biography of Erikson, Coles (1970) maintained that Erikson struggled with two identity crises: first, as an adolescent attempting to understand himself and his Danish-German world, and second, in America after writing *Childhood and Society.* Erikson was interested in investigating the identity development of famous individuals in different cultures. He analyzed the lives of Adolf Hitler (1962), Martin Luther (1968), and Mahatma Gandhi (1969). He also visited other cultures to better understand personality and identity development. Erikson viewed several cultures during his travels including two American Indian tribes. The following discussion will address some of Erikson's encounters with these tribes, his research methods, and cultural considerations.

TRAVELS IN AMERICA: THE SIOUX OF SOUTH DAKOTA

At the age of 35, Erikson in 1937 visited the Pine Ridge Indian Reservation in the southwest corner of South Dakota. Here lived 8,000 members of the Oglala subtribe of the Sioux (also called Dakota). Erikson traveled there with Scudder Mekeel, an anthropologist and guide. He gained information about the Sioux culture through observations, interviews, and an "interracial seminar." In the seminar, Mekeel and Erikson were joined by educators and social workers of both white and Indian origin. One purpose of Erikson's trip was to collect data concerning the system of child training used by the Sioux. Erikson used his psychosocial stages as a framework for understanding the Sioux's child rearing.

> The colostrum (the first watery secretion from the milk glands) was generally considered to be poison for the baby; thus the breast was not offered to him until there seemed to be a good stream of perfect milk. The Indian women maintained that it was not right to let a baby do all the initial work only to be rewarded with a thin, watery substance. The implication is clear: how could he trust a world which greeted him thus? Instead, as a welcome for the whole community, the baby's first meal was prepared by relatives and friends. They gathered the best berries and herbs the prairie affords and put their juice into a buffalo bladder, which was fashioned to serve as a "breastlike nursing bottle" (Erikson, 1950, p. 135).

One can see Erikson analyzing how the Sioux culture helped the infant cope with his first developmental challenge, Trust versus Mistrust. The giving of colostrum might engender in the infant feelings of mistrust in the world so the Sioux mother, relatives, and friends all banded together to help the infant have a trust-producing feeding experience. It was hoped that this positive feeding experience generalized to help the infant develop a trust in his world.

AMERICA: THE YUROK OF THE PACIFIC COAST

Erikson described the Yurok as "fishermen along a salmon river." He was accompanied by Alfred Kroeber, an anthropologist, after moving to California in 1938. The Yurok territory was situated about 200 miles north of San Francisco, near the Oregon border. The Yurok lived "in a narrow, mountainous, densely forested river valley and along the coast of its outlet into the Pacific." Kroeber acquainted Erikson with the Yurok territory, and introduced him to "informants" in the tribe. Erikson's methods of data gathering included observations, numerous interviews with native informants and consulting Kroeber's *Handbook of the Indians of California* (1925).

The main objective of Erikson's trip was to gain information and understanding about the training of children in the Yurok tribe. One major assumption held by Erikson in his study was that the Yurok's system of child training was neither arbitrarily lenient or cruel, but had a logic of its own. Erikson explained that systems of child training in different cultures

> . . . reveal mechanisms of an automatic mutual regulation of child training, tribal preservation and individual mental health. They represent unconscious attempts at creating out of human raw material that configuration of attitudes which is (or once was) the optimum under the tribe's particular natural conditions and economic-historic necessities (Erikson, 1943, p. 370).

In terms of his psychosocial stages, Erikson discussed the Yurok's attempt at accelerating autonomy in their young by early weaning ("forgetting the mother") and a general tendency to encourage the baby to leave the mother as early as possible.

> It begins in utero. The pregnant woman eats little, carries much wood, and preferably does work which forces her to bend forward, so that the fetus will not rest against her spine—i.e., relax and recline. Later, not only does early weaning further require him to release his mother; the baby's legs are left uncovered in the Yurok version of the cradleboard, and from the twentieth day on they are massaged by the grandmother to encourage early creeping (Erikson, 1950, pp. 175–176).

This attempt at accelerated autonomy is done to reduce the child's feeling too comfortable with and around his mother. The Yurok child is trained to be a fisherman, with nets ready for prey, the appropriate nice attitude, an ability to cry, and prayers in order to draw a salmon toward him. Autonomy, usually a developmental challenge in the child's second year of life according to Erikson, is made a first-year issue in the Yurok child's life seemingly to foster both a separation from the mother and an early identity as a "fisherman along a salmon river."

Erikson advanced our understanding of personality and identity development by including the influence of the person's sociocultural world throughout the lifespan.

APPLICATION OF ERIKSON'S IDEAS TO CULTURE, CURRICULUM, AND COMMUNITY

One of Erikson's major contributions was his emphasis on the intimate relationship between identity development, culture, relationships, and community. Children discover who they are through their interactions with significant others (especially parents and teachers) modified by the expectations and norms of the particular culture. Erikson highlights the importance of the development of self-esteem in children in different cultures.

> . . . their ego identity gains real strength only from wholehearted and consistent recognition of real accomplishment—i.e., of achievement, that has meaning in the culture (Erikson, 1950, pp. 235–236).

ALAN ROLAND: GEOGRAPHY

Alan Roland, an American clinician born 1930, is a cross-cultural psychologist and psychotherapist practicing and teaching in New York City. How did Roland become interested in studying and working with people from different cultures?

> Is there, however, any one true beginning? Beginners are often, in fact, journeys themselves, antecedents to new explorations not originally anticipated or even directly related. In 1950, after emerging from a year's experience in the Marine Corps and while in the throes of a late adolescent identity crisis, I came upon the writings of Vivekananda and Vedanta philosophy in my search for values and life's meaning. I transferred to Antioch College to study Indian philosophy and culture . . . took the few courses on India and the Far East, did a senior thesis on Gandhi . . . but it was the early 1950s, when graduate programs in South Asian studies were still few and far between. Instead I headed off into clinical psychology to deal more directly with the therapeutics of both others and myself, and to fashion a career (Roland, 1988, x).

Roland received a Ph.D. in clinical psychology from Adelphi University in 1960. Later Roland was strongly impelled to go to Japan as well as India. Although philosophy attracted him to India, it was art and aesthetics that drew him to Japan. On a trip to Japan in 1969 he met major Japanese psychotherapists with whom he later consulted on issues of cross-cultural psychology. While in Japan, Roland did etchings and watercolors of Zen gardens and studied wood-block printing. It is interesting to note that Roland's father was a recognized watercolorist who on occasion was mistaken for being Japanese. Roland's interest in India was also sparked by an unexpected event in March, 1971. After teaching a class in New York City, an intense-looking Indian man approached Roland about starting therapy because his identity was extremely fragmented. In the following excerpt, one can see how Roland, in the initial therapy sessions, was profoundly surprised by the powerful role culture played in shaping his new patient's beliefs and way of life.

> Thus began a several month collaborative therapy with an Indian novel-
> ist, Ashis. . . . I was immediately struck in those therapy sessions that the
> quality of his mind was of a different cast than that of any American
> patient I had ever worked with. Slowly, indeed, an enormous fracture in
> his identity did emerge between Indian and Western values and modes of
> being—both anchored, to be sure, within familial relationships, but nev-
> ertheless relating to profound civilizational issues (Roland, 1988, ix).

ROLAND'S PSYCHOLOGICAL THEORY

A brief summary of Roland's theoretical orientation starts with his foundation of Freudian psychoanalytic theory. Roland uses a "Freudian multimodel approach" which is embedded in Freudian structural theory (id-ego-super-ego); Freudian psychosexual theory (oral-anal-phallic-latency genital stages; the oedipal complex); the importance of the unconscious and dreams; the importance of transference (the patients projection onto a therapist of feelings or attitudes); the importance of countertransference (the therapist's emotional responses to the patient); and the psychoanalytic method of treatment. He also incorporates neo-Freudian theories, especially ego psychology (which includes the ego defense mechanisms and the signficance of ego functions in processes such as learning, perception, and decision making) and object relations theory. An "object" is something loved, usually a person. The term "object relations" means emotional attachments. "These attachments can exist in the outer world of reality or as residues of the past—that is, inner presences, often unconscious, that remain vigorous and very much alive within us" (Scarf, 1995, p. xxxvii). Roland also values developmental models such as Erikson's psychosocial theory as well as other neo-Freudian and Jungian positions.

As Roland began his journey doing clinical research and encountering the cultures of India and Japan, he also found himself starting a far greater rethink-ing of his own theory and treatment than he originally had anticipated. He dis-cussed the profound effect these cultural encounters had on him.

> Only much later in my reflections did I realize that not only did the
> norms and values of psychological functions, and psychological
> makeup itself differ, but the very categories in which I was thinking as
> a psychoanalyst differed from Indian cultural categories of thought
> about human nature . . . only now have I begun to appreciate how
> much of the theoretical structure of psychoanalysis is based on West-
> ern philosophical thought (Roland, 1988, xvi).

Roland's travels and study led to the publication of *In Search of Self in India and Japan: Toward a Cross-Cultural Psychology* in 1988. Roland's travels to India and Japan will be reviewed in the sections that follow.

TRAVELS IN INDIA AND JAPAN

One main purpose of Roland's study was to investigate profound changes in the structure of the self that takes place when persons are in intense contact with both Eastern and Western cultures; to do this he examined the nature of self from a cross-civilizational perspective. Roland compared the nature of the self in India, Japan, and the United States. Roland did his research and clinical work in India from 1977–1978 and then again in the summer of 1980. Most of his psychoanalytic work was done in cosmopolitan Bombay. His provided short-term psychoanalytic therapy with some thirteen Indian patients for periods of one to six months. The patients came from heterogeneous regional and religious backgrounds as described here.

> They were from five different religious communities: six were Hindu upper-caste persons, three were Parsees, two were Muslims from the Borah and Ismaili communities, one was Christian and another Jewish (Roland, 1988, xx).

He also did work in three other Indian cities: New Delhi, Ahmedabad, and in 1980, Bangalore. Regarding methodology, Roland consulted with social workers, psychiatrists, and social scientists reviewing valuable comments and critiques. He also attended case conferences and lectures, and gave presentations to mental health professionals on the initial formulations of his research. In the summer of 1982 Roland traveled to Japan and spent a month in Hiroshima as a participant in a working group of up to thirty-five psychoanalytically oriented therapists from many cities in the Inland Sea area. Roland led group supervisory sessions reviewing the therapy of five patients. There were lengthy exchanges and discussions both formally and informally. He had intensive discussions with several Japanese psychoanalysts on Japanese psychological makeup. Roland also met psychoanalysts in Tokyo and was allowed access to a psychiatric hospital.

ROLAND'S CROSS-CULTURAL CONCEPT OF SELF

In taking a cross-cultural perspective on the self, Roland compared and contrasted the development and functioning of the self in three societies: India, Japan, and the United States. As a result of his research and experience in the different cultures, Roland became convinced that the self must be divided into three overarching organizations: the familial self, the individualized self, and the spiritual self. He defines the familial self as "a basic inner psychological organization that enables men and women to function well within the hierarchical intimacy relationships of the extended family, community, and other groups." The individualized self is the predominant inner psychological organization of Americans, enabling them to function in a highly mobile society where considerable autonomy is granted if not imposed on the individual. The spiritual self "is the inner spiritual reality that is within everyone and is realized and experienced to varying extents by a very limited number of persons through a variety of spiritual disciplines." Summarizing his findings, Roland found that the traditional makeup of Indians and Japanese consists of integrations of a familial self and a spiritual self with little of the individualized self as discussed previously. This contrasts with the American makeup which has predominantly the individualized self with background chords of a familial self. According to Roland the familial self also manifests itself much more in Western women than in men.

APPLICATION OF ROLAND'S IDEAS TO CULTURE, CURRICULUM, AND COMMUNITY

Roland's findings underscore the importance of community-based and school-based mental health professionals exploring and understanding the varied religious, ethnic, cultural, and national characteristics of their clientele in order to be more effective service providers. A cross-cultural perspective needs to begin in the professional's training program, whether in counseling, psychiatric nursing, psychiatry, psychology, or social work. Through selected textbooks, guided readings, chosen lecture material, and field placements which have a diverse population, students can be exposed to the values and modes of being of persons from a variety of cultures. A cross-cultural perspective is becoming more important in the United States because the face of America is becoming increasingly diverse.

REFERENCES

Coles, R. (1970). *Erik Erikson: The growth of his work.* Boston: Little, Brown.

Erikson, E. (1943). Observations on the Yurok: childhood and world image. In S. Schlein (Ed.). (1987). *A way of looking at things* (pp. 446–480). New York: W.W. Norton.

Erikson, E. (1950). *Childhood and society.* (2nd. ed.). New York: W.W. Norton.

Jacobi, J. & Hull, R. F. C. (Eds.). (1973). *C. G. Jung: Psychological reflections; a new anthology of his writings, 1905–1961.* Princeton: Princeton University Press.

Jaffe, Aniela (Ed.). (1979). *C. G. Jung: Word and image.* Princeton: Princeton University Press.

Jung, C. G. (1928). *Contributions to analytic psychology.* New York: Harcourt, Brace & Co.

Jung, C. G. (1930). The complications of American psychology. In H. Read, M. Fordham, G. Adler, and W. McGuire (Eds.). (1964). *The collected works of Jung: Vol. 10. Civilization in transition* (pp. 502–514). Princeton: Princeton University Press.

Jung, C. G. (1939). The dreamlike world of India. In H. Read, M. Fordham, G. Adler, and W. McGuire (Eds.). (1964). *The collected works of Jung: Vol. 10. Civilization in transition* (pp. 515–524). Princeton: Princeton University Press.

Jung, C. G. (1939). What India can teach us. In H. Read, M. Fordham, G. Adler, and W. McGuire (Eds.). (1964). *The collected works of Jung: Vol. 10. Civilization in transition* (pp. 515–524) . Princeton: Princeton University Press.

Jung, C. G. (1944). The holy men of India. In H. Read, M. Fordham, G. Adler, and W. McGuire (Eds.). (1964). *The collected works of Jung: Vol. 11. Psychology and religion: West and East* (2nd ed., pp. 576–586). Princeton: Princeton University Press.

Jung, C. G. (1961). *Memories, dreams, reflections.* New York: Vintage Books.

Jung, C. G. & von Franz, M. L. (Eds.). (1964). *Man and his symbols.* New York: Doubleday.

McGuire, W. and Hull, R. F. C. (Eds.). (1977). *C. G. Jung speaking: Interviews and encounters.* Princeton: Princeton University Press.

Roland, A. (1988). *In search of self in India and Japan: Toward a cross-cultural psychology.*

Roland, A. (1997). *Personal communication.*

Storr, Anthony (1973). *Jung.* New York: Routledge.

Chapter 3

Beyond Values Clarification:
A Civic Ethic for Public Discourse
and Education

LELAND J. WHITE

I know I risk a new round of lawyer jokes—if not lawyer bashing. But what the American people need is more consideration of law as a primary resource for education in ethical matters. Our public discourse might become more civil and our understanding of professional responsibilities more workable if we followed the logic of law.

Nursing education is inevitably education for professionals who must in an ever changing society reassess how to provide ethical health care. It is also preparation for professionals in daily contact with often far less prepared fellow citizens who must weigh the pros and cons of life and death decisions with good consciences. In either case the health care professional must begin with some clarity as to the values and norms appropriate. We cannot assume that values and norms appropriate for one serving the public are identical to the values and norms that guide our individual private lives.

CORE VALUES, PROFESSIONAL NORMS, AND LAW

I will argue that our core social values and the norms suitable for professional life are enshrined more in our legal traditions than anywhere else. Moreover, when we look elsewhere to psychologically grounded processes such as values clarification, or to religious traditions, for example, we fail to meet our demand for ethical guidance as a society. As the argument develops, I hope that it becomes clear that the fundamental issues at play are at work in virtually all professions and areas of American life,[1] certainly not confined to nursing and health care.

Let us proceed in three stages. First, it is good to describe some of the less than adequate approaches we Americans take in dealing with the ethical issues that confront us, whether in health care, professional life, or elsewhere. The contention, I emphasize, is that they are less than adequate, not that they are either all wrong, or that we might replace them with completely different approaches. Cultures, I believe, are if not organic, at least systematic. Their strengths are embedded in the same perspectives as their weaknesses, their blind spots determined by their focus. Perhaps, Europeans or Asians do some things better. We are not likely to weave particular threads of other cultures

---

[1] A word of explanation for my focus on "American" life, law, and values, as well as what will certainly appear to be my underlying proposition that a coherent "American" culture can be described and, for our purposes held to be normative. Diversity, or better, pluralism, is certainly an ever more important dimension of U.S. life. Nonetheless, pluralism, the existence of a host of private choices in religious, aesthetic, or familial patterns, produces subcultures available to individuals who are part of the wider culture not as members of a subculture but rather precisely as individuals. For example, pluralistic U.S. cultural norms, embodied in law, guarantee me the right to choose to be Catholic, for another individual to be Buddhist; they do not give the Catholic Church or Buddhism any rights as groups. Groups in the United States exist insofar as individuals have the right to associate freely. In this context, then, the term "multicultural" is inappropriate (Weber, 1921/1978).

into the fabric of our culture without reshaping them beyond recognition. So we begin with a vision of the American ethical landscape. Having seen the ethical landscape, second, we will show how it is rooted in an overall values orientation. For this we will rely on the Kluckhohn-Strodtbeck model, which has the cross-cultural virtue of indicating not only our priorities but how our priorities differ from those of other cultures.

Finally, let us look at the U.S. legal tradition as a resource for conversation on the values that shape our social and professional lives. Preeminent in this tradition is our constitutionalism, the idea that norms, rules, and laws themselves are grounded in something more fundamental, which includes a fundamental law in which basic values are enshrined but also a process by which the relevance and salience of the basic values is tested and applied.

ROADBLOCKS: SOME U.S. ETHICAL LANDMARKS

Landmarks often come in the form of roadblocks, like ancient oaks that happen to stand in the middle of a heavily traveled, narrow city street. In what follows, keep in mind that anything important enough to be a landmark may also obstruct the view. Just as all lawyers are not ethical, admittedly a large measure of the legal tradition is not a particularly helpful source of ethical norms. Much of what we find in the law are mere rules, procedures that serve our overall legal objectives of justice and fairness only *in relatively circumscribed situations.* Clearly, following these rules does not in and of itself produce justice. Indeed, following the rules in some situations frequently results in inequities, sometimes even gross inequities. For example, under older rules nursing staff may have had no responsibility to take initiatives beyond the directions given by an attending physician regarding the medical regime. These rules *may* be questionable in the health care system we see emerging where the "attending physician" is very often a remote figure, who has not seen the patient for some time, or has been brought into the situation for the first time in the middle of an ongoing program of treatment. Without getting overly involved in specifics, any assessment of such situations that does not impose an obligation on *each* of these health care professionals (i.e., the physicians and the nurses) both to consult one another, and to insist on being consulted misses the point. Contemporary health care has made them interdependent members of a health care team. Rules derived from the era of independent professional life do not provide adequate protection to the patient.

NEW RULES? USEFUL?

In times of rapid change people, professionals included, readily enough conclude that rules must change. Nonetheless, the resulting disarray is disturbing, and especially so for professionals engaged in activities in which lives hang in the balance. Legal response, not always appropriate, to this disarray is understandable even if the resulting law has debatable merit. Patients, potential patients, as well as health care professionals, for example, confront health insurance company-based decisions to manage costs by restricting the length of hospital stays. The "There ought to be a law" response takes over. Well-intended, and in the circumstances perhaps necessary, *measures are enacted to require insurers to honor medical decisions in reference to disease X, or procedure Y.* What is the long-term prognosis for the use of these legal Band-Aids? Other unwarranted intrusions in—or forgetfulness of—patient care will always turn up. And the lengthened stay required today may be counter indicated in the future. The rule, however, especially if it is enacted into law, is likely to outlast its usefulness.

One response to this state of affairs is to rely more exclusively on the ethical judgment of each individual to discern their personal and professional responsibility to others and to act accordingly. This approach has both a long history and considerable appeal. Its history is embedded in some of the notions central to the concept of "profession." The concept has religious origins; the "professed life" in earlier Christian history was grounded in vows, solemn commitments made by its members. Reformation Christianity generally extended such solemn commitments to all believers who were considered "called" to their work in society as a whole. Modern and contemporary secularized understandings of *profession* retain the emphasis on the judgment of the professionals themselves—an emphasis justified only if we assume a relatively high level of personal commitment as well as education—when they distinguish professions from other forms of employment in terms of the profession's self-governing character.

Professionals today often complain that their independence and judgment is compromised by decisions imposed by agents outside their professions. What is new in the complaint is that decisions are *imposed by agents outside their professions.* This element of outsider power over the professional person needs to be pointed out because professionals, especially in the United States, have extremely high, if not unrealistic, expectations of personal autonomy that make them unwilling to acknowledge the controls that have always been a feature of professional life. In the past, individual professionals were considered self-governing not because the judgment of each individual was regarded as sacrosanct but because the professional was committed to self-regulation determined by standards and norms established by the traditions of the profession and the collective judgment of colleagues. When professionals thought of themselves as self-governing individuals—and therefore designed programs of professional education to equip individual professionals to make appropriate professional decisions—they deferred instinctively, as a matter of fact, to relatively elaborate standards and codes. Moreover, the general public relied on the fact that this was the case, seeing each professional within the wider framework of the profession as a whole.

PERSONAL INFLUENCE PREFERRED TO SOCIAL CONTROL

This state of affairs *was* taken for granted in large measure because the professions had, at least by comparison to the present situation, relatively settled turfs. Those in control of the professional's life were colleagues. Although we think of colleagues as our equals, their equality is not the equality of one person to another, one citizen with another before the law, but rather the common bond existing among persons who share the same language, language being taken here as far more than a vocabulary, as a whole way of organizing and investigating reality through the use of a system of symbols. The colleague has roughly the same education, acknowledges the same kinds of authorities, and relies on the same types of procedures in action as well as thought. Even when one colleague is invested with authority over another colleague, the colleague makes an appeal based on a presumed mutual understanding, an understanding that may be challenged in terms available to both parties. Ultimately the colleague employs *influence*, the ability to persuade others to think or act in a particular way before and usually instead of *power*.[2] Moreover, a professional's influence over the public stems in large measure from the fact that the public accepts an individual as a professional to the extent that professional colleagues appear to accept the individual as such. Influence is based on persuasion.

From the perspective of U.S. culture, morality is inherently individualist because we tend to assume that direct use of social controls is coercive, an exercise of sheer power. We tend to judge social controls legitimate to the extent that they are derived from individuals or individual experience. Matters of personal probity or lack of it are given great, if not exclusive, attention when we select public officials. We vote for the individual regardless of party, that is, without attending to socially elaborated public policy positions.

And we are likely to admire the person who independently refuses to compromise with others to do "some good" rather than holding out for what is right. In our aversion to the direct use of social control and compromise, quite probably we do not see ourselves as rejecting the option of some good; rather we instinctively trust our individual judgment which inevitably perceives less goodness or perhaps evil in the group proposal. We distrust the group proposal insofar as it seems to be the product of either coercion or half-hearted conviction. Individually unpersuaded, the most striking feature we attribute to the group option is its coercive power. That is, we resign ourselves to going along because the group has the power to enforce its will or because going along with the group will enable us in some measure to enforce our will on others. It is not surprising that the most eminent social ethicist in U.S. history, Reinhold

---

[2]One who wields *influence* must provide an explanation of the facts, know-why information; one wielding *power*, the sheer ability to get others to conform, needs know-how, specifically how to make decisions for others and get others to go along with them. In U.S. culture, even power tends to be exercised by a strategy of *inducement*, which means that power players have their effect by providing goods and services to others or by showing the link between compliance and such goods. See Malina, 1986: pp. 71–74, 81–84.

Niebuhr, would entitle a major work *Moral Man and Immoral Society.* The title sums up our cultural experience.

VOLUNTARY ASSOCIATION AND VALUES CLARIFICATION

Given this inherent cultural suspicion of group motivation, our favored form of social life is the voluntary association, the social group that is most completely dependent on the will of its members and prospective members for its very existence. We limit our sense of responsibility or obligation to those with whom we have chosen to relate rather than those related to us by blood or mere force of law. Spouses are obligated to one another and to their children because they have chosen these relationships. But children, unless and to the extent that they voluntarily enter into mutually acceptable relationships with parents or siblings, in a strict sense have no obligations, which is why very early on U.S. parents and parental surrogates (e.g., teachers) begin negotiating with their offspring, and why they highlight the benefits of such social graces as sharing and expressing appreciation. Instead of saying "You must" or "You should," the adult reasons and persuades, allowing the child to draw conclusions. Even at the end of life, U.S. parents are embarrassed to suggest, much less insist, that even their own children have obligations to them, something taken for granted in other cultures.

Adult-to-child discussions are in fact rooted in the same model of ethical education as values clarification. Values clarification techniques are designed to help the individual see what kind of a person they really are, that is, to identify the individual's goals and the means the individual would choose so that the person may develop more consistently. What is it that I do that makes me think well of myself, that expresses what I want to express about who I am and enables me to get what I really want? The values clarification technique assumes that the better stated goal is a more reliable guide to action, and that only clearer understanding will produce a clear statement. Also underlying this process is awareness that making the statement acknowledges or makes a commitment. The ground of social commitments is personal decision, voluntary.

In spite of the strong tendency of the religious right, along with some non-religious moral absolutists, to attack the values clarification approach for its subjectivism, many of those who rely on religion and religious moral codes to create the basis for a moral society are in essential agreement with the premise of the values clarification techniques. The common premise is that a society is as good as the personal lives, and therefore the personal moral resources and commitments, of its members.

GOOD PERSONS NO GUARANTEE SOCIETY IS GOOD

But a society only as good as the personal lives, personal moral resources, and commitments of its members is not good *as a society* (i.e., as a social whole). At one level, Americans tend to accept this assessment. We tend to think for example that the political system is corrupt, that business is not a realm where nice guys finish first, that the criminal justice system can do little about crime except to deter it by imposing harsh sentences or exacting vengeance on the criminals.

In those areas of life, by contrast, which are focused more directly on individuals, we make no such concessions. Thus, for example, schools could do a good job of educating our children if we let parents and teachers set their minds to it *without* the roadblocks created by the school systems and the teachers' unions. Medicine likewise could provide good patient care if we simplified the health care delivery system. The tax code would be fairer if it were simpler, and the poor would be better provided for if we let individual initiative replace the welfare system. In each of the cases, and in many more like them, our assumption is that moral rot appears wherever social institutions appear, presumably because social institutions get in the way of the otherwise good intentions and efforts of individuals or private groups of individuals.

The bias against social institutions is ingrained. Part of the reason is that we expect social institutions to function according to the same rules as interpersonal relationships (i.e., as face-to-face interactions). Our negative judgment on social institutions arises from the fact that this expectation is unrealistic. In fact, face-to-face interaction in the area of politics, for example, is characteristic of the tribe, not the state experienced by Americans. In tribal settings, people are always in person-to-person contact, seeing each other as fellow kin, perhaps fellow villagers. Those with authority, preeminently patriarchal figures, are immediately present to dependent kinfolk. Patriarchal authority, appearing to be grounded in natural life processes, is believed to come from God or some divine source, which makes it unquestionable. By way of contrast, the most apt description of relationships in the state as we know it is face-to-space, the state being above all a territorial entity in which persons interact not with embodied entities such as a patriarch, but rather with no "body." Squiggles on a page (print), light on a screen, or electrons coursing over the face of a TV or computer monitor confront us with advice, directives, regulations, and laws. In the democratic state all persons are fellow citizens with rights and obligations. In the democratic state some hold offices which they have *acquired* by election or some process certifying their qualifications, quite unlike the *ascribed* office once held by patriarchs by reason of descent or age. In intermediate stages between the tribe and the modern state, kings or the monarchy held office on roughly the same terms as in the tribal setting. This underscores the break that the modern state represents in political development, as does the fact that the modern state's authority is founded on the consent of the governed rather than divinely willed.[3]

---

[3]This analysis of political development, taken from James, is illustrated in Malina, 1994.

WHAT'S GOOD ABOUT BUREAUCRACY

Movable type and successively disembodied communications media along with the breakdown of the notion that certain persons differ from others by virtue of their access to either sacred wisdom or power, then, has produced the modern state. Fellow citizens do not seek favor from other persons, whether the blessing of a father (face-to-face), the grace of a patron with access to the king (face-to-grace) or the legal authorization of the monarchy's representative (symbolized by the mace, and hence labeled face-to-mace). Instead, fellow citizens confront impersonal institutional representatives (i.e., bureaucrats). Bureaucratic structures link persons and agencies to one another on the basis of officers having certain responsibilities, who must act according to written rules and regulations, using prescribed means of compulsion. Bureaucrats lack the arbitrariness of patriarchal and other authority systems founded on divine power. Indeed, what discretion bureaucrats have is restricted to choosing the best means to achieve a legitimate result, and even in the exercise of this limited discretion, bureaucrats are accountable, their actions being subject to later review.

The bureaucratic approach is the prime example of what Max Weber called formal rationality. Though Weber was generally gloomy about the effects of formal rationalization on human relations, he identified its chief virtues: efficiency, calculability, predictability, and the control it gives to nonhuman technologies, as opposed to human technologies, as means of controlling individuals. Nonhuman technologies include rules and machines, the rules and regulations rendering the actions of individuals as efficient, calculable, and predictable as the movements of the machinery that often replaced human labor. Human technologies, pens or hammers, for example, tend to be controlled by individuals and the results are far less predictable.

Burned by their experience of the British parliament and its agents whose grants of power derived from an unwritten constitution, American delegates assembling in Philadelphia after the revolution crafted a written constitution. Moreover, the text crafted by the framers of the U.S. Constitution enumerated powers for the Congress and reserved all other powers to the states or to the people. Likewise, it divided the officers of the federal government among three branches, assigning to each separate and generally limited functions; overall it made each branch serve partially as a brake on the others. While much has been made of the framers' Calvinistic distrust of human nature, the product of the Philadelphia convention is primarily evidence of their determination to control the wheels of governmental power by setting them firmly in a system of tracks, levers, and brakes. It was as rational a system as Henry Ford's assembly line or the franchising system epitomized by McDonald's.

What should be clear is that presidents, congresspersons or police officers who, following the rules of face-to-face interaction, decide to do whatever they feel moved to do or whatever a citizen or group of citizens desire, have overstepped their bounds. The law has tied their hands, as it also ties, though to a lesser degree, the hands of the businessperson who ignores rights established by law or contract in hiring, firing, promoting, or compensating employees. By the same logic, the professional norm ties the hands of the professional to exercise professional judgment, to restrict the more personal and intuitive response in accordance with professional standards. The more intimately the professional person's contact with others is, the greater the tension between acting as a friend and acting in one's institutionalized social role.

U.S. VALUES ORIENTATION IN CROSS-CULTURAL PERSPECTIVE

To get a more holistic view of the values orientation most characteristic of American culture, it is helpful to sketch a comprehensive view, and still more useful to do this from a cross-cultural perspective. This holistic view may be seen in the categories established by the Kluckhohn-Strodtbeck Value Orientation model.[4] How does U.S. culture look as a whole, and especially in comparison to others?

INDEPENDENT INDIVIDUALS

Americans see themselves as independent individuals. We see the individual as unique, totally different from all others—with the ironic consequence that all such individuals, being each irreplaceable, are equal and must be treated the same (i.e., with fairness). It must be pointed out that our sense of individuality is exaggerated, that we are not nearly as independent as we believe. Nonetheless, we are undoubtedly more individualist than any other humans have been or are. Independence does not negate relationships or membership in groups. Instead it qualifies our affiliations, which are typically both voluntary and more a matter of enthusiasm than they might be in a society where people think of themselves as having life-long ascribed relationships to certain groups. American groups must seek members, compete for them, give new members all the opportunities of long-standing members, including the opportunity to use the groups as vehicles for new objectives. In this, as in other aspects of U.S. social life, initiative is rewarded.

The premium Americans place on privacy would seem to conflict with our individualism and emphasis on taking the initiative. In fact, it may well simply be the flip side of the phenomenon. We guard fairly extensive portions of our lives and thoughts from others, especially the public as a whole precisely because we think ourselves unique and thus incomprehensible to others. In sum, the public areas of our lives are carefully circumscribed. We expect to make at best limited commitments to groups, which perhaps explains why in spite of the fact that we tolerate the widest possible range of personal opinions on politics, we are content to choose between only two somewhat middle-of-the-road

---

[4]For a description of this model see David M. Bossman, *Teaching Pluralism: Values to Cross Cultural Barriers.*

political parties. We are content with few public choices, provided we have the option of choosing that the public as a whole will have little to control.

ACTIVISM

U.S. culture is oriented towards action and work. "Don't just stand. there; do something!" is typical American advice. Work defines us not only as individuals, but as a people. Work orientation means activity planned to produce certain effects, the results being subject to test at its conclusion. While people in other cultures may find meaning in the realities around them (i.e., intrinsic to their lives) we find meaning primarily by finding purpose, some objective to be achieved.

This activist streak, which marks even our leisure, time-off, and vacations, appears at every income and social level. Among its effects is our growing sense that the inability to work renders life itself meaningless. Thus, what were once regarded as defining states, such as *being* a "cripple" or a "deaf-mute," in the United States have been reinterpreted first as being "disabled," then "handicapped," and now "challenged." The point is that the person is presumed to be an actor, a worker, and every effort is made to insure that he or she has every opportunity to fulfill the maximum possibilities this defining characteristic suggests.

PERSONAL CONTROL

Personal control over the environment, nature, and ultimately "Nature's God" is assumed. As individuals and as a people, we may not just stand there, because we are responsible. To think that the way things are is preordained is as close to un-American as anything could be.

Americans no longer believe in the power of Fate, and they have come to look at people who do as being backward, primitive, or hopelessly naive. To be called "fatalistic" is one of the worst criticisms one can receive in the American context; to an American, it means one is superstitious and lazy, unwilling to take any initiative in bringing about improvements. It is normal to seek a "cure" in a battle against disease, rather than "healing" by means of accommodating ourselves to an illness, just as we take it for granted that if humans want twenty-four hours of light in a day, and 365 days of temperate climate to live in, they could and should bring it about. It has been said that Americans feel compelled to do what the other seven-eighths of the human race have thought impossible apart from a supernatural intervention.

Bumper-sticker theology sums up our attitude towards the supernatural: God is my copilot. Lest anyone misinterpret this, over the course of our history we have become increasingly religious to the point that among the industrialized nations we are clearly the most religious by wide margins (Butler, 1990; Moore, 1994). God as copilot is, of course, the diametrical opposite of the biblical portrait of the divine-human relationship Americans would find in our best-selling book, the Bible, were we to read the Bible from the cultural perspective of its Mediterranean authors. But God as copilot expresses the sense of human control and responsibility shared by fundamentalists, liberal believers, and avowed secularists in the United States, as is evident in hymns, spirituals, and sermons on God and Jesus as "my friend." Contrast this with other cultures where God wreaks punishment on the disobedient and leads his faithful into battle. "What the world will be is up to us" is a conviction that cuts through bedrock to create canals, dam rivers, and make a landing base on the moon.

FUTURE ORIENTATION

We think in terms of the future, viewing change as positive. In spite of some indications that perhaps more Americans today than in the recent past are less optimistic about future prospects—how much great and lasting the shift may be being a matter of question—it remains undoubtedly true that we devalue the past and see the present as something of a launching pad for what may be. At the personal level especially, the span of time devoted to preparation and planning for first a career and then retirement is a considerable chunk of life. The initial phase of the educational process now takes up what would have been the entire average life span of peoples of other times, thirty years.

Change for us is strongly linked to development, improvement, progress, and growth, seldom if ever seen as destabilizing or threatening. The belief that we can do anything and the belief that any change is good—together with our belief in the virtue of hard work and the belief that each individual has a responsibility to do his or her best have led to a record of accomplishments. So whether these beliefs are "true" pales into insignificance before the historical reality of American impact on the world at large. The historical reality is that we have *considered* them to be true and, having acted as if they were, we have created a record of results less future-oriented peoples have scarcely been able to imagine. Nonetheless, because we so quickly consign even our most recent record to the past, we are always turning our attention to new problems to be solved. In so doing, we are typically insensitive to the fact that this renders us hypercritical and our social relationships unstable. After all, the team that created these new problems, that is, the team with the record of accomplishment, may not be the best team to solve them.

THE LEGAL TRADITION AS A RESOURCE

In the light of American future orientation, it may seem futile to appeal to any *tradition* as a resource for conversation on the values that shape our social and professional lives. I do so because what we call the legal tradition takes a not surprisingly different character in U.S. life from that of other cultures. To begin with, there is the fact that its roots are in Anglo-Saxon common law. Exactly what does this mean? Why does the Anglo-American legal tradition stand apart from the legal tradition of Europe? Second, American ingenuity reshaped the tradition quite early in a way that insures an ongoing process of legal development. Third, what has emerged is a sense of the law (i.e., a sense of what is normative), as a matter of facilitation, enablement, empowerment rather than as directive or controlling, or, perhaps better, as directive and controlling only for the sake of an ever broader empowerment of fellow citizens. Let us consider each in turn.

HOW ANGLO-AMERICAN LAW
BROKE WITH EUROPE

It is often supposed that Anglo-Saxon law developed so differently from continental law because of the unique spirit of the British people or because of their isolation on an island.

In fact, English and continental law diverged at the very time, the twelfth century, when England and English people were heavily involved in European affairs, its scholars at continental universities, its kings ruling and spending large amounts of their time in their continental territories, with French the court language and Latin still the language of scholarship and law (Van Caenegem, 1988, pp. 85–110). The reasons for the divergence of English from continental law are undoubtedly more a matter of the mode of English legal development than of any unique spirit or isolation. Common law, at least in England, is commonly spoken of as judge-made law, which means that it was built up decision by decision serving as precedent, a process that was ultimately derived from the various European tribal peoples who invaded England.

There is, however, a *lex communis,* or common law, derived ultimately from Rome that was codified and recodified on the continent. But there are significant differences between the way English common law and the *lex communis* functioned. The *lex communis* was seen as a universal law establishing principles for all the peoples (nations) on the continent, and these universal legal principles were the subject of university debate and elaboration, all quite largely in the abstract, and in any event not applied in ordinary local courts. At the local level, Europeans were governed by whatever local tribal traditions held sway. These differed greatly from place to place, nowhere taking standard form on a national level. It was quite different in England, where the king established royal courts throughout the land, and empowered all of the King's courts to dispense writs of judgment in the royal name following common law precedents as such precedents developed. In other words, English royal justice was national, but at the same time local, arising from particular cases rather than in an academic setting (Van Caenegem, 1988, pp. 88–90).

LAW SHAPED ENGLISH
AND THEN AMERICAN IDENTITY

At the same time—contradicting those who think common law is the product of the unique spirit of the British people—far from being the product of some mystical "Englishness," the common law probably shaped English identity and character to a significant degree. How else to explain what happened to England in the course of the twelfth century when the common law tradition was emerging? At the beginning, England was clearly one kingdom with at least two nations, the Anglo-Saxons and the Normans, who were commonly referred to at the time as Anglici and Franci in writs and charters. Danes and Welshmen were among other sizable populations. To use current terminology, England was multicultural; the conquering Normans ruled, and the natives (naïfs or knaves) were an underclass with little or no freedom. Within a hundred years, the "English" had emerged, free landowners no longer thinking of themselves as either Anglo-Saxons or Normans, intermarrying with one another and claiming the rights defended in the royal justice system (Van Caenegem, 1988, pp. 95–98).

Half a millennium later, English colonists in America claimed not universal human rights, but rather the rights of Englishmen when they spoke of things that were "self-evident." In assessing the blind spots in their revolution and constitution, this is significant. Thus, it was not a simple matter to square the rule of freedom for all under one law with the property rights of slave owners. Indeed, the bar to even a royal entry into one's home made the husband/owner master of all who dwelt there and still stymies advocates of women's and children's rights. Thus, two elements of the original tradition are still characteristic of U.S. common law, the sense of a national norm and its roots less in reason and logic than in empirical realities and relationships.

WHAT AMERICAN INGENUITY ADDED

American ingenuity, however, added to English common law the distinctive principle of judicial review. Judicial review, whether it was created out of whole cloth or understood as woven into the Constitution in Chief Justice John Marshall's *Marbury v. Madison* decision, asserts that the courts, ultimately the Supreme Court, as interpreter of the Constitution, is the arbiter of the constitutionality of any legislative enactment or executive order. In other words, both the making and execution of law is subject to review. To sum up this development, the review process was designed above all to see to it that all citizens receive due process. The Constitutional principle of due process reshaped the English common law tradition in a way that insures an ongoing process of legal development.

What Americans notice, especially in the major Constitutional cases, is the affirmation of one right after another, the right to free speech, freedom of religion, freedom of the press, reproductive freedom, and the like. Some people find some extensions of these freedoms to some types of activities, for example, free speech to flag burning or adult-theme artistic expression, distasteful. They complain of activist judges who are rewriting rather than merely interpreting the law. Even people quite comfortable with most of the concrete results may, however, wonder how such a collection of freedoms could serve as a resource for a conversation on values. After all, is not the effect more negative than positive, a series of statements about what people are free to do rather than a guide or norm of action? This is why I believe it important to identify a central constitutional concern in the whole activity of judicial review. The core constitutional concern or value is due process.

DUE PROCESS— OUR DEFINING CHARACTERISTIC

Due process is not easy to define or explain. It is difficult to avoid sounding circular when we discuss due process, because quite simply "due process is that process which is due, i.e., the procedures that ought to be taken in a given case with any person or persons." The fact that it is a matter of procedures (i.e., going through the legal forms) makes it unappealing even to many lawyers who recall how dull a course on civil (court) procedure usually is.

For the general public, more aware perhaps of criminal procedure, which they will likely label a "bunch of technicalities unscrupulous lawyers use to get people off," due process may appear largely immoral. For those who think of rights in terms of transcendent universals, such as the right to life extending even to the fetus, consideration of whether some individual, in this case the pregnant woman, has been accorded due process is a triumph of procedure over substance. We may acknowledge that all this and more is at work in due process. The more is what is significant, at least as a shaping influence on U.S. culture, and a value that may be seen as core in our social and professional lives.

The "more" is simply this: Due process is the norm that insists that every social relationship, especially every social institution, including the professions, adjudicate all disputes according to known laws and in such stages that all parties have a fair opportunity to have their claims considered. Due process places a burden on all parties, but especially on those with power over others, to make the public forum as open as possible to each and every citizen. Yes, this means an endless stream of inquiries: Who told this person to do that? Under what circumstances? Does the state have the right to an answer to such a question? If the state or perhaps some other social institution has a legitimate interest in regulating this or that activity, has it chosen the least restrictive means to do so?

What is "due" is always a matter of judgment. Even where the limits of social control have become relatively clear, there remains the judgment as to what actually happened in a given case. Interestingly, this crucial question of fact is reserved more often than not to a jury of one's peers rather than to a judge. Due process, thus, includes the idea that one's actions be assessed by those most likely to understand what was done.

RULES TO FACILITATE RATHER THAN CONTROL ACTION

The American sense of law, our norm for rules, is rooted in due process. Law and rules are meant not to control action, but rather to facilitate it, to enable and empower people, directing and controlling them only for the sake of an ever broader empowerment of all within the society. It should not surprise us— whether we think law shaped us or that, being the people we are, we shaped the law—to discover that the core value of according everyone due process embodies the individualist, activist, futurist character we have so far described as typically American. Nor should we be surprised that at first glance, it appears to be as ill-equipped to cope with society as society, social institutions as social institutions as we have indicated about the individual values earlier.

But the common law tradition, enhanced by judicial review focused on due process does, in a characteristically American way, address social life, at least by implication. First, it takes the empirical facts or realities in all social life as a given, insisting that what is to be judged is what is actually the case rather than a theory of what might be the case. It insists that this reality be sized up in all its particularity by those actually involved. Second, it makes every governmental intervention—and social intervention?—as a mater of principle subject to scrutiny, not presuming official wrongdoing, but certainly trying to prevent unwarranted coercion by the threat of subsequent review. Finally, it requires due consideration of all concerned.

NO FAVORS OR PRIVILEGES

Let it be noted as well that it takes full account of the face-to-space relationship characteristic of the democratic state and the bureaucratic social structure of virtually all sectors of contemporary life. Everything the citizen needs from the representative of the state is owed as a matter of law binding on the representative. Nothing is a matter of favor, favors being excluded in principle as unfair, unethical, illegal. The representative is faceless. But the representative who cannot not smile cannot frown.

What does the application of this legal paradigm mean in nongovernmental American life? It means, for example, that before doing anything to the consumer, the client, the student, the patient, or indeed one's colleague, the professional must receive the informed, not merely the *pro forma* signed, consent of the other, and that such consent, being as it is among equals, must accompany each significant stage of the relationship. Why? Because the process that is due is a requirement placed on the one intervening, who must ascertain what the other thinks is the case and make sure that the other has reason to understand what has been proposed. It is because it is subject to review that the burden falls on the intervenor.

PROFESSIONAL MAY NOT EVEN DO GOOD WITHOUT CONSENT

I have said that the legal tradition is a resource for public discourse and education. This requires a brief explanation at this point. Our laws provide thousands of examples, of varying quality and varying levels of difficulty for ordinary people and nonlawyers to understand, of the application of law to everyday ethical concerns. But these examples are only examples, merely illustrative. What is much more readily understood is the underlying premise of our law, the premise that social control is legitimate, or may be legitimate only to the extent that those involved participate actively in the decision-making process. This principle says I may not even do good to you against your will. It also says that you must allow others as full an opportunity to speak up as possible, and that the overall justice of any and all social life is whether or not conditions are created for all this.

Professional nursing educators might create the requisite conditions by so clarifying the services nurses provide and the role they play in relationship to other health care providers as well as to patients so that they will know not only the scope of their activities, but be able themselves to contribute to the ongoing redefinition of their role that an ever changing health care system will require. This will also require, of course, that they acquire the skills and attitudes necessary to communicate their sense of where their professional service lies not only for others with whom they work, but for the public as well. Success in professional life today is measured not by whether the condition of this or that patient or client is bettered, and certainly not merely by whether they experience the professional's warm concern, but by whether the patient or client is helped to demand suitable service from the next provider in the system, who may not be as caring, but who must nonetheless be held to a measurable standard of due care.

CIVIL DISCOURSE AT ROOT OF PROFESSIONAL SERVICE

If professional people lead the way in setting and being held to professional standards, they will enable those they serve to assess what they need from other social institutions, and learn how to articulate their needs in a reasonable manner. The resulting reasoned discussion and debate (i.e., civil discourse), which is a presupposition of due process, might enrich our social life as a whole. Aware that threats and condemnations, no less than rules of silence, eviscerate due process, educators in every area will be looking for instrumental values that embody due process, such as tolerance and the spirit of reasonable discussion.

REFERENCES

Butler, J. (1990). *Awash in a sea of faith. Christianizing the American people.* Cambridge, MA: Harvard University Press.

James, P. (1992). Forms of abstract "community": From tribe and kingdom to nation and state. *Philosophy of social sciences, 22,* 313–336.

Kluckhohn, F. & Strodtbeck, F. (1961). *Variations in value orientations.* Evanston, IL: Row, Peterson.

Malina, B. J. (1986). *Christian origins and cultural anthropology.* Atlanta, GA: John Knox Press.

Malina, B. J. (1994). Religion in the imagined new testament world. *Scriptura: Journal of bible and theology in Southern Africa, 51,* 1–26.

Moore, R. L. (1994). *Selling God. American religion in the marketplace of culture.* New York, NY: Oxford University Press.

Niebuhr, R. (1960). *Moral man and immoral society: A study in ethics and politics.* New York, NY: Charles Scribners Sons.

Van Caenegem, R. C. (1988). *The birth of the English common law* (2nd ed.). Cambridge, UK: Cambridge University Press.

Weber, M. (1921/1968). *Economy and society.* Totowa, NJ: Bedminster Press.

Chapter 4

Teaching Pluralism:
Values to Cross-Cultural Barriers

DAVID M. BOSSMAN

As I look back on the twentieth century, I see a century of unparalleled progress, both technological and social. Now is the time to focus on advancements and unfinished agendas in the social sphere, especially as it pertains to education for the twenty-first century.

The century began without women's suffrage, with racial, ethnic, and religious segregation and unfettered discrimination against many so-called societal minorities. Now, as the century draws to a close, those who forged progress in this century can rightly be proud of achievements in progressive antidiscrimination laws and growing public sensibilities: Women not only can vote but they have become operative in every branch of government. Serious efforts are even now underway to extend civil rights to members of society previously denied them, often with a claim that by nature or choice they are inferior. Women, for example, are denied equal rights by using the claim that, by nature, they are inferior to men; or to lesbians, claiming that by choice they are inferior.

As the twentieth century comes to a close, it is time to make an assessment of the age in which we have lived. The twentieth century has ushered in more advances than ever could have been imagined. But the disasters of this century similarly boggle the imagination. Using rapid advances in technology to act out various forms of bigotry and despotism, millions have been ruthlessly slaughtered in the name of ethnic cleansing (Weiss). Many more millions have been and continue to be deprived of their basic human rights of equal pay for equal work, equal access to jobs, to education, and to the requisites for advancement in employment (Jelin; Niebuhr; Mohr). Such enduring forms of prejudice and injustice, often fueled by hypocritical moral pretensions, even today linger in many communities of a nation that was populated to provide a home for the downtrodden, and structured to afford opportunities for all to seek and find justice.

But what is the agenda that we can derive from reviewing all this progress and recognizing such unfinished business? How can we, as educators of tomorrow's professions and social leaders now shape an agenda for educational advancement?

To answer this difficult question, I introduce the topic of values. Values drove the efforts and movements of our century because of their dynamic power for energizing and directing people (Baugh, Levinson). Thus the need to consider how the modern world has introduced a distinctive range of values for human society.

These values must be considered within the context of a world of dramatic development: radical changes in the conditions of life; unprecedented advances in the sciences, including the science of understanding ourselves; tremendous escalation in our capability to do damage to ourselves and our environment; new horizons for expansion and development in unthought-of realms of outer space, inner space, cyber space. The opportunities are many, yet the need for clarity and focus is real, especially for the professional educator whose task it is not only to teach technology but understanding.

The stakes are high—as high as we can imagine them ever to have been—for assessing the present in light of the past, and the future in terms of our best lights as human thinkers and educators today. If it is true to say that as a species we are distinguished by our ability to reflect upon the past and envision the future, then our task must lead us to a consideration of such questions as these: *What values motivated people in this century? What values will contribute to building a better future? And, how do we teach values that are best suited to advancing personal growth and enhancing social well-being?*

THE MEANING OF VALUES

What are values? Although we use the word frequently—as in family values, American values, social values, personal values, religious values—the dictionary gives us little sense of the power of values beyond a bland statement of "relative worth, utility, or importance." To tap the dynamism of values we must venture into more developed social sciences to pursue a fuller and more usable definition. Since values have both a religious and social base, I turn to biblical scholars John Pilch and Bruce Malina, who examine traditional religious literature using the critical tools of the social sciences. They describe values as "some general quality and direction of life that human beings are expected to embody in their behavior . . . a general, normative orientation of action in a social system . . . an emotionally anchored commitment to pursue and support certain directions or types of actions" (Malina & Pilch, xiii).

Let us take note of the several elements of this description. First, "a general quality and direction of human behavior" advances the notion that values move people to action. As normative in society, values are shared among people and thus lubricate social systems. By orienting people, values point people to a preferred mode of action within their social system. In light of these features of values, I suggest that values engage people for action in perceiving and working for a socially shared goal.

What is interesting, as we discover how different human societies are, is the realization that the human species has devised a range of systems for surviving and prospering—the goals of society. Within these diverse systems, values truly differ from one culture to another as social goals and strategies develop within human societies facing a variety of challenges and circumstances.

We thus see cultures as diverse systems that support human survival and growth, helping to shape the way people understand their world and learn how to address its challenges and opportunities together. Values embedded in diverse cultures are conventional in the sense that people within each culture learn to adopt the values that generate and sustain their particular culture (Hsu, 1972; Levinson & Malone, 1980). They are particular in the sense that cultures differ, and accordingly their conventional values serve as the social glue holding persons together and moving them to work as members of a society.

THE MEANING OF CULTURE

Next, we need to specify what experts mean by a culture. Anthropologist Clyde Kluckhohn describes culture as consisting of "patterns of behavior acquired and transmitted by symbols, constituting the distinctive achievement of human groups. . . ." He adds that "The essential core of culture consists of traditional ideas and especially their attached values. Culture systems may, on the one hand, be considered as products of action, on the other as conditioning influences upon further action" (Malina, 1986, p. 11; 1989). From this description, we learn that cultures are patterns which we can call systems—embodying both ideas and values. The ideas and values work together to bond people into a society.

The critical point now is to clarify how cultures differ as systems with their constitutive values. The television series *Crossroad Cafe* portrays individuals with different cultures working together in a diner. The program focuses on how persons of different cultures can work toward a common goal, and how they seem to coast through life on a sort of automatic pilot, which at times leads them onto collision paths with fellow workers. This is quite common in the United States. We're a country of immigrants, and each immigrant brings learned values and a particular culture. The key to our society's survival, however, is in recognizing, as we say, "E pluribus unum"—that from many cultures we become one society.

A poignant insight that Arthur Schlesinger, Jr., develops in his book, *The Disuniting of America,* is that most people come to America seeking to leave behind a society that was for them less suited for survival and growth and to enter one that has more opportunities for success. This motive led most immigrants to *want to be American,* and implicitly to learn what social values are inherent in becoming American. This often-repeated scenario is vividly portrayed for Chinese-American women in Amy Tan's book *The Joy Luck Club,* the story of Chinese immigrant women and their American-born daughters living in strained relationships because of cultural conflicts between China and the United States.

Schlesinger concludes that as long as immigrants sought to be American, this society grew and was enriched by the diversity of immigrants. This meant sharing the *value* of integrating into a cooperative social system composed of distinct individuals. The *disuniting* that Schlesinger laments results, he notes, when people later want to return to the collective culture of their ancestors, preferring that splinter group existence to the integrated American culture into which they had become—often slowly—individually incorporated.

This is a pivotal challenge today: understanding how a society can at once be built upon diversity of individuals yet be united in cooperative groups. The collectivist society assigns persons to groups by birth and role (e.g., an assigned gender or status role), creating thereby ascribed identities. The individualist society encourages persons to create their own identities by making personal choices (e.g., in education, career, relationships). Persons in the collectivist society remain dependent on the ascribing authority and can thus be described as codependent personalities. Persons in an individualist society are free to choose groups with which they find affinity by choice. Thus, individualists in practice do not normally remain isolated or self-serving, as traditionalists claim, but commit themselves voluntarily to action groups for both self-actualization and in a spirit of mutual benefit. It is this kind of individualism that Americans value.

SHARED VALUES

Let me explain this point through a consideration of what values distinguish American culture from other cultures. While Americans recognize the United States as a society composed of immigrants from many distinct cultures, they tend to agree on *shared values* that social scientists recognize as characteristically, but not exclusively, American (Watson).

Social anthropologists Florence Kluckhohn and Fred Strodtbeck studied values within diverse social world settings to determine whether there are distinctive values that differentiate social groups and how these might be specified, tested, and quantified. Toward this end, they devised a model composed of elements inherent in all human societies yet with a range of alternatives that help to distinguish the particularities of each culture. Thus, they were studying values cross-culturally, or within diverse cultures.

Their cross-cultural model was used to test distinct social groups by means of a set of questions intended to determine whether group members shared a value orientation for each of the value elements. Their study located values orientations that Americans tend to share as distinctive to their culture: orientations toward the values of individualism, action, the future, and controlling one's environment. Each of these values reflects a way of viewing core human issues, which each social world values differently. Each social group teaches members these distinctive value orientation, and group members effectively share an orientation toward these values.

Kluckhohn and Strodtbeck tested across cultural lines focusing on concerns inherent in all human societies. Within a given range of alternatives, what is the value orientation (preference) in the following areas:

1. Mode of relating to other people
2. Mode of viewing human activity
3. Temporal focus of human life
4. Relationship of humans to nature or Supernature

To the first question—the preferred mode of relating to other people—produced variations ranging from *lineal,* relating vertically as superiors and inferiors, *collateral,* relating horizontally as equals, or *individual,* relating voluntarily as independent entities. The first mode of relating is valued notably in traditional societies in which the elders, nobles, or rulers make decisions, presumably based on their wisdom (adherence to group values) or ascribed status (role) in society.

The second, relating to others collaterally, means that decisions come from the group as a whole when group members reach consensus.

The third refers to each person's acting independently as an individual, voluntarily agreeing to group action using such decision-making procedures as majority vote. These alternative preferences in effect are all values: the values that define as normative how people are expected to relate to one another: as linearly differentiated, as horizontally inclusive, or as voluntarily associated.

The second question: what is the preferred mode of human activity? This question can be answered in terms of *being*, that is simply membership in a particular group; or *being-in-becoming*, that is evolving toward fulfilling one's emerging state of being; or *doing*.

The third alternative is the value Americans seem to share: a sense that human activity is more highly valued if something is accomplished rather than if one simply is a particular group member. Traditional societies normally place great value on *being* group members. American society places less value on what group you belong to or are evolving toward and more value on what you succeed in accomplishing.

The third question: what is the preferred temporal focus of human life? This is also an interesting question that distinguishes one culture from another in terms of shared values. Some cultures value the *past* more than the *present* or the *future*.

These cultures seem to be ones in which the group is of primary focus, and the group's past gives the group its legitimacy and standards, which press the individuals to conform as group members. Other cultures seem to focus more on the present—a sense that the past is less important and the future is not within anyone's personal control.

The third value centers on the future—a realizable goal that can be achieved, normally viewed as the goals that individuals set for themselves or their children. The remote future is viewed as the group's domain, hence is linked with past as indicating the group's origin and ultimate dominance over outsiders.

The fourth question is: what is the relation of humans to nature, Supernature (divine person or order of being)? This question can be answered in terms of value preferences as *in harmony with* nature or God or the order of Nature—learning what laws govern life and complying with them in a harmonious relationship.

The second value preference is *subject to nature*: when people believe they cannot understand the workings of nature or God and simply must learn to accept what they take to be their fate in an erratic world. The third value preference is in pursuing ways to take an initiative in controlling one's circumstances—taking control of one's own life and taking responsibility for one's choices as well as joining forces to control such things as disease and disabilities. This taking control, or *mastering nature*, suggests that life is a challenge to be met rather than a script to be read. Taking control of one's life is characteristic of American values. It relates well with the other value preferences prevalent in American society, the actualized individual (*individualism*) over the dependent personality (lineal or collateral), and the energetic achiever (*doing*).

All these value preferences or orientations factor together in the professional education of medical personnel. The social world values of persons entering health-care programs will help shape their sense of what they need to learn and practice. Similarly, society sets up standards for these professionals that correspond to commonly held value orientations. This may well serve to differentiate American health-care practice from that of other cultures.

THE PLURALISTIC SOCIETY

The shared values characteristic of American society at large provide the normative orientation toward what has functioned as a progressively inclusive societal system. I add progressively inclusive to acknowledge that the values of a pluralistic system have emerged gradually over time. Slavery, segregation, prejudice, and discrimination of various kinds lingered even amid growing legal endeavors to eliminate them. The career of Supreme Court Justice William Brennan and his distinguished colleague on the Court, Justice Thurgood Marshall played key roles in advancing pluralistic standards of equal protection under the law, personal freedoms and equal rights among all citizens under the Constitution. As contested as these may have been by nativist proponents of a de facto class system, the move toward progressive pluralism remains a common cause supported across party lines within American society.

By pluralistic I mean at base that the society is composed of people from a variety of backgrounds and with diverse personal characteristics (Reck, 1990; Watson, 1990). This fact, however, may be observed in many societies that are not pluralistic. The critical feature that moves the simple fact of diversity to a pluralistic social system is that the diversity becomes subordinated to the operational goals of the society. Dominant values of achievement, individualism, future orientation, and a drive toward mastering problems inherent in "nature" take priority over the simple fact of diversity among people. These values displace and subordinate the fact of diversity to goals that do not rest upon the static features of a social order controlled by one or several dominant groups.

The picture is this: *e pluribus* means Americans derive from many cultures and are in reality quite diverse as individuals—religiously, ethnically, racially, sexually. This plurality is recognized not as a hindrance but as an advantage for the realization of society's values. *Unum* means that Americans become one culture, but not without continuing struggles against the traditions of collectivist, particularistic thinking and behaving. These traditional modes of social organization render the individual subservient to the group's dominance by identifying persons based not on personal differences but rather on the basis of the group into which they were born. Such collectivist thinking and behaving renders persons unable to relate person-to-person but only as representative members of the groups that give them their identity (Malina, 1989). In this system, stereotyping is the normal means for knowing a person—with the group's reputation being the means for knowing each person in the group. A pluralistic society necessarily regards such stereotyping of persons as antithetical to the social values constitutive of inclusiveness and individualism.

I view pluralism as having a high tolerance for diversity. This tolerance seems to revolve around the core questions I've quoted above. First, people have to be seen as having the ability to relate to one another as individuals rather than as branded group members. Individuality is the basis for human interaction in a pluralistic society: Recognition of personal diversity becomes the basis for relating to one another as individuals.

I view pluralism as characteristically having a dispersion of power. This means that power is not centralized within a ruler, a ruling class, or a ruling structure. Each person is assumed to have control over one's self, and to be individually responsible for the exercise of this personal power to act and make choices. Thus each person focuses the value of his or her human activity on a chosen accomplishment in the pursuit of personal goals. The group membership, again, is less important than the accomplishment. The collectivity does not control the person but persons voluntarily form the cooperative groups as means to shared goals.

I also see pluralism having a future time value, which correlates with the individual seeking to pursue personal or voluntarily shared goals. The future is the individual's future, not the group's. This means that while groups do exist, they exist for the purposes of present members—self-help groups, social action groups, community service groups. All these are rather specified in goal, voluntarily formed, and with future orientation aiming toward a realizable goal. I emphasize that the future is the individual's future. As noted above, some collectivist cultures see the ultimate future as the time in which the collective group is fully justified or duly in control. This undermines the shared sense of personal diversity characteristic of pluralistic societies inasmuch as the group would have prerogatives over the rights or benefits of individuals.

A pluralistic society, finally, is one that recognizes the larger capabilities of human activity. Those societies bent on group membership would perceive some superior power as controlling all life and being, bringing it into a subordination or submission. A pluralistic society values, rather, the kind of relationship between humans and the world of nature as having the potential for personal creativity and growth. This means that while each person pursues the value of being effective, he or she has some form of control over their own environment, and a constructive relationship with a God who does not control but participates as a friend in the process of the person's work.

These, then, are the values that undergird the United States as a pluralistic society. I don't begin to suggest that all Americans pursue these as preferred values, for many do not. But if you stand back and consider what Americans characteristically prefer, I believe that the Kluckhohn-Strodtbeck model does well describe American society as a whole. No other study, before or since, has been undertaken that so carefully quantified the sharing of values in a variety of social world context as this one does of value orientations studied cross-culturally.

Some might suggest that this is another form of collectivism, requiring all to share the same values. The objection is on surface true, that societies bond through sharing values. But as a pluralistic society, as a bonded society, Americans tend to share values that support individual initiatives and reward innovative achievement. These simply are not the kinds of values associated with collectivist patterns of thought. Collectivist values reward subordination and loyalty over initiative and upward mobility. Whatever the price this society pays for holding these values, or whatever internal regulations that such values require for their balanced implementation, they are nonetheless the values of an individualist rather than a collectivist social system. And for the individualist society, the future is of great importance inasmuch as it is in the personal future of individuals that development is achievable. For this reason, individualists think in terms of the future holding the possibility of positive change. Collectivists, on the other hand, believe that the past (referring back to the group's pristine origin) holds the greater authority. Progress in achievement of rights and the betterment of the human situation are thus solidly linked in a society marked by individualism. They are similarly key components of an immigrant society yearning to realize the dreams of immigrants who typically (but not always) come from what they perceive to be oppressive circumstances to what they intend to find in a free enterprise social system.

A further consideration here is whether I'm suggesting with a kind of nationalism or ethnocentrism that American society is best. For me, yes, this is true. And for many Americans as well. But, this is less true because of any ethnicity than because of the kind of system that Americans share—a pluralistic system that values diversity, supports personal freedom in the pursuit of individual goals, and rewards personal achievement over group pretensions. Collectivist cultures see people differently, and manifest thereby their own values and ends. And, there may well be other societies beside the United States in which pluralism functions a social system. I use pluralistic as a descriptive rather than as a synonym of American.

How might Americans today assess the merits of a pluralistic society? I believe we can do this by seeing what benefits accrue, and what weaknesses remain. In terms of merits, I believe that the gradual progress that this society has made toward recognizing and supporting a wide range of human diversity is real and productive. The diversity that exists among persons truly has surprised us all—even our own distinctive talents and potential for development is really quite amazing. This kind of society plays out much more justly—because it focuses on individuals who have rights rather than collectivities that have power—than a society that centers on the honor and prerogatives of a collectivity.

The collectivist society is one in which individuals must learn their place and their role, often thought to be so ordained by nature of God (Malina, 1986: pp. 22, 31). They must learn how to focus their lives on the group's past, on its inherent prowess, and on its ultimate vindication. To me, this is the seed ground for the kind of interracial and international conflicts that we have witnessed in the past and have witnessed in horrifying excess within our own century. I also believe that a system that recognizes and supports personal diversity is one that has the greatest potential for growth. Since individual persons truly are unique, and each person's development in many ways benefits each other person's quality of life, the pluralistic society offers an effective climate in which to express and develop creativity, originality, adaptability, and productivity.

Finally, what weaknesses can we identify within a pluralistic society? Surely the question of individuals out of control come immediately to mind. For this, the need is urgent for providing effective means for socializing individuals in ways of balancing personal goals with sensitivity to other persons who not only can help them toward their goals but also whose own needs must be recognized if one's needs are in like manner are to be recognized. This is not an easy task. We have seen notable examples in our history of individuals who simply take over, take control, and dominate others personally, economically, and environmentally. This potential for the individual "out of control" is real and must be addressed if a pluralistic society isn't to end in a state of reductionist egotism.

There are other potential weaknesses that we can sketch out in our own minds. Suffice it to say here that values for a pluralistic society result from the fact of diversity. They emerge in a society that seeks to recognize and benefit from diversity. And the chosen means for accomplishing this goal is to recognize diversity as inherent within individuals rather than within ethnic, racial, religious, or gender groups.

FOSTERING PLURALISTIC VALUES IN THE CLASSROOM

Education has the stated purpose of teaching people how to behave and survive in society. Needless to say, different systems of education match the operative values of diverse social systems. Alice Miller's stunning analysis of the traditional German educational philosophy focuses on the objective so characteristic of a society that teaches children to be subordinate to authorities. Ostensibly for the good of the child, the educator—parent, teacher, minister, government authorities—demand submission to authority. This philosophy of education aims to build a society of people for whom the lineal relationships of human society are valued over other value options. The effect, Miller argues as a child psychologist in Switzerland, is that persons so educated subsequently manifest characteristics of abused children. What was presented "for your own good" manifestly was not for the individual's good but rather for the operational model of societal authority. John Pilch examines how a similar philosophy characterizes the world of the Bible as well in biblical advice on raising children.

The case can well be made that the educational system should match the values of the social system within which it operates. And this can normally be assumed to be the case, but not always. The efforts to identify what values characterize American society should provide the basis for designing an educational model for preparing individuals to function effectively in a pluralistic society. This requires several key components:

1. Educators should recognize the rights and responsibilities of the individual student and encourage individual self-expression as a means to develop social skills necessary for independence and responsibility (Nell, 1991).
2. Opportunities for cooperative and interactive learning and research should be provided as stated means for learning how to work with other

individuals in settings with shared goals and the challenge to devise effective strategies for realizing them (Gerzon, 1997). This means that educators shouldn't take it upon themselves to do all the talking or presenting of class material, but should share the learning tasks with students through group research and presentation activities.

3. To develop requisite social skills in making personal choices that are effective for personal development, students should be encouraged to set goals for themselves, to state the desired outcomes and to test both the means they choose and the outcomes of their work. This assists students in recognizing the need to plan their actions, to take account of effects and consequences, and ultimately to realize their goals with greater facility and success.

4. Students need clarification about how merit, not relationship to persons in positions of authority, determines the value of class work. Some educators use student identification numbers in place of names on reports and examinations to help make the point that the work, not the person, is graded.

5. Efficiency in achieving goals requires adequate participation but not universal consensus in society. Hence, the classroom should reflect this priority of getting the job done with maximum participation but without delaying for universal acceptance. Just as the educator should not take on the role of power wielder in the classroom, so consensus is not necessary for the class to take action on its various tasks.

Each of these three thumbnail sketches of educational means to foster personal social development can best be achieved when the teacher clearly recognizes the underlying values of the society in which the classroom is a laboratory for growth and development. To avoid studying values because they are assumed to be parochial or arbitrary is to fail in a key element of any educational endeavor, awareness of what is really taking place.

One might assume that values drive all actions. The unexamined value is the one that is dangerous precisely because it is not driven by reason but by compulsion. The classroom is a setting for reason.

REFERENCES

Baugh, R. R. (1991). American values: the ties that bind. *Education, 112* (Winter), 217–228.

Bossman, D. M. (1991). Cross-cultural values for a pluralistic core curriculum. *Journal of Higher Education, 62* (Nov/Dec), 661–681.

Diner, H. R. (1993). Some problems with "multiculturalism"; or, "The best laid plans. . . ." *American Quarterly, 45*(2) (June), 301–308.

Ford, J. (1990). Systematic pluralism: Introduction to an issue. *The Monist, 73* (July), 335–349.

Frymer-Kensky, T. (1992). *In the wake of the goddesses. Women, culture and the biblical transformation of pagan myth.* New York: Fawcett Columbine.

Gerzon, M. (1996). *A house divided: Six belief systems struggling for America's soul.* New York: Tarcher/Putnam.

Gerzon, M. (1997). Teaching democracy. Doing it! *Educational Leadership,* February, 6–11.

Hsu, F. L. K. (1972). American core values and national character. In Francis L. K. Hsu (Ed.), *Psychological Anthropology.* pp. 241–62. Cambridge, Mass: Schenkman Publishing Company.

Jelin, T. G. (1990). Politicized group identification: The case of fundamentalism. *The Western Political Quarterly.*

Kluckhohn, C. (1961). The study of values. In D. N. Barrett (Ed.), *Values in America.* Notre Dame, Ind.: University of Notre Dame Press.

Kluckhohn, F. & Strodtbeck, F. L. (1961). *Variations in value orientations.* Evanston, IL: Row, Peterson and Co.

LeSourd, S. J. (1991). Integrating pluralistic values for reconstructing society. *Social Education, 55* (January), 52–54.

Levinson, D. & Malone, M. (1980). Toward explaining human culture: A critical review of the findings of worldwide cross-cultural research. New Haven: HRAF Press.

Malina, B. J. (1986). *Christian origins and cultural anthropology.* Atlanta: John Knox Press.

Malina, B. J. (1989). Dealing with biblical (Mediterranean) characters: A guide for U.S. consumers. *Biblical Theology Bulletin, 19* (October), 127–141.

Miller, A. (1983). *For your own good. Hidden cruelty in child-rearing and the roots of violence.* Translated by Hildegarde and Hunter Hunnum. New York: Farrar, Straus, Giroux.

Mohr, R. D. (1988). G*ays justice: A study of ethics, society, and law.* New York: Columbia University Press.

Nell, J. (1991). Values and the education of teachers: Challenges in a culturally pluralistic society. *College Student Journal, 25* (March), 466–469.

Niebuhr, R. (1932, 1960). *Moral man and immoral society.* New York: Charles Scribners Sons.

Pilch, J. (1993). Beat his ribs while he is young (Sir 30:12). A window on the Mediterranean world. *Biblical Theology Bulletin, 23*(3), 101–113.

Pilch, J. J. & Malina, B. J. (Eds.). (1993). *Biblical values and their meanings: A handbook.* Peabody, MA: Hendrickson Publishers.

Reck, A. J. (1990). An historical sketch of pluralism. *The Monist, 73* (July), 367–387.

Schlesinger, A., Jr. (1992). *The disuniting of America.* New York: W. W. Norton & Company.

Stewart, E. C. & Bennett, M. J. (1991). *American cultural patterns: A cross-cultural perspective* (revised edition). Yarmouth, ME: Intercultural Press, Inc.

Triandis, H. C., et al. (Eds.). (1980). *Handbook of cross-cultural psychology.* Six volumes. Boston, MA: Allyn and Bacon.

Watson, W. (1990). Types of pluralism. *The Monist, 73* (July), 350–366.

Weiss, J. (1996). *Ideology of death. Why the holocaust happened in Germany.* Chicago: Ivan R. Dee.

Chapter 5

Managed Care:
What, Why, Where,
and Whither Thou Goest?

FRED C. SMITH, JR.

Managed care which we will identify, analyze, and evaluate must be understood as a transitional concept, and a reflection of the industry it funds and controls to a much lesser degree than is perceived. It is at present mistakenly assumed to be the major change agent. It is only one of many; new models enter the field and others are discarded, only to be resurrected in a slightly different form with a new name and announced as today's panacea.

Health care professionals are not comfortable with the use of business terminology now applied to them and their services (i.e., industry, unit costs, service per hour, products, profit line, and bottom line). They prefer academic terminology that culturally they share with university, legal, and church operatives. They also prefer the traditional terminology and their resistance to change in philosophy of payment responsibility contrasts sharply with their practice of continuing easy adaptation and accommodation to the daily explosive changing technological advances they learn to use regularly. This self-misconception complicates the problems experienced in evaluating, accepting, and working within managed care and creates a major culture collision between "We serve" versus "We earn."

MANAGED CARE

Managed care is neither the greatest thing that has happened to the funding of professional service nor is it the worst. It is merely a changing position in a constantly evolving spectrum that has both economic and social considerations. Managed care is vastly different today than when it was given this current name just a few years ago. For-profit entities form nonprofit foundations while traditional nonprofit players, Blue Cross, Blue Shield, Health Insurance Plan (HIP) of New York, and others nationwide form for-profit organizations and/or merge with or into for-profit organizations. Their strengths of cost control and economic sanctions on waste are now used against them. Shortened or eliminated hospital stays, and ambulatory and home care service, although appropriate become political shibboleths. The anger America felt in 1980 about the soaring costs of health care and led to the reexamination of the prepaid group practice/HMO antecedents of managed care in a decade has turned against the organizations created to halt those rising costs. In an expected reaction, physicians who had the most to lose as a result of the new system reacted with a cry of "deterioration of quality" and loss of free choice of physicians.

The old adage that everything changes yet everything remains the same applies to "managed care" absolutely, including both its proponents and detractors. Even the name itself is merely the rechristening circa 1990 of "HMO," which itself had been rechristened in 1972, from the long established original 1890 title "prepaid group practice."

A major consultant for the health industry has called managed care a work in progress. How else would we have it? Health care—medical care and all its professions, hospital staffing, sponsorship, structure, and the services performed within it—are all works in progress. It is these very basic facts that mandate we review the payment for health and medical services. This will assist us to begin to understand the current state of affairs. More important, it will enable us to work effectively within managed care and allow us to contribute not only to the delivery of care within our expertise but help us participate in establishing the shape of the reimbursement mechanisms that fund it. This is vital since we must comprehend how something is to be paid for before we determine that a new service or procedure be undertaken. We must also accept the concept that cost is a prerequisite of our functioning at any level of health care. The myth of medical practice in isolation without oversight and controls of peer review is past.

The payment for the provision of medical care and allied services was originally handled on a private basis by the individual who had the means or through church, religious, or fraternal groups for those without fiscal means. This was truly reflective of the sociology of the times.

INSURANCE

Insurance, a concept European in origin, arose primarily in response to business requirements to protect against major losses such as those occurring in shipping or business failures. Lloyds of London, in the seventeenth century, is the company that comes to mind initially since it was one of the earliest syndicates that provided the mechanism where investors pooled funds for provision of payment against loss, charging sufficient premiums to cover loss claims, but also to make substantial profit for the investors.

HEALTH INSURANCE

Health insurance began in Sweden and Germany as government social schemes rather than insurance as it is known now. It was both a "Conservative" business concept (under Bismarck) and a populist or "Liberal" concept (Sweden). The insurance approach did not become widespread in the United States for almost a hundred years. Rather, here payment for care under contract, usually in advance, was the initial and prevailing methodology.

This is not to say that insurance was absent but was very limited. In the United States, the first health insurance policies were created to offset expenses connected with limited risk for the insurer but insured against costs connected with "dread" diseases such as cancer, tuberculosis, and serious infectious epidemic diseases prior to their eradication. These policies were written merely to offer persons insured for life, liability, and casualty some semblance of reimbursement. It was never comprehensive. These policies still exist along with accident policies that sharply defined and limited reimbursement for adversities such as the loss of eyesight and limbs all as adjuncts to life insurance. They were and are great profit generators for the insurance companies and played little part in the actual health funding that was to unravel in the later twentieth century and which is the great question mark as we reach the millennium in the next.

INSURANCE CONTINUED

The first serious application of the insurance principle to funding of care in the United States was the development of Workers Compensation that, although providing funding for medical and allied services, was also truly social insurance by providing subsistence income due to loss of wages during incapacity resulting from work-connected injury. Lest we forget, it was also a boon to employers since it protected them from undue litigation and made the resultant costs predictable by actuarial calculation. The rate was calculated for industries as a whole. Losses were averaged based on size. Competitive business disadvantage from adverse accidents could be minimized.

Some industries chose other schemes with substantial noninsurance concepts and from these grew what was to be the next several generations of funding for health care. The railroads, mine companies, and the logging industry, rather than lose the services of their employees, set up dispensaries usually on site and hired contract nurses and physicians who were not paid on a per-service basis to provide care of the sick or injured individual. This directly saved insurance costs, time lost, and litigation.

These physicians and nurses were paid either a salary or were compensated on a per capita (capitation) basis. Under this system, a payment is allotted per person listed whether or not service is required, regardless of the number of visits, how much time is spent in hospital, how many procedures are performed, or complexity of the service.

This concept puts the provider at risk as well as the institution providing the funding. A clash of the culture of fee-for-service or "piecework" is created where the provider has an incentive to do more (perhaps unnecessarily) as opposed to the incentive under capitation of doing less.

The original late-nineteenth-century philosophy is still basic to managed care in its present incarnation, whether offered by commercial insurance companies, Blue Cross/Blue Shield, Kaiser, Health Corporation of America, HIP of New York, or university plans such as that of the University of Medicine and Dentistry of New Jersey or New York Hospital/Cornell/Columbia University.

THE BUSINESS WORLD

However in the 1990s version, big business in the form of the corporate health care giants has tilted and compounded the philosophy from patient care as primary to profit as the motive. Fortunately some of the original players, HIP of NY, Kaiser, and Group Health of Puget Sound have pushed forward to establish national standards of care consistent with those originally in place, restoring the principles of prevention, easily available screening tests, and establishing systems to protect against abuse.

Initially, the employee was the only one covered as in Workers Compensation. As company towns developed and labor unions emerged and developed creating their own union health clinics and programs, family members were added, usually at employers' expense. This development had both economic and social impact.

In the case of the logging industry in the Pacific Northwest (Washington and Oregon), as the population surrounding the work places grew and diversified with support industry and services, the contract physicians needed associates and formed medical groups to offer their services to the general population. Two industries evolved within the same framework: capitated care for workers and later for their families; and medical group practice for the general public on a fee-for-service basis.

These groups combined on a county basis and were called medical bureaus. When solo practice physicians moved into the counties, the bureaus enlarged and became county medical societies. These county medical societies established schemes that combined the interests of the groups that had worked primarily with industry and the new solo practitioners who served the balance of the growing communities. These enlarged the old company plans and offered service through a panel of physicians on a prearranged fee or a specific fee schedule. The county societies, in time, set up these mechanisms statewide to accommodate the movement of persons from one company to the next or a change of residence. These county bureaus and state medical society organizations became the first Blue Shield plans.

As use of hospitals grew and was required by the advances in the scientific delivery system, hospitals formed first county hospital associations and then because of mobility and growth, state associations formed. They followed the lead of Blue Shield and formed what were to become the first Blue Cross plans. Nationwide, as this process took place, there were eventually over 180 plans. Very few of these plans covered both hospital and professional services. The merger of Blue Cross and Blue Shield took another forty years.

Compared to what takes place in the 1990s the work in progress of these early plans was comparable to the building of a cathedral next to the construction of prefabricated housing. This compares today to instant companies issuing instant policies and lining up instant panels of physicians and other providers who all may disassemble and form yet newer models later today or tomorrow.

Despite all the philosophical jargon, the essence of the earliest schemes and the managed care programs being offered today was and is to guarantee payment of physicians and institutional bills rather than to protect the individual patient. Although much lip service was paid to patient and consumer interest the provider came first.

The concept that led the parade was born of provider interests born of lost income or the Depression. The early plans maintained the connection with employers and usually were limited in size to protect them against adverse selection. Even though they were not insurance companies and were organized on a not-for-profit basis, they did use limited underwriting approaches so that the plan and ultimately the physicians who controlled them would not be hurt fiscally.

P H Y S I C I A N S ' M E D I C A L G R O U P S

During the 1930s, physicians in other parts of the country observed the local success and the plans spread. Most authors show Blue Shield as originating in 1939 in California. Actually the medical bureaus described above and a plan set up in Brooklyn, New York, in 1933, and another in Manhattan in 1935, are considered in the Blue Shield movement as the progenitors. It was in 1939 that the origins of the association that was to be Blue Shield brought California and the earlier plans together. These plans were initiated under the aegis of the state medical societies. In New Jersey in 1942, the state society not only formed the plan but also appointed the corporate directors for the next twenty years establishing almost absolute control.

The services covered by these programs varied greatly. In Brooklyn, the plan stressed coverage for home and office services, while plans in Manhattan and New Jersey leaned strongly toward physician specialization. This meant services in hospital, with extremely limited out of hospital care, were insured. Until the 1970s, the only services covered out of hospital were emergency accidental services with precisely defined benefits, and obstetrics and tonsillectomies. Blue Shield covered only physicians' services. Consideration was never given for the health-related providers or the institution. We will address hospital costs later.

Simultaneously, other groups were developing mechanisms to provide medical care to disparate patients and for the first time the goal was to move toward patient protection against rising costs and not with the providers as the prime movers and beneficiaries. This mirrored the development of cooperatives and the growth of union strength.

In Puget Sound, private citizens following the approach that preceded in the lumber industry formed a health care cooperative. Physicians were hired who would work on a capitated basis. In Minnesota and St. Louis, labor unions followed suit.

Henry Kaiser, through his company's medical director, set up medical groups for both aluminum workers in the western desert and for the shipbuilding employees on the West Coast.

At the same time, Mayor LaGuardia of New York City established the HIP of New York for the employees of the city. Again this was done through independent groups of physicians facing the fierce opposition of organized medicine. The principal reasons that these plans succeeded were that many physicians were returning from military service during World War II. They had been exposed to group practices in the service, and had become comfortable in patient referrals and to the fact that the practices they left had evaporated. A reasonable number of the physicians who joined had done so prior to military service, and had been associated with ethnic associations and workers guilds that had used either capitation or discounted fees.

Although arising from the same roots, prepaid medical care developed substantially two different profiles. The plans which came to be known as Blue Shield were organized and controlled by the medical societies through the creation of boards of directors. They slavishly held to fee-for-service and "free choice of physician" whether the physician was participating in the plan or not.

GROUP HEALTH PLANS

Group health plans on the other hand provided care directly through groups of physicians organized for this purpose as opposed to reimbursement for services already rendered. As stated earlier, these could be either salaried employees of the plan or those under a capitated contract with the plan. This latter format was followed by Kaiser, HIP, Group Health of Puget Sound, the St. Louis Union plan, and groups in Minneapolis.

These group health plans tendered to be more comprehensive and "generous" in benefits since the cost was tightly controlled by contract. Ancillary services and referrals to specialists were usually within the system and when sent out of the system these were to physicians who accepted a discounted schedule of payments. In most of these situations, the physicians were somewhat at risk, as was the plan. Case management and quality assurance were used from the earliest times, albeit by different names. It is from this prepaid group practice mode that the terms "managed care" and "gatekeeper" ultimately arose, although those individuals within the industry never used the terms.

All of the groups and prepaid plan organizations used other health-related disciplines long before it became general practice in the health industry. It was within these plans that much of the disease prevention programs and health studies in the areas of breast disease and coronary study originated. The earliest mammography, cholesterol, child immunization programs, and as stated earlier case management and quality assurance, were undertaken in large controlled populations. Continuity of care and common record keeping allowed for ease of reporting.

The substantial number of health-related professions worked in a freer environment of practice than occurred in the hospital or other institutional settings. Nutritionists, social workers, nurse practitioners, physician assistants, and physical therapists all contributed early on to the team concept replacing to some extent the traditional physician model.

COST CONTAINMENT

The control of costs had long been demonstrated over the years within the industry. But it took a study funded by the national Teamsters Union in 1964, that reviewed the utilization of medical services of all their members and dependents enrolled nationwide in a variety of Blue Shield, group practice plans, and commercial insurance companies, to highlight the issues.

This study demonstrated the need for a new look at the utilization of services for appendectomies, herniorrophies, and hysterectomies. Almost universally, patients in several different group practice plans had substantially lower frequency in these categories than did members enrolled in Blue Shield and the commercial insurance companies.

In addition, it was clearly demonstrated that patients enrolled in the non-group prepaid programs were hospitalized 25 percent more frequently and when hospitalized stayed 20 percent longer. This was thirty years before the great complaints and politically motivated cries concerning shortened hospital stays and the false alarms about decreasing quality care resulting.

It was this continuing attempt at efficiency that provided such a disparity in premium costs between the prepaid programs and other insurance approaches. It drew the attention of the federal government and after time led ever cost-conscious leaders to convince conservative lawmakers to support the creation of HMOs by President Nixon.

Twenty-eight years after the Teamsters study, when there were entirely different players on the field, HMO premiums in New Jersey averaged $3,643 per person compared to $4,406 for other coverage, a difference of 26 percent.

HIP patients in New York City and Kaiser patients in group health and other local community prepaid plans in other cities experienced the first major cuts in length of stay and admission rates following this example. It is interesting to note that independent plans new to the field following the broad scope of the earliest plans found similar success in controlling admissions and shortening length of stays.

So many things occur simultaneously; it becomes necessary to monitor who is doing what. When large corporations realized they were paying substantial amounts per person per year for their employees and families, up in some cases almost 300 percent of what they paid just a few years earlier, the bottom line became the prime mover. Decisions were made that traditional fee-for-service programs could not be sustained and that medical care inflation had to be stopped.

Complications arose almost immediately when too many different approaches were rushed into being. HMOs were created without recourse to existing entities. New structures were brought into being, and millions of dollars were appropriated for new comprehensive health programs. Some of these were new nonprofit organizations with no prior experience or expertise either in group practice or in insurance. They were predoomed and resulted in the loss of millions of dollars on start-up costs and buildings. After several years of losses and failure to dent the cost of care, preexisting group practice programs were asked to assume the operations of these failed operations.

At the same time, new for-profit organizations arose and began the merger of local hospitals and then attempted to form programs by use of the staff of these organizations. This created huge corporations, highly paid entrepreneurs had their try, and another rise in costs took place at points that had never been out of control before.

Here the complication goes into high gear. Costs at the delivery point are measured as never before. Controls are instituted to attempt to provide only appropriate care. All the while the complexity of the scientific equipment and diagnostic testing progresses geometrically. Cost becomes astronomical. Everybody wishes to ride the wave of technology. In order to pay for the equipment and tests, more and more services are requested by specialists and the institutions providing the new services.

Patients are becoming more aware of the opportunities to "solve" their problems and demand goes up as cost controls attempt to tamp down the explosion.

Under ordinary business circumstances, as the market place has more providers of service, competition drives cost down. Here is a direct contradiction of that theorem. With providers controlling the demand for their services in both the HMO and the fee-for-service world, a built-in confrontation begins between each of the players on the field: patient, provider, employer, paying mechanism, and government, all with an agenda that impinges on another.

THE RESPONSES

All this attention causes each of the players to react. Previous programs that had been retired and replaced are resurrected and refined. Both the nonprofits and the commercial programs start to use independent practice associations. These had been used under different names by the early nonprofit plans. These in effect are medical groups without walls where each physician or partnership contracts at a specified schedule or capitation to treat patients who use them within a prearranged reference network. They agree to certain cost containment mechanisms such as second opinions, prearranged referrals for high-cost testing procedures and prior approval before admission to hospital in nonemergent situations. They also agree to hospital-stay review among other stipulations. The attraction to the provider is the maintenance of the private practice plus, should a regular patient join the new insurance mechanism, they remain with the private physician and are not lost to a "foreign" HMO.

As the interest in HMOs grew, so did the perception of the for-profit hospitals and other noninsurance commercial enterprises as to the advantage of combining the pieces of medical expertise, hospital availability, and the dire need for more system in the health care which, combined, also meant profit.

Corporate HMOs such as Humana, U.S. Health Care, and the Hospital Corporation of America proliferated in those states that did not prohibit for-profit hospitals such as New Jersey. In those states, Physician Hospital Organizations (PHOs) were created around the hospital and their staffs.

Before proceeding we should now look at hospital care coverage and payment and see the repetitive forces at work. In the late 1920s and early 1930s, as a result of the Depression, the need for funding in hospital care became alarmingly apparent.

In Houston, Texas schoolteachers arranged a program with Baylor University Hospital in which they deposited a small amount of money with the hospital each payday. In Newark, New Jersey, the local hospital association in an effort to forestall hospital collapse formed the Hospital Service Plan in 1932. In 1935, the hospitals in New York City did the same and formed what they called Associated Hospital Service. Note the term's plan or service to separate the concept from insurance that these institutions had previously considered foreign to health care delivery and the payment for it.

The hospital plans, of which there were ultimately eighty-nine, adopted the name Blue Cross in the 1940s. Costs were contained by discounting payments made to hospitals. The policy and governance of these plans were either the local hospitals or their county or local hospital associations.

The guarantee of payment for the patients enrolled in the plan and the ability to get advances on payments gave the institutions fluidity since payment cycles could be advanced and their sense of control avoided the adversary role that exists in other payment mechanisms.

During the half century that prepaid medical care and hospital service mechanisms were developing and defining into very distinct branches, the federal and state governments continued to provide direct medical care for those who were the government's responsibility: veterans, members of the armed forces and their dependents, seamen in the maritime service, and Native Americans. Each group received care in separate systems, all independent of each other, duplicating in most instances and rarely if ever complementing the other. All services were directly rendered and were not handled on an insurance basis.

Following World War II, and gathering impetus in the 1950s, commercial insurance companies that previously basically ignored health coverage saw it now as an entry into customer accounts since they could apply cost-rating savings which were never available under the community rated nonprofit plans. Underwriting as done by insurance companies was little used by the Blues and other community and provider-oriented programs. The fundamental theory behind these organizations was to get the largest number of enrollees to avoid collection problems. In addition, the wage freeze of the 1950s encouraged unions to seek health benefits in lieu of wages denied them.

With the speedy growth of numbers of individuals with health coverage, the vast expansion of hospitals under the Hill-Burton Act, and the expanding medical school enrollment, the stage was set for an explosion of costs. The spectacular growth of medical technology and the concurrent training of the increasing available new graduates to use it compounded this. Another dimension was also present: the growth, diversification, and the professionalization of the health-related professions and the institutions that train them.

From the very beginning, the group practice plans offered programs for Medicaid as well as Medicare patients. In New York, the HIP of New York enrolled 100,000 Medicaid patients in the first year. Continuously since then New York State government has encouraged and succeeded in getting other plans to also enroll Medicaid members. So well did the plans succeed that in New York with HIP and in California with Kaiser, federal Medicaid authorities accepted the quality assurance programs of the plans and discontinued their own, only maintaining audit rights of the results of the programs.

In the 1990s, as states began to assume risk for welfare and Medicaid populations, other states such as New Jersey through its HMOs, commercial insurance programs, and the Blues began to follow this lead.

Early HMOs resulting from the 1972 HMO Act began to fail and were taken over by entrepreneurs. The new hospital corporations began to merge and were able to cross state lines and tempted the Blues to rethink their original mission and the mergers alluded to earlier became the "only" thing to do

Despite all the wonderful history of the early programs for payment of needed care, the ever-expanding payment mechanisms monumentally increased utilization from both real and perceived needs.

In 1993, the federal government and the people of the country decided to pretty much leave the current health system in place. Managed care in its many permutations is attempting to control costs and eventually cover the balance of the population while going in many directions at the same time.

Is it the culprit? Is it the answer?

The cultural clash between theories of payment and government versus private provision of care heats up, cools down, and begins all over again. In the meanwhile 35,000,000 individuals continue to lack the wherewithal to pay for health care.

REFERENCES

Access to health services for vulnerable populations. *Overview Health Care Financing Review,* USDHHS, 17(2), Winter 1995.

Benson, Barbara. (1997). *HIP stanches bloodletting.* Crain's New York Business. September.

Bigel, J. (1975). *Presentation to New York State Legislature: Health insurance plan of NY.* Program Planners, Inc. New York.

Davis, K. (1975). *National Health Insurance: Benefits, costs and consequences.* The Brookings Institution, Washington, D.C.

Kovner, A. R., (1990). *Health care delivery in the United States.* New York: Springer Publishing Company.

Lewis, C. E., Fein, R. & Mechanic, D. (1976). *A right to health.* New York: John Wiley & Sons.

Linden, R. M. (1994). *Seamless government.* San Francisco: Jossy-Bass.

Lindsay, C. M. (Ed.). (1980). *New directions in health care: A Prescription for the 1980s.* San Francisco Institute for Contemporary Studies.

Palmer, J. L. (1998). *Financing health care and retirement for the aged.* Washington, DC: The Urban Institute.

Rivlin, A. M. (1992). *Reviving the American dream.* Washington, DC: The Brookings Institution.

Schramm, C. J. (Ed.). (1987). *Health care and its costs: Can the U.S. afford adequate health care.* New York: W. W. Norton.

Sharp, A. M., Register, C. A. & Leftwich, R. H. (1994). *Economics of social issues.* Burr Ridge, Illinois: Irwin.

Smiley, W. G. (1951). An early prepayment plan for medical care. *Journal of the History of Medicine,* Vol. VI.

Starr, P. (1982). *The social transformation of American medicine.* New York: Basic Books, Harper Collins.

Chapter 6

Reengineering
and the Corporate Culture

C A R O L A . F A S A N O

REENGINEERING AND REDESIGN

Reengineering and redesign are two common words heard every day as organizations throughout the nation move through transition. Both terms describe the phenomenon of downsizing, the process of rapid resource reduction to reduce costs. Such a transition is necessary to keep up with economic constraints and the competitive business market of today. Change is inevitable, and historically, it is the process that most human beings resist the most.

For some persons, it disturbs their sense of well-being. For others, it is a challenge which they embrace with open arms and fly. Those who do not seize the opportunity will be left behind in the style of the old corporate world. A Boston business journal recently stated that, "Corporate culture is the eye of the needle through which change must pass" (Attridge, 1995). This statement captures the essence of what I am trying to convey in this chapter.

THE EYE AND THE NEEDLE

Historically, organizations fostered cultures which empowered a few and promoted powerlessness to the many (Attridge, 1995). An antiquated culture that is allowed to continue in today's corporate climate will contribute to the corporation's demise. Employees must be empowered to take action in situations that are a routine part of their job. No longer can employees wait for the manager to solve the problems and quickly respond to customer needs. Organizations that want to survive must employ a democratic structure that supports employees that perceive themselves as valued players, who can make a decision, and contribute to the overall economic growth of the corporation.

A PERSONAL EXPERIENCE

I was recently involved in a reengineering project and found that empowering individuals was the greatest challenge in this project's educational process. For many individuals, it is less stressful to let the managers handle a problem as opposed to confronting the issue themselves. With reengineering projects, employees should be provided with conflict resolution strategies, and be supported in the practice and implementation of these strategies. Empowered employees are vital, if reengineering is to be successful.

REENGINEERING DEFINED

What is reengineering? In the 1990s, the concept of Business Process Reengineering (BPR) became a popular strategy used in businesses nationally. BPR is a fresh start, or a new look at tasks and processes of a company with respect to how they should be accomplished and without regard to how they are presently done. The result is a completely new design (a "reengineering") of the tasks and processes. The primary purpose of this new design is to increase the effectiveness of accomplishing the company's management, administrative, and operations tasks, with the expectation that improved effectiveness will improve market position and increase profitability (Scott, 1995). More recently, BPR has filtered into the health care industry. Additional purposes of reengineering are to improve quality, to decrease costs, and to improve customer satisfaction thus increasing market volume and profitability.

A study, titled "Reengineering among the Fortune 500," commissioned by Pitney Bowes management services, found that, although the majority of companies report significant benefits with reengineering, the single largest challenge for employers is motivating and encouraging employees to change. In addition, the study states companies report that reengineering results in greater cost-efficiency, increased profitability, and improved customer service (Scully, 1995). The outcome that is especially interesting is that reengineering had significant workforce benefits including increased employee productivity and, an essential piece, empowerment.

Of most significance is the impact reengineering has on the culture of the organization. It is important that the culture and the change are congruent. The organizational culture has an influence on the employee's values and attitude toward the employer. The most productive employee is one who wants to grow and to be challenged. This is an individual with an inner drive that motivates him/her to seek new opportunities within the company, as well as the skills and knowledge to do the job. A second type of employee is the one who sees little need to do things in a different way. This is the employee who "talks the talk" but does not "walk the walk" of change. He/she tries to fit the new triangle into the old rectangle. A third type of employee is one who believes he/she is entitled to the job because the employer owes him/her for years of service. This type of employee evolves from the traditional paternalistic culture. It is not what can the employee do for the company, it's what can the company do for the employee. This attitude exists in many companies that have fostered a family attitude; that is, multiple members of a family work for the company and have worked there for years. Although loyalty is a quality employers want, this attitude does not contribute to the corporation's survival.

SPIRIT, REENGINEERING, AND COMMUNICATION

Employees who assume responsibility for developing their own careers help to develop a more flexible and employee ownership attitude at the same time (Jones, 1997). How can an organization develop this type of employee spirit in its culture while going through the process of reengineering? Anxiety among employees is common during reengineering. There is fear and resistance to change, fear of the unknown, of having to learn a new job, and/or to work harder. To improve employee spirit it is necessary for the employee to offset anxiety by anticipating it and providing adequate support systems.

Developing a greater tolerance for constant changes in the work setting is essential to being a satisfied employee. Support systems reduce stress and highlight the importance of connectedness to others (Hizer, 1996).

In planning reengineering, while considering employee anxiety and corporate culture change, it is imperative to promote an open communication system between management and the front-line employees. It is also important to assess carefully the educational needs of the organization and to develop a program that meets the needs of every level of employee. Table 6–1 lists the critical elements of reengineering curricula.

Outcome criteria developed to measure the knowledge base of the employee in performing the new tasks to assure quality, safety, and par work performance are most helpful. It is essential to provide middle managers with the tools they need such as current management strategies, problem-solving, empowerment, and team-building skills. Such skills foster communication with comfort and ease the commitment for change. Managers unable to adapt to the change are replaced with persons committed to bringing the message to the skilled employees and facilitating ownership of the change. The importance of skilled middle managers in a change process cannot be overemphasized. Adequate time must be provided to have all of the key players thinking, agreeing, and understanding before moving on with the process.

One key to positive change is communication that is clear and concise. Upper management should develop a system that assures that middle managers share regularly with employees the changes as they are discussed. Too often issues are communicated from the top but a block occurs that prevents the message from being received. This impedes progress, increases anxiety, and cultivates a "them versus us" attitude within the organization. Before throwing away the old culture and systems, consider which aspects have value and should be retained. Technology may "hardwire" an organization but relationships are the glue which hold it together (Attridge, 1995).

TABLE 6–1
Critical Elements of Reengineering Curricula

Concepts
1. Ownership
2. Empowerment
3. Critical Thinking
4. Decision Making
5. Conflict Resolution
6. Team Building

A PERSONAL EXPERIENCE

Recently, I participated in a reengineering project in a health care setting. I was a member of a work team that designed and implemented a curriculum for a patient care model redesign. The project involved decentralization of departments in the hospital and training employees to perform new skills in multiple roles. For example, a person who had worked as a housekeeper for twenty years had to reapply for a new position which included patient care activities, as well as housekeeping duties. In the process of designing the curriculum, the elements of quality, competence, and caring were stressed. The concept of empowerment was expanded and integrated as a thread throughout the training program. In addition, team building and conflict resolution were core elements of the educational program. It was the belief of the education team that these concepts were critical to the success of the redesign. The team also recognized that in order for the training to serve the organization's mission, the concept of ownership had to be ingrained in the minds of the trainers and managers to impact this concept in the minds of the trainees. This concept will enable the culture to evolve from a "you own me" attitude to a "we're in this together" attitude. This was the greatest challenge in the teaching phase and more so in the actual implementation of the model. Individuals who functioned in a system for a very long time that enabled dependency have a great deal of difficulty thinking in an independent way.

The program was designed in a methodical way to ensure that patients' needs remained the number one priority while being sensitive to the needs and fears of individuals going through the retraining process. Exercises in teaming and dealing with conflict were considered to be a crucial part of the core curriculum in which all individuals participated. The registered nurses were provided with multiple delegation exercises. In order for nurses to be successful in the new model, it was essential that they be safe, effective, and comfortable in their role as delegator.

Throughout the reeducation process the concepts were reviewed repeatedly. The true challenge came when the model went live on the clinical units. There was a great deal of enthusiasm in the beginning as the new skills were used. There were facilitators available on each clinical unit to coach the employees in the new roles. It was imperative to have the managers in place to keep the momentum moving forward when the dust settled and facilitators left.

The project was evaluated constantly, recognizing weaknesses and strengths, and making appropriate changes in a timely manner. It takes a commitment on the part of administration and the training team to work diligently revising entire units of teaching materials that were recognized as unsound and in need of revision. The problem areas were not identified until the workers were in the preceptorship phase. Areas deemed as unsafe must be changed immediately.

EMPOWERMENT AND CONFRONTATION

All employees must be able to feel empowered to make a decision within the boundaries of their job descriptions and to move the process forward. If fellow coworkers are breaking rules and taking shortcuts, each individual is responsible to confront and to attempt to resolve the conflict. If the problem is not resolved, the manager becomes involved.

In the situation just mentioned, it is very difficult for people to develop comfort and ease in the skill of confrontation. It is human nature for the average person to let someone else do this part of the job or to sweep the conflict under the rug. No longer in the corporate America of today do we have time for this type of behavior.

Success is achieved through critical thinking and decision-making skills as well as through exercises in confidence building and conflict resolution. Encouragement and praise are evoked in the training process. The training program for a reengineering project can be educationally sound, but without personal commitment and ownership to the change on the part of all concerned, change will not occur.

CHANGE, CULTURE, OPTIMISM, AND RELAXATION

Change is inevitable in health care organizations today. The uncertainty and flux in the health care environment are here and will not go away. Both managers and employees can practice optimism and positive expectancy (Rosenberg & Hizer, 1996). In addition to a positive attitude, stress reduction techniques such as deep breathing for relaxation, creative imagery, eating right, and getting enough sleep and exercise, can be incorporated as a part of the curriculum. These techniques will help to manage stress and contribute to an easier adjustment to change in the workplace.

A Chicago hospital undergoing reengineering developed "The Cultural Change Program." The program was designed to address the corporate culture of respect for each person within the agency. The program examined how the employees treated each other and how the hospital's current positive and negative norms impacted this treatment. The program was conducted by employees who volunteered to be trained and to conduct the programs for other employees. The management staff was provided with an opportunity to attend a two-day seminar which addressed their role in promoting positive norms, as well as to learn a process to redesign negative norms (Torrie & Houston, 1994). Such a program fostered a congruency of culture within the change environment.

It is essential to include individuals from every work level to participate in designing any new system. An open invitation to all levels is meaningful and ensures broad participation. A feedback mechanism builds consensus by identifying issues, dealing with rumors, and resolving uncertainty. Table 6–2 lists key management skills for the twenty-first century.

The basic building blocks of any organizational culture are values and beliefs. Core cultures are what the organization believes are good or bad for a particular situation (Nadler & Tushman, 1997). Truly focused cultures become deeply entrenched because with the passage of time, the values and beliefs they embrace become indistinguishable from those of the individuals within the organization (Nadler & Tushman, 1997). It is important to realize that cultures which

TABLE 6–2
Key Management Skills for the Twenty-First Century

Being able to
1. Think like an owner
2. Think creatively and independently
3. Be flexible
4. Be willing to take a risk
5. Create a vision and develop a plan to achieve it

previously worked for an organization can become outdated in the needs of today and can actually prevent the organization from moving ahead. Specific values that have enriched the culture should be threaded throughout the new. Reengineering not only has an impact on culture but in most instances an entirely new culture must emerge to be in concert with the organization's mission.

The research demonstrates that if an employer is loyal to the employees the result will be low absenteeism and a low turnover of employees. Note that employees who feel like the employer is their father do not see that profit to the organization is what will keep it afloat. It is important for employees to think more realistically that the organization is a place to work, a social network, and a means to personal fulfillment. It is not their family and should never be mistaken for such (Cole & Watts, 1997).

It is also very important to design a performance evaluation system that is congruent with the corporate culture change. It must incorporate the employee as an active participant in the evaluation process, with goals established mutually with the supervisor. A very important cause of unsuccessful change is related to performance evaluations not being linked to change initiatives and unclear understanding of the new role and accountabilities.

TWENTY-FIRST CENTURY EMPLOYEE

Reengineering and redesign projects must contain critical elements that will enable employees to move into the twenty-first century. What does the employee of the twenty-first century have to look like? This employee will have to adapt to new environments and cultures and be in charge of his/her own morale; be loyal to one position on Monday and another one on Tuesday; be flexible, open minded, and committed; assume more personal responsibility for the success of the entire enterprise, rather than focusing narrowly within the boundaries of the old job description; and act like an owner with a sense for managing the whole. The employee of the twenty-first century will have to personally help cut costs, better serve the customer's needs, and implement an innovative approach to each aspect of the job. An employee who has the power and inner drive to make things happen will excel and attain optimal personal satisfaction while contributing to the success of the employer (Pritchett, 1997).

As our descendants read American history in the future, I am sure the books will discuss how corporate America experienced a second industrial revolution during the turn of the twenty-first century which uprooted the systems in place since the first industrial revolution. They will also read that from a great deal of turmoil emerged a society of open-minded, independent thinkers who moved forward with no turning back and had a very positive influence on society.

References

Attridge, N. I. Human resources. *Boston Business Journal, 15* (28), 10.

Cole, J. & Watts, C. (1995). Last word/Is organizational loyalty dead? *Getting Results, 42*(2), 8.

Jones, B. Changing workplace. *Orlando Business Journal, 13*(38), 23B.

Pritchett, P. (1997). *New work habits for a radically changing world.* Dallas, TX: Pritchett & Associates, Inc., p. 18.

Nadler, D. A. & Tuschman, M. L. (1997). *Competing by design.* New York: Oxford Zenion Press, Inc.

Rosenberg, A. & Hizer, D. (1996). *The resume handbook: How to write outstanding resumes and cover letters for every situation* (3rd ed.). Holbrook, MA: Adams Media Corporation.

Scott, G. M. (1995). Downsizing business process reengineering and quality improvement plans: How are they related? *Information Strategies, 11*(3), 18.

Scully, E. (1995). Employee benefits/human report. *Cincinnati Business Courier, 2(5).*

Torrie, C. & Houston, S. (1994). Reengineering impact on organizational culture. *Journal of AHIMA, 65* (4), 47–48.

Chapter 7

Cyberspace: The New Culture

CATHERINE M. BOSS

Author William Gibson, in his book *Neuromancer* (1984), coined the term cyberspace as a metaphor to describe the place where electronic communication takes place, a notional information space in which geography no longer exists. According to Gibson, cyberspace is "a consensual hallucination experienced daily by billions of legitimate operators, in every nation . . . a graphic representation of data abstracted from the banks of every computer in the human system. Lines of light ranged in the nonspace of the mind, clusters and constellations of data." Connecting to the Internet and navigating this "information highway" is navigating through cyberspace. Cyberspace is considered by many to be a virtual community.

H O W

Jan Fernback and Brad Thompson have discussed the dimensions of community within cyberspace in a paper presented at the 1995 annual meeting of the International Communication Association. Communication, they identified, is the structural process that is associated with community. Both words stem from the Latin root, communis, which means common. Community and communications both revolve around the issue of bringing people together, exacerbating social divisions. The root word, common, contains elements of both. Community is communication. Without it, there can be no action to organize social relations.

Books were the primary way of communicating new ideas in the seventeenth century, the beginning of the science revolution. The scientific journal debuted in 1665. Much later, with the advent of computers, scientists began sharing ideas via computer networks using leased telephone lines. This method of communicating was not without problems. Scientists wanted to connect to different computers at different times. Leased telephone lines in the late 1950s had limited bandwidth, making networking of the increasingly large amounts of data that computer users wanted to send expensive and slow.

BEING AND BECOMING

Fathered by Cold War concerns of the late 1960s, the U.S. Department of Defense's Advanced Research Projects Agency (ARPA) began to explore packet switching. Instead of dividing up the telephone lines to transmit the data, ARPA experimented with dividing up the data into packets and forwarding the packets through the telephone network and reassembling the packets of data at their destination. If a part of the communications network was destroyed or damaged, the packet could take an alternate route, effectively maintaining data transmission. The military ramifications of this new technology was significant. Military communications could be maintained, even in the event that a nuclear war or sabotage interfered or destroyed a communications line. Splitting the data into tiny packets taking different routes would make the data hard to be eavesdropped on.

To economize on the expensive use of long distance leased telephone lines, the ARPA built a small packet-switching network to connect the many heterogeneous computers at four American universities in geographically distant locations—UCLA, Stanford Research Institute at Stanford, California, the University of California at Santa Barbara, and the University of Utah. By December 1969, the four were connected and the ARPAnet, the seeds of the Internet, was born. As an afterthought, researchers devised a way of sending messages through the network, giving rise to e-mail as it has become known, turning the network into a new method of communications.

The network grew, slowly at first, then more rapidly. Over the next decade, one new computer was being connected to the network every twenty days. Satellite and radio packet networks wanted to connect to the ARPAnet. New protocols, Transmission Control Protocol (TCP) and Internet Protocol (IP) were developed to interconnect these heterogeneous packet networks and determine addresses and routing of data packets through devices called gateways. By August 1983, there were 562 networked computers. The ARPAnet was then split into an unclassified, operating military network, Milnet, and a research-testing, nonmilitary network, ARPAnet. At the same time, other educational and research sites were forming their own networks, such as BITNET ("Because It's There" or "Because It's Time" network), EARN (European Academic Research Network), and CSNET (Computer and Science Network). The widespread use of TCP with IP allowed these many networks to become interconnected with the ARPAnet. This connecting of networks, or Internet working, gave rise to the term, Internet. Nowadays, people refer to the Internet as the "Net," as if were only one—one large "community" of computers.

The National Science Foundation, in 1987, established a national network of five supercomputer hubs, linked with a high-speed backbone network (NSFnet). A middle tier of regional, local, and campus networks could connect via the closest hub. This NSFnet superseded the ARPAnet, which was decommissioned in 1990 and is the framework for the Internet. Today the Internet is a worldwide community of computers, spanning over 240 countries and is still growing. According to network wizards, there are over 19,540,000 computer systems with an IP address connected to the Internet. About half of these networks are commercial and a third are associated with educational research. Attached to these networks are the millions of computers at thousands of sites. The network has been doubling in size every year since 1988. The World Wide Web has been a major contributing factor to this growth.

Tim Berners-Lee, at Cern, the European High Energy Physics Laboratory, developed the Web to display data as pages of multimedia objects. He included text, audio, video, and graphics in his documents, or pages, of the Web. The pages are linked together with pointers called hypertext pointers or hotlinks. One link leads to another document on the Web, which in turn may have other links. According to Berners-Lee, the "Web is intended to help people make information, resources, and services available to the widest possible community of users with a single connection." The Web has made it very easy for anyone to access all kinds of information. No communications medium has grown as quickly, not the fax machine nor the PC. For the estimated 25 to 30 million users of this medium, the Internet has revolutionized the way we communicate and obtain information.

CYBERCULTURAL DIVERSITY

Cultural diversity does not effect negatively the Internet's role as a community and as a marketplace. Cyberspace is a community a lot like the world—huge, messy, with some delightful places and some streets you don't want to walk down. The Internet allows heterogeneous communities of computers to talk to each other. Its users are a heterogeneous mix. Only a few years ago, the Internet user, according to Tom McNichol, was pictured as a young man with thick glasses, bad skin, and no Friday night date. Today, the Net looks more like America, with kids in elementary school, senior citizens, businesses, blue collar workers, professionals, political candidates, and housewives. The Internet allows people to exercise one of their most basic desires, to communicate, and to do so on an unprecedented scale—globally, openly, to one person or to many.

NEW CENTURY WATERCOOLER

The Internet has the remarkable power to make all of its users homogeneous, downplaying their cultural differences. The virtual community of the Internet does not acknowledge the color of one's skin, eyes, or hair, or one's weight, age, clothing, wealth, or other forms of alienation. Everyone is equal in cyberspace. What this virtual community of the Internet does is acknowledge our inner diversity by allowing for the formation of new communities, made up of people who share a special interest. List serves are discussion groups created to share knowledge and ideas on a subject. News groups provide access to topic-based discussion groups. Christians, Jews, Muslims, Buddhists, and atheists all have their own news group to discuss theology. News groups exist for any type of hobby or pastime. News groups serve as kind of an office water cooler where people gather to exchange the latest jokes. They offer an outlet for people to work through problems and personal issues in a productive way. People with all kinds of diseases are using the Internet to create support groups. This virtual environment, in a sense, provides a moratorium from reality that can be used for constructive purposes. In this virtual social experience, people feel most like themselves. Cyberspace helps users find a political voice for their ideas and views. According to Turtle, "having literally written our online worlds into existence, we can use the communities we build inside our machines to improve the ones outside them . . . like the anthropologist returning home from a foreign culture, the voyager in virtuality can return to the real world better able to understand what about it is arbitrary and can be changed."

CYBERLANGUAGE

People do not feel so alone on the Internet. In an increasingly fragmented society, McNichol points out, computer networks are recreating a small town

America where folks lean over the electronic fence to swap stories. These cyberspace communities have the warmth of a campfire and have developed a "global village that sometimes turns out to be Mayberry." These communities have developed their own jargon or insider's language full of abbreviations. Some of the abbreviations are meant to take the labor out of typing, for example, irl ("in real life"), btw ("by the way"), and ianal ("I am not a lawyer"). Letters are used to sketch emotions in this jargon. A wink, for example, becomes ;-), or a smile :).

The Internet can be used to communicate with friends and family in other countries, a help to America's diverse ethnic populations. E-mail is much cheaper than long distance phone calls and you don't have the constraints of time zones. One can send a message to Ireland this afternoon and have a detailed response the next morning. Parents use the Internet to keep in touch with their college kids. Nearly all colleges and universities provide Internet connections for their student populations.

CYBERPROBLEMS

Communicating on the Internet is not without its own set of problems. The main language of the Internet is English. Most of its key resources are written in English.

E-mail and other text areas are limited to roman characters, forcing many countries, such as Japan and China, to use complicated phonetic versions of their own language. Although global in nature, the Internet is narrow and local in focus culturally. Anyone with an Internet connection can go to Amsterdam's Digital City, Anderson notes, but they need to speak Dutch to get around. The Internet is a local outpost, built by and for the natives. This is true for the hundreds of local discussion groups, from German "Help Wanted" to New Zealand politics.

Fundamental to the Internet is the protection of free speech. Every news group has the right to be heard on the Internet. It is an altruistic place, providing a home for hate groups to culture bashers to sex of various kinds and giving rise to heated debate as to the scope and extent of access, particularly by minors. The flood of new users e-mailing and joining news groups has created some Internet prejudices. When a query to a news group or list triggers hundreds of responses, weeding of those messages is inevitable. Comments from those of similar, higher, or more prestigious cultural status tend to be read. Those messages from unknown, obscure, or different sources tend to be deleted.

CYBERGENEOUS

In the information revolution, the Internet has played a more positive role in making our diverse populations more homogeneous. The Internet has helped perfect strangers in finding information on their questions. The Internet has become a virtual utopia. Its interactive culture attracts people of all learnings. It has the power to make an ordinary person on a Web site an online celebrity.

If an Internet site is interesting enough, it might be visited by hundreds or thousands of people a day.

CYBERCATALOGING

Cyberspace, some say however, contains too much information to make sense. Peters and Sikorski, in their "Navigating to Knowledge" article make this observation:

> Imagine walking into the world's largest library, only to find all the pages from all the books dumped into one large pile on the floor. Add to this the fact that the librarian adds 200,000 new pages to the pile every day and periodically moves pages at random. How would someone be able to cut through the chaos to find a specific page on a particular topic?

This observation is why more than half of the Web users complain that information is hard to find.

Tools to help users search for information on the Internet's Web pages have been developed called search engines. One type of search engine is a Web catalog, which organizes the Web sites by subject classification. Yahoo and Excite are two such engines. Another type of engine is the Web database which indexes the contents of the Web pages and allows this content to be searchable. Lycos and Infoseek are examples of Web databases. These search engines help to put all Internet queries on equal footing. A new immigrant's need for health information in a language he or she can understand is no more special than a businessman's need for information on a corporation.

CYBERSCHOOL

The diverse populations in our communities have a wide range of information needs. The Internet can provide a wealth of opportunities for enhancing the way educators teach these diverse populations and the way students of these diverse populations learn. The Internet reaches beyond the internationalization of education. Events that will not be documented in textbooks for years to come can be found documented on the Internet. Students have the opportunity to collaborate with peers and professionals located around the world and even invite electronic mentors to participate in class projects, no matter where they live, with no time delay. Health care professionals can access useful information related to clinical practice, such as radiologic and diagnostic images, patient histories, or pharmaceutical research. Multimedia textbooks to support clinical decision making, distance clinical treatment sharing, electronic journals with continuing education credits, self-care and virtual conferencing are all possibilities. The Internet offers both health care professionals and patients with information that can be searched, retrieved, organized, and saved.

NEW CENTURY CRITICAL THINKING

Educators should integrate student use of the Internet into their curricula—Internet-ize. Online resources and Web sites could be included in "required readings." E-mailing by students could sharpen language and communication skills. If a curriculum goal includes any of the following tasks, Internet-ize:

- Recognizing and comparing similarities and differences between concepts, viewpoints
- Finding proof of a hypothesis
- Inferring unknown generalizations from observations or analysis
- Deducing consequences
- Analyzing errors
- Identifying an underlying theme or pattern of information
- Identifying personal perspectives on an issue
- Gathering information from human sources
- Working in teams

There are many Internet sites that provide educators with Internet projects. *Classroom Connect* is an excellent resource for educators, providing practical examples on Internet curriculum integration. In the October 1996 issue, a how-to guide for referencing such online sources and sample lesson plans are given. Why not have one class start a book chapter and have another class, geographically distant, add a chapter. Internet scavenger hunts work well. For projects, however, make sure that the group composition is as diverse as possible with regard to gender, race, or nationality. The Web site *http://www.cob.ohio-state.edu* has a wealth of information on teaching diversity and includes some hands-on teaching strategies.

Educators can use the Internet to network with other educators teaching the same curriculum content. The strength of cyberspace is in its numbers. The Internet grew because scientists wanted to share information. If only a few offer intelligent answers to a query, then the sum total of the knowledge on that query would increase. Don't be afraid to share what you know. If you develop a successful teaching strategy or lesson plan, share it via the Internet.

NET ETIQUETTE

Virginia Shea has developed some basic rules of Internet etiquette—Netiquette—that should be followed by anyone e-mailing:

1. Remember the human—the impersonality of the medium often changes ones behavior when e-mailing. "Humans exchanging e-mail often behave the way some people behind the wheel of a car do: They curse at other drivers, make obscene gestures, and generally behave like savages." The primary doctrine of Netiquette is simple: "There are real people out there—Would you say it to the person's face?"

2. Adhere to the same standards that you follow in real life. Be ethical. Behaviors may be different in some areas of cyberspace, but they should not be lower.

3. Know where you are in cyberspace. If you enter a domain that is new to you, get a sense of how the people who are there act, then go ahead and participate.

4. Respect other people's time and bandwidth. Don't expect instant responses to all your questions and don't assume that all readers will agree with or care about your passionate arguments. People have less time than ever today because there is so much information to absorb. Before you send a document, ask yourself if they really need to know. If the answer is no, don't waste their time.

5. Make yourself look good online. Pay attention to the content of your writing. Know what you are talking about. Be clear and logical, pleasant, and polite.

6. Share your knowledge. E-mail succeeds—it might help someone else solve a problem.

7. Help keep the "flame wars" under control. Flaming is what people do when they express a strongly held position without holding back emotion. Do not perpetuate flame wars. They get boring very quickly to those who are not involved.

8. Respect other people's privacy. Do not read other people's e-mail.

9. Don't abuse your power. Do not take advantage of others through the Net. Never print private e-mail.

10. Be forgiving of other people's mistakes. Give people the benefit of the doubt. Never be arrogant or self-righteous.

CULTURAL MINORITIES

The Internet can be of great value to migrant and minority students. In Texas, college students act as cybercounselors. Through e-mail, these cybercounselors give the migrant kids pep talks and help them with school work. As the migrant kids travel from one work site to another, the Internet enables them to overcome their geographical isolation. Academic, medical, and dental records can be sent via the Internet to wherever the migrants are located, a task previous difficult because of their nomadic lifestyle.

CYBERTOWNS

Entire towns are becoming Internet-ized. Blacksburg, Virginia, is one such town. On Blacksburg's Electronic Village (BEV), you can buy groceries, hear local bands, apply for a credit card, ask police to keep an eye on your house while on vacation, or chat with neighbors. The Internet has made Blacksburg a stronger community, according to Andrew Cohill, assistant professor at Virginia Polytechnic Institute and head of the BEV project. Senior citizens, who comprise 40 percent of Blacksburg's population have become more active and vocal because of the BEV. Townspeople feel that the BEV has led them to meet neighbors they couldn't ordinarily get to know. They visit the BEV business pages for goods and services. Sixth grade teacher Rich Beamish feels the BEV has helped him reach students and parents. He gets notes, comments, and questions, even homework online.

The rapid growth of the Internet has spurred dissatisfaction with the slowness of connections and of data retrieval. As a result, academics have embarked on a new project—Internet 2. This project began six months ago with thirty-four universities across America. The universities joined forces to develop tomorrow's Internet with high-speed electronic links to online research and teaching tools. The project was opened to any college or university that wanted to tackle the project, providing that it committed about $500,000 to connect its campus computers to the nearest Internet 2 hub and that it worked to develop new applications for the enhanced network. The project has grown to 109 universities and because of its size, according to Jones, Internet 2 will be difficult, technologically and administratively, to achieve success.

A project, Next Generation Internet Initiative, has been launched by the Clinton administration. If approved by Congress, the project would empower five federal agencies to work together to build a faster and better networking infrastructure. Monies have already been appropriated for federal support of networking upgrades. One of the main challenges of the twenty-first century will be the storing, retrieving, and representing of information. A national information infrastructure will be needed to meet this challenge.

LIBRARY

Benjamin Franklin's conception of the first lending library focused on the notion that every citizen is entitled to have unfettered access to the recorded, collected, and cataloged knowledge of mankind. Cost, space limitations, and proximity of the collection to everyone seeking the knowledge has made the realization of this nearly impossible until the birth of the Internet. The Internet has provided the solution that facilitates unfettered access to information.

CYBERSOCIOLOGY

The Internet has given rise to much debate by sociologists as to the nature of the Internet, this virtual community. Fernback and Thompson present the argument in "Virtual Communities: Abort, Retry, Failure?" —is cyberspace a form of real community, or is it a simulacrum of community. The notion of community has had a central place in our social fabric. Communities bring people closer together and exacerbate social divisions. Cyberspace allows people to experience and interact with one another in spite of physical isolation. The cyberspace community, therefore, according to Fernback and Thompson, encompasses the dimensions of community. Bulletin boards and conferencing provides for social interaction and solidarity. Romances and friendships blossom. Internet business transactions are made in cyberspace and political advice is exchanged. Culturally, people are exposed to the value and systems of other nations. Communities within cyberspace emphasize a shared belief in the principles of free speech, equality, individualism, and open access, the tenets of American democracy. Communities in cyberspace are usually bonded by a particular topic under discussion and oftentimes manifest themselves in political action or educational reform. It has been noted people in cyberspace do just about everything people do in real life, but we leave our bodies behind.

There is a fatalistic vision of cyberspace, according to Fernbach and Thompson. It is felt that cyberspace fragments society and insures that we never talk to people beyond our immediate friends or family on a personal level about anything. Cyberspace, McClennen comments, contributes to the decline of community. Cyberspace has created "mouse potatoes"—people who hide from real life and spend their whole life goofing off in cyberspace.

Despite this fatalistic vision, it is felt that the Internet virtual community will experience astronomical growth because of people's hunger for community, for a place they can gather for conviviality. According to Rheingold, the ability to network, gain knowledge, or find community within cyberspace is the social glue that binds formerly isolated individuals into a community. The same rituals or rites of passage that exist in real life can be found in cyberspace.

America is a multiracial, multiethnic hybrid society. Cyberspace is working to promote synergy amongst its diverse populations where there are no preconceptions based on appearance, and where there is equal access to the information conversations of its participants. The barriers to Internet access— affordability, intellectual accessibility, and time availability—need to be overcome to achieve this. Cyberspace is a the virtual community in which everyone should reside.

Vint Cerf, vice president of the Corporation for National Research Initiatives, and one of the original members of the Internet, said:

> All the world's a net: and all the data in it merely packets
> Come to store-and-forward in the queries a while and then are
> Heard no more. 'Tis a network waiting to be switched!

REFERENCES

Anderson, C. The accidental superhighway: A survey of the Internet. *The Economist, 336*:1–18 (July 1, 1995).

Betancourt, I. The more things change . . . library services to increasingly ordinary populations. *New Jersey Libraries, 31*(3): 11–3 (Summer 1997).

Britt, R. Going on-line. A beginner's guide to navigating the information superhighway. *Asbury Park Sunday Press,* Section C: C1, C7, C9 (April 10, 1994).

Broad, W. J. Communications network eliminates time, distance between scientists. *The Times & Observer,* p. 4F (May 23, 1993).

Dern, D. *The Internet guide for new users.* NY: McGraw-Hill, 1994.

Diamond, D. This town is wired. *USA Weekend,* pp. 4–6, (February 23–25, 1996).

Faughan, J. G., et al. Cruising the information highway: On-line services and electronic mail for physicians and families. *Journal of Family Practice,* 39(4): 365–71 (October 1994), pp. 4–6 (January 21–23, 1994).

Fernbach, J. & Thompson, B. *Virtual communities: Abort, retry, failure?* http://www.well.com.

Flower, J. Log on: A guide to the on-line world for healthcare executives, managers, clinicians and patients. *Healthcare Forum Journal* 39(5), 36–41 (July/August 1996), http://www.nw.com.

Internet basics, Part one. Infolink Technical Workshop Series-4.1. Lauren Technology Corp., 1996.

McNichol, T. Fellow travelers on the info highway. *USA Weekend,* pp. 4–6 (January 21–23, 1994).

Oren, A. http://muse.tau.ac.il/%Eavigail.

Palomo, J. All the difference in the world. *USA Weekend,* p. 16 (August 15–17, 1997).

Pastan, S. Evolution of the Net. *Guide to the Internet Lancet Supplement.* London: Elsevier Sciences, 1996.

Peters, R. & Sikorski, R. Navigating to knowledge: Tools for finding information on the Internet. *JAMA, 277*(6), pp. 505–506, (February 12, 1997).

Shea, V. Core rules of netiquette. Excerpted with permission. *Educom Review:* 58–61,(September–October 1994).

Turkle, S. Virtuality and its discontents: Searching for community in cyberspace. *The American Prospect, 24:*50–7, (Winter 1996).

Yerks, A. M. The Internet and pediatric nursing: Guide to the information superhighway. *Pediatric Nursing, 22*(1):11–5 (January–February 1996).

Young, J. B. Some participants in Internet2 fear it is becoming too large. *Chronicle of Higher Education,* p. A23 (June 27, 1997).

Chapter 8

Unknowing

PATRICIA L. MUNHALL

This paper has been adapted from "Unknowing: Toward Another Pattern of Knowing in Nursing," published in *Nursing Outlook,* 1993;41:125–128, with permission.

In this chapter the reader is introduced to the concept of suspension of one's own beliefs and the possible misunderstandings that can result from finding you have agreements or disagreements with the individual you are attempting to understand. "Unknowing" is presented as an art concerned with the creation of an authentic encounter between or among individuals from different cultures.

COMING TO UNKNOW

"What's it like looking back?" Two literary excerpts answer with different subjective perceptions of a phenomenon and present us with a rationale for a pattern of knowing acknowledged as "unknowing." The art of unknowing is discussed as a de-centering process from our own organizing principles of the subjective world. To be authentically present to a patient is to stand knowingly in one's own life and interact with full "unknowingness" about the other's life. The intersubjective intelligible whole is discussed from the persepective of intersubjective conjuction and disjunction. Unknowing is presented paradoxically as another pattern of knowing essential to empathy, understanding, and caring.

> As I sit on this hard bench I suddenly yearn for one last long look, and not only of the phenomenon of little Joe and little Michael, but of the others too, Ellen four and Annie, seven months sharing a peach. . . . As I watch them now as adults the fact that I will never see their toddler selves again is tormenting (Smiley, 1989).

> When you are thirty, the child is two. At forty, you realize that the child in the house, the child you live with is still. When you close your eyes, or the moment he has walked from the room, two years old. When you are sixty and the child is gone, the child will also be two, but then you will be more certain. Wet sheets, wet kisses. A flood of tears. As you remember him the child is always two (Beattie, 1989).

The foregoing literary excerpts illustrate the power of individual perceptions and the different structures of subjectivity that call for a knowing in nursing to be acknowledged, as "unknowing." Many nurses have endorsed in our nursing literature and in some curricula a structural, categorical approach to knowledge, reflected in Carper (1978) *Fundamental Patterns of Knowing in Nursing*. Indeed these four patterns of knowing are part of Fawcett's proposed "metaparadigm" for nursing (Fawcett, 1984).

This chapter is focused on the state of mind of unknowing as a condition of openness. "Knowing," in contrast, leads to a form of confidence that has inherent in it a state of closure. The "art" of unknowing is discussed as a de-centering process from one's own organizing principles of the world (Atwood & Stolorow, 1984). Unknowing is not simple, but it is essential to the understanding of subjectivity and perspectivity. These concepts are discussed, and a suggestion is offered that for understanding to emerge, the perceptual field that evolves when two or more personal universes come together must be clearly focused upon by the involved individuals. It is also proposed that in this perceptual field of two or more subjective perspectives, called the "intersubjective space," all sources of human understanding, empathy—and also conflict—can and will evolve.

THE ART OF UNKNOWING

Unknowing, paradoxically, is another pattern of knowing. Knowing that one does not know something, that one does not understand someone who stands before them, and perhaps this process does not fit into some preexisting paradigm or theory is critical to the evolution and development of knowledge.

To engage in an authentic encounter, one must stand in one's own socially constructed world and unearth the other's world by admitting, "I don't know you." "I do not know your subjective world."

When a nurse stands with another human being, forming impressions, making a diagnosis, formulating a perception, and knowing what is best, she/he may indeed practice an efficient type of nursing based on the empirical, ethical, personal, and eclectic patterns of knowing.

However, knowing of this kind leads to a form of confidence that has inherent in it a state of closure. To be authentically present to a patient is to situate knowingly in one's own life and interact with full unknowingness about the other's life. In this way unknowing equals openness (Figure 8–1).

This by no means is easy. Unknowing as an art is not presently acknowledged and calls for a great amount of introspection. However unknowing remains essential to the understanding of intersubjectivity and perspectivity. In other words, it is essential that we understand our self and our patient to be two distinctive beings, one of whom the nurse does not know.

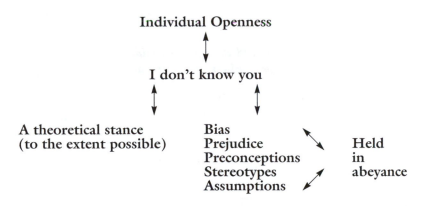

FIGURE 8–1.
The Art of Unknowing

Placing aside a cogent argument that might speak to just how well nurses know themselves, there can be little doubt that they do not know the patient. Each patient has a unique perspective of their situated context and a unique perspective of who they are as a person in the world. This is their perspectivity, their worldview, and this is their reality. When nurses and patients meet, two perspectives of a situation need to be recognized. Thus the process of intersubjectivity begins to create the perceptual field (Figure 8–2).

Personal Universes—Subjective Views of Reality

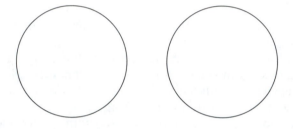

Intersubjectivity—Two Views Interact

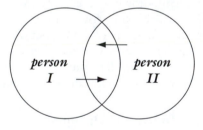

A Shared Perceptual Field
Where Subjectivities Interact

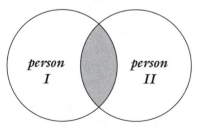

FIGURE 8–2
Personal Universes, Intersubjectivity, and a Shared Perceptual Field

INTERSUBJECTIVITY

Intersubjectivity is not a difficult concept to understand, though many writings about it seem intent at making the concept complex. What is challenging is practicing it in a wide-awake manner.

Intersubjectivity is the verbal and nonverbal interplay between the organized subjective world of one person and the organized subjective world of another (Patterson & Zderad, 1990). It is one person's subjectivity intersecting with another's subjectivity. In each person's subjective world is organization of feeling, thoughts, ideas, principles, theories, illusions, distortions, and whatever else helps or hinders a person. Individuals do not know about another's subjective world unless they are told about it, and even then one cannot be sure. Figures 8–2 and 8–3 illustrate visually the concept of intersubjectivity.

In Figure 8–3, the illustration depicts where many nurse theorists say nursing takes place. Sometimes this is called the "in-between," but visually it depicts a connection that for the purpose of this chapter is called a "shared perceptual field." When this shared perceptual field is pulled out by the nurse, it becomes a whole, as shown in Figure 8–4.

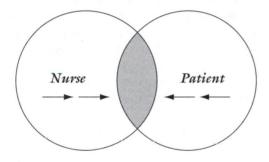

FIGURE 8–3
The Nurse–Patient Shared Perceptual Field

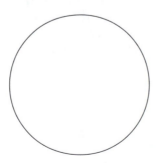

FIGURE 8–4
Perceptual Field

As was discussed, it is in this field that caring, understanding, empathy, conflict, and misunderstandings take place. This, then, is no small matter. For caring to be realized, this perceptual field that emerges, this intelligible whole or intersubjective space, must be clearly focused on, mutually analyzed, and mutually interpreted. The mutuality here reflects the nurse and patient communicating, reflecting, and validating the meaning of the patient's world. The unknowing stance of the nurse is primarily motivated by the intent to come to know the patient's world. The patient "knows" the nurse as one who is engaging in the process of coming to know so that the nurse can better understand, empathize, and care in an authentically individualized manner.

A DE-CENTERING PROCESS

This art of unknowing when two subjective worlds intersect is discussed as a de-centering process, one that de-centers us from our own organizing principles of the world (Atwood & Stolorow, 1984). This unknowing art enables empathy of the situated context where nurses understand the actual essence of meaning the patients' experiences hold for them.

Figure 8–5 might be what Sartre thought of as utmost importance in understanding and evaluating his concept of the human situation. This is called "being for others." Sartre feared in this the loss of self, but what is portrayed here as de-centering is a temporary suspending of self as the nurse allows the patient's subjective structure of reality to become known. The nurse is metaphorically eclipsed by a patient in order to "know" the patient. Nurses encourage patients to reveal their perspectives without interruption or the introduction of alternative interpretations. Nurses allow patients to be seen and heard.

DE-CENTERING AS UNKNOWING

These ideas of unknowing and de-centering are very practical realities to nursing practice and research. Without extensive examination and introspection of and about the substance of the intersubjective space, two dangers might occur that are counterproductive to understanding and to patients' health, growth, and becoming. Nurses must understand that their perceptions of the world and of health may or may not assist the patient. Stemming from the nurses' subjectivity, if not eclipsed temporarily by the patients', are two dangers of knowing. They are intersubjective conjunction and intersubjective disjunction (Atwood and Stolorow, 1984).

INTERSUBJECTIVE CONJUNCTION

In the instance of intersubjective conjunction the nurse is alerted to this circumstance by feelings of comfort with the patient. Immediately the nurse needs to understand that this comfort is originating from their own perceptions of knowing. We have yet to explore the meaning of this comfort for the patient. Although this initial compatibility may feel good, it could cause problems unless an attitude of questioning and unknowing precedes the continuation of the perceived shared subjective stance.

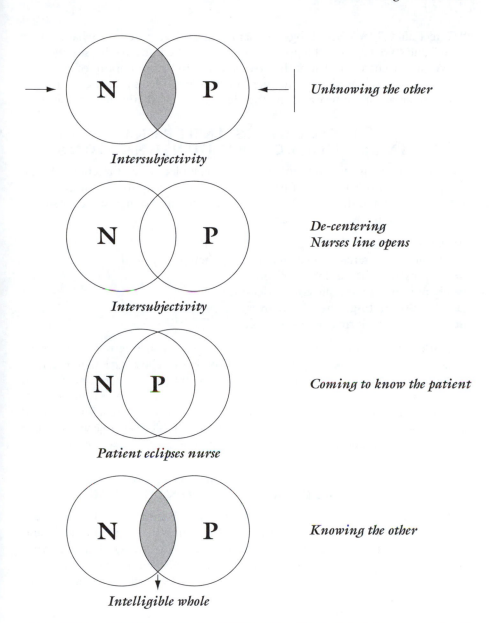

FIGURE 8–5
Knowing the Other

In this space of intersubjective conjunction is a situation in which it seems the two subjective interpretations of the world match. The patient is an analogue model of the nurse, or vice versa. Thoughts such as "We think alike,"

"We feel alike," "We see things the same way," "We agree on what's to be done," and "We have good rapport" should alert the nurse to this situation.

What is occurring is that both persons share similar perceptions of the experience. However, before going further, it is suggested here that the nurse proceed with an air of mystery and an attitude open to alternative interpretations.

DIFFICULTIES INHERENT IN INTERSUBJECTIVE CONJUNCTIONS

Closure is the main difficulty inherent in intersubjective conjunctions. While two persons (in this instance a patient and a nurse) may share common attitudes, the whys and the histories may be very different. So then shared assumptions of reality, or conjunction can:

- Close further exploration
- Achieve the status of objective reality (when it may not be so)
- Represent a shared defensive solution
- Represent a shared illusion or delusion
- Close off testing other alternatives
- Eliminate exploring origin of perception

An example of this could be a nurse and a patient sharing negative feelings about various things—people, places, or an experience. Their agreement becomes an agreed-upon truthful objective reality. In actuality, these shared perceptions could be a way that both these individuals project inner difficulties onto the outside world. The danger, of course, is that the inner difficulties are left unexplored and the conjunction becomes collusion. It is critical in this intersubjective space to go beyond or underneath the agreed-upon perceptions of the experience.

THE ART OF UNKNOWING IN INTERSUBJECTIVE CONJUNCTION

Unknowing can be the impetus to finding out. Where there is agreement about the world, nurses should de-center, hold their beliefs in abeyance, and allow others to tell their stories. Nurses allow others to enlarge their construction of their social reality. Before, nurses said, "I know how you're feeling," which is doubtful anyway, the knowing part comes from allowing the other to be known from individual perceptions, not those of the nurse. So agreement in the intersubjective space does not mean mutual knowing. Unknowing is essential to "knowing," just as in intersubjective disjunction.

INTERSUBJECTIVE DISJUNCTION

In the instance of intersubjective disjunction there is disparity and disagreement with the subjective perceptions of the two socially constructed realities of individuals. It is in this disjunction that misunderstanding and conflict may be counterproductive and nontherapeutic for patient. In disjunction, nurses believe that their interpretation of a situation is the better one and that the patient's interpretation would be improved if it were altered. Rather than assuming an unknowing posture regarding the patient's perception, the nurse attempts to change the subjective meaning for the patient. In contrast, then, to conjunction, in which there is agreement about the world (which may be obstructional as well), in disjunction there is disagreement, and this too may be extremely counterproductive to understanding and empathy.

THE ART OF UNKNOWING IN INTERSUBJECTIVE DISJUNCTION

Where there is disjunction, there is the potential for misunderstanding the meaning an experience has for a patient. If the nurse "knows" what is best and attempts to communicate this to the patient, the patient may feel misunderstood, conflicted, and may become resistant to the "knower." After all, the patient is a "knower" as well.

Again, nurses must hold their own beliefs and assumptions aside. For instance, if a nurse believes the situation to be hopeless and a patient is hopeful despite all evidence, to be empathetic and to help the patient feel understood, the nurse too should attempt a hopeful attitude. Many nurses can speak to a patient they had every cause to believe to be hopeless as far as improving or becoming more differentially integrated only to find that their "knowing" was based on usual cases in similar circumstances. The danger here is obvious, in that the self-fulfilling prophecy may be operating and the patient may begin to perceive his circumstance as the nurse does.

DIFFICULTIES INHERENT IN INTERSUBJECTIVE DISJUNCTION

The danger in disjunction or disagreement is mainly one of the projection of a nurse's perception on a patient. Once again, closure to the meaning and desires of the patient takes hold. In these instances, the disagreed-upon assumptions of reality, or disjunction can:

- Close further exploration
- Become self-fulfilling
- Alter the patient's perception of reality
- Give the patient the impression that he is wrong
- Interfere with patient's defense mechanisms

An example of this could be "knowing what is best" for the patient. A case that comes to mind is a nurse who discouraged a patient from marrying a man who was obviously a poor choice for this patient. The patient did not marry and had a series of psychotic episodes. Would they have happened anyway? We do not know, but de-centering here to find out what was going on with this patient from her perspective is essential. Instead of diagnosing and prescribing, the nurse needed to unknow, listen, and understand the meaning of this patient's perceptions.

THE FIFTH PATTERN OF KNOWING— UNKNOWING

"Knowledge screens the sound the third ear hears, so we hear only what we know" (Kurtz, 1989).

Indeed, our listening characteristics are often those of diagnosing and prescribing. The diagnosing and prescribing comes from our knowledge and our subjective perceptions. This then can lead to premature closure to other possibilities, interpretations, and perceptions. The fact that this occurs is a result of someone else's knowing. Someone else teaching us to know, to put together, to make sense. But it is not altogether freeing and, indeed, can be constraining.

"The compulsion to make sense is a resistance to unknowing" (Kurtz, 1989, p. 7). The pattern of unknowing can lead to a much deeper knowledge of another being, of different meanings, and interpretations of all our various perceptions of experience. The intent of bracketing in qualitative research is one in which the researcher assumes the posture of the naive listener.

Huxley (1982) stated:

Sit down before fact like a little child, and be prepared to give up every preconceived notion, following humbly wherever and to whatever abyss nature leads, or you shall learn nothing.

COMING TO AN OPENNESS

Knowing is wonderful, but it is just a guiding means. This chapter has focused on the essential state of mind of unknowing as a condition of openness. This unknowing in the intersubjective space of two people or people of two cultures allows others to be. This art of unknowing may enable the nurse to understand empathetically the actual essence of the meaning an experience has for a patient. This pattern of unknowing focused herein on the intersubjective whole between patient and nurse is applicable as well to learning in a more formal sense. To be open to learning one needs to posture oneself in a position of unknowing to hear a colleague, a teacher, a student. To provide and find openness is to be able to say, "I never thought about it that way," and at once experience the wonderment of coming upon an "unknown."

REFERENCES

Atwood, D. & Stolorow, R. (1984). *Structures of subjectivity*. New Jersey: Lawrence Erlbaum Associates, Inc.

Beattie, A. (1989). *Picturing will*. New York: Random House.

Benner, P. & Wrubel, J. (1989). *The primacy of caring, stress and coping in health and illness*. Menlo Park, CA: Addison-Wesley.

Buber, M. (1970). *I and thou*. (Translated by Walter Kaufman). Charles Scribner's Sons.

Carper, B. (1978). Fundamental patterns of knowing. *Advances in Nursing Science*, 13–23.

Fawcett J. (1984). *Analysis and evaluation of conceptual models of nursing.* Philadelphia: F. A. Davis.

Huxley, J. H. (1982). *Space, time and medicine.* (L. Dossey, Editor). Boulder, CO: Shambhala.

Kurtz, S. (1989). *The art of unknowing.* New Jersey: Aronson, Inc.

Leininger, M. (Ed.). (1988). *Caring: An essential human need: Proceedings of the three national caring conferences.* Detroit, MI: Wayne State University Press.

Moccia P. (1986). *Theory development and nursing practice: A synopsis of a study of the theory-practice diabetic.* In P. Moccia (Ed.), *New approaches to theory development.* New York: National League for Nursing.

Paterson, J. D. & Zderad, Z. J. (1990). *Humanistic nursing.* New York: National League for Nursing.

Polanyi, M. (1958). *Personal knowledge.* Chicago, IL: University of Chicago Press.

Sartre, J. P. (1966). *Being and nothingness.* New York: Washington Square Press.

Smiley, J. (1989). *Ordinary love and good will.* New York: Random House.

Travelbee, J. (1971). *Interpersonal aspects of nursing.* Philadelphia: Davis.

Watson, J. (1985). *Nursing: Human science and human care.* Norwalk, CT: Appleton-Centry-Crofts.

Part Two

CURRICULUM

Chapter 9

The Internationalization of Higher Education

D A V I D   M.   G I B S O N

> In the past . . . it was usually only the rich who could send their sons to university to fit them for playing a full role in society, rather than for acquiring a narrow academic training. Now a minority privilege is becoming the need of the majority. This means that universities will have to provide a different and broader kind of education than much that is now given: with the emphasis on turning out useful citizens who can adapt to our complex, changing society, rather than specialized scholars.
>
> *(Chomsky, 1963)*

THE ROOTS OF INTERNATIONAL EDUCATION IN THE AMERICAN ACADEMY

Foreign exchange programs are hardly new to higher education in the United States. Their origins, however, had more to do with administrators and faculty studying abroad than student exchanges. American college presidents and faculty, who studied in European universities during the late antebellum and postbellum periods, did so to either improve American higher education or to further their own academic careers. Indeed, the configuration of higher education in the United States has at least some of its roots in English, French, and German universities as academic leaders scrutinized the American academy from the mid and waning years of the nineteenth century to early years of the twentieth. As early as 1851, Henry P. Tappan, a professor at the University of the State of New York (now New York University) and later president of the University of Michigan, touted the preeminence of the German universities as "model institutions" (Hofstader & Smith, 1970). Elsewhere and later, a great educational leader and founder of Cornell University, Andrew D. White, extolled French higher education as typified at the Sorbonne or the Collège de France as well as in Germany and England (Hofstader & Smith).

From the middle of the nineteenth to the beginning of the twentieth centuries, graduate students often sought to study in foreign colleges and universities where they surmised that their particular concentration of study would be enhanced by such experiences. Many of these students were, in fact, tutors in American colleges. To further their careers and to create a more disciplinary career, during the 1840s and 1850s these tutors sought advanced training in European universities. At Brown, for example, during the mid-1850s nearly one-quarter of the faculty took leave to study in Europe (Finkelstein, 1984). Hence, in its very beginnings from the charter for Harvard College in 1636 to the emulation of the great universities of Europe during the nineteenth and twentieth centuries, American higher education was inchoately international, albeit somewhat unilateral.

GROWING A SHARED VISION OF INTERNATIONAL HIGHER EDUCATION

More recently, the importance of the community of universities throughout the world has been underscored by the initiation and continuance of the International Association of University Presidents (IAUP). Founded in 1964, the association serves as an example of the ends common to those who aspire to collaborate in higher education. According to the association, its primary purposes are "to promote peace, well-being, and security for all humankind through education; to generate friendship, understanding, and confraternity among educational leaders; to encourage joint research and exchange of professors and educational materials; to facilitate cultural exchanges and to aid generally in maintaining world peace and cultural progress for the benefit of humanity" (IAUP brochure). It is germane to the current discussion to quote Resolution VI, passed by the IAUP at its Fourth Triennial Conference which was conducted in Boston, Massachusetts, in 1975:

> Whereas, A group of 500 college and university presidents and chancellors from all over the world met in Boston in mid-November 1975, representing the International Association of University Presidents and the American Association of State Colleges and Universities,
> Be it resolved, That these presidents and chancellors affirm their faith in higher education as the most important single long-term investment in promoting world peace and maximizing human fulfillment, and that they further affirm their belief that international educational cooperation and the internationalization of education in every country are essential goals in the process of improving the quality of life and in contributing to the survival of the human race (de la Rosa, 1996).

Hence, with this social mission in mind and with an electronically shrinking global village, educational leaders were sensing an urgency to expand higher education as an international enterprise and in so doing, grapple with deep socioeconomic issues. Elsewhere in the IAUP history, there are numerous resolutions pertaining to the preservation of human dignity, the place of women in higher education, the role of universities and colleges in advancing peace and the importance of advancing common values across cultural, ethnic, and national boundaries. Indeed, in 1996, the IAUP issued a statement noting the "imperative need to internationalize higher education and promote its sustained implementation as critical to quality education in our increasingly interdependent and multicultural world" (de la Rosa, 1996). Elsewhere, the IAUP stresses the importance of student and faculty exchange programs to foster greater international and multicultural understanding.

Another concern which may have contributed to the sustenance of the IAUP and shared as well by nonaffiliated higher education leaders is the so-called brain-drain phenomenon felt most acutely by developing countries which were losing their best and their brightest young students to developed countries, particularly to the United States. In the twelve-year period between 1970 and 1982 the number of foreign students pursuing their education in American colleges and universities doubled from 145,000 to 321,000 (Kelley, 1983), many of whom remained in the United States. According to *The Chronicle of Higher Education's* 1996 Almanac, sixty countries sent more than one thousand students each to American colleges and universities during the 1994–1995 academic year, for a total of 413,542 students. The total foreign student head count from all countries was given as 456,000 or 3.1 percent of the higher education student population (*The Chronicle of Higher Education* Almanac, 1996). Since 1982, then, there has been a 42 percent increase in foreign student enrollments in American colleges and universities. The largest increase, however, was during the twelve-year period between 1970 and 1982 when the foreign student enrollment jumped by just over 82 percent.

Today, more than ever, colleges and universities throughout the world are providing various foreign exchange programs for undergraduate studies. Students from colleges and universities in the United States are increasingly taking advantage of opportunities to study abroad. Indeed, the United States is the largest importer and exporter of students in exchange programs (Bollag, 1996). Although 62 percent of American students still study abroad in western Europe, there is a definable trend to other countries. The percentages of students studying in certain regions have increased significantly in certain regions. For example, the number of American students has increased by 25 percent in Africa, 39 percent in Oceania, 14 percent in Latin America, and 9 percent in Asia (open doors, 1995–1996). At the same time, many countries are building or reengineering their colleges and universities more often than not as private or independent enterprises or at least with some requirement for student payments and institutional accountability. Such is also the case at home as calls for more accountability prevail and the dependence of higher education on public funding competes with other state obligations (Kent, 1995). Still others are seeking to formalize agreements with peer institutions abroad. The shift from the almost exclusive professorial exchange to student exchanges has been dramatic and it does not appear as though it will abate anytime soon. It remains to be seen what all the implications this cross-migration may have on colleges and universities, but one may surmise it will strongly affect the world view of our students—be they foreign and studying in the United States or our citizens studying abroad. It may well have both positive and very negative implications for higher education institutions' stature at home, their curricula, and the quality of instruction and student life. If one's view of the role of higher education is rather narrowly circumscribed in economic terms, the issue of accessibility may widen the gap between the "haves and have nots." On the other hand, a failure to recognize the strain of the higher education enterprise on the nations' economies without regard to other sources of support, subjects institutions to the vagaries of the marketplace. In some cases the creation of new private colleges or universities without appropriate governmental oversight may be more advantageous to students studying abroad than to their counterparts in the countries in which they are guests.

In the May 9, 1997, edition of *The Chronicle of Higher Education*, the author recounts that from 1970s to the present the number of colleges in Costa Rica has grown from five to more than thirty. Notwithstanding this rapid growth, the increased numbers of colleges has not enhanced access for the population of Costa Rica. In a country with a literacy rate about equal to that of the United States, the new colleges make no promises to assure that the citizens of Costa Rica will benefit from their creation and presence. They are private and many are for-profit. Hence, they are put beyond the reach of many Costa Rican students. Conversely, Costa Rica has become increasingly popular for foreign students who can afford this tuition dependent education (Magaro Rubin, 1997). Former Soviet-aligned countries are also seeking ways in which they can establish independent colleges or universities or redesign their current institutions of higher education. Similarly in the Middle East, governments are grappling with ways in which to improve higher education or to make it less dependent on government purse strings. For example, this author has been negotiating with the president of MISR University for Science and Technology established recently in Egypt. This latter case exemplifies a switch in the conception of higher education as a free governmentally sponsored enterprise. It is funded privately and has instated a tuition program, unlike the free universities in Egypt such as Cairo University or Suez Canal University. MISR University is also actively seeking to promote student exchange programs, faculty exchanges, and even joint degree offerings. This change in the fundamental concept of tuition-free universities is being challenged elsewhere as well. In Great Britain, for example, a bipartisan commission has recommended the termination of "free tuition" in the country's universities (*Chronicle News Bulletin*, 1997).

ELECTRONICALLY YOURS: BRINGING THE CLASSROOM HOME

As mass electronic communications improve, it seems almost inevitable that higher education will become increasingly and more intensively internationalized. Just as higher education institutions in the United States are rushing to find ways in which they can collaborate through shared networks of distance learning technologies, so too are colleges and universities throughout the world looking to ways in which they can increase accessibility for students, widen educational opportunities, and share resources. The very challenges, however, that American higher education leaders are facing in attempting to implement electronically driven distance learning will be compounded as one attempts such enterprises across national and continental boundaries. Some of these concerns come almost immediately to mind. For example, capital expenditures; the appropriate use of technology or the correct technology to use; linguistic and cultural differences; administrative support for faculty and students;

and inclusiveness in curricular designs and models come almost immediately to mind as legitimate concerns.

Since not all students will be able to afford international exchanges, there is little doubt that the role of electronically generated distance learning programs will become an increasingly key component for the internationalization of higher education. As is the case with live exchange programs, there are certain cardinal principles adapted from the Commission on Higher Education, Middle States Association of Colleges and Schools "Guidelines for Distance Learning Programs" that must be maintained, they are:

1. Maintenance of fidelity to the institutions' missions
2. Similarity of student outcomes to those derived from more traditional modes of instruction
3. Curricular adaptation and appropriate faculty development in the utilization of distance learning
4. Faculty and student accessibility to appropriate learning and library resources including, if necessary translation services
5. Parity of measurements of the efficacy and outcomes of electronically derived learning with those derived from its traditional counterparts (Commission on Higher Education, 1997)

The reality of distance learning in international higher education is exemplified by the establishment of the European Association of Distance Teaching Universities (EADTU) established in early 1987 by Europe's major distance teaching universities. It is a seventeen-member organization representing fifteen European countries. It is an extensive system of higher education made up of a network of Euro-Study Centers to create the European Open University Network. It is no small enterprise either in student enrollments or in its scope of delivering courses as may be noted from the following:

> More than 350,000 degree students are registered with member institutions and a further 195,000 students are taking continuing education courses. The network of local and regional study centers has an educational staff of 3,500 academics . . . Activities relating to the transnational delivery of courses include the provision of distance education programs and courses offered by other European distance teaching universities; the provision of new distance study offerings to be developed by the EADTU members (in the areas of languages, cultural background, and social and cultural sciences); and the adaptation of European distance study offerings to individual local and regional specifications in close cooperation with faculties of the responsible universities. International events for students, mentors/tutors, and professors may include study days, face to face events, etc. (Pronk, 1996).

European nations and the United States are not alone in the growth of information technology. Michael Hudson, a Georgetown University professor of

Arab studies, suggests that Egypt serves a hub for information technology into the Middle East because communication cables from Europe connect the continents. So too, the higher education communities in Latin America, Mexico, Canada, and across the African continent have been engaged in the design and implementation of various forms of distance education. As global communications become more sophisticated and the costs for technology stabilize or even lower, educators are seeking ways in which they can transform their colleges and universities into network learning sites.

The ubiquity of computers as one source of information, however, brings still some other challenges. Professor Hudson also notes that a number of the Arab countries are tightening access to the Internet by censoring selective information to their citizens (McCollum, 1997). This issue brings to bear some thorny problems on what we, in the United States, consider academic freedom and how that is interpreted in other countries. As educators attempt to bridge international boundaries, issues of what is culturally seemly to some peoples may be very much the opposite to others. Certainly, great care must be exercised in the design and delivery of Internet courses, faculty and student exchange programs, and other forms of international exchanges. Certain courses, especially in the humanities and social sciences, may unwittingly carry with them some culturally insensitive materials to at least some participants in exchange programs, whatever the medium of transmittal may be.

There can be little doubt that the increased use of electronic media and its refinement through digitalization has had and will continue to have far reaching implications for all of higher education and for enhanced opportunities for shared resources both nationally and internationally. At the same time the rapidity with which it is appearing virtually on every continent in some form or another and its ubiquity in business and in homes have caught educators between the ivy halls and the university without walls. Does the rise of distance teaching, made easier through electronics, predict the demise of traditional colleges and universities? As well-endowed colleges and universities invest huge sums of money to globalize themselves over electronic pathways, how well will less well-endowed small liberal arts colleges or, for that matter, large research universities fare in an increasingly competitive higher education marketplace? Opportunities for combined and interdisciplinary research have grown and clearly areas for international research via this medium are almost a natural fit in the environmental sciences or in health fields such as is evident in the American Cancer Society's GLOBALink. What impact such transcontinental research will have on universities is still not clear, but one might surmise that the pooled talents of the best may well force the reduction of the lesser players in certain areas of research which lend themselves to international collaboration.

CHALLENGES AND OPPORTUNITIES

There are both dark clouds and rays of sunshine hovering above the field of international education. For one, the increase in private institutions which lure

American students abroad may not be all that good an educational experiment if their creation causes a decrease in accessibility to natives of the host countries or if they are founded on less than solid standards of higher education. For another, our immigration laws have some disturbing components regarding nonimmigrant foreign students and scholars, including the imposition of a special fee to be collected by colleges and universities from both students and scholars. These fees, however, are targeted for the benefit of the U.S. Immigration and Naturalization Service for updated tracking systems of foreign nationals while studying in the United States. Indeed, Stevan K. Trooboff, president of the Council on International Exchange notes: "We seem to be doing everything we can to keep people out. . . . The way we now treat foreigners, we make people sorry that they came" (Desruisseaux, 1996).

Part, at least, of the past rationale for exchange programs was derived from the Cold War but now there has been a shift from a focus on physical to economic security, albeit some of the restrictions in the new immigration laws have at least part of their roots in the World Trade Center bombing (Desruisseaux, 1996). A caveat may be in order here inasmuch as the laws on immigration regarding higher education are from a governmental perspective that may only partially converge with the views of academicians dedicated to the concept of internationalizing higher education. For example, Gary D. Hays tersely stated in a letter to the editor some of the perennial values of international education:

> As the world becomes increasingly global in its focus, the manner in which colleges and universities draw upon the ethnic, cultural and national diversity of their students, and not simply the numbers of students defined by any given category, is what will enable us to build greater understanding and empathy and to help develop stronger relationships among the business, community, and political leaders of tomorrow. These are the sorts of goals we in higher education should strive to attain (Hays, 1997).

Although Hay is president of United States International University, there are numerous other American institutions of higher education still committed to international higher education. In the reference to *The Chronicle of Higher Education's* 1996 Almanac, Boston University leads the four-year institutions in the enrollment of foreign students. In the same city, Boston College has created a very successful Center for International Higher Education. The center's primary aim is to provide the public with information about international colleges and universities with a related mission to the Jesuit tradition of higher education; nonetheless, it has:

> a broader mission to be a focal point for discussion and thoughtful analysis of higher education. The center provides information and analysis for those involved in managing the higher education enterprise internationally through publications, conferences, and the

maintenance of a database of individuals and institutions. The center is especially concerned with creating dialogue and cooperation among academic institutions in the industrialized nations and those in the developing countries of the Third World (Forest, 1995–1996).

There are yet other heartening developments in international education which may serve as stimuli for greater collaboration and resource sharing. In the December 20, 1996, publication of *The Chronicle of Higher Education*, Burton Bullog reported that the Convention on the Recognition of Qualifications Concerning Higher Education in the European Region had completed a draft treaty to simplify foreign-degree accreditation. Remarkably enough, the treaty had representatives from forty-nine countries to discuss issues ranging from credit-hour allocations to simplification of foreign academic credentials (Bullog, 1996). Similarly, urgent and ongoing discussions in South Africa are aimed at seeking consensus on curricula, the research mission and its relationship to the national agenda, and the insistence on interinstitutional collaboration and international exchanges, particularly for faculty (www.NCHE). Although there are a myriad of challenges facing global higher education ranging from the requirements of specialized accreditation to language barriers, there remains, nonetheless, ample opportunities for growth and innovation. Moreover, whatever the challenges may be, the trend toward the internationalization of higher education is most likely irreversible.

INTO THE FUTURE: AT HOME ABROAD

The questions that seem germane to ask about international education appear too simplistic: What and how does or will international education create a more informed world citizenry with enhanced tolerances for cultural differences; what roles will colleges and their faculties play in reshaping the academy; and can our colleges and universities maintain or create a past-to-future continuum but also help maintain certain American cultural values while teaching students to respect apparently conflicting values held by others? Although the questions at first blush may seem simple enough, it is readily apparent that the answers are not coequally simple.

In whatever form international education is conducted, educators will need to recognize that the creation of an informed citizenry has different meanings to different political systems. In this regard some international exchanges, by whatever methods, may of necessity be limited. Academics used to almost total freedom in their classrooms may simply have to curtail some of this freedom in recognition of geopolitical, cultural, and religious realities. This is not to suggest that faculty should engage in some disingenuous teaching strategies. Rather, the long-term view of the ends of education should be paramount to the enterprise of international education. The International Association of University Presidents has sponsored symposia on questions of human dignity, woman's role in society, and other sometimes thorny social or economic issues, as have other higher education associations. It may not, however, be particularly prudent for a professor engaged in international exchange programs to raise issues without regard to cultural and belief systems' differences. Just as nutritionists oftentimes must recognize cultural eating habits, not infrequently tied to religious beliefs, before making recommendations for dietary changes, so too must educators engaged in various cultural settings recognize and respect the rights of peoples to their own beliefs and cultural identity. The reality is that the growth of international education will require the professorate to become diplomatically adroit.

As the impact of technology and its relationship to trans-border education continues to mature, faculty members and administrators will find themselves facing some rather difficult decisions. Technology, first of all, is not inexpensive. As colleges and universities become convinced of the need to invest in advanced teaching technology, it will soon become apparent that they will have to hire new support staff, technological gurus whose price tags may well be above that of some faculty members. International education, whether through exchange programs or via distance teaching or a combination of both also brings further expenses to the campuses and can also bring troubling social upheavals. College administrators may have to make some very difficult decisions through which technology investment, including technology personnel, win out over faculty hires or replacements. It is, therefore, no mean challenge to faculty to help reshape the academy when, indeed, they may feel that it is being reshaped all around them. The faculty are, nevertheless, the content experts who as a whole are a rich corporate treasure. Their active and supported input will assure the reshaping of the modern globally conscious college or university.

In addition, students coming to the campus or leaving the campus to study need special attention and guidance. In response, colleges need to assure that exchange or distance teaching programs meet their own academic requirements, with due regard to differences in teaching strategies, grade assignments and values, and students' learning needs or habits. In this regard, the leadership of the institutions must be firmly committed to the implementation of international educational opportunities which afford their students opportunities for an enriched education and help fulfill the mission of their institutions. It is no small undertaking to enter into global education. Hence, the governing boards must back these ventures and be wholeheartedly convinced that these endeavors are a natural extension of their institutional missions. Governing boards must join with their academic leaders to support as fully as possible the faculty's efforts to globalize their educational mission and to provide institutional commitment to support students enrolled in such programs of education. From initial planning to technical and design support services and program implementation, the sustained commitment of the president and members of the governing board of the institution must be sustained to assure success. In other words, a successful international program is a corporate enterprise.

The past-to-future continuum is implicit in the preceding paragraph inasmuch as the key to this continuity is in maintaining adherence to the institutional mission. If formalized international education is inconsistent with the mission of a college or university, its introduction, wedged awkwardly into the curriculum, will diminish the mission's value and most likely doom the endeavor to failure, at any rate. If, on the other hand, the introduction of international education is a fit to the institution's mission, the values of the institution are all but guaranteed. Such American values as individual rights and liberties can, in reality, be enhanced through international exchanges. Students from abroad studying in our colleges or universities may be quite surprised at the rights accorded to individuals in our society and, for better or worse, they will have seen this particular value lived out, and not too infrequently, perhaps, violated. Conversely, our students studying in countries where the common good may override individual freedoms may find some legitimacy to such a societal underpinning value. On the other hand, they may discover how much they have taken for granted individual rights and liberties. In either case, all of the students, be they Americans abroad or foreign students here, will have had their education enriched and hopefully all will have gained respect for the differences among the peoples of the world.

If people of good will remain committed to the ideal of international, shared education—through whatever media—perhaps Noam Chomsky will be right: We will have helped to turn "out useful citizens who can adapt to our complex, changing society. . . ."

REFERENCES

Almanac Issue. (1996). *The Chronicle of Higher Education*, V. XLIII, N. 1., p. 20.

Bollag, B. (1996, December 20). European draft treaty simplifies foreign-degree accreditation. *The Chronicle of Higher Education*, December 20, 1996, p. A39.

Chomsky, N. (1963). Editorial, *Observer*, as quoted from Kenneth Minogue, 1973. *The concept of a university.* Berkeley and Los Angeles: University of California Press, p. 186.

Commission on Higher Education, Middle States Association of Colleges and Schools. (1997). *Guidelines for distance learning programs.* Philadelphia, PA, pp. 1–6.

Ibid. Desruisseaux, P. (1996, November 29) *New U.S. law makes foreign students, scholars feel unwelcome.* Section: International, pp. A45.

Finklestein, M. (1984). *The American academic profession.* Columbus: The Ohio State University Press, p. 18.

Forest, J. (1995–96). The Boston College Center for International Higher Education: A new initiative in higher education. The Trustees of Boston College, Boston, Forest@alumni.stanford.org.

Ibid., Hays, G. D. (February 7, 1997). *Foreign students at U.S. institutions.* Section: Opinion, pp. B12.

History of the IAUP: The first thirty years. (May 1996). Printed in Guadalajara, Mexico under the supervision of Dr. Alvaro Romo de la Rosa, pp. 45–46.

Ibid., pp. 371.

Hofstader, R. & Smith, W. (1970). Henry P. Tappan on university education, 1851. *American higher education: A documentary history*. Chicago: The University of Chicago Press, p. 488.

Ibid. The "Cornell Idea" Forms in White's Mind, 1860–1865, pp. 550–551.

Institute of International Education. American students abroad: Americans studying abroad in record numbers to diverse destinations. *Open Doors*, 1995/1996, p. 1.

Keller, G. (1983). *Academic strategy: The management revolution in American higher education*. Baltimore: The Johns Hopkins University Press, p. 13.

Kent, R. (1995). Two positions in the international debate about higher education: The World Bank and UNESCO. Paper for presentation at the Latin American Studies Association's meeting, Washington, DC, September 28–30, 1995.

Magaro Rubin, A. (1997). Costa Rica finds that having more colleges does not translate into better access. *The Chronicle of Higher Education*, V. XLIII, N. 35, pp. A 47–A 50.

McCollum, K. (1997, July 17). Scholars watch as information revolution sweeps Arab nations of the Middle East. *Academe Today, The Chronicle of Higher Education*, Washington, DC.

News Bulletins. (1997, July 22). The future of higher education in Britain. *Academe Today, The Chronicle of Higher Education*, Washington, DC.

Peace, welfare and security for mankind through education. International Association of University Presidents, Regional Council for Africa and the Middle East (informational brochure).

Pronk, N. (1996). The EuroStudy Centre (ESC) Network. In M. M. Thompson (Ed.), *Internationalism in distance education: A vision for higher education*. The American Center for Distance Education, The Pennsylvania State University, University Park, pp. 67, 69.

WWW, NCHE. A Quality Assurance System for All Higher Education.

Chapter 10

Bringing Diversity
into the Curriculum:
Successes and Problems

FRANK NAUGHTON

When I recently asked an older relative if his daughter and son-in-law had finished renovating their stately old house, he replied that they had progressed to where they finally could live in the house—but added that they would have to work on it for years to come. The situation with bringing diversity into the American higher-education curriculum is similar. Over the past three decades much success has been achieved—but much remains to be done.

This article discusses results of past efforts to introduce into our undergraduate courses and programs those issues and materials that provide significant learning experiences in the perspectives, lives, and insights of communities of people largely excluded from this curriculum in the years before 1970. More specifically, I describe specific changes that have been implemented and some major social forces contributing to this implementation. The article also delineates a fundamental problem that continues to affect efforts to establish diversity within the nation's higher-education curriculum, and it suggests some steps to be taken in dealing with this problem.

CHANGES ALREADY IMPLEMENTED

In its first issue for 1992, *Change* magazine presented an important report on the extent to which the topic of diversity (or multiculturalism), and questions associated with it, had already been introduced onto American campuses. The report was based on a survey of 196 colleges and universities selected to be representative of American higher education. Characterizing changes focused on diversity as constituting a "quiet revolution," the report presaged the 1997 observation by Nathan Glazer, the prominent observer of racial and ethnic issues in American society and its educational institutions. Glazer concluded in 1997 that multiculturalism had "established a powerful position in higher education . . . ," this being done apparently despite an abundance of negative reactions toward the introduction of diversity, including a 1987 best-seller on the subject by Allan Bloom. The *Change* survey generated eleven findings about multiculturalism in colleges and universities. Of these, the following were focused on curriculum:

1. Thirty-four percent of American colleges and universities maintained a multicultural general-education requirement. Most institutions (57%) included in their requirements both global and domestic diversity; fewer (12%) focused on domestic diversity;
2. At least 33 percent of colleges and universities offered coursework in ethnic and gender studies. But departments and programs in these areas were rare;
3. Fifty-four percent of all colleges and universities had introduced diversity into their departmental course offerings;
4. Public colleges and universities had surpassed private institutions in efforts toward introducing multiculturalism;
5. Multicultural programming existed in every region of the country;

6. Multiculturalism in the curriculum was a major topic of concern on campuses across the country. Seventy-two percent of vice presidents and deans surveyed said that they talked about multiculturalism frequently or continually.

The same issue of *Change* presented an article by Jerry Graff, senior staff member of the Association of American Colleges. It reported results from an earlier study of three hundred colleges and universities in America. Graff found multiculturalism to be "very much on the ascendancy," with schools requiring "more study of international topics or other cultures, more courses on racial and ethnic minorities . . . , and greater attention to gender in human affairs." Still another article on educational issues inherent in multicultural education presented the conclusion that the multicultural wars remained a hot topic in the press. On campuses, however, multiculturalism had won. The question "is no longer whether students should learn about diverse cultures, but how."

There is little reason to believe that the facts regarding curriculum matters presented in *Change* during 1992 have altered significantly in recent years. A review of *The Chronicle of Higher Education* over a two-year period from mid-1995 to mid-1997, for example, turns up few reports, letters, or opinion-statements about the introduction of diversity into the curriculum of American higher education (in contrast to coverage of diversity issues centered on changing faculty and student populations). It appears that the tongue-in-cheek title of Nathan Glazer's newest book on diversity in American education (*We Are All Multiculturalists Now*) can be taken as representing accurately the effects of changed attitudes and curriculum alterations that have brought diversity into the higher-education curriculum.

These transformations have not occurred, however, throughout all aspects of the higher-education curriculum and institutional structure. According to the *Change* survey report, alterations were not taking place across all academic departments. They were largely occurring in English, history, and within "an assortment of social sciences." Moreover, where modifications were being implemented within disciplines, they were being done though adding new material to existing courses (at, for example, 34 percent of two-year institutions and 51 percent of four-year institutions). Among all these institutions fewer than 50 percent surveyed for the report offered separate courses in women's studies, Hispanic studies, Native-American studies, Asian-American studies, and gay and lesbian studies. Among four-year institutions, only, did more than half (56 percent) offer courses in African-American studies.

Thus, with respect to changes already made in introducing diversity issues and materials into the American undergraduate curriculum, it seems that historian Lawrence Levine was correct in 1996 when he suggested through the title of his book that an "opening of the American mind" has been taking place. While work remains to be done, many institutions have already taken steps toward altering their curricula. Important modifications to general-education programs and to courses in some larger academic departments have been accomplished, and current attention seems concentrated on implementing approved changes and getting a qualified, diverse teaching faculty, rather than on defending the change itself.

WHY CHANGES HAVE TAKEN PLACE

To assess possibilities for continuing success in bringing diversity into the higher-education curriculum, and to help discern future problems, it is necessary to examine briefly why past successes took place. Why have general-education requirements been altered? Why has course content been changed? Why, in fewer cases, have new courses and some new programs been developed?

At the outset it is important to note that the transformations occurring since 1970 are not the only changes that have been made in what is taught, and how teaching occurs, in American higher education. As Christopher Lucas and others have made eminently clear, the curriculum has been changing quite continually (but not without controversy) since the turn of the last century at the latest, when Charles William Elliot succeeded in implementing his long-sought elective system at Harvard University. For nearly a century the higher-education curriculum has not been characterized by an immutable canon. Rather, it has been the creature of larger forces and ideas which themselves changed with transformations in the American social and economic scene. So the major variables contributing to the increased attention to diversity issues in our colleges and universities probably comprised a mixture of on- and off-campus developments, and the changes resulting from these developments are a continuation of an irregular but transforming process that has been operating for some time.

What are some developments leading to recent changes with respect to diversity in the curriculum? One major element has been the change in socioeconomic characteristics of the American undergraduate population over the past three decades. Since the mid-1960s, American college and university students increasingly have come from class, ethnic, racial, and gender backgrounds that were, in some cases, hardly represented on campuses earlier in the century. For example, according to sources cited by Levine, during the period 1960–1988 the percentage of college students from minority groups in America grew from approximately 6 percent to almost 20 percent of the student population. In the years 1960–1990, the percentage of women students earning bachelor's degrees increased from 35 percent to 54 percent, while the percentage of women going on to earn PhDs grew from 10 percent to 37 percent. An additional aspect of the changing socioeconomic characteristics of the undergraduate population is the noticeable presence of first- and second-generation students from cultural backgrounds that were largely underrepresented in higher education during the first two-thirds of the twentieth century. Children of families from a variety of Asian and Latin American countries, for instance, have increasingly entered our colleges and universities since the late 1960s.

Obviously, changes in the student population have reflected ethnic and racial changes in the total American population, as well as altered expectations about who should continue their education beyond the secondary-school level.

As more students from older and newer minority communities have attended colleges and universities, and as increasing numbers of women students have been present, they have been an important source of pressure and support for changing the curriculum to include subject matter and perspectives reflecting their intellectual and social concerns. Their statements and occasional demonstrations on behalf of curriculum changes (like those at Columbia University in the spring of 1996) have not, of course, reached the magnitude of student movements during the 1960s—but they are representative of student pressure and support for curriculum modifications.

An additional variable contributing to curriculum changes emerged from major intellectual shifts and new viewpoints being formed in certain academic fields. In history, for example, the appearance by the early 1970s of the "new history" with its emphasis on social history and attention to previously neglected communities and social categories contributed to establishing the discipline's appreciation for, and professional interest in, sociocultural complexities and diversities within American society, particularly those emerging from gender, class, and ethnic and racial communities. Eric Foner, in introducing a 1990 book on the "new history," characterized this change as a ". . . fundamental transformation of history itself. . . ." Similarly in sociology, major criticisms during the 1960s of the reigning structural-functionalist paradigm and its focal points, along with growing attention to different social issues (e.g., power structures and sources of social conflict) resulted in a modified agenda for this discipline. By the 1990s, the changed agenda had altered the sociological curriculum to the present point where it includes more courses on issues of gender, race, class, and global diversity. Thus, intellectual shifts in some fields have made them increasingly receptive to confronting issues of diversity and to modifying their viewpoints and the content of their curricula.

Clearly, a third variable contributing to curriculum changes since 1970 is comprised of the various social movements that grew or emerged in the 1960s. These represented, among other things, a new cultural assertiveness on the parts of several groups and communities, and eventually impacted on the attention (or lack of attention) given to these groups and communities in the higher education curriculum. These movements generated much of the intellectual drive (and in part the subject matter) for altering existing courses and, less frequently, creating new courses and programs of study in American colleges and universities. As a result of these modifications, there has been a notable increase in academic attention to the expressions, experiences, and situations of a greater variety of groups, categories, and social communities.

A KEY PROBLEM TO BE FACED

As we have seen, substantial alteration associated with diversity has occurred in American undergraduate education over the past three decades. As American society has become more differentiated and modified its attitudes about groups and communities once experiencing invisibility, our colleges and universities have modified what they teach. Among the problems remaining to be faced with respect teaching about diversity one question is central, namely, how to convince institutions that courses, programs, and departments focusing on diversity should be not only present in the curriculum, but be continuing and fully integrated parts of the curriculum.

The key problem of how fundamentally to integrate diversity into higher education is vital to making effects of the "quiet revolution" described earlier widespread and enduring. As we noted, most curriculum changes concerned with diversity have been what one observer in *Change* magazine referred to as "course add-ons," that is, new materials about diversity have been inserted into existing course frameworks within some humanities and social science programs. In contrast to such modifications, few new courses—to say nothing of new programs and new departments—have been assembled. Where programs and departments have been developed, support levels and organizational development have been weak, at least into the middle of the present decade. It is clear that the academy in bringing issues of diversity into its teaching has hardly given these issues the same status as that of, say, politics, economics, or languages. One is tempted to suggest that what Lucas might call a "window-dressing strategy" has been employed. Worsening the problem are the facts, as Glazer noted, that most colleges and universities have put issues of diversity within structures that make them optional for many students, and that those academic programs where attention to diversity is presently centered (humanities and social science programs) are particularly subject to changes in intellectual fashion.

Further compounding the problem of truly integrating diversity into the curriculum is the fact that much of the social activism and drive associated with earlier social movements have now weakened or disappeared. While students on a few campuses in recent years have publicly demonstrated on behalf of establishing or maintaining courses or programs related to the larger subject human diversity, these actions typically have been narrowly focused and, at times, tied only to a locally popular faculty member or local issue. Thus, there has been a diminishment of national attention and concern about working on behalf of diversity in the higher-education curriculum. Individuals and groups concerned with diversity today consequently are faced with different circumstances than those existing ten or twenty years ago. As a result of these altered circumstances, confronting the question of integrating diversity into the curriculum requires new and complex actions.

It is not possible within this article to suggest a meaningful strategy for fundamentally integrating the issues and subject matter of diversity into higher education. It is clear, however, that any successful strategy must take into account the need to convince curriculum review committees and other academic decision makers that courses, programs, and general education requirements which teach students about the phenomenon of diversity are central to offering high-quality educational experiences.

What will convince decision-makers of this reality? One tactic would be to demonstrate that such courses and programs directly address valued, long-standing goals of American higher education (e.g., to help students expand their understandings of the human condition and alternative reactions to problematics associated with it); a complementary action would be to demonstrate that such courses and programs can provide students with a range of skills effective in interacting successfully with individuals from a variety of social and cultural backgrounds. For example, a general-education diversity course could introduce students to how people from different class and ethnic communities deal with issues universally part of being human (e.g., socializing the young, constructing and maintaining social institutions, controlling social problems, explaining human suffering and mortality). The course could also contain learning experiences to help students acquire basic skills important for communication and relationships with individuals from different backgrounds. It might, for instance, teach students how to become acquainted with other people's basic conceptualizations and language, their major values and norms, and contemporary issues important to other peoples. Actions such as these will be important in developing and making secure the place of diversity within the curricular arrangements of American higher education.

The past three decades have seen significant changes in the extent to which issues associated with the diverse categories, classes, and communities of people within the United States, and outside this society, are present in our higher-education curriculum. These accomplishments in making students more aware of the range of human possibilities and realizations will benefit everyone, but presently such accomplishments need reinforcement by action on behalf of full integration and reasonable levels of administrative support. This is the work that has to go on.

REFERENCES

Bernstein, R. (1994). *Dictatorship of virtue*. New York: Alfred A. Knopf.

Bloom, A. (1987). *The closing of the American mind*. New York: Simon and Schuster.

Change. January, 1992.

D'Souza, D. (1991). *Illiberal education*. New York: Free Press.

Foner, E. (Ed.). (1990). *The new American history*. Philadelphia: Temple University Press.

Glazer, N. (1997). *We are all multiculturalists now*. Cambridge, Massachusetts: Harvard University Press.

Levine, L. (1996). *The opening of the American mind*. Boston: Beacon Press.

Lucas, C. (1996). *Crisis in the academy*. New York: St. Martin's Press.

Chapter 11

Primary Care, Education, and Research Integration: A Vehicle for a Culture of Health

FRAN QUINLESS

GETTING IT

As a nursing educator for over twenty years, I can safely say that I have written hundreds of course objectives indicating that students will effectively ". . . analyze the social, political, religious, economic, and legal issues impacting health care delivery . . ." upon completion of various courses. In fact, I realize that hundreds of students have, over those same twenty years, quite effectively identified and analyzed these cultural variables which so critically and intimately affect the lives and health status of individuals and communities. Despite this intellectual appreciation, however, I have frequently felt an uneasiness about students' lack of lived experiences in integrating these variables in actual community-based client encounters. In short, have students been allowed to "get it"—to deeply understand the integration of these variables in the lives of individuals and families? I don't think so. In fact, I believe that they have danced around the periphery of these issues and have been fairly sheltered from seeing the negative impact of these social class differences and health behaviors, particularly in the lives of inner-city minority residents.

REALITIES

Given my perspective, you will readily understand my drive to establish community-based health service programs in the cities of Newark and Camden, New Jersey. As dean of the School of Nursing (SN) within the University of Medicine and Dentistry of New Jersey (UMDNJ), I have been fortunate to work with faculty, staff, and students equally committed to the goal of improving the health status of inner-city residents. In 1993, the university's mission statement was amended to include community service alongside education, research, and patient care as core missions. SN correspondingly amended its mission statement and included community service as a core value and goal. Faculty endorsed a five-year strategic direction document to reflect our intent to establish nurse-managed community health services programs in Newark and Camden. Such programs were intended to serve the dual purposes of improving residents' access to primary care services and of increasing students' clinical rotations in community programs. Access to primary care, in our programs, incorporates the underlying assumption that health risks are decreased among residents exposed to health promotion programs which effect positive changes in health behaviors. Of course, in the backdrop of this surge to become increasingly responsive to our host communities' needs were two key realities—first, residents' demands for increased health care services to meet specific needs of minority neighborhoods (i.e., a common town-gown phenomenon noted by academic health science universities), and second, the revolution in managed care with its corollary impetus to offer less costly primary care in ambulatory settings. In essence, these realities reflect vast cultural differences deeply embedded in conflicting cultural norms and mores. Cultural differences are clearly noted in the university's definitions of "health care delivery" versus the communities' definitions of the same; such differences lead to vastly conflicting expectations of what services are delivered, how services are to be delivered, and even where they should be delivered. In addition, the managed care system superimposes yet again another cultural difference—that of the corporate business culture with its emphasis on bottom line productivity, a norm which clashes with both the university's expectations as well as those of communities.

Our community health services initiative was fortunately planned at a time when other independently occurring phenomena were also becoming realities. For instance, both academic nursing and medicine were encouraging schools to emphasize primary care and community services. The previously frowned upon generalist specialties were gaining momentum over the subspecialties due to health care reimbursement methodologies. The concept of a health "team" trained in an interdisciplinary manner and mutually exposed to differentiated practice in community settings was gaining favor among health care accrediting agencies, including the National League for Nursing and the Licensing Council for Medical Education.

SAYING YES

In 1993–1994, the moment was right to establish nurse-managed centers. On several occasions, we answered "yes!" to community agencies' requests to offer on-site health services, sometimes before we were really sure about resources. As of summer 1997, SN has opened four health centers in Newark and two in Camden. They are in various stages of development, utilization, and maturity. In all sites, however, there is one given—the centers are mutually designed, implemented, and evaluated by our host community partner(s) and SN. Our community partners range from churches, to HeadStart programs, to schools, to housing projects. The success of the centers is positively correlated with the partners' level of real involvement, from minor decision making regarding site renovations to the major clinical services to be offered on-site. Please note also that "success" of a health center is defined differently by residents in different neighborhoods of these two cities. The variables of local unemployment rates, housing availability, street violence and crime rates, availability of social welfare systems, extent of participation in church activities, level of acute and chronic illnesses, and quality of educational systems interact mutually in a holistic definition of health. Thus, our centers provide holistic health services, ranging from educational workshops, to providing job skills, to providing immunizations, to offering pregnancy prevention workshops, to providing on-site acute and chronic illness treatment, and to offering health promotion and disease prevention screenings and workshops.

SN currently offers a community health services program in Newark and Camden which employs its own professional staff so that students will ultimately be inculcated with the values of community service and residents will experience increased access to primary health care services. The school's delivery arm supports the education, research, patient care, and community service missions of the university. This paper will explore the services offered on-site as well as how we galvanize resources to maintain a stable professional staff and nonsalary clinical supplies. Right or wrong, we did not meticulously anticipate, or plan, each detail of our programs—we believed we were doing the right thing, and thus we simply closed our eyes and dived in! For the most part, we have surfaced unscathed; at other times we took risks and failed. However, we continue to move forward with the realization that there is never time to make anything perfect, and that action is invariably preferable to inaction. Interestingly, as we sometimes went down a path leading to failure, we seemed unable to change our course, even though we intellectually could predict that our behavior would lead to failure! The force of our deeply inculcated norms arising from both our individual ethnic cultures (the majority of our faculty and staff come from white, middle-class backgrounds) as well as our shared beliefs on what constituted good health care at times was so strong and powerful that we seemed unable to behave differently despite our intellectual awareness of the sociological phenomenon we were living. This paper describes our continuing adventure—an adventure in appreciating and accepting different cultural values and norms so that nurses can assist residents to inculcate new, positive health promoting behaviors into their belief systems. We can only effect long-lasting, health-promoting behavioral changes via a cultural shift in which such behaviors become norms emanating from a new "valuing" of health.

LOCATION, LOCATION, AND LOCATION

As real estate experts often say, the trick to selling a business is location, location, and location. The same is true if one wishes to establish a health center. Our centers in Newark and Camden service specific local neighborhoods, some primarily African-American and at least one essentially Hispanic. Each center is located in a busy downtown area surrounded by accessible bus routes, local strip malls, schools, churches, and other social service agencies. People live, work and/or worship near the sites. Sites have been chosen on the basis of invitation by community residents, local accessibility (e.g., bus routes), proximity to acute care hospitals, and relative lack of accessible culturally competent health services. Basically, if a community invited SN in, SN accepted. Our first site was within the St. Columba Neighborhood Club (i.e., the "Club"), one of five Hispanic community-based organizations (CBOs) in Newark. The Club had invited the university to offer on-site health services to the Hispanic community in 1995. SN responded affirmatively for the university by opening an on-site health center in the summer of 1995. We made many mistakes with our first community venture. In looking back, I am embarrassed to write that we were obviously paternalistic at best and condescending at worst in our attitudes and behaviors. We knew best what residents needed in relation to health! Clearly, our first initiative was viewed by the community in our first year of operation as a university "transplant"; that is, a program imposed by SN and operated according to our norms, values, and needs rather than according to the Hispanic neighborhood's defined needs. In short, we almost failed miserably in year one. Several cultures clashed: socioeconomic, educational, professional, and ethnic. We were very different from the people in the neighborhoods that we were attempting to enter. However, our Hispanic neighborhood patiently helped us mature and conduct business in a real, tangible manner.

Our downhill slide into failure was turned around by the recruitment of Spanish-speaking professional staff and a major door-to-door community-needs assessment aimed at determining residents' perceived needs. Subsequently, the Club's health center has enjoyed steady business with referrals to many local providers, drug and alcohol counseling centers, the university's acute care services, and women's programs. Our center began to move with the feelings and pace of the community. We adapted our rhythm and they moved along with us.

From the Club, SN expanded services into two housing projects in Newark in predominantly African-American neighborhoods. One project, the Roberto Clemente Shalom Towers, is located on a main business avenue next door to a fast food restaurant and houses approximately 1,000 residents with multigenerational families. The other project is New Hope Village located on the opposite end of town next to a strip mall. The Village is closely associated with the New Hope Baptist Church, the largest Baptist church in the city with a stable, dedicated group of "church nurses" who extend health services to the church population. Most recently, SN joined forces with our medical school and contracted with the Newark Pre-School Council to offer on-site health services at a large HeadStart program offered in a nicely furnished location referred to as Alberta Bey. Thus, SN offers health services in two housing projects, one HeadStart Program, and one Hispanic CBO in Newark.

Since the university has a statewide mandate and academic health centers located in the major urban areas of Newark, Camden/Stratford and New Brunswick/Piscataway, SN expanded its baccalaureate and graduate programs to the Camden/Stratford campus in 1994. Once the academic programs were solidly established, the SN faculty and staff on that campus began negotiating with community partners to offer on-site health services in local neighborhoods in Camden. Our initial impetus was provided by involvement with the church nurses organized in Camden through the city's large network of over 160 churches. In 1995, an informal leader of the ministers in Camden approached SN to develop and offer on a regular basis a ten-week curriculum to educate the local church nurses on basic first aid, health screenings, and health promotion and disease prevention strategies. The goal was to educate these locally respected lay providers with information on healthy lifestyles and prevention so that they would infuse residents with this knowledge. In the Camden community, as in many urban communities, church nurses or parish nurses, are critically important individuals who have been given status and informal power—cultural tools valuable to employ in efforts to positively impact health status of residents! Working through the church nurses as a cultural vehicle, we recognized that we could effect change. Ultimately, the faculty and students developed a program which is now regularly offered each semester throughout the churches in the city. Through this activity, one minister offered SN space in his church for a one-station examining room. This "center" subsequently led to relationships with the local HeadStart program and a second center was established in the largest HeadStart facility in Camden. Currently, these sites are staffed by a professional nurse who divides her time between activities offered at the church and the HeadStart program. Religion and education are major sociological institutions deeply embedded in setting behavioral norms; they thus become mediums through which health care may be delivered.

These health centers were basically established on the basis of handshakes and verbal commitments. Apart from our Alberta Bey site, SN does not have any formal legal contracts with our community partners which spell out the details of our relationships. Instead, we have learned that being there on a predictable basis, and offering services mutually determined as needed, solidifies relationships with community partners more firmly than legal documents. Operationally, SN does not pay rent to use the space provided at these sites; rather, we barter with our community partners to offer needed services in exchange for space and other necessities. For example, at several sites sinks needed to be installed, along with air conditioning systems for air quality control. To ensure that our sites meet state health safety requirements, SN and its community partners have negotiated with each other to pay for, and install, necessary equipment, plumbing, and HVAC systems. In some instances, SN received small grants from local companies and employed local community contractors to complete necessary renovations and installations. In other instances, we have split costs with our partners. Essentially, the health centers are mutually owned by SN and its community partners. They have invested in the centers and thus, have a critical stake in their success. In the housing projects, residents have agreed to give up space in their community rooms to accommodate the health centers. We were surprised at first by residents' easy willingness to give up space. However, we began to appreciate over time that their willingness emanated from what they believed they would get from a health center. Basically, to many tenants, a health "center" was a different type of community room. Since health status is not viewed as an individual phenomenon by many of our communities but rather as a group phenomenon, the community room simply takes on additional "group" health functions—thus, the space itself is not lost, it is simply altered in function. These types of negotiations have been spearheaded by tenant associations.

By common medical practice standards, SN's health centers are "cozy and basic" at best and primitive at worst. What do our centers literally look like? Each is a one-room shop, with a sink, examining station with attached wall diagnostic equipment, file cabinets, desk, several chairs, and cabinets for storage. All comply with the health department's regulations on ambulatory care practice sites, including regulations on disposal of medical waste. In order to properly equip each site, our "nursing learning practice laboratory" on the

Newark campus was dismantled and the equipment appropriately divided among the various sites. This step was a radical one for a school of nursing; however, it completely corresponded with our utilization of the community health center sites as "learning laboratories." This dismantling of an artificial practice environment to a live site was critically important—it reaffirmed two values. First, it conveyed the reality of our community centers as integrally important to our academic programs. Students would now "practice" on people in real settings, rather than on models in safe environments. This reality orientation builds confidence, critical thinking, and problem-solving skills. In real practice, students must think flexibly and be ready to make clinical decisions often with an incomplete database. Thus, conducting health screenings, health fairs, and physical examinations on community residents became learning activities in skills courses in the undergraduate and graduate programs. Secondly, it reaffirmed community-based learning in which practice and education are integrated phenomena. Since some nursing faculty have chosen to engage in faculty practice within the health centers, students are linked with them as they expertly role model either generalist or advanced practice behavior. In a practical sense, the lack of a practice lab drove home both the importance and the reality of our centers. This shift from a practice laboratory to a live setting was a huge cultural change for faculty who had been accustomed to a much different, safer environment. This shift, therefore, was a major change responded to in various ways—some faculty enjoyed the "realness," spontaneity, and unpredictability of the setting while others were uncomfortable and outlined numerous reasons why the hypothesis would not work. Students, however, walked into the settings as clean slates—they had no expectations other than those we had given them in class. Thus, students did not struggle with the shift as much as faculty did. In fact, some students even volunteered to work in the centers at different hours just to extend services.

INFRASTRUCTURE TO HEALTH CENTERS

Once the first health center opened, we realized that the school had just gotten into the health care delivery business. The university's signage was placed at each site and each became listed as components of the institution's ambulatory care network. The delivery world moves at a faster pace than the academic environment—the patient care issues are immediate, decisions must be made quickly, supplies must be readily available, and continuity of care must be assured. Our attention diverted for a significant amount of time to create an adequate administrative infrastructure to fully support the clinical activities of the centers. These issues primarily revolve around human resources, policies and procedures, adequacy of clinical supplies, continuity of care issues, and proper utilization of students. The first, most critical matter was that of obtaining a dedicated professional staff to provide culturally competent, linguistically appropriate health care. Not an easy task—both in terms of recruitment and funding. Our first recruit was a Spanish-speaking nurse practitioner of Hispanic background. We quickly realized that although she was "linguistically and culturally appropriate," she was uncomfortable in the role and did not aggressively pursue getting involved in the community. Ultimately, we hired a white, Jewish, registered nurse from the suburbs who spoke Spanish. What made her an immediate success in our Hispanic center was her easy willingness to get involved, her flexibility, her enthusiasm for people, and even her ability to blend into the environment by choice of clothing. Thus, we learned that speaking the language was basic; but what is more essential to success is an open willingness to join in the community and respect for its norms. We developed job descriptions of professional staff included as a delivery unit of SN. Once approved by human resources, we worked with our community partners to recruit the professional staff for the centers. A separate cost center within the school was assigned to the health center initiative and funds were internally reallocated from a variety of revenue streams to fund the program. At the present time, two nurse practitioners, two nurse clinicians, and one public health representative staff the centers. In addition, the "professor-in-residence" program was established among the faculty. One nurse practitioner faculty member holds this title on the Newark campus. She has moved her primary location from the campus to a community health center and students rotate to her at the site. Similarly, another faculty member in the southern region acts in this capacity at the Camden sites. Other dean's office staff members were assigned specific tasks to assure that the centers' needs would be met.

Once full-time staff were on board, we shifted our attention to the practical details of center management, including the development of forms (all seventeen of them!), a continuous program improvement plan, policies and procedures related to equipment management and operational flow, and health regulations compliance procedures. A detail that was time-consuming and costly was the mandate to install the appropriate ventilation system for tuberculosis control; this required some small grants from local businesses to purchase the necessary equipment. Installing an air conditioner in one setting was a tricky task; not from a construction viewpoint, but rather from a human viewpoint. Why were we so special that we deserved air conditioning when so many other areas were not and people simply put up with the inconvenience? Our need for compliance with air exchanges for tuberculosis control ultimately was an important rationale for our installation of air conditioning. One matter particularly difficult was recruiting professional staff at university salary rates to work hand-in-hand with other professional staff employed by the Club—a community-based organization highly dependent on grant funds. Our staff have higher salary bases than the Club's staff. This incongruence remains. However, we openly acknowledged this incongruence right from the beginning. Due to the high productivity of all staff, this financial matter has not created undue internal stress. Concurrent with the steps of staff recruitment and program management, we also developed a method of obtaining the necessary nonsalary components to make the centers functional. Relationships were developed with the local departments of health to offer immunization fairs. Our own hospital was approached to provide nonsalary funding of recurring clinical and other medical supplies for the centers. As major feeders referring patients to our hospital, the centers have become important outreach arms of our acute care hospital. The vice president and chief executive officer of the hospital agreed to assume these costs related to the operation of the centers. We have also not been reticent to ask for help from major companies in the state that produce clinical supplies— we have experienced variable success through sophisticated begging. Although we do seek "giveaways" from companies now, I must admit that I did not let staff engage in this behavior for almost a year. I have learned that to survive as a neighborhood health center, one must sometimes "look the other way." I now tell staff to be as resourceful as possible in making our centers viable.

CONTINUITY

Continuity of care issues are consistently at the forefront of our centers. At present, the centers serve residents primarily through health promotion, disease prevention, health maintenance, advocacy, and referral functions. The nurses have canvassed their neighborhoods to determine the perceived health needs of residents and have developed programs centered on these needs. They have developed links to community social and health agencies to ensure that residents can be immediately referred for drug and/or alcohol rehabilitation, financial health benefits counseling, psychiatric services, domestic abuse services, and other issues. It has not always been easy to be a patient advocate. Our health system has erected many elaborate, sophisticated barriers to easy access to care. For example, for mental health referrals, we had to deal with "catchman" areas, invisible boundaries surrounding geographic areas within which care is provided for local residents. What to do, however, for patients with immediate needs (i.e., someone expressing suicidal ideation as a walk-in to one of our centers) living outside of a catchman area with particular services available only to those living inside the area? We faced this particular issue for drug and alcohol detoxification programs. Our staff have handled such issues by developing interpersonal relationships with the nurses at the other ends of phone lines—they make it close to impossible for our patients to be refused for particular services. This only works, however, because the staff are intensely interested in "their residents."

In order to provide primary care services, collaborative practice agreements have been developed with both community and university physicians to enable certified nurse practitioners prescriptive practice through protocols. These nurse practitioners are currently being reviewed for clinical credentialing within the appropriate departments at University Hospital. Since SN has a Medicaid provider number which incorporates these practitioners as providers, the health center sites may now be reviewed by insurers to assess whether or not they meet the standards set by the industry as ambulatory primary care sites. Once approved, the centers can be designated as primary care locations with nurse practitioners credentialed as primary care providers by various insurers. The next step will be to market our nurse practitioners as primary care providers within our neighborhoods so that residents choose them as their designated "first contact" providers within their Health Maintenance Organizations (HMOs). Concomitantly, it will become important to work with HMOs to encourage them to include nurse practitioners as primary care providers on their panels. At the present time, some HMOs credential nurse practitioners and others do not; the essential task will be to educate HMOs regarding the state's designation of nurse practitioners as primary care providers. In addition, given that nurse practitioners function in New Jersey through collaborative practice agreements, we have worked out in advance the financial disbursement arrangements for revenue generated by our nurse practitioners. Essentially, we have agreed to reimburse our collaborating university physicians a certain preestablished percentage of revenues collected for their services. This work is being done to provide residents with quality continuity of care services. It is our intent to work well and closely with our University Hospital and physicians to provide direct on-site primary care within a network of specialty services and sophisticated acute care management. Given the morbidity within our populations, the establishment of such arrangements is essential for quality, ethical care.

Finally, the incorporation of students (nursing, medical, dental, and allied health) within the centers is an important practical matter for our centers. How should students be incorporated? What learning experiences can be shaped appropriately for students? How can experiences in the neighborhood centers and in residents' homes be structured to meet both the students' needs as well as the centers' needs? What continuity of care experiences between and among the community center, the hospital, community social and health agencies, and the home can be structured for students to "see" the forces at work that shape health status? What interdisciplinary rotations can be arranged via the centers? After all, since the centers were originally established to meet educational objectives of students, these questions have become paramount. And, as health profession educators clearly know, students both extend services and slow you down in the delivery of those same services! At present, we have named one staff member the clinical coordinator—she will coordinate all student rotations, review learning objectives with faculty, structure program activities to initiate through students, orient new students, and provide an overall evaluation of students' rotations at the completion of each semester. Students clearly face culture shock by involvement in the lives of poor urban residents. For example, when conducting the community needs assessment in Newark, rarely did residents mention HIV/AIDS as a health issue. However, the neighborhood has a high incidence of HIV/AIDS. Interestingly, students began to understand that HIV/AIDS is NOT viewed as a health problem in the neighborhood because it is considered almost a given. As some residents have indicated, they "have the virus, but they don't have any health problems." All of our professional center staff have been reviewed for faculty appointments to the School of Nursing on the Clinical Track; in fact, all but one have already received UMDNJ board of trustees–approved appointments as clinical faculty. Our traditional orientation to education will change from passive to active learning—faculty will eventually provide service with students at their side rather than in the classroom. This, however, currently operates through our "professor-in-residence" program. One faculty struggled over a two-year period to define her role as the professor-in-residence and remain accepted as a member within the faculty ranks. Initially, she was clearly ostracized by her willingness to take risks, do business differently, and spend more than the usual hours in her role. In time, the concept will become a reality.

SERVICE PROVIDED BY HEALTH CENTER IN A NEW MODEL

The health centers offer a variety of services under a very broad definition of "health." Given that our community partners include churches, schools, CBOs, and housing project tenants associations, their definitions of "good health" include such variables as spiritual health, lack of street and domestic violence, being "clean" of drugs and alcohol, having adequate income and social benefits, being HIV "free" or "virus free," having children remain in school and off drugs, controlling asthma, and keeping hypertension in check, among others. In all of our communities, we have conducted needs assessments of the local residents served. Not surprisingly, our beliefs about what the needs were differed somewhat from residents' stated needs. Most importantly, residents requested a consistent presence of the same personnel at each site in order to gain confidence in their commitment and competence. Being there on a consistent, daily basis was almost as important as the services themselves. Residents clearly did not want a "drop-in" university presence; they requested, in fact, demanded, that "their nurses" were culturally appropriate and recruited from their neighborhoods. They wanted providers sensitive to their cultures and needs *on their terms, not on our terms.* The challenge to us in meeting this demand was great. In fact, we were able to recruit a nurse from the Hispanic neighborhood at one of our centers; however, since she did not meet the university's criteria for the job title nurse clinician, we had to hire her under a different title (i.e., public health representative).

Since opening our doors in 1996, we have dealt with an array of resident problems spanning acute drug and alcohol detoxification to suicidal ideation to teenage pregnancy and sexually transmitted diseases (STDs). Generally, our services are offered under the following broad categories: health promotion, health maintenance, referral, and advocacy. With the addition of nurse practitioners on-site, primary health care services are also provided. Our health promotion activities include such events as street health fairs, immunization days, health screenings, and educational workshops and seminars. Health fairs are organized by our nurses at the sites with assistance provided by students, residents, and other local health agencies. The Newark and Camden Departments of Health coordinate immunization fairs at our centers on a regular basis. They provide both the staff and the equipment to immunize the children. One of our goals is to provide a "one-stop shopping" mall during these immunization events—that is, we intend in the future to offer other needed social and welfare services to mothers as they wait to have their children immunized. We also provide regularly scheduled health screenings, including screenings targeted to the specific populations living within the vicinity of the centers. Thus, breast and cervical cancer screenings are provided by coordination with our medical school's women's wellness center. Screenings for hypertension, hypercholesterolemia, diabetes mellitus, asthma, and cancer are also provided.

Major emphasis is placed on education and training. The staff frequently offer group seminars/workshops on topics raised by residents, including STDs, HIV/AIDS, drug and alcohol rehabilitation, signs and symptoms of various diseases, healthy eating, weight reduction, smoking cessation, and oral health, among others. Such programs are planned as short sessions in which residents are actively involved and only essential information is presented in clear, bulleted fashion. Pre-tests and post-tests are conducted to assess learner knowledge. Nursing students are routinely scheduled to provide a standard menu of educational programs within the local elementary schools surrounding the centers. In one center, small groups of seventh and eighth grade students meet weekly throughout the academic year to problem solve, to express their concerns in a safe environment, and to learn coping strategies for dealing with the issues intrinsic to urban living in high-crime neighborhoods. These groups have been offered by psychiatric nursing faculty with psychiatric back-up services provided by the university's Behavioral HealthCare system. A major emphasis is on monitoring behavior to see change—changes which reflect valuing of health, health promoting behaviors, and self-care responsibility for health status. Our health outcomes research component is focusing on this aspect; we are still too early to predict data trends.

One particularly important educational program provided in the centers is the adolescent pregnancy program. This program is multifaceted and deals with the real issues of teenage pregnancy, STDs, and HIV/HBV/AIDS in minority populations. The program has two goals: (1) to decrease the incidence of teenage pregnancies and repeat pregnancies in teens and (2) to provide them with the appropriate prenatal, intrapartum, and postpartum care if pregnant. The "Baby Think It Over Program" is a computerized life-like baby doll (available in all ethnic variations and specific health variations including cocaine addicted), which is loaned to seventh and eighth grade children for up to one week. Their activities with the doll are recorded by the doll's computer; thus, neglecting, shaking, hitting, etc. will be duly noted by the computer.

Our pre- and post-test data on our participants demonstrates a dramatic shift from wanting to be pregnant given cultural norms and expectations of positive parenting to gaining a deeper appreciation for the realistic demands placed on mothers and fathers of babies. This program is linked with a workshop series on STDs, pregnancy prevention strategies, HIV/HBV/AIDS, and preteen/teenage pressures and "saying no" techniques. Such techniques include role-playing sessions among teens during which they enact situations involving peer pressure and learn various ways to saying no firmly.

Two other important services offered within the health centers include referral and advocacy. Many of our referrals are to other community agencies, the city departments of health, mental health agencies, drug and alcohol counseling and rehabilitation agencies, and our own specialty physician network. Given the pervasiveness of drug and alcohol addiction in the cities we serve, much time has been spent locating, and establishing relationships with, counseling, and rehabilitation services for these residents. Knowing the names of responsible individuals in these agencies is critical; establishing relationships with them is even more important. The nurses in our centers have developed strong relationships with specific agencies; often enjoying "preferred referral" status among the triage nurses in rehabilitation centers. Additionally, the nurses play an important advocacy role. For example, residents sometimes seek their advice as to what questions they should pose to their physicians when they go on either a routine visit or an acute illness visit. They seek a great deal of information regarding medications (e.g., main effects, side effects). Very frequently, the nurses teach residents about the appropriate use of antibiotics and antihypertensives, including educating them about continuing to take medications although symptoms have abated. Adolescents frequently seek guidance and counsel on contraception, STDs, dealing with parents, domestic violence, etc. The nurses also become involved in assisting residents obtain financial assistance, such as applications for Medicaid and charity care. The advocacy role often feeds into the educational role—frequently asked questions may become the focus of a workshop or program.

In summary, our services span a wide spectrum—from education, to primary care, to referral, to advocacy, to simply "being there" when someone needs help or a confidential listener. As our relationships and referral networks develop both within the community and within the university system, our services are expanding to ensure continuity of care. Once our centers had developed some roots within our communities, we began rotating nursing students through them for experiences in community health, psychiatric/mental health, pediatrics, and obstetrics (through the Healthy Mothers/Healthy Babies program). Students have offered health education classes in HeadStart, the elementary grades, to parent groups, to parishioners, to church nurses, and to residents. They have participated in door-to-door community assessments of health needs, including data analysis, data management, and interpretation of findings. They have enthusiastically offered street health fairs and immunization fairs. Volunteer medical students have also participated in educational classes to adolescents. In the beginning of this paper, I asked the question: "Do students 'get it'?" After dealing with urban residents on a daily basis in their neighborhoods and on their terms, I can say that they are beginning to "get it." In fact, students enjoy the experience and frequently ask to volunteer—one graduating student asked if we had job openings. Our faculty are integrating the community health centers in their programs of study at the associate degree, baccalaureate degree, and graduate level. The research questions are so abundant that often it becomes frustrating that one simply doesn't have the time to do all that needs to be done. Simply put—it's working!

HOW DO WE KNOW
WE'RE DOING QUALITY SERVICES?

A key in all of this is: Are our community health centers making a difference? From a curriculum perspective, students and faculty evaluate their experiences positively. From a provider perspective, our staff are satisfied with their jobs and are eager to become even more involved in community activities. From a patient perspective, our "client satisfaction survey" cards completed after each encounter indicate a high degree of satisfaction with the services. Our clients have indicated that they are "satisfied" with our services as long as we are consistently kind, predictable in scheduling, open to their suggestions, able to handle their health needs as they arise, and willing to deal with a wide array of resident issues.

However, from an overall program evaluation perspective, how well do the programs effect the health status indices of residents in the communities we serve? We are at the beginning of our Continuous Performance Improvement Plan implementation. We do not yet know to what extent we positively impact the predictable level of illnesses within our communities. We need a predictable, routine database and regular analyses. We do not have that yet. We also need to discern what are the best screening programs and health maintenance programs to offer for our target populations. We must study the epidemiological patterns in our communities and make informed decisions as to where to spend money wisely on screenings. Up to this point, we have screened based on national disease data; not on local neighborhood data. Additionally, we plan to collect qualitative data obtained by focus groups of residents and users of services (e.g., Club users, HeadStart families and teachers, and church parishioners). Although we know these issues, we do not at present have the time and resources to do what we know we need to do. Our plan is to capitalize on our partner institutions to help us obtain the expertise we need to get this job done.

SUMMARY

When a community invites you in, say "Yes"—even if you're not sure how to do it. When a faculty wants to help, say "Yes"—even if you can't see the fit at first. When people say you're wasting time on "divergent" issues from academics, ignore them. When people say you don't have the expertise, laugh. When you doubt yourself, just get used to living with ambiguity and go on.

REFERENCES

Abdal, K. A., Aday, L. A. & Walker, G. M. (1996). Patient satisfaction in government health facilities in the state of Qatar. *Journal of Community Health, 21*(5), 349–358.

Anderson, A. (1996). Nursing clinics in urban settings. *Home Healthcare Nurse, 14*(7), 542–546.

Andres, T. L., Baron, A. E., Wright, R. A. & Marine, W. M. (1996). Tracking community sentinel events: Breast cancer mortality and neighborhood risk for advanced-stage tumors in Denver. *American Journal of Public Health,* *86*(5), 717–722.

Attridge, C., Budgen, C., Hilton, A., McDavid, J. C., Molzahn, A. & Purkis, M. E. (1997). The Comox Valley nursing centre. *Canadian Nurse, 93*(2), 34–38.

Cole, F. L. & Mackey, T. (1996). Utilization of an academic nursing center. *Journal of Professional Nursing, 12*(6), 349–353.

Frenn, M., Lundeen, S. P., Martin, K. S., Riesch, S. K. & Wilson, S. A. (1996). Symposium on nursing centers: Past, present and future. *Journal of Nursing Education, 35*(2), 54–62.

Glick, D. F., Hale, P. J., Kulbok, P. A. & Shettig, J. (1996). Community development theory: Planning a community nursing center. *Journal of Nursing Administration, 26*(7–8), 44–50.

Glover, S. H., Shi, L. & Samuels, M. E. (1997). African American administrators in community/migrant health centers. *Journal of Health Care for the Poor and Underserved, 8*(2), 153–169.

Hill, L., Patrick, K. & Avila, P. (1996). Training physicians to care for the underserved: Preventive medicine residency-community health center linkages. *American Journal of Preventive Medicine, 12*(3), 156–160.

Kaufman, A., Galbraith, P., Alfero, C., Urbina, C., Derksen, D., Wiese, W., Contreras, R. & Kalishman, N. (1996). Fostering the health of communities: A unifying mission for the University of New Mexico Health Sciences Center. *Academic Medicine, 71*(5), 432–440.

Kerekes, J. J., Jenkins, M. L. & Torrisi, D. (1996). Nurse-managed primary care. *Nursing Management, 27*(2), 44–47.

Oldam, D. (1997). Nurse-led asthma clinic in an Asian community. *Nursing Times, 93*(13), 58–59.

O'Malley, A. S. & Forrest, C. B. (1996). Continuity of care and delivery of ambulatory services to children in community health clinics. *Journal of Community Health, 21*(3), 159–173.

Pierce, C., Goldstein, M., Suozzi, K., Gallagher, M., Dietz, V. & Stevenson, J. (1996). The impact of the standards for pediatric immunization practices on vaccination coverage levels. *Journal of the American Medical Association, 276*(8), 626–630.

Rieber, G., Benzie, D. & McMahon, S. (1996). Why patients bypass rural health care centers. *Minnesota Medicine, 79*(6), 46–50.

Schauffler, H. H. & Wolin, J. (1996). Community health clinics under managed competition: navigating uncharted waters. *Journal of Health Politics, Policy and Law, 21*(3), 461–488.

Shanon, A., Reisner, S., Paswell, J., Friedman, N. & Koren, N. (1997). The role of a secondary pediatric ambulatory care service within the community. *Pediatric Emergency Care, 13*(1), 50–53.

Smego, R. A., Jr. & Costante, J. (1996). An academic health center-community partnership: The Morgantown Health Right free clinic. *Academic Medicine, 71*(6), 613–621.

St. Martin, E. E. (1996). Community health centers and quality of care: A goal to provide effective health care to the community. *Journal of Community Health Nursing, 13*(2), 83–92.

Watson, L. J. (1996). A national profile of nursing centers: Arenas for advanced practice. *Nurse Practitioner, 21*(3), 72–74.

Chapter 12

Culture Learning and Unlearning: Creating a Culture Supporting the Development of Transcultural Nurse Managers

SUSAN W. SALMOND

The Graduate Program in Nursing at Kean University prepares practitioners interested in clinical management. These individuals assume roles such as managers, directors, case managers, and project coordinators in settings where the focus is delivery of a clinically based nursing or health care service. The focus of the clinical manager is to establish the environment or the climate and culture, which facilitates quality health care delivery and patient and provider satisfaction. The philosophy of the program is that role effectiveness of clinical managers is grounded in a transcultural approach. The goal of our program is to prepare leaders who provide culturally congruent care to their customers—their staff and the patients they serve.

Learning to think, act, lead, and work productively in partnership with people of different cultures, styles, abilities, classes, nationalities, races, sexual orientations, and genders goes beyond acquiring new skills and attitudes (Miller, 1994). It requires that the individual give up familiar ways of thinking, expectations, roles, and operating patterns which they have come to assume are routine for all. The curriculum and teaching methodologies used in the program are selected to both assist the student to learn new information about cultural worldviews and cultural care and to unlearn or become aware of their own tendency to look at the world through their own cultural lenses. The unlearning process involves the students' developing an awareness that each culture has its own arbitrary mode of interpretation of social tradition—what makes sense to one group may seem mysterious or unusual to another. With the arbitrariness recognized, the key is to appreciate that there is equal validity to the differing approaches. It is not necessary to adopt or even to approve of the different approach but to acknowledge that their reality is coequal with the mode of our own culture (Vail, 1996). Using process approaches, the faculty assists the students to catch themselves in the act of judging and inquire about the source of that judgment. This leads to an openness whereby the individual can now see around their cultural lenses. Cultural congruent leadership and care becomes more possible within this framework.

This chapter will describe the strategies used within the graduate program to build a culture which values diversity and academically prepares the clinical manager to practice in a culturally congruent manner. This process can be transposed to other settings where leaders are attempting to create organizational cultures supportive of multiculturalism.

CULTURE DEFINED

An initial task was to reach agreement as to what culture and cultural competent leadership meant to the faculty and how it would be shaped in our department and in our curriculum. Achieving this goal was not as simple as it appeared on the surface as everyone came to the table with different definitions, preferences, and feelings regarding transcultural care and transcultural concepts. Repetitive dialogue brought us to a shared definition, which then served to unite us toward a common understanding. As we tried out this new definition in our courses and our own faculty practice, we came to see it as a successful categorization for nursing and leadership practice. Through this reinforced success we developed a shared value for an encompassing definition of culture.

Culture consists of shared beliefs, values, and attitudes that guide the behaviors of group members. The operational definition of transcultural in our program has a broad meaning, encompassing sex and ethnic groups along with groups based on such attributes as nationality, professional discipline, common health problems (i.e., patients with chronic illness, patients with a handicap), social class, and age groupings (i.e., adolescents, the elderly). Culture manifests as behavioral norms and expectations associated with the shared beliefs and values (Cooke, 1989). An understanding and appreciation of these different shared beliefs and values is needed for effective nursing and leadership interventions. Individuals and groups as well as organizations are viewed and analyzed within a cultural context.

CULTURAL COMPETENT LEADERSHIP

Cultural competent leadership requires an increased appreciation and consciousness of differences associated with the heritage, characteristics, and values of many different groups while at the same time respecting the uniqueness of each individual (Morrison, 1992). The culturally competent leader does not have the objective of assimilating people (i.e., patients or staff) into the organization nor into the mainstream of medical care so that they think and behave alike and comply with the norms and tenets of practice as prescribed by the dominant group. A bicultural focus recognizes the validity of different worldviews/approaches and engages in ongoing negotiation and accommodation at the personal and organizational level to create a reasonable fit between the individual's personal values and those of the professional discipline and organization (Salmond, 1996). To achieve biculturalism, the leader focuses on self-knowledge and understanding of their own contextual responses and cross-cultural interpersonal skills along with an understanding about other groups and the organizational contextual response. In this process, the leader creates new norms of openness that are supportive of a wide range of worldviews. Polarization is a lesser problem in the organization because so many groups and types of differences are recognized. The organization is strengthened by leveraging a host of significant differences (Morrison, 1992).

LEADING REQUIRES LEARNING

Faculty discussions regarding culture reinforced that although the faculty was knowledgeable, to effectively lead others in transcultural nursing leadership there was a need for continued learning and development in the area of transcultural care and cultural competent leadership. Realization of the need for ongoing learning on the part of all faculty was critical to the creation of a departmental culture supporting multiculturalism. By acknowledging our learner status we were open to new information and new approaches. Active dialogue challenging our perceptions and interpretations was accepted. Although this dialogue was often heated, the outcome for many faculty was a growing awareness of the tacit knowledge (taken for granted aspects of culture) which we all used in interpreting situations and solving problems. A simple example of this tacit awareness came from a discussion of what was an acceptable handshake. The majority of faculty believed that a firm grasp and moderate hand/arm motion was preferred. Many identified that this was a factor they paid attention to in interpersonal situations, especially upon initial meeting with an individual. Judgments were made regarding individuals with weak handshakes such as "wimp," lacking authority, lacking confidence, and unassertive. This was especially true if the individual with the weak handshake was a male. This awareness of the judgments we make on something as common as a handshake facilitated our awareness of the multiple areas for misinterpretation and misunderstanding. The need for "unlearning" so that we would be open to new learning regarding different forms of tacit knowledge became apparent.

To further our learning, a resource development approach was adopted. After identifying the theory base that would drive the curriculum, we identified books, videos, journal articles, and qualitative methodologies that would assist all faculty to gain a holistic understanding of culture. This resource approach allowed for self-directed learning according to the unique needs of the faculty.

Cognitive learning was drawn from the texts and articles and provided a common language and theoretical framework for addressing the issues inherent in transcultural care. Additionally, our university is committed to the success of a multicultural student population, and faculty could avail themselves to a variety of university-sponsored workshops on diversity training and multicultural teaching strategies.

However, the faculty recognized the limitations of the cognitive approach alone and realized there was a learning curve associated with experiencing and applying this information. Faculty sought out experiential learning to assist them in understanding and applying transcultural theories. A very successful approach was the pairing of two faculty members, one expert in nursing management and one expert in anthropology. Together they participated as change agents on a clinical unit in an acute care hospital unit where the staff was experiencing multiple conflicts related to cultural misunderstandings and team dysfunction. This experiential, "on-line" learning experience allowed the faculty to experience and explore the conflicts as experienced by the staff and to gain a deeper understanding of the meaning and reasons surrounding the conflict. The faculty partners mentored and challenged each other to suspend their initial interpretation assigned to events and open themselves up to the situation as it unfolded. Interpretations were later discussed and analyzed among each other and with the staff. Ultimately, transcultural leadership and change approaches were then proposed, implemented, and adapted within the context of helping the staff to appreciate cultural differences and improve cross-cultural communication. The outcome for the staff was a team demonstrating cultural synergy that was more responsive to both their personal needs as well as the needs of the patient. The outcome for the faculty was the successful experience in culture brokering leadership approaches that broadened our thinking and reinforced the efficacy of a transcultural leadership approach.

MULTICULTURAL GROUPS: ESSENTIAL TO MULTICULTURAL UNDERSTANDING

If we are to develop multicultural practitioners then it is essential that we require continuous learning and discussion of different perspectives. This is best achieved when faculty and students in the class come from a variety of cultural backgrounds. An active recruitment effort targeting multicultural nurses was initially undertaken. The goal was to admit diverse cohorts of students with variations in demographics including but not limited to nursing backgrounds, ethnicities, gender, and age groupings. It is this diversity which brings richness to the teaching approaches used in class. This same principle applies to the health care organization. Effective and innovative transcultural care best emerges from a diverse workforce who are actively engaged in dialogue regarding nurse and patient satisfaction from a multicultural perspective.

Admitting a diverse group of students or employing a diverse staff is not enough. Retention of diverse students or staff requires a culture that truly appreciates diversity and which recognizes that diverse students/staff have diverse needs. This translates into innovative and flexible policies, teaching strategies, and support services.

ORGANIZATIONAL POLICIES AND PRACTICES: IS THERE AN ORGANIZATIONAL PREFERENCE?

Organizationally, academia tends to be rather rigid and this rigidity often is a barrier to multiculturalism. Genuine reflection as to the purposes and underlying values and assumptions of our educational policies and approaches was an important faculty task. It is the faculty who are the leaders in creating the culture supporting diversity. This can be compared to the manager or administrator of an organization. These leaders must gather data from their customers, shareholders, and stakeholders regarding their perception of the cultural sensitivity of policies and practices within the institution. Being open to exploring the reason (i.e., underlying context, values, and assumptions) behind the policies, preferences, and practices and recognizing that the need for these approaches may no longer exist is important to designing new policies and practices which are culturally relevant. This process that the leaders must go through is an unlearning and learning experience.

Some of the policies which the nursing faculty examined had to do with admission requirements (need for GRE or MAT entrance testing), clinical practice experiences (the assumed need for the separation of work and academic experiences), and policies regarding prerequisite requirements. The reason (contextual foundation) for the policies was discussed and we attempted to infer the underlying values and assumptions that these practices were grounded in. We were open to the reality that the culture of our professional discipline and the university itself influences the image of what a successful student or successful graduate-prepared nurse would be like (organizational preferences), and that the choices we make in terms of policies and teaching strategies are geared to favor these images. We looked for data on the relevance of our policies and debated whether there was cultural bias in the policies of our entrance exams and entrance requirements.

An outcome of our discussions was the growing commitment to the belief that diversity is not egalitarianism. Treating everyone the same and following the "golden rule" worked when the group was homogeneous. The paradigm of a color-blind or gender-blind approach does not work within heterogeneous groups and acknowledging this and embracing a new paradigm was needed. Decisions were made by the faculty to have multiple admission factors that could be looked at as a whole instead of limiting choices to GRE/MAT test scores and undergraduate grade point averages. Consequently, admission to our program allows for consideration of work references, portfolio data, writing samples, and personal interviews. Through this more open process, we became more inclusive.

Promoting Educational Biculturalism: Teaching Strategies Supporting Multiculturalism

Valuing diversity requires not only attention to course content, but also to teaching methods and strategies. Traditional, didactic lecture and evaluation of individual performance is not a culturally neutral approach to teaching. These methods favor students from the dominant culture who have been socialized in an "individualistic, competitive, man-can-control nature" worldview. For the student socialized outside of this framework, the classroom can be a potentially alien place fraught with self-doubt, confusion, and anxiety. Women, students of color, and students from linguistic minorities in particular may experience a bicultural dilemma as they attempt to balance the behavioral expectations of the traditional college classroom (stressing individual performance, reasoned argumentation, and impersonal objectivity) with their own cultural norms and values which generally value affective and relational approaches (Pacquiao, 1996; Adams, 1992). A teaching method which incorporates a variety of learning approaches, both individualistic and group-centered, will assist the student in bridging the bicultural dilemma and provide the faculty with a broader set of experiences to get a true representation of the students' abilities. Taken as a gestalt, these approaches are examples of culturally relevant teaching styles that facilitate student empowerment.

Teaching strategies, which encourage active involvement versus passive listening and note taking are encouraged. Although all of the same content is actually taught, it is accomplished in a more interactive way, with students discussing the content and ideas and faculty filling in where student interaction did not cover an area. Generally these interactive sessions are augmented by handouts that outline the content in an organized, rationale, step-by-step analysis of the material. The result of this approach has been more active student involvement and a higher level of critical thinking for all students, regardless of their cultural background.

Common statements I hear from faculty are, "I can't compromise my standards because someone can't understand," or, "this wouldn't be fair to the other students who understand and are ready to go faster." It must be made clear that there is no compromise in standards or quality when different approaches are used. In fact, the interactive approach benefits all cultural groups and when the curriculum is grounded in transcultural theory, this methodology is even more relevant. White students find the interactive approach and the use of "storytelling" to be highly effective as it increases the connection between their work world and the "theoretical" world. Furthermore, they gain a greater understanding and appreciation for differences as they listen to other classmates tell their story. For example, when discussing effective communication when intervening with an employee regarding a practice issue, a typical story told by a nurse from the dominant group is something such as:

My nurse manager asked to see me when I was finished with patient care. We went into her office. She closed her door and told me that she needed to speak to me about a problem regarding my care with a patient who was on our floor for chronic back pain. She told me that the patient had complained that I did not believe that he was truly in pain and that my manner had been rude and disrespectful and that I did not give the pain medication on time. She then gave me a chance to tell my side of the story. After that she shared that this was not the first time that she had heard this complaint and she expected my behavior to change. She told me that if I needed resources on effective strategies with the chronic back pain patient that I should use the library and that she would discuss the issue with me in another month.

This approach was seen as effective because it was private, direct, and allowed for participation in that the nurse was able to tell her side of the story. Furthermore, it was made clear that a change in behavior was expected and that there would be follow-up on the matter.

Another student, from a nondominant cultural group, told her story of what she considered to be an effective approach by a nurse manager when a problem was identified.

The nurse manager was told by a patient that he had not seen his nurse, only the assistant, and it was three hours into the shift. The nurse manager had heard this complaint before so she approached one of my colleagues (who was my friend and of the same ethnic background). The nurse manager thought that my friend had a better understanding of what was expected by patients and by the hospital then I did and asked her to talk with me about it. Later, the nurse manager said to me that she was aware that I had met with Marietta and she knew that I would be sure to see all of my patients within the first hour of my shift. The nurse manager followed up on this and found that I was doing my rounds in the first hour.

This approach was seen as effective because it was indirect and respectful of the person's cultural background in using a peer mentor as compared to a direct approach by the hierarchical leader that was perceived as confrontive and not supportive of the nurse. The communication from the nurse manager set the expectation but in an indirect manner which "saved face." The situation was followed through.

These two stories represent two very different ways of handling a similar problem. Both interventions achieved the desired outcome while being culturally sensitive to the nurses involved. Students were encouraged to discuss their responses to both approaches and faculty guided the students in understanding that the preferred interactions were grounded in the cultural norms and values and operationalized as social traditions and expectations of behavior. Both modes are equally valid for each cultural group. Bicultural leaders must be able to see around their own cultural lens and recognize alternative modes of interaction and flex their style to achieve optimal results. If the interactive mode of teaching was not the preferred approach, it is likely that the students would not be engaged in these stories and the differences would not be appreciated.

CREATING A CLIMATE OF TRUST: FACILITATING PARADIGM SHIFTS AND RISK TAKING

A bicultural educational teaching methodology opens up students' thinking such that commonly held paradigms and beliefs regarding how people should behave or fit in are challenged. Having experienced the unlearning and learning process themselves, faculty is cognizant of the anxiety attendant upon unlearning processes that were previously successful. The need to create within the department and within the classroom a sense of "psychological safety" is essential (Schein, 1996).

Our courses are structured using consistent cohorts of students. They come to know each other and to recognize that the faculty cares about them. With this trust level it is possible for faculty and students to challenge each other when they respond in an ethnocentric or judgmental fashion. It is very common for individuals (students and faculty alike) to be blind to their own ethnocentricity and biases and to feel anxiety when confronted with this. It is a trusting climate and a nonjudgmental confrontation that leads to the unlearning and learning which is needed for multicultural competence.

Faculty can use examples from their own experience, from student experiences, or from what is happening in the classroom to facilitate an understanding of biases and paradigms used. One example in which this author used in-class group dynamics to highlight group differences occurred when a group of students were preparing for an in-class presentation. The group consisted of two Anglo nurses and two nurses from Jamaica. As one Anglo nurse spoke, the nonverbal message of two of the Jamaican nurses included rolling of eyes, crossed arms, and occasional frowning and tense looks. The Anglo nurse appeared to pick up on this nonverbal communication and continued to talk, however, her rate of speech increased, she became very red in the face and only maintained eye contact with me. The students were ignoring the tension. Recognizing that there was a possible conflict, I asked the group to pause and reflect on what was happening in the group. I asked the nurses to describe the nonverbal communication that was present and to discuss the meaning of the messages. This revealed that although both agreed as to what the nonverbal message meant (e.g., rolling of eyes, crossed arms, and frowns indicated frustration and anger, whereas rapid speech and blushing indicated nervousness), there was not agreement on the intensity of the message. The message sent by the Jamaican nurses was overinterpreted by the Anglo nurse as signaling severe frustration and anger when in fact it was rated by the Jamaican nurses as mild. A discussion of cultural differences in expressiveness ensued resulting in an understanding that the conflict, in part, resulted from misinterpretation of the nonverbal message. As we continued to analyze the situation, the "I versus we" orientation (individualistic versus group centered) was discussed. The Jamaican nurses identified that their frustration began when the Anglo nurses continued to use the pronoun "I" as they discussed what the group project would be. The Jamaican nurses viewed this as competitive and individualistic with one person trying to take individual credit. The situation was further aggravated because the Anglo nurse shared with the group that she had a "surprise" ending for her presentation that she did not want her partners to know about "because it would ruin the impact." This was perceived by the Jamaican nurses as trying to take all the credit and not willing to work in a group. Stepping back from the situation and discussing the interaction, the students were able to discuss the individual-versus-the-group value orientation. The Anglo student was comfortable with preparing on her own and taking charge of assignments. She was not as comfortable discussing what her part of the presentation would be as part of a group negotiation. The Jamaican students were very comfortable in the group discussion and had much greater anxiety concerning their own individual presentations and gained support by discussing what should be involved in that presentation. A bicultural understanding was reached as the faculty reviewed the different value orientations and the students were assisted seeing the different behavioral expectations that they held because of these values. Bicultural appreciation was achieved as they were urged to suspend judgment and come to a negotiated agreement on how they should work as a group. This resulted not only in a better presentation but an unlearning that their own approach was not the only approach and a learning about alternative strategies and ways of being.

Further insight was gained as I challenged the group to move beyond value orientations and be open to the fact that another area of conflict was perceived biases. Initially this was met with uncomfortable silence. However, I encouraged them to reflect honestly on how they were responding to each other and to consider whether past experiences may have resulted in prejudices they may have brought to the situation. The end point of the discussion was the realization that the Anglo nurse may have judged the Jamaican nurses as not as intelligent because of their more unassertive responses and because of their accents. Additionally, the Jamaican nurses identified that the moment the Anglo nurse began to assertively share her ideas, it triggered past experiences where their ideas were not valued, and they contributed less as a result. Having shared these insights, all involved experienced the unlearning and the learning process. They were able to identify how their own ethnocentrism and linguocentrism, which led them to perceive and to judge different behaviors as not as valuable, was a barrier to successful group performance. They were then able to open themselves up to accepting these differences and using them constructively in forming a culturally synergistic group.

Significantly, because the climate of trust existed, the students allowed this encounter and discussion to be presented to the larger group. The class as a whole responded in an active discussion of the differences in value orientations, stereotypes, and biases, and trigger experiences. If traditional teaching approaches were used, this depth of understanding would never have been achieved.

SUPPORT STRATEGIES PROMOTING MULTICULTURAL SUCCESS

Acceptance of a bicultural focus requires that faculty provide extra time and assistance in the form of 1:1 educational counseling with students, especially with those from nondominant cultural groups. Pacquaio (1996) found that students from diverse ethnic backgrounds equated hard work, persistence, and tenacity with success and highlighted the cognitive and affective dissonance that students felt when their grades did not match their effort. This has been our experience with students as well. In returning papers to students, we attempt to schedule 1:1 conferences. If the paper is not acceptable (receiving below a B), we begin a dialogue about the time and effort spent in preparing the paper. Acknowledgment of the importance of this effort and recognition of the student's efforts provides the lead-in to providing specific feedback about strengths and weaknesses.

Faculty must be cognizant of the fact that many students indicate that they understand when in fact they do not. Faculty must understand the context of this situation. For students from different cultural backgrounds, telling faculty that they do not understand what you are trying to say is viewed as disrespectful. For other students, it is difficult to relate lack of understanding for fear of being viewed as stupid or unable. It is imperative that faculty use innovative ways to explain the content and to seek student feedback until faculty is assured of understanding. It is my experience that providing students with a scenario or case study and asking them what they would do in the situation and what theory or research they are using to support that action is helpful because it makes the exchange more concrete. The discussion can then challenge the student to explain why this approach or theoretical model was used. This moves the student into having to provide their opinion, rather than simply rote feedback of theory, and facilitates their critical thinking. Taking the verbal conversation and assisting the student to turn it into a structured paragraph helps the student understand the expectations of the written work.

Although this extra support may seem quite apparent as necessary and philosophically, most faculty feel that any student having difficulty should receive this support, the reality is that frequently students are on their own. Pacquiao (1996) found that faculty valued students who were self-directed, who independently problem-solved issues, and who took the initiative when they felt that help was needed. It requires a significant shift in teaching style to approach students who do not initiate this contact and to provide the time that is truly needed to support these students. Creativity, patience, and perseverance are important for both the faculty member and the student. When one student, for which English was the second language, experienced consistent difficulty writing papers, we referred her to the university's bilingual program. After evaluating the student, the bilingual department did not feel there was a deficit. We then referred her to a campus-wide tutorial program which, although they worked with her for a short period, did not feel that her deficits were as great as other students and released her from the program. As both the student and the faculty member recognized both the writing difficulty and the student's potential, she was advised to take a semester off from the program. In this period, a faculty mentor gave her weekly or biweekly professional writing assignments in which she had the opportunity to practice her writing skills while receiving faculty guidance. She was readmitted after her leave and successfully completed the program.

I believe that if we are to truly facilitate success among nurses from different cultural backgrounds, then this must be a requisite faculty strategy. Institutions and departments committed to this philosophy may have to address resource utilization so that faculty or other support personnel are available to assist students.

WALKING THE TALK: TRANSCULTURAL LEARNING IS MORE THAN ONE SEMINAR

Having redefined new norms for transcultural understanding, faculty was aware of the importance of rewarding individuals for taking the initiative to explore themselves, their interactions and their organizations from a new perspective. New rituals whereby time was set aside in the classroom and clinical seminar to discuss the past week's reflections, learnings, and experiences was established. It was in these sessions where multiple examples associated with ethnocentrism, linguocentrism, organizational preference, and cultural bias were raised that students both gained greater insight and were reinforced for their new awareness. A sense not only of the student's new knowledge base but of their new feeling level for the content was evident.

Another ritual implemented in a class dealing with cross-cultural communication allowed for a safe method of identifying trigger words or trigger stories. As students discussed work or clinical experiences, if the accounting of the story was viewed by another student as triggering an emotional reaction because of the words or incident reminded the student of previously negative experiences, the student would get up during the discussion and on a designated easel record what the trigger was. If triggers were identified during the class, time was set aside during the end of class to discuss them. This ritual reinforced the importance of continuing to gain insight into the complexity of cross-cultural communication.

SUMMARY

As with all other learning, transcultural learning is not a destination but a journey. It is a journey for both faculty and students as we challenge traditional ways of thinking and open ourselves to alternative ways of being. Creativity is the key in discovering and designing teaching strategies and clinical experiences which value transcultural care and transcultural leadership. Transcultural competence is not a one-time learning experience but an ongoing process of unlearning and learning which must be integrated into all course work, clinical experiences, and faculty-student interactions. This integration reflects the deep-seated values held by the department regarding the importance of transcultural care and contributes to the culture supporting the development of transcultural nurse leaders.

REFERENCES

Adams, M. (1992). *Promoting diversity in college classrooms: Innovative responses for the curriculum, faculty and institutions.* San Francisco: Jossey Bass.

Cooke, R. (1989). *Life styles inventory.* Plymouth, MI: Human Synergistics.

Miller, F. (1994). Forks in the road: Critical issues on the path to diversity. In E. Cross, J. Katz, F. Miller, & E. Seashore (Eds.), *The promise of diversity* (pp. 38–45). New York: Irwin.

Morrison, A. (1992). *The new leaders: Guidelines on leadership diversity in America.* San Francisco: Jossey Bass.

Pacquiao, D. (1996). Educating faculty in educational biculturalism. In V. Fitzsimons & M. Kelley, *The culture of learning* (pp. 129–162). New York: NLN Press.

Salmond, S. (1996). Master of science in nursing: Curriculum development: Clinical management with a transcultural focus. In V. Fitzsimons & M. Kelley, *The culture of learning* (pp. 209–214). New York: NLN Press.

Schein, E. (1996). Leadership and organizational culture. In F. Hesselbein, M. Goldsmith, & R. Beckhard (Eds.), *The leader of the future.* San Francisco: Jossey Bass.

Vail, P. (1996). *Learning as a way of being: Strategies for survival in a world of permanent white water.* San Francisco: Jossey Bass.

Chapter 13

A Dream Realized: An African American Woman's Experience

SANDRA SEALS MCQUEEN

FOUNDATION FOR A DREAM

As a child growing up in a small Midwestern farming community, I was free to roam the woods and fields with the younger two of my seven brothers. We explored caves, fished, and hunted squirrels, rabbits, and various birds. We lived a life of freedom. I spent many spring days enjoying the new beginnings of every kind of tree, flower, and shrub. Those were the days my father referred to as my "white bread" days. In his childhood, if you had a loaf of bread made from white refined flour, you were living well.

My mother was a believer in the benefits of a "mess of wild greens" as a spring tonic. Much of my time every spring, at age six or seven, was spent picking wild greens and learning the difference between edible greens and poisonous weeds. It was important to know how much of each kind to pick to avoid the greens having a bitter taste. It was something that had to passed down generation by generation. Little did I know that this was the beginning of my career as a member of a caring and healing profession and my first lessons in herbal therapy and holistic health. It was always understood that my goal in life was to become a nurse.

JOURNEY TO A DREAM

Neither of my parents completed their formal education. My father completed the sixth grade and my mother completed the eighth grade of elementary school. They both believed that a formal education was "the colored person's" answer to all the inequalities of the country. I can still hear my father saying, "They can't take away anything that you have learned." So, I became an avid reader. I have been told that I read before I ever attended school, probably attributable to my status in the family as number nine of ten children. My older siblings taught me invaluable lessons that could not be learned in school. My earliest memories of school are of a building that had two large classrooms separated by sliding doors. These two classrooms housed nine grades; kindergarten through eighth grade. We had two teachers, a principal, and an art teacher, who came to our school once a week from the white school.

I was four years old and was eager to start school. I would get up every day, get dressed, and follow my older brother and sister to school. The school was literally across the street from my home. The community was a rural farming community and was racially segregated. Our teachers knew every family and attended the same churches as most of the families in the community. I was a free-spirited and independent child, and my father supported these traits. Family members cautioned him to place some restrictions on me. His response in my defense was, "She may become the first colored president of the United States." However, that was never my aspiration. In school, the teachers always taught us that limitations existed and encouraged the girls who showed promise to become teachers or nurses. Perhaps, they were trying to protect us. My father, on the other hand, always preached to us that *"we could be whatever we wanted in life."* The seed of my dream to become a nurse was planted when my aunt, who was also my godmother, gave me a little red nurses' kit complete with stethoscope, plastic "pretend" syringes, pill bottles, and a cap. She would always comment on how I cared for the children of my older brothers and sisters when they visited us, and how neighborhood children, when they fell and had cuts, would come to me to clean and dress the wounds of childhood. Many injured animals found their way to me, too. I never really knew at that time how I was going to make my dream a reality. It was simply a dream.

THE ROAD

In the late summer of 1957, I looked forward to starting school in an integrated school system. The Civil Rights Act which was passed guaranteed me equal education opportunities. I started the new school year with little understanding of how difficult it would be to attain that which was guaranteed to me by law. The integration of the schools in Missouri changed my whole world. We left the comfortable familiarity of our community to go into what had always been foreign to us. My father was very positive about the benefits of school integration for his children. I was not convinced, but I made a valiant effort to believe him as I went to school every day knowing that we were not wanted there.

In 1959, as I was about to complete my tenth grade year, I went to my guidance counselor to set up my classes for my eleventh grade year. I shall never forget that day. I told him of my dream to become a nurse. I explained to him that my classmate, who was white, and was also planning to attend a nursing school, advised me of the need to take chemistry, biology, and algebra. I was told by the counselor that, "Because of your inferior elementary education, you will never be able to become a nurse." He further advised me that I would do better to think about a business course after high school. Consequently, I was set up to take general science and general math. At that time, I had already achieved honor roll status consistently, and had been told by the principal of the high school that I was the first Negro student to do so since the school had been integrated. Something did not compute. I shared the counselor's opinion with both my parents. Needless to say, it angered my father who was always my champion. I really was not aware of what wheels were set in motion at that time, but I do know that all my life I have believed that God has had a plan for me. No matter what my "free will" put in place or what others tried to put in place for me, if it was not what God had planned for me, it wouldn't work anyway.

During the spring of 1959, my older sister, her husband, and her five children visited us from Colorado. Another older brother who lived in California had been visiting and was returning to Los Angeles and my parents made plans to send me to Denver with him as soon as the school year ended. At fifteen years old, I had never traveled more than fifty to ninety miles from my home. The prospect of this trip filled me with a sense of adventure. As far as I knew, I was only going for a visit. When September came, I was enrolled in school. My sister and her husband obtained legal guardianship of me and I was tested and placed in a college prep track. Manual High School was very culturally diverse even in

1959. I was relieved and surprised that I had done so well on the entrance exam-inations. I had begun to believe the counselor. My entire schooling at that point had been considered to be inferior and how could I ever hope to rise above those inferior beginnings? As a matter of fact, I had heard rumors that students coming from rural schools were often "put back," meaning to be placed in lower grades for remediation. I can't really explain my feelings at that time, but in retrospect, it gave me a new lease on my dream of becoming a nurse.

Developmentally, fifteen is a rough time to be uprooted from all that is familiar and comfortable. I was uprooted from the freedom of a community where everybody knew everybody else, and looked out for each other, a com-munity that provided a certain sense of protection and being cared about. It was wonderful to be part of that kind of community. Moving to a large urban area and being restricted in many ways was the beginning of learning a whole new set of values. My young mind was boggled.

TURNING THE CORNER

Although Denver was a clean city, it was overwhelmingly large to me. This was compounded by the fact that I would have to make new friends. My sister cau-tioned me about everything. I was cautioned to always keep doors and win-dows of the house locked, and to come right home from school. At all times, my family had to know my whereabouts. Adjustment was to address both the change in available outdoor recreational activities, as well as to adapt to a full integration of all facilities and schools in Missouri which were mandated by law to be integrated. Being able to go anywhere to buy a hamburger or ice cream cone was a new and wonderful experience and changed my life forever. I began to grow and meet new people. My sister, who had lived in Denver for many years, set about educating me to the ways of the world outside my little Mid-western community. She had accepted the responsibility of another child and that child was chronologically fifteen, but very naïve socially and not at all adept at dealing with people who were city bred.

Denver was the epitome of the "melting pot." I met and became friends with many people from ethnic groups that I had only read about. They were just like me in many respects. It was wonderful. My self-image improved and I devel-oped a sense of cultural identity that allowed me to have self-pride. I could now be proud of being colored/Negro/Afro-American (to my father we were always colored to the day he died in 1994). I no longer had to try to emulate my white counterparts. I remember Robert, who was Mexican; Spiros, who was Greek; and Janie, who was Japanese. One of the most notable of my classmates was Norm Rice, future mayor of Seattle, Washington. He was *Head Boy.* This was a coveted title for which one campaigned and which was viewed by the school as part of the education process to educate students about politics and democracy.

I was encouraged by the Dean of Girls to pursue art as well as some area in the health profession. This was based upon aptitude tests conducted by the guid-ance department. The Dean of Girls, named Mrs. Henry, was a very kind Caucasian woman. She was genuinely interested in my becoming all that I could become. I felt as if she was genuinely interested in **me.** My ethnicity was not a factor in our relationship. I was offered an art scholarship and a substantial nursing scholarship. I was accepted into Mercy Hospital School of Nursing. Needless to say, I accepted the nursing scholarship from a local black social organization.

As I look back over my life, and my entry into nursing, and reflect upon today, I can truly say that I have come a long way. It is not because the educational system was designed to include a black female, but in spite of it. I believe that education and self-esteem are linked. Throughout my nursing education, when I learned about Florence Nightingale and other notables in nursing history, I never knew there were notable black nurses (such as Mary Seacole, a Jamaican nurse who also served during the Crimean War). I learned the history of black nurses many years into my nursing career. The way one is educated can be a factor in how one sees him/herself. Having developed critical thinking skills early in my life helped me to realize that I should not believe everything I read in books. I knew that I had several role models in nursing. A cousin by marriage often told me of her positive experiences in the Army nurse corps. Another young woman from my hometown in Missouri, whose family pooled their resources to send her to a segregated hospital school of nursing in Kansas City, was held in high esteem by many black people in our community. My sister had a very good friend who was a nurse in one of Denver's leading teaching hospitals. She was a great source of support and encouragement to me. I knew that I could attain my dreams no matter what the obstacles, because of their encouragement and my family support.

My father always thought that education was the great equalizer in the world. It was the less than equitable educational process that sent to me the message of invisibility and that I didn't really count in the larger society. I have learned through multiple personal experiences that it is a difficult task at best to be accepted by the larger society on your own terms. Until recently, blacks were not portrayed in a positive way on television, in newspapers, textbooks, and other media. Many black females in all walks of life have the same story as me, of being passed over for jobs that you are better qualified to perform by experience and education, in favor of a white person with lesser qualifications and experience. I realized early in my life that I would have to be strong and determined in order to become a success. I always had to be cognizant of the fact that I could become immobilized in the face of challenges. I reminded myself often that I was a competent and educated nurse and I would make my own path to acceptance, recognition, and success in the nursing profession.

FACING THE NEW CENTURY HORIZON

It has always been a challenge to me personally to keep a realistic image of myself and of whom I am. I have always struggled to maintain an image and view of myself as capable, competent, and able to achieve anything that was important to me. This was and still is difficult in a system that has historically neglected to give black women healthy competent images of themselves. Today, there are books authored by black nurses about black nurses' contributions. Ethnic culture sensitivity is being taught as part of the curriculum of many nursing programs. Our black nurses are more informed as nursing students and will obtain advanced degrees and model the way for other black nurses who continue to struggle within an educational system that for the most part is designed to fail or push out the average black nursing student.

As a black nurse who has attended Kean University for much of the last fifteen years, earning two baccalaureate and one graduate degree, I can honestly say that I have observed the university become more "user friendly" to the black nurses enrolled in higher degree programs. The black nursing student can look at the faculty and see someone who "looks like them" and someone who has been where they are trying to go. This Department of Nursing is actually "walking the walk" that they talk.

CHARTING A NEW ROAD

These programs have provided me with a quality education and concepts that I utilized to chart my career. After completion of each level of education, I am inspired to greater heights. I am more conscious of the fact that I practice nursing in ways that are much different than when I started nearly thirty years ago. My life is better because of how I have integrated my knowledge base into all aspects of my life. In addition, I believe that I have enough to give back to other black nurses and the community.

Today I am employed as an educator and am planning to pursue a doctorate. I sometimes have the desire to go back to my hometown in Missouri, find that guidance counselor who tried to steal my dreams, and let him know how wrong he was to discourage my dream. Instead I turn to my spirituality and thank God for direction, guidance, and strength I was given to make this journey and continue to be able to effect positive outcomes in health care service delivery.

Completing the baccalaureate and graduate programs has made me refocus my role as a black American who is a contributor to the economic, political, and social health of the United States. In addition to my being a nurse, I see community activism and community development as tools that can be used to alleviate the high infant mortality rate in black communities, and to help rid these communities of violence, drug abuse, and AIDS. I have begun to realize through the educational process that as a member of this society and as an African American, I will need to assist the black community by responding to their health care needs as they perceive them and in a manner that is acceptable to the black community; this instead of the current trends of imposed efforts from outside of the black communities that are often foreign to its members.

REALIZATION OF THE DREAM

Education, both formal and informal, has been a life-long process for me. I seem to be like a sponge; I soak it up where and when it happens. This is an unceasing process. I owe so much to my family, friends, mentors, and instructors. My clients have been my instructors, too. I am thankful for all who touched my life and were part of God's divine plan for me. I am grateful to my alma mater's chairperson of nursing for giving me an opportunity to share my experiences as an African American proceeding through the educational system. She made me aware of a time-honored tradition in higher education. And that is to photocopy my Master of Science in Nursing degree and send it to the guidance counselor who said that I couldn't do it. That guidance counselor, way back in 1959, has that photocopy coming to him. I have come this far by faith and I still have a long way to go. So, I will end this chapter with titles from the writings of one of my heroes, Maya Angelou, "I Wouldn't Take Nothing For My Journey," "And Still I Rise."

REFERENCES

Angelou, M. (1993). *Wouldn't take nothing for my journey now,* pp. 5–139. New York: Random House.

Angelou, M. (1993). Poems. *And still I rise,* pp. 121–123. New York: Random House.

Carson, B. (1992). Think big: unleashing your potential for excellence, pp. 259–260, 268–278. New York: Harper Collins.

Edelman, M. W. (1993). The measure of our success—a letter to my children and yours, pp. 3–97. New York: Harper Collins.

Clovis, D. L. (1994). *Struggles for freedom: An anthology of multicultural experiences,* pp. 143. Orange, NJ: Bryant & Dillon.

Cole, J. B. (1993). *Conversations. Straight talk with America's sister president,* pp. 1–3, 76–80. New York: Doubleday.

Parks, R. & Reed, G. (1996). *Dear Mrs. Parks. A dialogue with today's youth.* New York: Lee & Low Books.

Vanzant, I. (1995). *The value in the valley. A black woman's guide through life's dilemmas.* New York: Simon & Schuster.

West, C. (1993). *Race matters,* pp. 35–46. Boston: Beacon Press.

Chapter 14

Revisiting the Men's Health Curriculum

D AVID A NTHONY F ORRESTER

This chapter is dedicated to the memory of Frederick W. Bozett, RN, DNS.*

> The first wealth is health.
>
> *Emerson, "Power,"* The Conduct of Life *(1860)*

About a decade ago, the late Fred Bozett and I published "A Proposal for a Men's Health Nurse Practitioner" in *Image: Journal of Nursing Scholarship* (1989). This article described the educational preparation of a men's health nurse practitioner (MHNP) and prescribed the MHNP's knowledge, skills, and scope of practice in providing comprehensive primary care for men from a holistic perspective. Thus began our formalization of the need for the MHNP and delineation of the unique health needs of men.

Since that time, much has happened. The role of nurse practitioners in delivering advanced practice has further evolved to include: (1) increased participation and collaboration with physician's and other health providers in the areas of assessing, diagnosing, treating, evaluating, and referring health consumers; and (2) an increased focus on culturally sensitive health interventions designed to address consumers' health needs within the context of their community.

Not only has the role of nurse practitioners grown and developed, but the expectations of society and men have further evolved, along with health care itself and the economy: (1) changes have occurred in society's notion of men's roles (e.g., the continuing growth and development of the men's movement which began in the early 1970s); (2) men have become increasingly aware of the gap between their expectations as health care consumers and the health care options available to them in meeting their expectations; (3) health care reform (or revolution, if you prefer) has rocked the 1990s—insurance and reimbursement mechanisms have changed dramatically, institutional restructuring through mergers and closures, downsizing, new skill mixes, and new providers have changed forever the nation's health care delivery system; and (4) in response to these social and economic changes, men have taken the initiative themselves and continue to take increasing personal responsibility for their health by making changes in their personal lifestyles and life transitions. It seems timely, therefore, to take this opportunity to revisit the men's health curriculum from the broader perspective of men's health considered within the context of culture and community rather than from the somewhat narrower perspective of the educational preparation of any one particular health professional charged with meeting men's complex health needs.

MEN'S HEALTH: CULTURE AND COMMUNITY

Within the context of culture and community, at least two important factors need to be considered regarding the men's health curriculum: (1) as previously stated, there exists a gap between men's expectations as health care consumers and the health care options available to them; and (2) there are compelling patterns of morbidity and mortality among men indicating a dynamic relationship between stereotyped male role behavior and men's health in contemporary American society.

MEN: THE HEALTH CARE GAP

The total health care needs of men are currently not being met. Several factors contribute to this health care gap: (1) health care providers are not skilled at getting behind the male facade to assist men in dealing with problems and concerns they are unable or not willing to share; (2) health providers do not provide total holistic health care to men; and (3) increased specialization within health care has left men at a loss for their nonspecialist types of problems (Bozett & Forrester, 1989).

The traditional medical frame of reference has been the biomedical model, involving: (1) delineating pathological findings; (2) formulating medical diagnoses; and (3) addressing those medical diagnoses through treatment of the pathologies identified. The intent of medical education is, therefore, not comprehensive health care, which includes health education, maintenance, prevention, and restoration. Thus, physicians are as ill-prepared to assist their men patients in other than the biomedical domain as they have been with women. This, because the biomedical model applies as narrowly to men as it does to women. Although men may seek care for their hearts from cardiologists or treatment for their prostates from urologists, problems requiring a nonspecialist or more holistic approach often go unattended. Like most men, male health practitioners and their men patients have difficulty getting beyond the superficial. Dealing with the personal affective responses of other men is often perceived as threatening. Additionally, many men have difficulty to one degree or another admitting to less than perfect physical or mental health. Men commonly conceal their emotions and often deny physical and emotional symptoms. Thus, men may not seek care for problems such as stress management, occasional impotence, and emotional upsets because they are socialized to avoid emotional vulnerability and intimacy with strangers in general and with other men in particular.

MEN: MORBIDITY AND MORTALITY

Men in contemporary American society are socialized to engage in high-risk activities as a means of validating their male social status. This often times results in stereotyped compensatory masculine role behavior which may be characterized by unnecessary risk-taking, aggression, and violence, along with a greater incidence of smoking and excessive alcohol consumption. Also detrimental to the well-being of men are such factors as lack of physical exercise, excessive weight, stress associated with personal and work relationships, the social environment, and a perceived lack of meaning and purpose in life (Leafgren, 1990). Men's morbidity and mortality data provide compelling evidence of the profound impact that such stereotyped male role behavior may have on men's health.

Men have significantly higher morbidity rates than women for accidental injuries, coronary artery disease, emphysema, hernia, and peptic ulcer. In spite of these statistics, men seek health care less frequently than do women (Forrester, 1986). Men die more often than do women from five natural causes: (1) malignant neoplasm of the respiratory system; (2) chronic obstructive pulmonary diseases (COPD); (3) chronic ischemic heart disease; (4) acute myocardial infarction; and (5) cirrhosis of the liver. Four external causes of death also occur more frequently among men than among women: (1) homicide; (2) suicide; (3) motor vehicle accidents; and (4) other accidents (Bozett & Forrester, 1989; Forrester, 1986).

The men's health curriculum of necessity must focus on comprehensive primary health care provided by health care professionals who possess knowledge and a genuine appreciation for the multiple physiologic, psychologic, and sociocultural variables that influence men's ability to seek, obtain, and maintain their optimal health. The men's health curriculum should, therefore, include health education, health maintenance, preventive screening, and data regarding those specific acute and chronic illnesses that have a high incidence and prevalence among men.

MEN'S HEALTH CURRICULUM

Introductory courses in the men's health curriculum should focus on men as holistic human beings and should include content regarding the socialization of men into contemporary American society. Both primary socialization (i.e., in the home within the family) and secondary socialization (i.e., outside the home within the community) need to be addressed. Students should have the opportunity to investigate and gain a greater understanding the dynamic relationship between biology and environment in the psychosocial development of men; and, how masculinity is understood differently by men in various social, ethnic, and economic groups (Femiano, 1990; Forrester, 1998).

Among the essential topics included in any comprehensive men's health curriculum should be: (1) the history and development of masculine sex roles; (2) myths of masculinity; (3) men's health problems and concerns; (4) men's concepts and values of health; and (5) men's health promotion beliefs and behaviors. Additional men's health topics should specifically address issues regarding men's sexuality (e.g., men's health and sexuality and gay/bisexual men's health).

This course of study should focus on the needs men have for promoting and maintaining their health. It should concentrate on men's biologic, psychologic, and sociocultural development as these interact with their lifestyles, life transitions, and their impact on men's health. Some of the lifestyle and life transitions issues discussed might include: (1) career advancements and failures; (2) mother-son and/or father-son relationships; (3) developing significant other relationships (e.g., straight, gay, bisexual, or transgendered); (4) marriage, divorce, and widowerhood; (5) parenting; (6) age-specific transitions;

and (7) changing identities (e.g., becoming a father or coming out into society as a gay man). Men's roles and responsibilities in family participation also need to be addressed (e.g., father-present versus father-absent households).

Time should be allocated within the men's health curriculum to address men who are healthy but at risk. These are well and worried well men who are seeking general or specific health information. Some examples include: (1) men requesting sexual counseling (e.g., straight, gay, bisexual, or transgendered); (2) men changing careers, retiring from their careers, or with dual or nontraditional careers; (3) men experiencing grief associated with the loss of their partners through separation, divorce, or death; and (4) men at risk of human immunodeficiency virus (HIV) infection or developing acquired immune deficiency syndrome (AIDS).

In addition to the men's health content already described, students in the men's health curriculum should have opportunities to develop expertise in assisting men in improving their abilities to function within the physical and mental limitations imposed by physical and/or psychosocial illness or accident. Here, curricular emphasis should be placed on the concepts of prevention, maintenance of function, and client participation and collaboration. Of particular interest here are men experiencing long-term chronic or progressive illnesses or injuries needing supportive management, periodic evaluation, and referral or follow-up care and evaluation. Examples of such physical/psychosocial illnesses and injuries are arthritis, diabetes, hypertension, COPD, substance abuse, HIV/AIDS, loss of limb or paralysis resulting from trauma, and affective disorders including depression and suicidal ideation.

Numerous special topic areas are also worthy of inclusion in the men's health curriculum. Among these are: (1) minority men's health—in which the health implications of membership in racial/ethnic minority groups are identified and studied; (2) men at work—which should address the occupational and environmental hazards men encounter and their implications for men's health; (3) men in the family—which would offer an exploration of the health implications of the familial roles men play as husbands/partners, fathers, sons, brothers, etc.; (4) men and religion—which would address men's religious involvement as it relates to their and the community's health; (5) men and violence—again, as related to individual men's health and the health of the community; (6) men and incarceration; and (7) men and homelessness. For a brief discussion of many of these topics as they relate to minority men's health, refer to the chapter, "Minority Men's Health: A Review of the Literature with Special Emphasis on African-American Men," which appears elsewhere in this text.

EDUCATING MEN TO CHOOSE HEALTH

According to Leafgren (1990, pp. 265, 274), "Educating individuals to choose lifestyles that will facilitate health and well-being rather than lifestyles that foster the potential for illness is a goal of wellness." He advocates holistic health care for men which integrates and balances the total whole person's mind, body, emotions, and spirit. Inherent in this model of men's health are the notions of social, physical, occupational, intellectual, emotional, and spiritual wellness. "Wellness in all these dimensions is essential for well-being. Wellness in any one of these dimensions contributes positively to wellness in the other dimensions. A lack of wellness in any one of these dimensions can diminish one's well being in other dimensions" (Leafgren, 1990, p. 268).

Social wellness emphasizes interdependence with others within the family and community, as well as interdependence with the environment. Participation through volunteerism with community agencies such as schools and churches is encouraged—as is environmental sensitivity and concern for natural and community resources such as our water, air, land, and cities.

Physical wellness encourages knowledge and personal responsibility for healthy food and nutrition, physical activity and fitness, and self care in general. This wellness dimension discourages our use of tobacco, drugs, and excessive alcohol consumption.

Occupational wellness relates to attitudes about work and career. Here the primary concern is for our personal satisfaction and life enrichment through fulfilling career choices and work role behaviors.

Intellectual wellness involves the use of available resources to expand knowledge and improve skills. Creative, stimulating mental activities which enhance our individual capacity to contribute to the community and culture are encouraged. Examples of intellectually stimulating activities include reading, travel, and involvement in the arts.

Emotional wellness refers to a generally positive self-regard. It includes: how we feel about ourselves and our lives, awareness and acceptance of our feelings, the development of personal autonomy, the realistic assessment of personal limitations, and our ability to maintain positive relationships with others.

Spiritual wellness includes our personal values and ethics and extends to our understanding of the meaning and purpose of our lives. This is a limitless dimension which may be expressed through involvement in an organized religious group or simply communing with nature.

CONCLUSION

The ultimate goal of the men's health curriculum must be to produce health care professionals who can educate men to choose health. Men are deserving of expert, comprehensive health care provided by health care professionals who are sensitive to the special needs of men and who have an education that prepares them specifically to diagnose and treat men's unique and often complex health needs in today's society. More important than which specific health professional provides men's health care, is that men's health care is provided by practitioners who know that health can be taught and that health can be modeled by those who are teaching (Leafgren, 1990). Such health care providers would no doubt make innumerable valuable contributions in virtually every setting in which health care services are rendered—acute care hospitals, extended care facilities, the home, and the community.

*AUTHOR'S NOTE:

In October of 1987, I attended the American Nurses' Association Council of Nurse Researchers International Nursing Research Conference in Washington, DC. Among the presenters in attendance was Frederick W. Bozett, RN, DNS. Fred presented a most provocative research paper regarding the social control of identity by children of gay fathers. This was the latest of literally dozens of textbook chapters, articles, and invited scholarly paper presentations Fred had to his credit regarding gay and lesbian parents.

After his presentation, I introduced myself and congratulated Fred on a job well done. We talked about our mutual interest in men's health and decided that we would collaborate on a paper about men's health nurse practitioners (MHNPs). What followed that casual introduction was one of the most fulfilling collegial and scholarly collaborations that it has been my privilege to be partner to in all my professional nursing career.

Everything about our next few months' work was a true pleasure—even the editorial process. Donna Diers was then editor of *Image: Journal of Nursing Scholarship,* and letters with heavily annotated manuscripts were freely exchanged among the three of us in an effort to see that our paper was of the highest quality possible for the time. To date, this has been my most important lesson in true professional generosity and scholarly exchange through discussion and debate—a lesson I try to model with my students and colleagues.

A decade has passed and others have picked up our banner for the men's health curriculum. Medical and nursing schools have incorporated some of the basic tenets of Fred's and my original work into their curricula. Other behavioral science scholars have published numerous articles, chapters, and entire books contributing to our growing body of knowledge about men's health.

Thank you, Fred.

REFERENCES

Bozett, F. W. & Forrester, D. A. (1989). The men's health nurse practitioner: A proposal. *Image: Journal of Nursing Scholarship, 21*(3), 158–161.

Femiano, S. (1990). Developing a contemporary men's studies curriculum. In D. Moore & F. Leafgren (Eds.), *Problem solving strategies and interventions for men in conflict* (pp. 237–248). Alexandria, VA: American Association for Counseling and Development.

Forrester, D. A. (1986). Myths of masculinity: Impact upon men's health. *The Nursing Clinics of North America, 21*(1), 15–23.

Forrester, D. A. (1999). Minority men's health: A review of the literature with special emphasis on African American men. In M. L. Kelley & V. M. Fitzsimons (Eds.), *Understanding Cultural Diversity.* New York: Jones & Bartlett National League for Nursing Press.

Leafgren, F. (1990). Being a man can be hazardous to your health: Life-style issues. In D. Moore & F. Leafgren (Eds.), *Problem solving strategies and interventions for men in conflict* (pp. 265–275). Alexandria, VA: American Association for Counseling and Development.

Chapter 15

What Is a Freshman?
Helping Faculty Relate
to the Freshman Culture

HENRY L. KAPLOWITZ

John Silver buttoned his tweed jacket and nervously straightened his club tie as he rushed off to meet his Introduction to Political Science class for the first time this semester. Although he had been teaching at Queen State College for over thirty years, the first day of classes always made him anxious. In fact, he started to realize that for some reason he had become more tense about his classes in recent years than he used to be.

He entered the classroom, introduced himself, and handed his syllabus to a student in the front row asking that it be passed out. As the copies of the document slowly made their way from the front of the room to the back, John scanned the faces of his students and began to form an impression of them.

"God, do they look young! Each year the freshman class looks more and more juvenile," he thought to himself. This impression was immediately confirmed when he looked at the group of "girls" in the back who were giggling and whispering instead of reading the syllabus. The diversity of this class also did not go unnoticed by John, as he remarked to himself that this looked more like the United Nations than the classes he had taught in the "good old days" at Queen State.

After going over the syllabus, he decided to take attendance. Calling out each name from the roster had become a new challenge. He had mastered the popular African-American names like Tamika, Shareeka, and Tariq. His high school Spanish prepared him for the Hispanic names, but he was at a complete loss in dealing with Indian names. Was Siddhartha going to be a male or a female? He guessed female, but was wrong. "Why can't people living in this country use American names?" he complained to himself.

Professor Silver had planned what he considered a "real grabber" for today's lecture; he was going to engage the class in a dialogue about the headline story in this morning's *New York Times*. "What do you think about the Secretary of State's visit to the Middle East? Will she be successful?" he asked the class.

The lack of response puzzled him. He decided to ask a more basic question, "How many of you read this morning's *Times*?" Again, silence. "Who knows the name of the Secretary of State?" No response. Professor Silver sat down in his chair as if he was critically wounded. He had assumed that this class would be difficult, but now his mind kept racing with thoughts of early retirement.

WHO ARE TODAY'S FRESHMEN?

The above anecdote, thankfully, is fictitious. However, on many campuses there are elements of this story occurring with great regularity. A cultural chasm frequently exists in the classroom between faculty and students. Part of it is due to age differences. Certainly clothing styles, music preferences, and linguistic colloquialisms change dramatically with each generational cohort. More subtle, but no less important, are the different values and assumptions that influence the behaviors of faculty and students.

Most college professors experienced their college years as full-time students, usually on residential campuses. If they worked at all, it was only a few hours per week. They were usually serious students, and certainly were successful enough in their studies to get into graduate school and complete their terminal degrees. If asked, most would unembarrassedly admit that they love their field of specialization. It is not surprising then, that many assume that their students should be just like they were. In fact, when they first started teaching (perhaps as graduate teaching assistants in the research university where they received their doctorate) many students were just like them.

Students in today's classrooms, especially in urban colleges and universities, are much more diverse than in the past. Most students are working over fifteen hours per week and many are keeping full-time jobs as well as pursuing full-time studies. They don't have the luxury of devoting their "spare time" to campus activities or cultural pursuits as they need to work to earn the money to make their car and insurance payments just to get to campus. An increasing number are single parents who are faced with child care expenses in addition to maintaining a home. These students typically are in school to get the necessary credentials that will allow them to get a meaningful job. They often see courses as barriers that must be surmounted as they pursue their degrees, rather than as enjoyable intellectual experiences. Their pragmatism is evidenced by the question that professors dread after an enjoyable discourse on a tangential subject: "Will that be on the test?"

Whether they are recent immigrants or have been in this country for many generations, the typical urban college student is the first generation of his or her working-class family to go to college. Their parents take pride in this accomplishment, but don't have the experiences to provide their children with the support and guidance that many middle-class, college-educated families do. It is not unusual during freshman registration for students to come back to their advisors saying that their parents refuse to pay for general education courses in History and English, since they don't seem necessary for Accounting majors. Many young women living at home report that their families expect them to increase the time they devote to household chores since they only have sixteen hours of classes over four days—obviously, a less time-consuming schedule than high school. No one is telling these students to spend their free time in the library, or that they should expect to put in three to four hours of work for every hour that the course meets. It is dubious that many students from this background would grow up in a home where the *New York Times* was read daily.

TEACHING OLD PROFESSORS NEW TRICKS

At Kean University, we became acutely aware of these cultural differences when we were faced with training faculty members to teach a newly required Freshman Seminar course. The goal of the course was to reduce the freshman drop-out rate by providing new students with an informal classroom orientation to the college experience. Research by John Gardner of the University of South Carolina and by Lee Noel of the American College Testing Program had shown that such a course could dramatically reduce attrition.

These "success" courses provide students with both information and values about the academic environment that are critical in helping the student make a smooth transition between high school and college. This is done in an encouraging environment by warm, empathetic faculty members who are trained to use small group exercises to create "support groups" in the class where students feel comfortable discussing their adjustment problems. The interpersonal relations that develop in this course are at least as important as the information that is transmitted.

The problem that we faced as trainers was that a number of the faculty members who volunteered to teach the course were motivated by low enrollments and canceled sections in their own disciplines rather than by a desire to bond with and help freshmen. In some cases, they openly espoused a "sink or swim" philosophy in dealing with students rather than providing a nurturing relationship. We could easily equip these professors with the necessary materials to teach in class and train them in running small groups, but how could we make them more empathetic and interested in bonding as mentors to their students? If, in fact, we were dealing with different cultures, how could we get our instructors to recognize these differences as legitimate and not impose their own values? In the most extreme cases the question became: How could we make some faculty aware of their xenophobic tendencies to disparage members of any culture that differed from their own?

The solution we came up with to deal with these problems took the form of a one and one-half hour experiential workshop that was given to Freshman Seminar instructors during their mandatory two-day training program. We called it, "What Is a Freshman?" The unwritten goal of the workshop was to break through the cultural barriers that keep some faculty from relating to their students with concern and personal interest. The strategy used was to work in both the affective domain as well as the cognitive domain where professors are typically more comfortable.

THE AFFECTIVE APPROACH: BACK TO THE FUTURE

The first part of the workshop involved an exercise that required faculty members to sit in a circle of five colleagues and share their recollections of what their first week as a college freshman was like. In particular, they were asked to recall how they felt about any emotional experiences that may have transpired.

Each time the workshop has been run we have found that participants take to this exercise with relish. After the first volunteer breaks the ice and shares his or her own personal account of feeling lost, or homesick, or foolish, the remaining members of the group eagerly compete with each other to tell even more pathetic stories about their experiences. It is hard to imagine, unless you were there, how certain paragons of sophistication, who normally would only talk about their academic accomplishments in boastful tones to their colleagues, could now share incidents that make them sound like naive, emotional adolescents, which, of course, they all were as freshmen.

The specifics of the anecdotes vary dramatically, but certain themes occur frequently. For example, feelings of loneliness and homesickness were often described and in a number of cases the person wanted to or actually did leave college in the first week. Many of the incidents involved fear of exposing his or her lack of knowledge. That may have taken the form of wandering the campus looking for a classroom building and being so afraid to ask for directions that he misses class. Another variation on that theme was buying a parking lot permit from an entrepreneurial upperclassman for a nonexistent lot and feeling too embarrassed to try to get her money back.

After the members of the small groups share their stories, a reporter from each group summarizes to the larger audience what transpired in his or her group. Through the debriefing of the exercise, the faculty begin to understand that the naiveté and fragile self-esteem that they commonly experienced as freshmen was a normal part of the developmental process of adolescence. They recognize that their foibles were acceptable and, perhaps, even endearing.

Now they are ready to relate these feelings toward today's freshmen. Seeing their students from the perspective of what they themselves were like when they were eighteen strips away the veneer of sophistication that often inhibits empathy. They could now understand why students are reluctant to participate in classroom discussions.

We then ask the participants to compare and contrast the cultural norms and shared experiences that existed in their freshman subculture with current freshman norms and experiences. Although at first glance it may appear that the two different cohorts are worlds apart, when we go back to the same developmental level and speak to the similarities—common fears, common goals, etc.—our participants see a part of themselves in that diverse freshman class.

GIVE ME JUST THE FACTS

In addition to the affective approach, we offered hard data to paint a statistical portrait of the freshman class. Many of our faculty members learn experientially when they are discussing emotional issues in small groups. Others, however, need hard facts to be moved. They want to see the data! In the second part of the workshop we provide our participants with survey items culled from the ACT Entering Student Survey that is administered to all entering freshmen. We ask the faculty to rank the items the way they believe an entering freshman would (Table 15–1).

After the faculty members have ranked the items the way they believe our current freshmen would, we have them share their guesses and reasons within their small group about which items will be the top three reasons for attending college. We then present them with the most recent data available showing the percentage of students who chose each of the items as a Major Reason for attending college (Table 15–2).

Over the years of doing this exercise, the item "to meet educational requirements for my chosen occupation" has always been the most strongly endorsed by our students. Many of our faculty guess this correctly, and this

TABLE 15–1
What Is a Freshman?

Part of what a freshman "is" might be indicated by her or his needs, wants, and expectations of college. To examine some of these, please rank each of the categories below <u>AS YOU THINK A FRESHMAN JUST ENTERING THE COLLEGE WOULD RANK THEM.</u>

A. What were your reasons for entering college? (RANK FROM ONE TO TEN, WITH ONE BEING THE STRONGEST REASON.)

   <u>RANK OF REASON</u>

   _____ Parents/relatives wanted me to continue my education

   _____ To take part in the social life offered at college

   _____ To develop independence from my parents

   _____ High school teachers/counselors suggested I continue my education

   _____ To study new and different subjects

   _____ To meet new and interesting people

   _____ To meet educational requirements for my chosen occupation

   _____ Couldn't find anything better to do at this time

   _____ To increase my earning power

   _____ To become a better educated person

B. What type of class format do you prefer? (RANK FROM ONE TO FOUR WITH ONE BEING THE MOST PREFERRED.)

   <u>RANK OF PREFERENCE</u>

   _____ Laboratory (with hands-on experience)

   _____ Independent study (self-paced study)

   _____ Small-group format

   _____ Lecture

---

provides us with a springboard to discuss the occupational focus our students, the number of hours per week that our full-time students are employed, and the cultural values of working-class families.

The item that usually comes in second among our students, "To become a better educated person" is often missed by the faculty. They often presume that our students are more motivated by social and financial goals rather than intellectual pursuits. This data gives them an opportunity to reassess their assumptions about our students' values and to see them in a more positive light.

TABLE 15–2
What Is a Freshman?

Part of what a freshman "is" might be indicated by her or his needs, wants and expectations of college. To examine some of these, please rank each of the categories below <u>AS YOU THINK A FRESHMAN JUST ENTERING THE COLLEGE WOULD RANK THEM.</u>

A. What were your reasons for entering college? (RANK FROM ONE TO TEN, WITH ONE BEING THE STRONGEST REASON.)

   <u>ACTUAL STUDENT RANKS</u>

   __8__ Parents/relatives wanted me to continue my education

   __7__ To take part in the social life offered at college

   __6__ To develop independence from my parents

   __9__ High school teachers/counselors suggested I continue my education

   __4__ To study new and different subjects

   __5__ To meet new and interesting people

   __1__ To meet educational requirements for my chosen occupation

   _10_   Couldn't find anything better to do at this time

   __3__ To increase my earning power

   __2__ To become a better educated person

With regard to the items on class format, our faculty are usually shocked by the high proportion of students who prefer small groups (50%) rather than lectures (13%), laboratories (10%) or independent study (6%). The majority of freshman classes are taught using the lecture format. These data often lead to a valuable discussion about learning styles and teaching styles.

The response to this workshop has been overwhelmingly positive. In fact, it was adopted as part of the orientation program given to all new faculty members for a number of years with one adjustment. The data section that was presented to new faculty showed breakdowns for Caucasian, African American, Hispanic, and Asian students. This helped new faculty members realize the many similarities and occasional cultural differences that exist among our ethnically diverse students and how they can teach to these strengths.

REFERENCES

Astin, A. (1975). *Preventing students from dropping out.* San Francisco: Jossey-Bass.

Gardner, J. (1986). The freshman experience. *College and University,* 1986, 61(4), 261–274.

Greene, E. (1987). South Carolina's Garner: Self-appointed spokesman for the 'largest educational minority'—freshmen. *Chronicle of Higher Education,* 34(6), A41–A43.

Kean College of New Jersey comprehensive freshman retention program. (1991). In *A compendium of successful, innovative retention programs and practices: 1989 and 1990 winners of the Noel/Levitz retention excellence awards.* Coralville, Iowa: Noel/Levitz.

Noel, L. (1978). *Reducing the drop-out rate. New directions for student services,* No. 3. San Francisco: Jossey-Bass.

Robinson, L. F. (1989). The effect of freshman transition-to-college/orientation courses on student retention. *College Student Journal,* 23 (Summer), 225–229.

Chapter 16

Holocaust to Be Taught in the Schools of New Jersey

R OSE T HERING

With Executive Order No. 17, Governor Thomas H. Kean, on October 5, 1982, created a New Jersey Advisory Council on Holocaust Education to assist and advise in the implementation of education programs on genocide and the Holocaust in the schools of New Jersey for a period of four years. On March 30, 1987, Governor Kean issued Executive Order No. 168, extending the Advisory Council until 1990 and ordered that:

> The Advisory Council shall be authorized to resurvey the extent and breadth of Holocaust and genocide education being incorporated into the curricula of the school systems of the State and, upon request to assist the State Department of Education and local educational agencies in the development and implementation of Holocaust and genocide education programs. In furtherance of this responsibility, the Advisory Council shall be authorized to contact and collaborate with existing Holocaust and genocide public and private nonprofit resource organizations and may act as a liaison concerning Holocaust and genocide education to Federal and State legislators.

At least ten years earlier, in 1973, Holocaust education efforts began in New Jersey. Individuals from two school districts, Edwin Reynolds in Northern New Jersey (Teaneck) and Richard Flaim in Southern New Jersey (Vineland), met at a school conference and discovered that each was exploring efforts in the area of Holocaust studies. They approached the State of New Jersey Department of Education and were able to obtain a small grant under Title III, Innovative Grants to develop curriculum. Their task which was to develop curricula and training programs, was completed in about four months. A series of statewide workshops were organized to present the material to teachers. The curriculum that was field tested was published in 1983 by the Anti-Defamation League, and titled: *The Holocaust and Genocide: A Search for Conscience* (Winkler, 1993).

This Holocaust program activity was in progress when Thomas Kean was elected governor in 1981. Governor Kean, a historian and teacher, saw the great need for teaching the Holocaust. A group of educators, survivors, and legislators met with Governor Kean. It was in 1982 that Governor Kean formed his Advisory Council. Through the efforts of key legislators an appropriation from the State of $125,000 was given to the council for its ongoing efforts. A staff was assigned by the Department of Education to coordinate the recommendations of the council.

During the next ten years, executive orders were signed annually and community representatives were appointed by the governor. Since its creation, I have been privileged to serve on this Advisory Council, and now on the Commission. Leaders may ask: Why Holocaust education? Has not there been too much emphasis on this topic? Why cannot Jews forget this period of history? And there are still others who deny that the Holocaust—the attempted annihilation of an entire group of people—ever took place.

The rationale and purpose for including Holocaust education in the curricula of our schools has been stated poignantly by a survivor of Hitler's killing programs, "the final solution," of all European Jews. Haim Ginott (1993, p. 37) writes:

Dear Teacher, Educator, and Parent:

I am a survivor of a concentration camp. My eyes saw what no man or woman should witness:

Gas chambers built by learned engineers.
Children poisoned by educated physicians.
Infants killed by trained nurses.

Women and children shot and burned by high school and college graduates.

So I am suspicious of education.
My request is: Help your students become more human. Your efforts must never produce learned monsters, skilled psychopaths, or educated Eichmanns.

Reading, writing and arithmetic are important ONLY if they serve to make our children more human.

More than half a century has passed since Adolph Hitler launched his genocidal slaughter of Jews in Europe and other peoples deemed "inferior" or "undesirable" by the Third Reich. Today, the horrors of the Nazi death camps are becoming a distant memory. For some, Nazism is seen as a historical aberration unlikely to be repeated. For others, like the "historical revisionists," the Holocaust never happened.

These so-called historians seek to discredit the Holocaust and to rewrite history in spite of thousands of witnesses who are still alive—namely, survivors, rescuers, observers, and bystanders, not to mention our own American soldiers who liberated the concentration camps at Dachau, Ordruff, and Buchenwald among others.

The State of New Jersey has served and continues to serve as a model for Holocaust education; other states look to New Jersey for assistance. Thousands of teachers in New Jersey have taken the Holocaust courses, workshops, and institutes offered at various colleges and universities: Ramapo, Kean, Brookdale Community, Monmouth, Rider, Rutgers, St. Elizabeth's, or Seton Hall. Each summer ten-day workshops prepare teachers to teach this important topic. Since I was a part of these teacher training programs, I witnessed an encouraging response from the participants.

Governor Kean holds that teaching this period of history "is a sacred responsibility of the New Jersey school system." In assessing what has been done, he writes: "New Jersey is in the leadership of moral-ethical education, employing the tragedies of the Holocaust . . . as the centerpiece of its educational effort." He pleads: "We must all work together—the entire community—to present a faithful recounting of the twentieth century's darkest period. We must ensure historical accuracy in order to prevent a posthumous triumph for Adolph Hitler."

A grant program was established in 1985 whereby classroom demonstration sites could be founded wherever successful instruction on the Holocaust was occurring. There are approximately eighteen demonstration sites including the two original districts, Vineland and Teaneck. The teaching strategies include infusion programs, full courses, special programs, and other forms of Holocaust education through art, music, literature, as well as social studies and history.

Grants were made available also to Holocaust Centers located in institutions of higher learning. The purpose of these centers is to provide materials, consultations, resources, and training to teachers to prepare them to teach the Holocaust. Seventeen colleges and universities participate as designated centers; well over 15,000 teachers have received special Holocaust education.

In 1990 the Advisory Council initiated efforts to make the Council a permanent State entity. In June 1991, Governor Jim Florio signed legislation establishing under New Jersey law a Commission on Holocaust Education. Between 1991 and the present, objectives were reestablished, and primary efforts continued in the preparation of a basic curriculum on Holocaust and Genocide Studies for grades K through 12.

The major change occurring within the Commission was the in-depth discussion regarding the question of mandating Holocaust education in the schools of New Jersey. In the spring of 1993, the Commission voted to do all in its power to encourage the mandate for teaching the Holocaust. The efforts were successful. Working with the educational committee of the State Legislature and the State Department of Education, on March 10, 1994, the State Legislature accepted Senate Bills No. 710, 621, and 563 to mandate Holocaust education. The Holocaust Genocide Mandate bill was signed into law by Governor Christine Todd Whitman.

During 1994–1995, proficiencies for grades K through 12 relating to the teaching of the Holocaust were developed, and a curriculum to meet the proficiencies was completed. To orient the educators and assist them in meeting the mandate, a series of workshops in the spring of 1995 were conducted in all areas of the state. Activities of the 1995–1996 school year included working with local districts in their implementation plans.

In the fall of 1996, the Commission endorsed other curricula that may be used in the study of genocide, including the Great Irish Famine and the Armenian Genocide. Lessons derived from a study of the Holocaust will awaken educators and students in New Jersey to the realization that the destruction of peoples and nations through hatred and bigotry is an ongoing tragedy which must be addressed through continuous education and public awareness. Other curricula available for genocide instruction include the Ukranian Famine, the Native American tragedy, African Americans in slavery and the genocide in Cambodia. These curricula will make it possible for teachers to draw on other examples of racism, and students will learn about and respect each other's differences.

Because teachers have responded to the mandate, schools in New Jersey have made Holocaust education a definite part of the curriculum. In many schools an interdisciplinary approach introduces these studies not only in the social studies areas such as history, sociology, and psychology, but also in the humanities (e.g., literature, art, music, and the sciences). In parochial schools, Shoah studies are a part of religious education.

Principals of New Jersey schools seek to involve the entire population of their schools in a culminating experience after a unit of Holocaust studies. I have participated in such programs at Millburn Junior High School, West Orange Public Schools, Kimberly in Montclair, Pingry in South Jersey, South Orange Middle School, Montclair Public Schools, Newark Educational Center for Youths, Union City High School, and Watchung Regional High School, St. Joseph School, Maplewood, St. Raphael's, Livingston, and Yeshiva schools in New Jersey.

New Jersey teachers have the opportunity to apply for graduate tuition scholarships for graduate courses in Jewish-Christian and Holocaust Studies at Seton Hall University. The Sister Rose Thering Endowment has made possible tuition scholarships for teachers since 1994.

The Holocaust (Shoah) is a compelling case study of human potential for extremes of both good and evil. Only by internalizing the lessons of the past can our youth of today help to shape a new future and reduce the possibility of a recurrence of the horrors of the Shoah.

"Never Again" is our motto; that is the reason Holocaust Education must be a part of every curricula.

REFERENCES

Ginott, H. (1993). *Teacher and child.* New York: Simon and Schuster.
Winkler, P. (1993). *Brief history of holocaust education* (unpublished manuscript).

Chapter 17

Externship—
Moving Real Life
into Professional Life

MARY L. KELLEY

WHAT WE ARE ABOUT

Educators in the nursing profession have an excellent opportunity to provide students with relational correlations between earning a livelihood and the knowledge, cognitive skills, and affective skills requisite for practice. Designed for student success, these educational programs integrate students from culturally diverse backgrounds into the common cause of healing and caring through clinical experiences that best mirror the workplace to which the students will eventually contribute and where they have, at least in part, the support of a familiar context. Education's finest challenge is to help mold the generations that ensue, epitomizing in many respects the Jeffersonian construct to provide an informed citizenry. It is uniquely so for nursing educators, who also impart knowledge, skills, and competencies that will add dignity to their students' lives and to those they serve.

> It is one o'clock in the morning. The place is a busy coffee shop in an inner-city next to a major hospital. The two extern instructors had just driven twelve students home to various locations. Twelve midnight was far too late to let these women, all nursing students, wait for and then take public buses (sometimes needing two or three buses) home. These two nursing educators were exhausted and thrilled. It was the end of an eight-week program and these students, the majority of whom were minorities and at the lower end of the economic ladder, had succeeded.

And this is the story of the Extern Program that moved struggling students toward the behaviors and thinking processes, and so toward the culture, of nursing. Many of the strategies are not the standard, routine activities of a nursing course. However, these students are not middle and upper-middle class learners with resources to support themselves.

These were minority students, who had been caught in the cycle of failure. They came alive academically when immersed in clinically intensive extern programs. When challenged, and paid for their clinical work, they responded with maturity, independence, and competency, and then, with academic success (Nelson, 1996).

Our schools enroll predominantly minority students. The inordinately high rates of minority students failing out of the programs exacerbated the far too low rates of minority registered nurses in our region.

REALITY ORIENTATION

Meet students' needs and the students will succeed. Knowing the needs of the minority learners is the first, and the key, step in seeing the unique needs of these men and women (Pacquiao, 1996).

Our students are very poor. There are only twenty-four hours in a day. These students care for families, work twenty to forty hours a week in addition to school hours. Many of them struggle with academic skills. Their reality as students is our reality as teachers. Reality demands that the students' life situations be an important part of the teaching/learning focus.

MONEY

Working at jobs unrelated to nursing and at minimum wages left the students exhausted, with little energy left for their studies. The skills attendant to these jobs did nothing to improve their nursing skills. The Extern Program did two things: It paid an above-the-minimum wage salary, and it had a strong orientation to learning. The work and learning were associated with their educational program and with their growing familiarity with the nursing agency.

The students used the salaries to give up their fast food and grocery store jobs. Their salaries were used to pay tuition and book fees. In addition, after they had completed the Extern Program, they were able to secure positions as unit secretaries or nursing assistants. The program had prepared them for these positions that would be available to them on a part-time basis when school was in session. Having an opportunity to apply for jobs as they were posted enabled the students to feel as if they were a part of the organization. It also gave them an edge. The hospital was pleased that they needed little additional orientation for these positions. The externs were traditionally offered nursing positions at graduation. This occurred because of the excellent employee evaluations in their personnel files and due to the fact that many of them were still in part-time positions and were current employees. The program had an excellent reputation in the community. The externs functioned well and were safe beginning practitioners. Other agencies found the externs to be readily available to work because of their extern experiences. And so many additional avenues for earning money opened up for them. When the struggle for a cash flow was eased the attention to learning was a possibility.

CURRICULA

Our purpose was to have a curriculum focus no matter what nursing unit the student was assigned to. This was accomplished by identifying five core curriculum principles present in every nursing course and applicable to every nursing unit. This was easy. Five core principles were targeted:

- Use of the nursing process
- Patient/client safety
- Communication skills
- Ethics/legal concerns
- Comfort care
- Technical skills

With these core nursing actions as priorities, the externs could function on every unit of the hospital and provide prioritized, coherent, client-centered care. These five core principles enabled the learners to focus on the clients' needs in a systematic and organized manner. They began to understand the nursing process from a professional and cognitive dimension. With caseloads of up to six or eight patients, the externs were able to assess, plan, complete interventions, record, and evaluate the nursing care they designed. With the exception of distributing medications, the externs completed all treatments and other care modalities.

The assignment of full patient loads had a number of advantages for the learners. The demand for pulling together considerable information in a sequential manner moved the externs into quick thinking and decision-making modes. As they stated, "I felt like a part of the nursing team, and so I acted like a part of the nursing team. I felt like a nurse." The staff offered support by sharing organizational and functional tips. Externs expressed considerable appreciation for the spirit of collegiality each had with the other. And, as all nurses learn, the patients were the most supportive of all.

FACULTY

Choosing faculty for the Extern Program was unique. The teachers were chosen because they wanted to work in this innovative program. They were not necessarily the faculty in the school of nursing and so did not have these students in class or on clinical units related to coursework.

Extern faculty were outstanding clinicians themselves. They had extensive knowledge of the units they supervised and knew the personnel on those units. Faculty were carefully oriented to their roles. They, in turn, had the challenge of orienting the staff on the units. From Head Nurse to Nursing Assistant, the role of the extern was explained, discussed, reinforced, and evaluated.

An overall 1:10 faculty to student ratio was present. Each extern was supervised doing treatments and procedures. There were periodic pre- and post-conferences with case presentations and discussions.

Extern faculty served as mentors and role models. They taught at the bedside and clarified the role and competencies of the externs to the staff. It was an ongoing process of nursing, teaching, supporting, and validating the students' progress.

OUTCOME

The bottom line of the project was that students' academic scores as well as clinical competencies soared. Specifically, the students reported an increase in self-confidence and self-image as a neophyte nurse. Improvement in nursing skills made the nursing clinical components of their classes far less stressful. Improvement in "thinking like a nurse" and just thinking more quickly enabled these externs to learn more in the classroom setting. As concrete thinkers having had hands-on experiences, they were able to correlate lecture material to clinical experiences. They took great pride in being able to relate anecdotes from their clinical experiences that demonstrated ever-improved cognitive abilities. When their own clinical performance stress was diminished, they became more available to their patients as caregivers and to their studies as learners.

The combination of focus on the nursing process, and safety and technical competency provided excellent opportunities for these extern learners to develop a high level of proficiency in their physical skills. All procedures were tested and approved in the skill laboratory before going on the units as externs. Opportunities for doing the skills lead the externs to higher levels of competency with the skills as seen in accuracy, speed, patient comfort, and ability to evaluate and record outcomes.

Externs took great pride in being able to apply a full scope of nursing theory to their practice. They used their textbooks to research patient needs and were able to articulate the application of lecture material to their patients. The lectures began to make sense. Test scores improved.

Improved organizational skills enabled opportunities to refine nursing judgment. Confidence in clinical competency supported the externs' therapeutic communication skills. Health teaching and health counseling skills improved as communication skills became more relaxed. Competency supports further competency.

The externs reported that functioning, as a team member was a superior experience. Teams included both the hospital's staff members as well as their own groups of externs. It was very important that the older externs (Extern II) worked closely with the younger externs (Extern I). These relationships addressed the affective needs of the minority learners. Extern II students served as role models and peer teachers in some situations, helping the Extern I to feel confident. The Extern II had valuable feelings of pride and accountability toward his/her less experienced colleagues. On one particular respiratory unit with many tracheostomy patients, Extern II students demonstrated high levels of skills with aseptic technique and suctioning and tracheostomy care. They could be with the Extern I student and model the procedure for him/her. The Extern I not only was able to observe fine nursing care in the Extern II, but could visualize him/herself reaching for the same level of competency. Peer learning within the minority student group has a most positive, multiplying effect for the learners.

STUDENTS' VOICES IN PERSONAL VIGNETTES

In their personal stories, subjective and from their hearts, the externs praised the Extern Program for its ability to provide a vehicle for them to gain confidence, feel at ease in giving nursing care, and being able to "get close to the patients." The externs appreciated the opportunity to have continuity in the care that they rendered. After several days of taking care of the same group of patients, the externs reported that they valued knowing the patients as individuals.

Above all, the externs valued the knowledge and nursing judgment that they developed. As they gained speed in giving care, they actually performed better with more accuracy and more complexity in their views of care.

Peer relationships, so important in minority student learners retention rates, built quickly and strongly. They felt like nurses and they loved it. Feelings of competency lead to feelings of having job security. In fact, they identified the experience more than just a job, but rather as a beginning of a career, a professional level perception.

Improved competency lead to greater independence and less direct supervision. The externs were able to identify their own learning needs and to make their own assignments to meet their own learning needs.

They certainly enjoyed the relationship with the extern faculty and the attention to a "teach, don't supervise" approach to the relationship. Once on the unit, the tension of being evaluated was replaced with a mentor relationship. The externs reported that fear was greatly reduced and "steps of procedures fit together." Feeling competent is a positive upward spiral. The externs loved to see the results of their work. They saw patients heal. They saw patients and families deal with life-threatening situations.

The externs reported a particular pride with "learning the language of nursing" and "thinking fast on the unit." They appreciated the relationship with the faculty that halted their feelings of inferiority. They became persons with rank and achievement. They bonded with their colleagues, socialized with them at meals, and identified themselves as students who were moving into the registered nurse role at graduation.

With all of the externs' many reports of achievements, there was no talk of money. Their need for money were great, but their need for self-affirmation was even greater.

REFERENCES

Nelson, L. (1996). The work/study experience: A phenomenological inquiry. In V. Fitzsimons & M. Kelley. *The culture of learning*. New York: NLN Press.

Pacquiao, D. (1996). Educating faculty in the concept of educational biculturalism. In V. Fitzsimons & M. Kelley. *The culture of learning*. New York: NLN Press.

Part Three

COMMUNITY

Chapter 18

The Many Faces of Homelessness

PAULA DUNN TROPELLO

The best thing we can do is make wherever we are lost in
look as much like home as we can.

Christopher Fry (1996)

PREFACE

In the interest of shattering stereotypes, I will refrain from talking about "the"
homeless, as they are indeed a very diverse culture. Placing "the" in front of a
descriptive noun tends to label and place homeless persons in a particular box.

In the six or more years of working with this population, I have come to see
their rich and varied strengths. Their ability to survive and cope with overwhelming odds against them is demonstrated repeatedly.

A marginalized but fast growing group in our society, those who are homeless need recognition for their resilience and will as well as assistance through
collaboration between the private and public sectors. "Charity must reach out
to join hands with justice" (Olson, 1994).

INTRODUCTION

Although homelessness is one of the fastest growing social problems for our
nation and profound in its impact, the actual numbers are illusive and the once
stereotypic derelicts and bag ladies no longer seem to apply. Approximately 50
percent of today's homeless are families with children, most of which are
headed by single parents (Thrasher & Mowbray, 1995). The working poor,
veterans, runaway teens, single men and women, substance abusers, battered
women, some migrant workers, and the mentally ill comprise the remaining
portion of this population, estimated to total between 700,000 and 3 million.
Many homeless go unidentified, living in temporary quarters, even cars, and
moving on a regular basis as they wear out their welcomes with different relatives and contacts. Also, many do not wish to admit to this stigma so that they
delay applying for housing assistance and are never counted in homeless statistics. Most programs that serve homeless persons only address the literal homeless and not those who are precariously housed in motels or doubled up with
friends and relatives (Lewit & Baker, 1996, p. 149). However, the lack of good
data on homelessness cannot be utilized as the excuse for society not dealing
with a problem of this magnitude.

The diversity of images seen with homeless populations has not always been
portrayed by the media. Certainly it is easier for the public to classify homeless
persons as the unfortunates who have simply made poor choices or have been
victims of a poverty ridden past, destined to a cycle of misfortune. It is harder to
believe they could be former neighbors or part of a working class community.

Popular culture is very good at giving readers and viewers what they want
and excluding those images which cause guilt and discomfort. It is acceptable to
portray do-gooders serving up trays to the hungry in soup kitchens or ill-shaven,
slovenly old men sleeping in cardboard boxes, keeping warm with steam from

the city tunnels or with their bottles of booze. But it is not so comfortable to view a young mother with several children sleeping in a tent at a park in order to keep her family together and avoid a shelter situation. It is much easier to believe homelessness is confined to the underground tunnels of large cities than to accept it as part of suburban and rural America.

DEFINITION AND SCOPE

The Committee on Community Health Services (Weitzman, 1996) substantiates the existence of homelessness in virtually every community, as well as its negative impacts on developing families. Homeless populations are often described as subpopulations and subcultures. These words are further disappointments, for the prefix "sub" already implies being down or under another group. Homeless persons must constantly fight just to stay above water and move beyond their situational crisis. They are a culture worthy of recognition.

Many definitions exist on homelessness and exact tracking of statistics is difficult and misleading due in part to how one defines homelessness. The fact remains that no agency is in charge today of keeping track of the numbers who are homeless (Lewit & Baker, 1996).

The Select Committee on Hunger of the 1987 U. S. Congress defines homelessness as being without permanent domicile that can be secured without special assistance (Sullivan, 1994). The Department of Housing and Urban Development (HUD) defines it as those who live on the street or in shelters, as well as those at risk for being homeless.

According to Lewit and Baker (1996), there are two major groups of homeless persons: those who are "literally" homeless and on the street or in a shelter situation, and those who are "precariously housed," in other words, those who are in danger of literal homelessness because they have no place of their own to live.

ROOT CAUSES

Just what has led to the tremendous surge of homeless families in the last two decades? Many fault the very people who are so often victimized for laziness or poor choices when, in reality, most homelessness is a direct result of increasing numbers in poverty coupled with a lack of decent, affordable housing. In *The Choice Is Ours: Housing or Homelessness* (National Coalition for the Homeless, 1996), it is stated that low-income families have little chance of stable housing with a neighborhood school and stable friends as a result of the new low-wage economy, coupled with a reduction in the affordable housing and a simultaneous rise in demand. According to this document, out of 15 million households who qualify for federal housing assistance (HUD), a little over 4 million receive it. Many pay over half their incomes for housing, so that wages are not keeping pace with rent costs and those in poverty are becoming homeless at a rapid rate. Government housing subsidies have decreased while the numbers of working poor have drastically risen. Many are one paycheck from homelessness, so that a sudden layoff or rent increase is devastating in its impact. Many must then choose food or necessary medical expenses over housing.

Often listed as causes of homelessness for the "new poor" are domestic violence, eviction, unemployment, substance abuse, and mental disorders. High on the list is the remarkable increase in single parent families whose incomes are below 51 percent of the poverty line, up from 1 million in 1974 to over 2. 5 million in 1991 (Lewit & Baker, 1996).

FAMILIES WITH CHILDREN

The U. S. Conference of Mayors reported in 1994 that families requesting shelter increased some 21 percent and these same families are typically headed by women of preschoolers. Projections are that most of the U. S. homeless will be single mothers with children (Hatton, 1997). This demographic shift has tremendous implications for the welfare of children caught in this crisis.

Confirmed by Thrasher and Mowbray (1995), women with children constitute the largest group of homeless families in the research on homeless persons. They are also the most vulnerable and costly to society as well as the fastest growing segment of the homeless population. Weitzman (1996) states it is imperative for children to have permanent dwellings if they are to thrive. With the 1995 Welfare Reform (Personal Responsibility Act), there are even further impacts on families with children, in particular, that will change the picture of the present homeless population and perhaps make it even more difficult to secure stable housing. Touted as a social experiment (Geltman, 1996), Clinton's pledge to end welfare as it is presently known will decrease Aid to Families with Dependent Children (AFDC), forcing low-paying jobs and underground economies. This has a tremendous societal impact and, therefore, greatly affects both the educational and health care systems as these children enter in such vicarious positions, often underfed and nonimmunized.

Because shelter is such a basic human need as defined by Abraham Maslow (Lindberg, 1994), it is not surprising that Lewit & Baker (1996) found homeless women to have more low birth weight infants than other similar poor women with housing; and homeless children to have double the health problems, developmental delays, hunger, depression, and behavioral problems. In addition, Hatton (1997) found homeless women suffered from more problems, including mental disorders and drug addiction, than did their counterparts in the nonhomeless population.

Sullivan (1994) found for children that homelessness meant a disruption in normal life patterns that in turn caused deficits in meeting basic needs, family breakdown, poor performance in school, and lack of support groups. Therefore, rather than lack of home, it meant lack of structure, disrupting and impacting the child's life. However, the children in Sullivan's (1994) phenomenological study found safety and security in shelters that protected them from the events preceding homelessness. They often perceived the shelter as home, and meeting basic needs was the center of their identified hopes and dreams.

When the Stewart B. McKinney Homeless Assistance Act was passed by Congress in 1987, it made money available to states for the same free and appropriate education of homeless children as that given other children, but awareness of this act is a problem. With at least one-fifth of children under eighteen living in poverty in the United States (Bassey, 1996), teachers must deal with social problems brought to school from home, learn to recognize tell-tale signs, and intervene when appropriate. Learning frustrations, according to Bassey (1996), can manifest themselves in maladaptive behaviors, which often can be curtailed by the use of active, creative activities versus passive ones. In addition, many poor children do not perform well in school because they do not understand middle class values, attitudes, and language that is so often the tacit hidden curriculum, so that social inequities become academic ones (Basset, 1996). According to Wassermann (Bassey, 1996), emotional deprivation and stress of poverty often leads to low academic achievement from emotional insecurity and low self-esteem. The twin chronic problems of homeless children, identified by Kozol (Bassey, 1996) from teachers, are falling asleep and not completing homework assignments. Interestingly enough, truancy is not mentioned. James et al. (Bassey, 1996) also identified as key problems for poverty-stricken homeless children learning difficulties, developmental delays, and speech and language delays.

Pawlas (1996) estimates one in five homeless children are not enrolled in school and that many enter later or have poor attendance records. Pawlas (1996) also advocates for a "life skills" curriculum that assists those in school to listen, follow instructions, ask questions, learn social skills, and develop self-esteem. Many present curricula based on competitiveness do not work in his research with homeless children. Most read at below grade level and score two years behind in math, making them often older chronologically than their counterparts in grade level. School-based services can be helpful to this population since there is continuity and accessibility all under one roof.

Because the 1987 McKinney Act was the government's first attempt at recognizing the problems of homelessness and was particularly geared to assist needs of homeless children, much early research centered around monitoring its implementation by the local child placement agency. Later literature is finally addressing ways to effect change within the social system.

NAVIGATING THE SYSTEM

Although precariously housed for some time, many do not readily access social services since many do not choose to further stigmatize themselves or their families by admitting loss of residence. In August 1997, a family in rural New Jersey was threatened with removal of their handicapped foster children if they continued to allow a homeless family of four to share their residence (Parker, 1997). This skirmish with the social system made several papers as headlines, further placing fear into those at risk for homelessness. They fear being charged with neglect and having their children removed if they give in to being homeless even though applying to the board of social services could get them the assistance they need to get back on their feet. Rather than assist those who are in need nonjudgmentally, many times the system tries to place middle class values onto cultures who do not understand or appreciate middle class ways.

Just the experience of applying for emergency assistance can be harrowing with criminal and drug background checks, the need for a social security number for all members of the family, and trying to get transportation. All this makes the system difficult to access and adds to an already stressful situation. However, emergency placements can usually be arranged by social services until the necessary paperwork is in place.

Some choose to remain doubled up at friends or family, in tents or cars, with possessions in plastic bags and boxes until the cold weather. Often this, with school starting in the fall, is motivation to navigate the system and become those who are officially counted in homeless statistics.

The General Accounting Office's (GAO) estimates of the homeless population relies on indicators of service utilization so that those not utilizing social services such as shelters are not included in counts. HUD showed the number of shelters in 1984 to be at 1,900 while in 1988 the number had grown to 5,000 shelters. Obviously, the newest data on emergency and transitional (service-enriched, long-term) shelters have far surpassed this number as homeless families now wait to enter. Recent statistics indicate that at least 8 percent of poor families with children in the United States utilize homeless shelters at one time or another in the course of the year (Lewit & Baker, 1996).

Life at a shelter often gets a bad rap but essentially some prefer shelter life in order to have a place for possessions and a schedule that gives some control to their lives. Shelters also provide for basic needs such as security, warmth, food, and a place to sleep. But there can be great disadvantages such as loss of privacy, especially in emergency shelters.

Two main types of shelters exist: those considered emergency placement for short-term use, and the more recently developed transitional shelters that usually have services on site and provide long-term placements for approximately one year or more. Neither type of family shelter situation typically allows single males or sometimes any males. This adds to the problem of family disruption and may deter the family from seeking shelter life.

Far from the typical connotation of nonproductivity, laziness, or boredom often associated with homelessness, observations at shelter sites prove them to be highly structured and organized, geared to productivity and management of daily living activities. This structure seems necessary in order to coordinate resources involved and to maintain safety, efficiency, and control.

Many families find they not only have to crowd bunks and cots into one room and share baths, but that their parenting skills are constantly under scrutiny or perhaps undermined when volunteers are present. It is important for volunteers to be sensitive to the issue of not hovering or clustering around a homeless family and to honor their privacy. Times can be found to do counseling, parenting classes, tutoring, and the like without bombarding or overwhelming them. Coexisting peacefully is a challenge for all involved in shelter life, and a balance can usually be achieved.

Typically vans are available for transportation to an extent at most shelter sites and in some cases social workers may be liaisons with the school system. Mobile health vans exist on a part-time basis in many urban areas, but illness is still considered an inconvenience in a regimented system. There is difficulty accessing daycare for an ill child in particular, although many transitional shelters now have a preschool program on the premises.

Smoking is often an issue, especially because it is a safety hazard in many older buildings that are utilized. Most shelters allow smoking in designated areas outside and adhere strictly to this rule. Also, there is absolutely zero tolerance for drugs and alcohol.

Phone calls usually are made from pay phones, and interviews with volunteers form certain religious networks who assist homeless families indicate phoning to be a difficult area to control, thereby resorting exclusively to coin phones.

Although control may appear to be impugned from an outsider's perspective, there are few complaints from those who have experienced being precariously housed or literally homeless prior to having a stable shelter residence. Adaptability and coping skills seem to take over and difficulties overcome. And although most homeless families are temporarily displaced by unemployment, natural disaster, family breakup, or problems with money flow, many still remain homeless for years and are unable to find and keep affordable housing even with assistance from social service. Somehow this trend must be reversed and the root causes of homelessness addressed.

WHAT CAN BE DONE TO REVERSE THE TREND

The shelter system has become acceptable and housing is truly not being addressed in Washington. There seems to be a tacit agreement that the poorest are able to live with less. In "An Invitation to Action," a speech by Helen Dunlap, newly appointed president of the National Low Income Housing Coalition, she states:

> We must stop stereotyping low income people and patronizing the recipients of federal dollars. We need to move beyond direct services and take a holistic approach so that housing, jobs, and daycare are thought of as something people deserve—not as something we allow the government to ration (*Hospitality*, 1996).

However, McLaren (1989) speaks to the myth of democratic schooling and calls for theories that allow teachers to question value judgments. McLaren says our educational system is a "loaded social lottery, in which each student gets as many chances as his or her parents have dollars." He also believes the real issue is that our system gives better chances to those who begin with certain advantages. Therefore, it would be of great value to interview school nurses, social workers, counselors, and teachers of homeless children to determine if there was shared knowledge of their social situation and to observe these same children in the school system to see if they receive special intervention. Is there or should there be a confidentiality issue in this situational crisis, and is homelessness a stigma that can track a student accordingly, thereby transmitting a hidden curriculum and preventing growth? According to Sullivan (1994), many homeless children, despite recounting violence, abuse, family breakdown, and multiple moves, still did not perceive themselves as homeless and were able to function in a chaotic, inconsistent environment, often claiming the shelter their home. They showed remarkable resilience and adaptability. Do children cope so well that their education does not suffer if they are regularly in school? Do they convey cultural capital to the educational system? Are they known and assisted by school personnel? How are they viewed by their peers? Should year-round school be available for this high-risk group? There is an enormous need for study in this area as the homeless population soars. Presently, there exists only a paucity of research to assist us in policy making for this vulnerable population.

Due to the recent shift from emergency to transitional, service-enriched shelters for the homeless, effects of these versus emergency shelters need to be looked at over time. In addition, the effects of the 1995 Welfare Reform legislation on the poor, with reduction in AFDC are also worthy of following as they impact the numbers of homeless as well as their quality of life.

Self-interest in our society can no longer be tolerated. Just as lifestyles no longer define the person, "politics of difference" (Guarasci, 1997) should no longer define a democracy. According to Banks (1994), the canon needs transforming and an aim for socially oriented curricula needs to fill schools and colleges to increase cultural tolerance, reduce bias, and begin forming a committed citizenry in which all can "enter public life with equal dignity, no matter what our social or economic status might be" (Gabelnick, 1990). Partnerships and commitment to community can reverse the cycle of homelessness and build a culturally competent nation.

TALES OF THE HASSIDIM[1]

An old rabbi once asked his pupils how they could tell when the night had ended and the day had begun.

"Could it be," asked one of the students, "when you can see an animal in the distance and tell whether it's a sheep or a dog?"

"No," answered the rabbi.

---

[1] From *Peacemaking: Day by Day*, Pax Christi USA, 348 East Tenth Street, Erie, PA 16503.

Another asked, "Is it when you can look at a tree in the distance and tell whether it's a fig tree or a peach tree?"

"No," answered the rabbi.

"Then when is it?" the pupils demanded.

The old rabbi told them, "It is when you can look on the face of any woman or man and see that it is your sister or brother. Because if you can't see this, then it is still night."

REFERENCES

Banks, J. A. (1994). *An introduction to multicultural education*. Boston: Allyn and Bacon.

Bassey, M. O. (Fall, 1996). Teachers for a changing society: Helping neglected children cope with schooling. *The Educational Forum*, Vol. 61, pp. 58–62.

Bigras, M., et al. Discriminant validity of the parent and child scales of the parenting stress index. *Early Education and Development*, April 1996, Vol. 7, No. 2, pp. 167–171.

Dohrn, B. (1991). *A long way from home: Chicago's homeless children and the schools*. Legal Assistance Foundation of Chicago, IL.

Fry, C. Quote in *The Educational Forum* (Fall 1996), Vol. 61, p. 23.

Gabelnick, F. (1990). Educating a committed citizenry. *Learning communities: Making connections among students, faculty, and disciplines*. San Francisco: Jossey-Bass.

Geltman, P. L., et al. Commentary: welfare reform and children's health. *Health Policy & Child Health*. Special Report, Spring 1996, Vol. 3, No. 2, Center for Health Policy Research, pp. 1–5.

Gudrasci, R. & Cornwell, G. (1997). *Democratic education in an age of Difference*. San Francisco: Jossey-Bass.

Hatton, D. C. Managing health problems among homeless women with children in a transitional shelter. *Image, Journal of Nursing Scholarship*. Vol. 29, No. 1, First Quarter 1997, pp. 33–36.

Horowitz, J. A., Hughes, C. B. & Perdue, B. J. (1982). *Parenting reassessed*. New Jersey: Prentice-Hall.

Hospitality (1996), Vol. 7, Issue 2, pp. 1–4.

Lewit, E. M. & Baker, L. S. (1996, sum/fall). Homeless families and children. *The Future of Children*, 6(2):146–158.

Lindberg, J. B., Hunter, M. L. & Kruszewski, A. Z. (1994). *Introduction to nursing: Concepts, issues and opportunities*. Philadelphia: Lippincott.

McLaren, P. (1989). *Life in schools*. New York: Longman.

National Coalition for the Homeless. *The choice is ours: Housing or homelessness*. Dec. 1996, Washington, D. C.

Olson, K. (1997). From the president. *Hospitality*, 8(1), 1–4.

Parker, Jr., C. (1997). Readington family told: Remove homeless or else. *The Hunterdon Review, 101*(39a).

Pawlas, G. E. (1994). Homeless students at the school door. *Educational Leadership, 51*(8), pp. 79–82.

Pawlas, G. E. (1996). Homeless children: are they being prepared for the future? *The Educational Forum*, Vol. 61, pp. 18–23.

Sullivan, L. M. (1994). *The meaning and significance of homelessness to a child: A phenomenological inquiry.* (Dissertation).

Thrasher, S. P. & Mowbray, C. T. (1995 May). A strengths perspective: An ethnographic study of homeless women with children. *Health and Social Work, 20*(2): 93–101.

Weitzman, M. (1996). Health needs of homeless children and families. *Pediatrics, 98*(4):789–791.

Chapter 19

A Walk in Beauty:
Strategies for Providing
Culturally Competent Nursing Care
to Native Americans

KAREN A. JOHO AND ANNE ORMSBY

> I will be happy forever, nothing will hinder me.
> I walk with beauty before me, I walk with beauty behind me,
> I walk with beauty below me, I walk with beauty above me,
> I walk with beauty around me, my words will be beautiful . . .
>
> *Navajo Beautyway Chant*

Cultural understanding of the nearly 2 million American Indians living on or near reservations in twenty-eight states must begin with an awareness of the historic oppression and excessive attempts at cultural assimilation experienced by the descendants of the original inhabitants of the United States. From the arrival of the first European explorers and Christian missionaries, immigrants have dominated the American Indians. Presently, the federal government continues to play a bureaucratic and paternalistic role in tribal affairs, despite the Indian Civil Rights Act of 1968 and the Indian Self-Determination and Education Assistance Act of 1975. The intent of the latter legislation is to return to the American Indian people the responsibility for internal governance and various services that they require, such as health care and education. This is a slow process, keeping in mind that there are approximately 510 federally recognized Indian tribes, bands, pueblos, and villages. A unique feature of a federally recognized tribe is that the tribe has signed a treaty with the U.S. government providing eligibility of the tribe to participate in federal programs, such as the Indian Health Service (IHS) while at the same time placing the land once occupied by the American Indian in trust to the U.S. government, thus the term reservation. Not all American Indian tribes have treaty rights and are not recognized by Congress.

EFFECTS OF OPPRESSION AND FORCED ASSIMILATION

Examples of forced cultural assimilation to the Anglo-American's way of life abound. Boarding schools for American Indian children became popular public policy in the late nineteenth century. These schools were developed to facilitate the suppression of the American Indian culture and religion, thereby easing the assimilation of the American Indian into the Anglo-American culture. American Indian children were taken from their homes and transported off the reservation to attend school. Vacations and holidays were spent living with Anglo families. Traditional American Indian religious ceremonies were denounced as pagan practices and the fall-out from speaking a tribal language was corporal punishment.

The Sun Dance, a holy ceremony performed by the Plains American Indians was horrendously misunderstood by Anglo-Americans. This ceremony, in which voluntary suffering was offered to the Great Spirit, was outlawed in 1892 by the Bureau of Indian Affairs (BIA) as offensive. The passage of the American Indian Religious Freedom Act in 1979 implies that the American Indian is free to practice their ceremonies and rituals, however, this has come into question with the use of peyote as a harmonizing agent by the Native American Church in sacred rituals. It must be reported that the use of peyote as a sacrament within the Native American Church is a highly controlled practice and the tenets of the Native American Church stress moral and ethical precepts and behavior (Beauvass & LaBouff, 1985).

Another example of the historical oppression experienced by the American Indian is the "Long Walk." During the Civil War, Commander James H. Carleton and Christopher "Kit" Carson marched 8,000 Navajo men, women, and children over 300 miles to live four years in exile with substandard housing and insufficient food and water. The "Long Walk" as it is referred to by the Navajos and resulting massive annihilation was sanctioned by Abraham Lincoln who had been convinced that the Navajo land contained gold and precious metals which would help finance the Civil War—the war against slavery.

To comprehend the consequences of oppression is to understand the present-day American Indian. A social consequence of oppression is poverty. The by-products of poverty, which include malnutrition, lack of health care, low self-esteem, depression, substance abuse, and violence, are visible throughout the reservations. According to Spector (1991), one-third of all American Indians live in poverty. The U.S. Census Bureau (1990) reports that the median household income for reservation-based families was at $16,800 while among the general population the median household income was at $30,000. A behavioral consequence of oppression is a distrust of the dominant society, in this case the Anglo-American society.

Wars, imprisonment, oppression, and excessive attempts at cultural obliteration of the American Indian have not eliminated this unique heterogeneous community. While many common elements exist among the various tribes, within each tribe and their members there is a plethora of regional differences in language, living patterns, myths, and religious beliefs. This contrast can be seen between the coastal settlements of California and the nomadic big game hunters of the Plains. These variations in behavior, history, and culture preclude any standard notion of American Indian.

TRADITIONAL AMERICAN INDIAN VALUES AND BELIEFS

So who are the American Indians? To be identified as an American Indian, an individual must be an enrolled member of a tribe and/or living on a reservation. For example, to declare oneself a Navajo, lineage must include one-quarter Navajo blood. Other tribes have different criteria. For census-taking purposes, self-identification is the method of choice since no legislative definition for American Indians exists.

Although the American Indian has incorporated some values and beliefs from the Anglo-American culture and diversity in tribal rituals and traditions abound, there are basic tenets that apply to traditional American Indians. It can be stated that American Indians are a people who share a belief system based on the reciprocal relationship between man and nature. The following highlights these suppositions.

Respect for age. Children are expected to care for their elders, and this includes extended family members such as aunts and uncles. The leadership position in the family is held by an elder, most likely the eldest female member. The elderly are consulted for their wisdom and life experiences.

Present-minded. Each day is lived to its fullest. The individual has little control over the future. Planning for the future is futile.

Value of extended family and clan system. The function of the family is for creation and caring. There is nothing more important than the family or clan. To be poor by American Indian standards is to be without family. In some American Indian tribes all women who were instrumental in the development of an individual are referred to as "mother." In other tribes, first cousins are treated as brothers and sisters.

Decision making. Problem solving and decision making is a group rather than an individual experience. Decisions are based on what is best for the community not necessarily the individual.

Cooperation. Competition is devalued and discouraged as it weakens the cohesiveness of the group. Sharing is a core value of American Indians.

Time. The completion of a task takes precedent over appointments or meetings. Time is a continuum with no beginning nor end. It is not unusual for an American Indian home to be without clocks.

Status of role. Relationships are based on personal integrity not role, status, or the accumulation of material goods. To the American Indian the concept of being is more important than the concept of achieving.

Natural resources and the environment. All of nature exists in harmony. Everything has a spirit. The American Indian uses only those resources needed to survive and does not change the environment to fit the needs of man, but lives and accepts the environment.

Health. The basis of health and well-being is to live in harmony and balance within the world. Health is not the absence of illness or disease.

These principles have been extrapolated from the many spiritual beliefs and practices of the American Indian which are woven into the fabric of American Indian life. Unlike the Western culture, which separates religion and medicine, the American Indians believe that faith and healing are joined. It must be reiterated that diversity is present in the healing practices of all tribes and it remains difficult to determine purity of these practices since the acculturation process did not occur in an orderly manner. An understanding of the following spiritual orientations that have influenced the traditional healing practices of the medicine man or woman will assist the professional nurse in incorporating these traditional practices within a health care facility. To the American Indian the world is animistic, in other words, everything has a spirit. Mother Earth with her insects, snakes, and trees, to Father Sky with the rain and lightening. There is a sense of brotherhood with all living things and respect is paid to all living things. The existence of a supreme spiritual creator or creators and lesser spiritual beings are central to the majority of traditional American Indian beliefs. Taboos have been communicated to man from these spirits. The breaking of a taboo, such as misusing a sacred object or violating proscribed behavior, will result in disharmony with the universe followed by illness and disease.

Life is circular with physical death moving the individual toward another life. The spirit of the individual continues to exist in various places. The natural progression of sickness and death are but one aspect of the life processes and are not to be feared but revered. The concepts of illness and death do not necessarily represent disharmony but can exemplify a fulfillment of the natural cycle.

It is preposterous to assume that American Indians do not recognize the benefits of allopathic health care and that antibiotic therapy is necessary to cure a beta hemolytic strep infection. However, to rid the body of the bacteria is only the first of many steps to the healing process. Illness and disease are not value or meaning free. In other words, according to Western health care practices, the etiology behind the infection is bacteria. The question answered by the American Indian healer reveals the experience or object that resulted in the individual's disharmony with nature that ultimately culminated in illness. For the individual to return to a state of balance and reintegration into the spirit world, the act responsible for the unbalanced state must be diagnosed and treated.

With these beliefs in mind, it becomes apparent that the traditional healer's task is to mobilize the client's psychological, spiritual, and bodily resources. This is achieved vis-à-vis a ceremony, chant, or sing. The client must have hope and faith in the healer and an awareness of being embraced by loved ones and significant others. The use of amulets and symbols during the ceremony contributes to the effect of the ceremony on the client. Traditional healers fall into two categories; the diagnostician and singers or medicine people. For the purpose of this discussion, the term medicine man will be used, however, bear in mind that some of the world's most powerful healers have been and continue to be women. The diagnostician, using a type of meditation determines the cause of the illness or disease. These individuals are often referred to as hand tremblers, crystal gazers, or star gazers depending upon their method of diagnosis. The second type of healer, the medicine man or singer, provides the cure and treatment of the illness and may perform the necessary treatment, such as a ceremony, chant, or sing. An additional type of healer, the herbalists are individuals that have been bestowed with an ability to prescribe herbs for healing purposes. Many families have elder members that have been given this ability and it is not unusual for the herbalist to be the first person approached during illness or disease.

Generally, the healer is an individual who is believed to have experienced divine intervention and has chosen to live a life in continued harmony with one's surroundings. The traditional healer has been entrusted with powers not available to everyone. After the acquisition of these powers, it requires years of mentoring with an elder medicine man to learn all the treatments. This may account for the dwindling numbers of contemporary traditional healers.

The rituals of the healing ceremony must be performed in a precise manner in order to be effective, and not all medicine men can perform all ceremonies. Sings are group ceremonies which involve the individual, the medicine man, his assistants and the immediate and extended family members. Again, the underlying principle of the ceremony is the belief that the illness or disease is a direct result of a lack of harmony between the person and his or her environment. The ceremony may involve the laying on of hands and the use of ritual objects such as eagle feathers, drums, whistles, rattles, and/or corn pollen.

The expense of the ceremony becomes the duty of the family and the offerings can range from a few dollars to thousands of dollars. The family is also responsible for feeding the ceremonial participants, with some ceremonies taking nine days to complete. The individual is the focus of the ceremony. Family members and significant others are expected to put aside all other obligations for the ceremony. This may include taking time off from work or school. Healing, not curing, may be the objective of the ceremony, however ceremonies are performed for births, deaths, entrance into puberty, for departing the reservation as when students leave for college, and for those who may have violated a tribal taboo.

STRATEGIES FOR INTERVENTIONS WITH AMERICAN INDIANS

Strategies for nurses to practice culturally competent care of the American Indian client begins by transcending the cultural universals of the American Indian and learning as much as possible about the specific tribal rituals and traditions for each client. Ask the client and family about traditions they may desire since a common American Indian does not exist. Question the client and family on their previous use of traditional healing modalities. The development of a cultural assessment tool that addresses the specific traditions and rites of the American Indian tribes that seek health care at a given facility guides the nurse in appropriate questioning. Knowledge about the tribal customs can be obtained through indigenous nurses and unlicensed assistive personnel. Culture brokers are individuals who assist non-American Indians to understand the cultural issues important to the various tribes (Buehler, 1993). They work with health care providers during orientation to the tribal hospitals and Indian Health Service facilities. They are also consulted when educational materials are developed and marketing strategies employed for preventative health within the reservation.

A current trend among younger American Indians is to migrate from the reservation to urban areas. High levels of unemployment, the lack of post-secondary education on the reservation, and high rates of poverty account for this movement. A nurse providing care to an American Indian in a non-Indian Health Service facility needs to be aware that American Indians, upon leaving the reservation, may have forfeited health care services provided by the IHS. As such, the client and family may be unfamiliar with health care services available off the reservation and concerned about the financial obligation incurred with an illness or disease. A social service referral is imperative to assist the client in navigating the complex health care system.

Another issue related to the relocation of American Indians off the reservation is the lack of access to traditional healers. The nurse must know the client's previous use of healers and if a traditional healer is desired by the client. Total healing of the client will not occur if the client is denied traditional healing rites. Any health care facility that treats and admits American Indians should have available a list of qualified medicine men.

Due to the strong ties to the nuclear and extended family, the American Indian requires a liberal visitation policy. If the client's condition does not permit visitors, then periodic updates on the client's condition and treatment regime should be initiated by the registered nurse providing care in attempts to help alleviate the family's anxiety.

Keeping in mind that the family becomes involved with decision making, obtaining a consent may require discussions with multiple family members. It is the nurse's responsibility to determine the gatekeeper of the family and to include this person in discussion provided that permission is first obtained from the client. In emergency treatment or surgery, the time for group discussion and decision making is limited. The nurse needs to find ways to include the family in the preparation for the treatment. For example, staying with the client through the induction of anesthesia or allowing the traditional healer into the surgical suite.

From time to time the facilities of the IHS must air transfer a client to an urban medical center for contracted specialized treatment. This often results in confusion, fear, anxiety, and possible culture shock for the client and family. Information and assistance with arrangements for short-term living needs of the family members accompanying the client must be provided and information about the client's cultural beliefs relayed to the new facility.

Communication and the use of language also varies within the tribes. For the most part, the American Indian, excluding the elderly, speak English. Today, with over 150 languages and dialects, the majority of American Indians cannot speak their tribal language. The following suggestions are generalities that can be made in regards to verbal and nonverbal communication with American Indians.

If the client is elderly, their ability to speak the English language may be limited. Prior to answering any questions they need to translate the question from English to their native language, translate their answers from their native language back to English, and then attempt to answer the question orally. This takes time and will slow the admission process or interview. In the event that a translator is required, a child or younger member of the family should not be used as this is considered disrespectful to the older family member.

Storytelling, anecdotes, and the use of metaphors are commonly used by the American Indian to explain situations and during history taking. Realizing this, extended time must be allowed for all oral interactions with American Indians. Silence is considered a trait of maturity. Individuals who interrupt, speak before thinking, hurry the conversation, and interject opinions are considered immature and rude. The American Indian has been taught to think before speaking and may have periods of silence before answering a question.

Body language is as important to the American Indian as periods of silence. A brief handshake with an introduction communicates acceptance, but the handshake should not be a firm grasp with vigorous hand shaking. This sign of strong character to the Western culture denotes aggression to the American Indian. Smiling represents reassurance and acceptance but may not be returned by the American Indian. Eye contact is expected during the initial handshake and periodically throughout the conversation, however staring into the eyes of the individual is considered vulgar and disrespectful.

During hospitalization, space and privacy can be arranged for the client and family desiring a ceremony or sing. In the event that a more elaborate sing is required, discussion with the health care team on the feasibility of an earlier discharge may be necessary. A healing room in which ceremonies can be conducted has been recently constructed at the Chinle Indian Health Service Hospital in the center of the Navajo Nation. Lacking a healing room, many ceremonies can be conducted at the client's bedside. As it is considered an act of rudeness, privacy during ceremonies and prayers will not be asked for by the American Indian. It becomes the nurse's responsibility to assure privacy and to not participate in the experience unless asked by the client or family.

An area that requires the cultural sensitivity of the nurse is in the identification of individuals who may have participated in a ceremony prior to arriving at the health care facility. The processes of the ceremony may continue for days despite the conclusion of the medicine man and group participant. Indicators of a ceremony include body art with ash, corn pollen, animal fat, or paints. The client has been marked in a specific manner to represent a holy spirit. Removal of these markings disrupts the healing process and removes any protection the individual may have had from evil spirits. Generally, the use of herbs can be detected by their distinct odor. Herbs when used together with Western pharmacological agents may result in deleterious outcomes. A thorough assessment includes the use of oral and topical herbs at home and herbs that may be continued during the hospitalization. Taking the time to discuss with the client and family the detrimental effects the herbs may have with the allopathic treatments and to consult with the healer who prescribed the herbs to determine a compromise or substitute is advisable so no further taboos are broken or the processes of the ceremony disrupted.

Medicine bundles are small animal skin bags carried by an individual to ward off evil spirits and to act as a preventive health practice. These bundles are worn around the neck or can be attached to the clothing. Inside the bundle, objects such as wood, feathers, corn pollen, or any number of items that have been deemed by a healer to carry protection from evil may be found. The pouch and contents are not to be casually questioned, removed, examined, or admired. They are to be treated as a sacred object.

SUMMARY

For generations the American Indian has walked in beauty despite widespread oppression and forced acculturation. Contemporary nursing has always been in the forefront of accepting alternative methods of healing and to continue this valuable trait, we must recognize and appreciate the sacristy of the traditions, rites, and rituals of the American Indian. Together with Western health care practices, nurses will be able to provide culturally sensitive and competent nursing care for the attainment of health and happiness for the American Indian.

Cultural Assessment for the American Indian

This should be used as an example only as cultural variations are expected.

1. In previous illness or disease have you consulted a medicine person?
   ☐ Yes   ☐ No
   Comments_____

2. Have you consulted a medicine person for this illness/disease?
   ☐ Yes   ☐ No

3. If yes to question 2, what did the medicine person say?
   Comments_____

   _____

4. Do you desire a medicine person while in the hospital?
   ☐ Yes   ☐ No

5. Have you used any herbs/roots to help with this illness/disease?
   ☐ Yes   ☐ No

6. If yes to question 5, what type of herbs/roots were used?
   Comments_____

7. Do you wish to continue with their use while hospitalized?
   ☐ Yes   ☐ No

8. Do you wish any hair that is removed returned to you?
   ☐ Yes   ☐ No

9. Do you wish any nail clippings returned to you?
   ☐ Yes   ☐ No

10. Do you wish any body fluids returned?
    ☐ Yes   ☐ No

11. Do you wish a ceremonial hair washing?
    ☐ Yes   ☐ No

12. Do you wear your hair in a traditional hair style?

    ☐ Yes   ☐ No

13. Do you desire to keep any sacred objects in your room?

    ☐ Yes   ☐ No

**Assessment questions for woman experiencing childbirth may include:

14. Do you desire the umbilical cord to be returned to you?

    ☐ Yes   ☐ No

15. Do you desire the placenta returned to you?

    ☐ Yes   ☐ No

16. Do you wish us to save your child's first stool?

    ☐ Yes   ☐ No

**Assessment questions for the dying patient may include:

17. Do you wish to be positioned toward a cardinal direction?

    ☐ Yes   ☐ No

    Direction_____

18. Do you desire an opened window?

    ☐ Yes   ☐ No

19. Do you wish your family present during death?

    ☐ Yes   ☐ No

20. Can the deceased body be prepared in the hospital room before individual visitation takes place?

    ☐ Yes   ☐ No

    Comments_____

REFERENCES

Beauvais, F. & LaBoueff, S. (1985). Drug and alcohol abuse intervention in American Indian communities. *The International Journal of the Addictions, 20*(1), 139–172.

Buehler, J. (1993). Nursing in rural Native American communities. *Nursing Clinics of North America, 28*(1), 211–217.

Spector, R. E. (1991). *Cultural diversity in health and illness* (3rd ed.). Norwalk: Appleton & Lange.

U.S. Department of Commerce, Bureau of the Census (1990). *Census of the population: Social and economic characteristics.* Washington, DC: U.S. Government Printing Office.

Chapter 20

The Filipino American Culture: The Need for Transcultural Knowledge

VIRGINIA VILLANUEVA
AND ANUNCIACION S. LIPAT

CHANGE IN HEALTH CARE SYSTEM— NEED FOR TRANSCULTURAL KNOWLEDGE

Nurses today are confronted with the rapidly changing health care delivery system. With clients being in their own homes and in their own territory, they are demanding more control and an increased role in decision making in relation to their care. Clients expect health care providers to understand their cultural practices, their values, and needs and to incorporate them into the health care services (Leininger, 1991).

The way an individual behaves is within the context of one's cultural pattern. It is essential that the nurse has a basic knowledge of the characteristics of the client's particular ethnic group, the dominant traits, traditional beliefs, and practices that have an impact on their health promotion practices, their perception of illness, and their relationship with the health care providers.

As migration to the United States continues, demographic features will continue to change. Demographers estimate that by the twenty-first century one-third to one-half of the population will be of descent other than Euro-Caucasian. The reversal is predicted where groups categorized as minorities will collectively comprise the majority (Shake & Redman, 1997). Knowledge of cultural diversity is important. In this pluralistic society nurses are faced with the increasing challenge that being culturally sensitive is no longer sufficient. Health care services must also be culturally safe. Paxton (1967) stated that interventions without cultural consideration are not only unsafe but also inhumane.

Among the various cultures that nurses will be encountering in the community will be Filipino Americans. They comprise the third largest Asian group only exceeded in the number of population by the Chinese Americans and Japanese Americans. According to the 1990 Census, there are 1,406,770 Filipinos in the United States; 70.5% reside in the West, 11.3% in the South, 8.1% in the Midwest, and 10.2% in the Northeast (U.S. Bureau of Census, 1990 Census of Population).

NEED CURRENT INFORMATION ABOUT FILIPINO AMERICANS

When learning about the Filipino American culture the nurse has to utilize information from contemporary research findings or literature. Although earlier findings from various studies appeared empirically valid there are questions regarding their applicability to the Filipinos in the current situation and in today's world. Having a broad understanding about the Filipino culture will provide the knowledge to avoid a stereotypical approach. Not all Filipino Americans behave in a similar manner typical of their ethnic category.

DIVERSITY OF FILIPINO GROUP

Intracultural differences exist among Filipinos because they differ in dialect, geographical origin, social class, and the degree of acculturation to the dominant society. Some Filipino Americans retain their traditional traits, religious beliefs, and kinship values, while others adopt a way of living and values characteristic of the Anglo-American culture. The degree of acculturation and behavioral modification is influenced by various factors such as age, gender, educational attainment, and socioeconomic level.

GENERAL BACKGROUND

Philippines is composed of 7,107 islands, with three major islands that are densely populated, namely: Luzon, Visayas, and Mindanao. The temperature ranges from 76 to 84 degrees with 60 degrees centigrade in the mountainous areas. There are various dialects that are spoken by distinct ethnic groups. While Tagalog or Filipino is the national language, the formal language of instruction is English (de la Costa, 1965).

CULTURAL/RELIGIOUS INFLUENCE

Filipino culture is a blend of diverse heritage and colonization experience. Filipinos are essentially Asian with complex Malayan and Indonesian descent. The influence of Spanish colonization for 300 years and 50 years of American occupation are incorporated by the Filipinos in their culture, their world views, and their actions. Furthermore, countries that have a trading relationship with the Philippines such as China, Japan, and Korea have affected the practices of the Filipinos today (de la Costa, 1965; Spangler, 1991). European colonization converted Filipinos to Christianity making it the only Christian country in the Far East. The majority of people are Christians and 90 percent are Roman Catholic.

VARIED GROUPS OF IMMIGRANTS IN THE COMMUNITY

There were three major waves of Filipino immigration to the United States. The first wave was pioneer immigrants drafted primarily as farmers or unskilled laborers. The second group of immigrants was the families of the soldiers who served in the United States Armed Forces during World War II. The third group migrated after 1965 as a result of the liberalization of the immigration quota. The majority of these immigrants were professionals and relatives of earlier immigrants (Orque, Block, & Monroy, 1983).

It is important for the nurse to recognize that earlier immigrants will present different characteristics and health needs and an entirely unique world view that is very different from that of the more recent immigrants.

DOMINANT TRAITS

Despite the mixed heritage, there are basic traits that predominate among Filipino Americans. One of the most notable characteristics of the Filipino society is the tradition of family loyalty. This is reflected in the absence of nursing homes and orphanages. With a strong sense of kinship support and familial commitment, children are socialized to depend on one another for mutual support, emotional assistance, and intervention in times of crisis (de Gracia, 1979). Individual goals are often sacrificed and subordinated to that of the group and family objectives take precedence over the interest of a particular member. Strong kinship relationship is also extended outside that of the nuclear family.

Honor of the family and religion are highly revered. At an early age, children are oriented to preserve family dignity and to avoid any impropriety. Children are disciplined by invoking shame and guilt in the family name (Galanti, 1991).

Another trait that is pervasive among the Filipino Americans is deference to elders and persons of authority. Elders are regarded with high esteem and their wisdom viewed with utmost consideration. Children are expected to respect their parents, older siblings, and senior relatives.

Additionally, a trait that permeates in social interactions and life activities is maintaining smooth and harmonious interpersonal relationships. Any open confrontations, conflicts, or disruptions are regarded as undesirable and noncaring.

DOMINANT TRAITS INFLUENCING HEALTH BEHAVIORS

Pido (1986) cited five significant values that influence the health behaviors of Filipino Americans: *utang na loob, bahala na, hiya, amor propio,* and *pakikisama*.

Utang na loob—mutual reciprocity

Utang na loob refers to debt of gratitude, mutual reciprocity, or giving assistance in time of need. It is a traditional cultural expectation that children are to care for the elderly parents or their sick family members. In the hospital it is not uncommon to see clients with the family members actively involved as caregivers. Nurses need to recognize the importance of kinship support and to consider the family system when doing health services. Kinship support is obtained from within and outside the nuclear family.

Utang na loob is also evident with the Filipino Americans feeling morally obligated to repay the kindness and services provided by the nurse. To express their appreciation, they display generosity, hospitality, and giving of gifts. The nurse has to be gracious in acknowledging their gesture of gratitude. *Utang na loob* can play a significant role in a client's compliance to the health management. A client may commit to the treatment because he or she is indebted to the caring nurse.

Bahala na—leaving one's fate to God

Bahala na, is leaving oneself in the hands of God. Filipinos are deeply religious, which is their source of strength in time of illness, uncertainty, or adversity. The following clinical situation illustrates how this value operates when a client is dealing with illness. Mr. D. was admitted to the coronary care unit with an acute myocardial infarction. During his critical stay in the unit he coped with his heart attack by leaving everything in the hands of God. He contended that there were external factors that were beyond his control. With God's intervention he was optimistic that he would recover positively.

When caring for Filipino Americans, it is important for the nurse to assess religious affiliation, rituals, and practices. Filipino Americans are predominantly Roman Catholic due to the influence of the Spanish missionaries in the Philippines. The nurse can encourage the family to bring religious medallions, rosary beads, scapula, and figures of saints. The priest has to be contacted to provide spiritual support and oftentimes to offer a Mass as requested by the family.

Filipino Americans believe the etiology of illness as caused by natural factors such as lack of moderation as in overeating, poor diet, excessive smoking, imbalance in nature, decrease in resistance to germs, and unhygienic practices. Others perceive illness as due to a supernatural cause such as punishment from God or from the angry spirit (Hart, 1966; Vance, 1995; Wilson, 1994).

A 65-year-old male Filipino was admitted to a medical surgical unit for cellulitis of the foot. Despite the gross swelling of the affected limb, he never asked for the prescribed analgesics. Upon questioning by the student nurse, he expressed that his illness was a punishment for his past wrongdoings. Attributing his illness to an external cause beyond his control, he patiently endured the pain.

Like any other clients from a diverse background, the nurse assesses the Filipino Americans' behavioral reactions and views to illness. They may appear pain free or stoic, which is a culturally ascribed response. In addition to nonjudgmental acceptance of their beliefs, pain medications have to be offered and the importance of adequate pain management explained.

The role of cultural differences in illness behavior is best illustrated in the clinical incident cited by Leininger (1995, p. 87) involving the Italian, Chinese, and Filipino clients who had major surgery. The Italian client asked for the pain medication. The Chinese client got angry when offered the medication saying, "I don't need anything." The Filipino client on the other hand did not request medication, but explained to the nurse, "*bahala na* (God's will) and I can bear the pain Jesus gave me. From *bahala na*, Filipino Americans believed that God will give them strength to bear pain or sickness (Orque, 1983). Filipino elderly endure the pain associated with chronic illness and resist hospitalization as long as they are ambulatory (Caringer, 1977).

Hiya—maintaining privacy and confidentiality

Hiya refers to value placed on maintaining one's privacy and modesty. Filipinos feel embarrassed when exposed unnecessarily or when taken care of by health providers of the opposite sex. Female clients may postpone having a regular gynecological check-up such as a Pap smear or mammography. In addition to privacy, *hiya* further denotes confidentiality. Filipino Americans are uncomfortable discussing topics dealing with personal matters, sex, tuberculosis, and socioeconomic status (Gutrie & Jacobs, 1976).

Assigning to a nurse of same sex and cultural background has to be considered when providing service in the community. There is evidence that staff and client having similar cultural beliefs and practices tend to readily identify with one another. This enhances the initial work phase of a nurse-client relationship.

Furthermore, there is less anxiety. Sharing similar culture can also support feelings of mutual concern for one another (Leininger, 1978).

A practitioner of similar gender and cultural background may encourage more Filipinos to take advantage of the preventive health screenings services (Miranda, McBride, & Spangler, 1998). Regarding sensitive topics, it is essential that the nurse establish a rapport with the client prior to the discussion. The nurse needs to assess their readiness and to determine if they are receptive to discuss the issues. Because of the family centeredness of the Filipino Americans, often talking about their children and their achievements prove beneficial in alleviating their discomfort (Orque, 1983). While Anglo-American culture emphasizes an action-oriented approach, the Filipino American culture values establishing socio-interpersonal relationships prior to any intervention. Filipino Americans respond to social amenities prior to any intervention (Leininger, 1994).

Hiya

Hiya denotes shame on any action perceived to bring dishonor to the family. Filipinos will try to conceal conditions they feel bring disgrace to its members. Ailments such as AIDS, or any sexually transmitted disease, or tuberculosis are kept secret. Pregnancy out of wedlock may be hidden from friends within the community. They are found to be reticent to share information with outsiders (Wilson & Billiones, 1994).

The nurse may encounter difficulty obtaining complete information if discussions of these topics are guarded. Interventions may not be sought appropriately if conditions are sheltered from people without any filial relationship.

Amor propio

Amor propio refers to self-esteem, sense of personal dignity, self-respect, honor, and pride of one's accomplishment. Filipino Americans are very sensitive to criticism. To preserve one's *amor propio*, Filipinos avoid confrontation, criticism, or depreciating oneself or others. Others may show protective behaviors to preserve self-esteem or engage in smooth or deferential interpersonal relationships. A Filipino who is *amor propio* is wounded and will preserve his or her dignity in silence or aloofness (de Gracia, 1979), or one will react to the nurse's action in an extremely agreeable manner.

Scholars vary in their interpretation on the root of this defensive behavior. One claimed that a Filipino has a frail sense of worth as a person. Another attributed it to an inferiority complex instilled by the Caucasian colonist. Others contended that it due to overprotective upbringing within the family (Miranda, 1992).

Pakikisama

Another dominant trait characteristic of Filipinos is *pakikisama,* which means getting along and maintaining smooth and harmonious relationships with others. Filipino Americans may not approve of the health management system developed by the nurse, yet they may be hesitant to confront the nurse in order not to ruin the relationship. If the treatment is in conflict of what they believe to be valuable, they will revert to their traditional practices. Some may utilize their indigenous treatment simultaneously with the Western modern medicine, especially if it works (McKenzie & Chrisman, 1977). While Anglo-Americans value assertiveness and direct confrontation, Filipinos avoid open conflict and disagreement (Spangler, 1991).

DIETARY PRACTICES

As the Filipinos settled in the United States, some have blended their traditional dietary patterns and adopted the American culture. First-generation Filipinos usually adhere more closely to their ethnic food habits than the subsequent generations. Others follow their practices only on holidays and at family gatherings. Chinese influence pervades in food preparation as in use of soy sauce. Filipinos are fond of *patis*, which is an extract from fish and shrimp; soy sauce; and *bagoong*, a salted shrimp.

The traditional dishes for Filipinos include *adobo, lumpia, pancit, dinuguan,* and *lechon. Adobo* is both a dish similar to a stew and a style of cooking. It involves chicken or pork simmered in soy sauce, white vinegar, garlic, and peppercorns. *Lumpia* is a deep-fried egg roll. *Pancit* is rice or wheat noodles sautéed with vegetables, chicken, shrimps, or pork in a soy sauce. *Dunuguan* is made of entrails, guts, or other inside organs with pork blood, seasoning, and spices; and *lechon*, which is a roasted pork served with sauce (de Gracia, 1979; Alejandro, 1982).

Health care providers need a baseline understanding of the dietary practices of the Filipino Americans. Clients identified as having health risk factors need nutritional teaching and dietary modification as the primary initial approach.

PREVALENCE OF DISEASES AND HEALTH CONSIDERATIONS

Hypertension

There were various studies conducted showing a prevalence of hypertension among Filipino Americans (Stavig, Igra, & Leonard, 1988; Klatsky & Armstrong, 1991). The findings of Requino (1981) revealed incidence of hypertension ranking second to African Americans.

Drawing from these studies, efforts need to be directed toward controlling cardiovascular risk factors. Modifying health behaviors, an increase in the appropriate use of preventive services and dietary management are important.

Traditional high-sodium diets with foods such as soy sauce, *patis*, and *bagoong* should be used in moderation or products with lower sodium content provided. Clients on restricted sodium need advice on how to prepare *adobo* by marinating the meat overnight in mixture of lemon juice, onions, garlic, sugar, and crushed peppercorns (Orque, Block, & Monroy, 1983, p. 434).

Diabetes mellitus

The study conducted by Sloan (1963) showed that the incidence of diabetes mellitus is three times higher in the Filipino population than in the Caucasian population. Prevention must be emphasized and those identified as at risk need to use the health screening services. For those afflicted with the disease, teaching on proper physical activity, diet, and medication is vital. The nurse needs to inform clients of the existing community resources. Through adequate education Filipino Americans who may be feeling loss of external control (*bahala na*) may gain self-efficiency in managing the condition rather than feeling controlled by it.

AIDS

Research by Woo, Rutherford, Payne, and Lemp (1988) in San Francisco indicates an increased incidence of AIDS among Asians and Pacific Islanders. The degree of occurrence of AIDS among Filipinos was reported to be 92 per 100,000. This statistic indicates the importance of addressing sex education among Filipino Americans. Traditional families are uncomfortable discussing this topic which may contribute to their children's lack of education of safe sexual practices.

Genetic variations

Some Filipinos experience distention, cramps, flatus, or diarrhea after ingesting milk. Motusky et al. (1964) found that there is high prevalence of glucose-6 Phosphate Dehydrogenase (G-6 PD) deficiency among Filipinos. The deficiency of this digestive enzyme, lactase, can lead to calcium deficiency. Filipinos are encouraged to avoid foods high in lactose and substitute with yogurt, milk with acidophilus added, or milk treated with Lactaid. Intake of calcium from sources such as green leafy vegetables, canned sardines, salmon with bones, and calcium-fortified milk is important (Dudek, 1997, p. 529).

NURSING CONSIDERATIONS

Since elders are revered in the Philippines, they expect caring, compassion, respect, and gentleness. Elders are sensitive to the tone of voice and find it offensive to have younger persons answering back. In the Tagalog speaking regions, to convey respect "Ho and Po" are used when addressing them (Orque, 1983). "Ho and Po" are designations which are the English equivalent of "madam or sir" (Gutrie & Jacobs, 1976).

When providing health teaching in a group setting, the nurse has to realize that Filipino Americans may be hesitant to ask questions for fear of losing one's face. They can benefit from one-to-one teaching, with the use of audiovisual aids and written materials.

When visual aids are used to augment teaching, attention should be given to selecting those with appropriate cultural meanings (Angrosino, 1987). Filipino Americans may have difficulty articulating themselves verbally but they comprehend materials in English since in the Philippine schools instructions are conducted in English. The nurse should assess their comprehension by return demonstration rather than by verbal feedback. A hesitant yes could be a no to avoid a direct blunt no (de Gracia, 1979).

The nurse must assess use of folk medicine. If the client is taking antihypertensive medication and utilizing ginseng as a tonic, untoward conditions can occur. Without informing the health care provider, the client can develop an adverse reaction from its combined diuretic effect. Use of beneficial alternative treatments should be considered and incorporated into the development of care as desired by the client.

REFERENCES

Alejandro, R. (1982). *The Philippine cookbook.* New York: Putnam Publishing Book Co.

Angrosino, M. V. (1987). *A health practitioner's guide to the social and behavioral sciences.* Dover, MA: Auburn House Publishing.

Branch, M. F. & Paxton, P. P. (Eds.). (1976). *Providing safe nursing care for ethnic people of color.* Englewood Cliffs, NJ: Prentice Hall.

Carringer, B. (1977). Caring for the institutionalized Filipino. *Journal of Gerontological Nursing, 3,* pp. 33–37.

Cimmarusti, R. (1996). Exploring aspects of Filipino American families. *Journal of Marital and Family Therapy, 2*(22), pp. 205–217.

Clark, M. J. (1996). *Cultural influence on community health nursing in the community.* (2nd ed). Stamford, Connecticut: Appleton & Lange.

de Gracia, R. (1979, August). Cultural influence on Filipino patients. *American Journal of Nursing,* pp. 1,412–1,414.

de la Costa, H. (1965). *Readings in Philippine History.* Manila: Bookmark.

Dudek, S. (1997). *Nutrition handbook for nursing practice.* (3rd ed.). Lippincott: New York.

Ennis, T. & Inaba, M. (1977). *Philippines: In the volume library.* Nashville, TN: Southwestern company.

Galanti, G. (1991). Caring for patients from different cultures: Case studies from American hospitals. Philadelphia: University of Pennsylvania Press.

Giger, J. N. & Davidhizar, R. E. (1995). *Transcultural nursing assessment and intervention.* (2nd ed.). St. Louis: C. V. Mosby Inc.

Gutrie, G. & Jacobs, P. (1976). *Childbearing and personality development in the Philippines.* University Park: Pennsylvania State University Press.

Hart, D. V. (1966). The Filipino villager and his spirits. *Solidarity, 1,* 66.

Klatsky, A. & Armstrong. (1991, November). Cardiovascular risk factors among Asian Americans living in northern California. *American Journal of Public Health, 81*(11), 1,423–1,427.

Landa-Jocano, F. L. (1966) Rethinking "smooth interpersonal relations." *Philippine Sociological Review, 14*(4), 282–291.

Leininger, M. (Ed.) (1978). *Transcultural nursing: Concepts, theories & practices.* New York: Mc Graw-Hill, Inc.

Leininger, M. (Ed.) (1991). *Culture care diversity & universality: A theory of nursing.* New York: NLN Press.

Leininger, M. (Ed.) (1995). *Transcultural nursing: Concepts, theories & practice.* (2nd ed.). New York: Mc Graw-Hill, Inc.

McKenzie, J. & Chrisman, N. (1977). Healing herbs, gods and magic. *Nursing Outlook, 25,* 326–328.

Miranda, D. (1993). Buting pinos. (Probe essays on values of Filipinos). Philippines: Logos Publications.

Miranda, B., McBride, M. & Spangler, Z. (1998). Filipino Americans. In *Transcultural health care.* Philadelphia: Davis & Co.

Motusky, A. et al. (1964). Glucose 6-phosphate dehydrogenase (G-6-PD) deficiency, thalassemia, and abnormal hemoglobins in the Philippines. *Journal of Medical Genetics, 1,* 102–106.

Orque, M. S. (1983). Nursing Care of Filipino American Patients, in *Ethnic Nursing Care: A multicultural approach.* New York: C. V. Mosby Inc.

Orque, M. S., Block, B. & Monroy, L. S. (1983). *Ethnic nursing care: A multicultural approach.* St. Louis: C. V. Mosby Inc.

Pido, A. J. (1986). *The Pilipinos in America: Macro-micro dimension of immigration and integration.* Staten Island, NY: Center for Migration Studies.

Shake, K. & Redman, R. (1997). Nursing science in the global community. *Image: Journal of Nursing Scholarship, 29,* 11–15.

Sloan, N. (1963). Ethnic distribution of diabetes mellitus in Hawaii. *Journal of the American Medical Association, 183,* 419–424.

Spangler, Z. (1991). Culture care of Philippine and Anglo-American nurses in a hospital context. In M. M. Leininger (Ed.), *Culture care diversity & universality: A theory of nursing.* New York: NLN Press.

Specter, R. E. (1996). *Cultural diversity in health and illness.* (4th ed.). Norwalk, CT: Appleton & Lange.

Stavig, G. R., Igra, A. & Leonard, A. R. (1988). Hypertension and related health issues among Asians and Pacific Islanders in California. *Public Health Reports, 03*(1), 28–37.

Tripp-Reimer, T. (1989). Cross-cultural perspective on patient teaching, *North Clinic of North America, 24*(3), 613.

U.S. Bureau of Census, Statistical Abstract of the United States: 1996 (116th ed.): Washington, DC.

Vance, A. R. Filipino Americans. (1995). In J. N. Giger & R. E. Davidhizar (Eds.), *Transcultural nursing. Assessment and intervention.* (2nd ed.) (pp. 417–438). New York: C. V. Mosby Inc.

Wilson, S. & Billiones, H. (1994, August). The Filipino elder: Implications for nursing practice. *Journal of Gerontological Nursing, 20*(8): 31–36.

Woo, J. M., Rutherford, G. W., Payne, S. F., Barnhart, J. L. & Lemp, G. F. (1988). The epidemiology of AIDS in Asian and Pacific Islander populations in San Francisco. *AIDS, 2*(6), 473–475.

Chapter 21

Hispanic Client Satisfaction with Home Health Care: A Study of Cultural Context of Care

DULA F. PACQUIAO, LUDOVINA ARCHEVAL, AND ELLEN E. SHELLEY

It is predicted that the percentage of ethnic and racial minority composition of the total population in the United States will increase from the current 26 percent to 38 percent by 2025. Approximately 23.7 percent of the population 65 years and older will consist of minorities in the year 2025 (U.S. Bureau of Census, 1995). This demographic trend is accompanied by the shift in health care delivery from acute care settings toward community-based ambulatory care. In fact, the seminal document, Healthy People 2000 (U.S. DHHS, 1992) emphasizes primary prevention and health promotion in the community with a goal toward cutting disparities in health outcomes between population groups. The combined demographic and health care delivery changes require different knowledge and abilities from health care practitioners of the future. An area needing scrutiny is the development of culturally competent health care givers who will be able to manage not only an increasingly diverse workforce but also a highly diverse clientele.

As the setting for health care moves into the community and the home, practitioners need to understand the pivotal role of clients, their families, and groups in defining quality care. Achievement of health outcomes in a timely and cost-effective manner hinges upon the provision of collaborative and client-centered care. Central to providing outpatient or home-based services are health care consumers whose expectations, preferences, and lifeways define satisfactory and effective health care. The impact of context of care as defined by consumers' own values, beliefs, and practices need to be discovered in order to provide care that is meaningful and achieves lasting positive influence in their lives.

BACKGROUND OF THE CLASS PROJECT

The study originated as a research project for graduate students at an MSN program who set out to look into home health care. The two-pronged study was undertaken as a class project for two consecutive research courses. Students selected a general topic to study for their project based upon their understanding of future trends in health care delivery. This was followed by the first phase which was a review of literature and development of a research study proposal. The review of the literature revealed very minimal documentation of the *emic* worldviews of consumers regarding satisfaction with health care. Most studies employed tools derived from *etic* descriptions of satisfaction with health care by health practitioners. Based on these findings, the second phase began with the selection of a qualitative method to obtain the clients' own descriptions and evaluations of the care they receive at home. The concept of satisfaction as used in this study is a highly personal, subjective, and contextual experience. As the literature has suggested, patient satisfaction is an "outcome from the patient's point of view" (Reeder & Chen, 1990, p. 171).

Hence, designing effective health care services responsive to the needs of a growing home care population must be informed by insights into clients' needs, wants, and preferences about the care they receive. Any tool measuring clients' satisfaction must be drawn from their perspectives. Thus, this study was aimed at generating qualitative descriptions of satisfaction with home health care by those who experienced such care first hand. Specifically, the study aimed to identify descriptors of satisfactory health care at home by clients.

REVIEW OF LITERATURE

A client satisfaction survey in home care drawn from health professionals was designed by Reeder and Chen (1990). This same instrument was used by Laferriere (1993) to identify domains of client satisfaction. In another study, Forbes and Brown (1995) developed a questionnaire to evaluate effectiveness of nursing care provided in an outpatient surgery center. Surveys were developed based on the domains of caring as continuity of care, competency of nurses, and education of patients and family members with input from nurses, not from the clients.

Dansky, Brannon, and Wangness (1994) designed a questionnaire to ascertain the influence of organizational factors on quality care as measured by patient satisfaction. The surveys were mailed to patients upon discharge by the home health agencies. The questionnaire elicited responses from clients using predetermined categories.

None of the studies cited used interviewing clients in their homes. The *etic* perspectives of the health care providers were used to develop the surveys which were then mailed or distributed to clients.

Studies by Williams and Associates (1990) and by Hays (1992) defined the needs of home care clients based upon data that were collected from nurses' notes. Very little was noted about what the clients receiving home care perceived as important or what their expectations of home care were.

These studies attempted to measure client satisfaction, yet their design excluded generation of their authentic input. An important gap in the literature was the lack of data about how clients themselves define or describe their own experiences with health care and how they attribute meanings to their experiences.

STUDY SIGNIFICANCE

The significance of the study lies in its discovery of indexes of satisfactory care as defined by clients and their families. In particular, the study examined clients' perceptions of their experiences and how they interpret meanings of these experiences. Obtaining this data is a prelude to gaining understanding of their expectations which serve as a basis for future research on client-focused care and in designing models of care delivery at home.

The study serves as a guided student experience in discovering the nature of *emic* worldview and of culture as a variable in client satisfaction. As participant-observers, students gain immersion in the naturalistic and holistic context of culture in shaping clients' perceptions and attributions of health care.

METHODOLOGY

A qualitative method has been chosen to seek the clients' *emic* perspective of satisfactory home health care. Qualitative methodology generates holistic and contextual nature of their experiences, which is necessary to capture the authentic meanings of events. Interviewing clients at home preserves the integrity of the events within the natural setting. Interviews are used to generate thick descriptions and promote saturation of relevant phenomena.

An interview guide was used to gather informants' *emic* perspectives consisting of open-ended, focused, and contrast questions (Spradley, 1979). Questions covered informants' demographic data, experience with hospital and home health care, perceived meaning/impact of illness, satisfaction with care, and perceived ongoing needs.

Participants' role in this study was that of informant. They were the storytellers whose experiences and interpretations of meanings provided the data for this study. The researchers' role was to facilitate unfolding of their unabridged stories about their experiences.

Thick descriptions were gathered using tape recorders and journals. Data were then transcribed verbatim to capture the informants' own descriptions of events. Informants were encouraged to describe experiences with professional and nonprofessional caregivers in both hospital and home settings. This attempted to obtain insight into the contextual variables that may have influenced their experiences. Other family members, significant others and caregivers present at home were also interviewed. This protocol allowed for triangulation of data from various sources using descriptions in various contexts. Triangulation helped insure reliability and validity of data.

Transcribed data were analyzed for recurrent patterns from which themes were drawn. Themes were categorized according to similarities and differences. From these categories, more inductive generalizations into theoretical concepts were drawn. Theoretical frameworks were then examined for relevance to the themes that emerged.

A small convenience sample was used. Informants were selected through professional contacts at local hospitals and Visiting Nursing Agencies as well as those known to the researchers. Thirteen informants were obtained by professional contacts, and five were obtained through individual researcher's contacts.

Informants were interviewed from one to three times, with each interview lasting from one to three hours. Informants ranged between 29 to 87 years of age. They were residents of Queens County, New York, several counties in New Jersey (Essex, Bergen, Hudson, Monmouth, Union, and Middlesex counties), and Baltimore, Maryland.

FINDINGS

Informants described situations at their homes that typified those when they felt *most comfortable, satisfied, and positive with the caregiving*. Their narratives unfolded indexes of their definitions of home care that gave them feelings of satisfaction. Thematic analysis revealed salient commonalities in their conceptualizations of home care that approximated the quality of their expectations.

Theme 1. Care is given with respect for lifeways and is consistent with personal and cultural values. Eighty-year-old Peruvian emigre, Carmen

Marbella, receives home care services following hospitalization for gastroenteritis. She describes how home care enables *her daughter to be an active participant in her care*. She is comforted by the fact that her daughter keeps her valued tradition of caring for family members. She took care of her husband until he died and thinks that caring for family members is done *out of love and a sense of duty*. Without the assistance of her homemaker, she believes that she would have ended up in a nursing home since her daughter has to go to work twelve hours every day.

Despite the daily assistance given by her homemaker, her daughter is the only one who helps her with her bath and prepares her meals every morning before she leaves for work. The value of modesty among Hispanic women is exhibited by Carmen's preference for her daughter to provide for her personal hygiene care. Her daughter appears to accept this obligation matter-of-factly as part of her daily routine, unworthy of alternative planning to suit her work schedule. As has been documented in the literature, group-orientation among Hispanics is manifested in how Carmen and her daughter have repatterned their daily activities based on mutual interdependence rather than individualized priorities. The homemaker in this case is utilized to reinforce their core values within their situated context. Carmen's situation depicts the value of familism found among Hispanics wherein family members serve as primary caregivers. Caring is expressed primarily as actions provided by others rather than by oneself (Villaruel & Leininger, 1995). The family plays a significant role in all aspects of the ill members' life including rejection or acceptance of healthy life change among Hispanics (Andrews & Boyle, 1995).

Reliance on family members for care needs is observed with Jose Ramirez, a 65-year-old Mexican male who had a knee replacement. He depends on his wife and sisters-in-law to assist him with activities such as shopping, laundry, and cleaning. The nurse has offered to get Juan help, but he and his wife refused stating that, *"they could manage with help from the family."* Distinctly different roles between men and women and orientation toward extended family systems have been found as a common theme among Hispanic groups (Andrews & Boyle, 1995). In Jose's situation, family is inclusive of extended kin outside of consanguinal relations. Extended family ties including fictive kinship are common among group-centered cultures such as the Hispanics.

Carmen's homemaker allows her private time every morning. She states, *"I pray to God every day that I may live to be 105 years old."* Magico-religious beliefs and practices are documented to be indigenous to Hispanic groups. Health is generally regarded as a gift from God and conversely, illness as punishment for wrongdoing (Spector, 1996).

Joan Smith, a 65-year-old white female with chronic obstructive pulmonary disease was hospitalized for pneumonia. She also discusses how it is important for her to be able to pray whenever she gets depressed. She believes that having faith in God is important for her health and well-being. *"I keep the rosary beads in my pocket and whenever I feel the need, I pull them out and use them."*

It is evident that the home environment allows for holistic assessment of informants since many artifacts and natural activities are observed at home which define their unique personality. In their own natural habitat, their life-ways are unraveled. Authentic value premises are allowed expression like the rituals of praying when ill. Such rituals are prevented from being openly prac-ticed in a contrived setting such as the hospital where patients have to abide by the norms of the unfamiliar environment.

Another informant, Martin Hill, a 76-year-old white male who had home care following quadruple bypass surgery described the nurse's respectful atti-tude toward his lifestyle. He stated, *"I continued to smoke and the nurse knew it. She would take my blood pressure and asked if I was still smoking, and if the blood pressure was elevated, she would let me know, but not in a derogatory way."*

In fact, Leininger (1991) has identified three sequential phases for nursing actions and decisions, namely, cultural preservation, accommodation, and restructuring. The nurse in this case knows that Martin, at his age, may not be able to stop smoking altogether. She is aware that he knows the relationship between smoking and his condition and the consequences from continued smoking. She works around his chosen lifestyle, pointing out some cues for possible negotiation with his lifeway. She understands that restructuring is a negotiated stance which hinges upon Martin's own choice for a changed life-style. Restructuring according to Leininger is a last resort requiring value change, time, and effort. The nurse herself had to undergo repatterning of her professional decision making, not to impose a new value, which is considered highly beneficial for Martin, but to negotiate a change while respecting his learned lifeway.

Clearly, the home environment sets the tone for cultural preservation and negotiation before restructuring. As pointed out previously, the home is the context by which nursing care is given. The patient is in his own territory and within his turf, he defines the norms and rules of caregiving. Territoriality has been linked with humans and animals alike (Hall, 1973). Territoriality enables informants to influence the context of the care being provided by professionals.

Theme 2. Care is congruent with perceived needs and attentive to the unique needs of the individual. Lucien Warnewski discussed how his nurse was able to keep him informed about the progress of his surgical wound. Although he was able to care for himself after his discharge from the hospital, visits from one particular nurse were most appreciated. Although all the other nurses provided competent wound care, he felt most satisfied and assured by that one particular nurse who kept him informed of the progress of his wound. He stated, *"She looks at it and explains to me what's going on."*

John Apple described how the nurse's visits after his son died in the hospi-tal meant so much to him and his wife. He related how she sat with them and *"listened to our sadness. She was there when we most needed someone to talk to. She was kind and understanding."*

These two informants defined caring according to their perceived needs, which may be independent of or integral to the treatment regime. Their satis-faction with the caregiver and the care they received was premised upon their own *emic* interpretation of what is meaningful to them. The value of any therapeutic regime is embedded in the situated context of their lives.

Harry Sills, who has Lou Gehrig's Disease, appreciates the individualized attention he receives. *"My nurse knows special things about my condition which makes me more comfortable. My respiratory therapist knows exactly how to change my tracheostomy and I don't bleed when he does it."* Harry communicates via a computer through a breathing straw. Before being severely incapacitated, he led an active life and was a sports enthusiast. He looks forward to his nurse's visit because of her own interest in sports and her computer skills.

Another informant, Leslie Worth, stated that the lab technician *"was very accommodating in switching his schedule to come and draw blood in the late morning, as there would be no one at home to let him in until the homemaker arrived. The nurse monitored my blood pressure and would call the doctor as needed."*

Both Harry and Leslie underscore the importance of valuing differences and uniqueness of informants by caregivers. This process promotes mutual and symbiotic relationships between them. As caregivers value their individuality, they in turn value their care. Both informants and caregivers act as partners in achieving mutually satisfying outcomes. Informants embellish the essence of their satisfaction with home care not in the treatment regimes per se but in the manner by which the caregivers accommodate their functional abilities, schedule/routine, and preferences.

David Mitchell stated that his wife is disabled, and if it was not for the home care services he received, he would not have been able to come home immediately after discharge. He noted that having his family around and being in his own surroundings assisted in his recuperation. Home care in this respect enabled and facilitated David's ability to continue his significant role in his family early in his recovery phase. His perceived needs were intertwined with his wife's needs at home. Hence, his definition of satisfactory home care was one that supported his ability toward early resumption of his caring responsibilities at home.

Informants define the context for satisfactory home care. The meanings attached to their satisfaction tend to be highly integrated in their own value orientations, situational context, and phenomenological, *emic* worldview. Their home as the natural setting for caregiving enables care providers to appreciate varied parameters of knowing them as unique cultural beings whose value premises shape the meanings they attribute to their experiences. These intangible values are given life in their home environment through their uninhibited interactions supported by sensitive and facilitative caregiving.

It is evident that their satisfaction is enhanced by the extent to which their lifeway and personal identities are integrated in the treatment regimens. Central to the therapeutic effectiveness of any care regimen are informants' perceptions or attributed meanings to these measures within the framework of their existence. Satisfaction with care is associated with the nature of caring itself, one that promotes a sense of safeness (*sic*), security, and feelings of mutuality (Larson & Dodd, 1991).

Theme 3. Care promotes trust because it is responsive, competent, and consistent. Informants identified having a sense of trust in the caregiver as the care given was validated by responsiveness to their perceived needs, congruence with their expectations, and consistent with the outcomes they experienced. One informant stated, *"My wife's homemaker was trustworthy. I was comfortable in leaving my house at any time while she was there."*

David Mitchell stated, *"The nurses showed me exactly what would transpire, and whatever they said was going to happen, happened. My nurse took the time to explain things, and anything I would ask for or if I needed an explanation, she was right there with me."* Trust in this case enabled David to have a sense of control of the unknown and the ability to predict the future.

Several informants verbalized that receiving information on how their condition was progressing from the nurses and therapists was comforting as these accurately affirmed the changes they experienced. Laurel Pickett stated, *"The physical therapist would tell me how well I was progressing."* Peter O'Brien also stated that he received progress reports from the nurses as they did his wound care. *"The nurse would inform me as to how my wound was healing."*

Caregiving may be conceptualized as an interpersonal process involving interactions, relationships, and transactions between caregivers and clients. Healthy interpersonal relationships foster conditions that lead to a climate of trust. This means that each individual must examine his/her self in relation to others. Mitchell (1973) has noted that there is growing evidence that the quality of interpersonal contacts has an influence on the person's becoming ill, coping with illness, and becoming well.

The examples provided by Laurel and Peter illustrate how the effect of caregivers' encouragement of informants moved from mere reinforcement to trust as further validation is achieved by consistent observations from other caregivers and affirmed by informants' own feelings of progress. Hence, trust is facilitated by cumulative evidence of congruence between caregiver behaviors and informants' perceptions and experiences.

Watson speaks of human caring *"as originating in an attitude which must become something more, a will, an intention, a commitment, and a conscious judgment that manifests itself in concrete acts"* (Sherwood, 1991, p. 85). As demonstrated by the foregoing vignettes, human caring is in the eyes of the informant rather than the caregiver. The prerequisite of human caring is for caregivers to accept the premise as has been asserted by Leininger that informants are cultural beings whose orientations provide the context for the potential outcomes of the interactions that transpire between them and their caregivers. Hence, the effect of caregiving on informants is ultimately judged by their situated context and orientations.

Theme 4. Care transforms intangible qualities into concrete acts that make a difference in informants' life. Robert Holt discussed how he tried to obtain an electric wheelchair for his wife. *"It took eleven months, but we finally got it. The nurse and physical therapist pushed and persisted until we finally got it.*

Whatever we asked for, the nurse was right there calling the doctor to make sure it was taken care of." Jean Snyder stated, *"They would do more than was required of them."* She recalled how the homemaker even shoveled the front of the house after a snow storm.

Robert and Jean describe the essence of caring which originates from an attitude, commitment, and intention that are translated into concrete actions (Larson & Dodd, 1991; Sherwood, 1991). Here the tacit values of caring are made tangible by the concrete actions or outcomes derived from a process of mutuality and of becoming.

Jean Snyder also described how the homemaker would recognize if she was feeling down. *"She would say to me . . . Hey, what are you doing, and I would say, just thinking. She would then make me a cup of tea, talk to me, and try to lift my spirits."*

Another informant receiving physical therapy and homemaker services discussed how the physical therapist also encouraged his wife to get dressed up and put make up and jewelry on every day. *"It made her feel good. Having the homemaker around was good for her. She would do nice things for both of us, talked, made us laugh, or just made us a cup of tea."*

Watson (1979) has proposed that the practice of caring goes beyond the performance of actions for clients but rather involves the nurse as an interactive agent in a rather total way. According to this perspective the presence of the nurse is the central focus of nursing actions. Presence in this case is not merely being there but to use oneself in a creative way to achieve results.

In both of the last two situations, the homemaker uses the ritual of social gathering over a cup of tea. Her presence is accentuated by the atmosphere associated with a cup of tea. The ritual is associated with talking and socialization, which is distinct from having tea with meals. The effectiveness of the ritual however is enhanced by her caring presence and by the meaning of the ritual to the informants.

The home environment provides opportunities for caregivers to appreciate their clients as cultural beings. Symbols and rituals are made evident, which can then be used by an observant caregiver as creative ways to enhance their presence. Creative caregiving and presencing are made effective when they are congruent with informants' attributions and lifeways. The home environment enhances the role of the caregiver into that of the participant-observer within the world of meanings of the client. It is an ideal setting for transforming caregiving actions into caring that is meaningful to clients.

CONCLUSION

Leininger (1995) sees care as the essence of nursing and a distinct, dominant, central, and unifying focus. She defines caring as actions and activities directed toward assisting, supporting, or enabling another individual or group with evident or anticipated needs to ameliorate or improve a human condition or lifeway or to face death (p. 105). Informants in this study affirmed the same attributes of caregiving that they considered as satisfying. Like the author, informants described caring behaviors as those that provide comfort, compassion, concern, empathy, trust, presence, interest, and involvement.

Culture Care Theory (Leininger, 1991) stipulates that caring is a universal concept with culturally defined expressions. Leininger states that while caring is a universal phenomenon that is essential to human growth and development, caring behaviors vary transculturally according to cultural expression, priorities, and needs satisfaction. As demonstrated in this study, informants described universal parameters of satisfying home care. Expressions or manifestations of these parameters, however, were contextually defined. For example, individualized care was translated in many ways, each time fitting the cultural knowledge, values, and beliefs of the individual which were contextually differentiated by their situations. Hence, discovery of informants' *emic* descriptions of satisfactory care at home allowed for interweaving of the many variables embedded in their cultural definitions of caring. By listening to their stories, we gained understanding of the authentic meanings of caring. Meanings of caring were within the informants and not with the caregiver. Congruence was made possible by knowing their *emic* worldviews about caring—highly personal, subjective, and culturally defined phenomenon.

The goal of home care is to support clients in their recuperative process and assist them to resume their previous lifeways or facilitate their transition toward a familiar, stable existence. Informants in this study felt most comfortable in their own homes where they have control of their lives, live within the comfort and security of their loved ones, and resume continuities in their lives. The essence of home care is that it has allowed for culture to play a significant role in the health experiences of informants. It is the context where valued lifeways had a chance to thrive and flourish. Illnesses are discontinuities in one's secure lifeway, and caring, to be meaningful and satisfying, must be instructed by the cultural values, beliefs, and practices that provide direction and explanations to one's existence. Home care minimizes turbulent disruptions in one's being by providing a supportive, restorative, and assistive caring environment.

The home provides the context for culturally congruent and competent care to occur. Caregivers can easily transform their roles into that of participant-observer, which preserves the authentic and continued lifeways of people. It is the natural environment conducive to unfolding people's intangible value premises into concrete and observable rituals and symbols that can be incorporated in caregiving regimes. There is of course a place and need for hospitals and institutionalized care. As the context for caregiving, however, becomes more contrived and artificial to the clients, more effort is required to appreciate them as cultural beings and create a fit between their tacit values and concrete acts of caregiving.

RECAPITULATION

During phase two of the study, students realized the critical role of gatekeepers in obtaining informants and gaining entry to their homes. As they reviewed the verbatim transcripts of their interview data, they became aware of differential abilities among them in interviewing informants, the critical influence of repeated contacts with informants, and the need for minimizing the "stranger" effect of their presence in the environment. As the class progressed toward data analysis, students appreciated the value of thick descriptions by informants in the quality of themes that emerged. Several sessions were devoted in inductive analysis of data to detect recurrent patterns. For most students, this was sheer enlightenment since they were mostly trained in the quantitative methodology with predetermined and predictable responses which either verified or refuted their hunches.

As expected, the theoretical concepts selected to support or refute the themes reflected those that they had been previously exposed to or had read about. This stage required much assistance since students did not have the opportunity to look at theoretical formulations following the study except those they came across during their literature review.

The most significant learning from the experience is the appreciation of culture in the context of care, discovering its parameters and realizing that beyond established quality of care criteria lies the subjective and phenomenological conceptualization of satisfactory care which informants themselves define within the context of their lifeways. Students also appreciated the meaning of clients' role as informants and their own role as learners of *emic* worldviews. This was an experience in perspective-taking, encouraged by a natural environment for caring.

Indeed, the study enriched students' appreciation of the nature of culture and the benefits of the home as the setting for health care. The experience refined their ability to be open, and assume the role of a genuine listener and keen observer of the many aspects that influence caring outcomes. Clients' natural habitat, their homes, allowed for their cultural lifeways to be manifested and expressed in ways that made sense to outsiders (students).

LIMITATIONS OF STUDY

The study used a small, convenient sample. Larger samples with longitudinal follow up of informants would strengthen or validate findings of this study. Generalization of findings is limited to the population involved focusing on their home care experience. Although findings of the study gave some comparisons between their experiences in hospital and home care, a more rigorous comparative study of their *emic* perspectives of satisfaction between home and institutionalized care is needed.

REFERENCES

Andrews, M. M. & Boyle, J. S. (1995). *Transcultural concepts in nursing care* (2nd ed.). Philadelphia: J. B. Lippincott.

Dansky, K. H., Brannon, D. & Wangsness, S. (1994). Human resources, management practices and patient satisfaction in home health care. *Home Health Care Services Quarterly, 15* (1), 43–56.

Forbes, M. L. & Brown, H. N. (1995). Developing an instrument for measuring patient satisfaction. *AORN Journal, 61* (4), 737–743.

Hall, E. T. (1973). *The silent language.* New York: Anchor Books.

Hays, B. J. (1992). Nursing care requirements and resource consumption in home health care. *Nursing Research, 41,* 138–143.

Laferriere, R. (1993). Client satisfaction with home health care nursing. *Journal of Community Health Nursing, 10* (2), 67–76.

Larson, P. J. & Dodd, N. J. (1991). The cancer treatment experience: Family patterns of caring. In D. A. Gaut & M. M. Leininger (Eds.), *Caring: the compassionate healer* (pp. 61–78). New York: NLN Press.

Leininger, M. M. (1991). *Culture care diversity & universality: A theory of nursing.* New York: NLN Press.

Leininger, M. M. (1995). *Transcultural nursing: Concepts, theories, research and practices* (2nd ed.). New York: McGraw-Hill.

Mitchell, P. H. (1973). *Concepts basic to nursing.* New York: McGraw-Hill.

Reeder, P. J. & Chen, S. C. (1990). A client satisfaction survey in home health care. *Journal of Nursing Quality Assurance, 5* (1), 16–24.

Sherwood, G. (1991). Expressions of nurses caring.: The role of the compassionate healer. In D. A. Gaut and M. M. Leininger (Eds.), *Caring: The compassionate healer* (pp. 79–88). New York: NLN Press.

Spector, R. E. (1996). *Cultural diversity in health and illness* (4th ed.). Stamford, CT: Appleton-Lange.

Spradley, J. (1979). *Ethnographic interview.* New York: Holt, Reinhart, & Winston U.S. Bureau of Census. (1995). *Statistical abstract of the United States.* Washington DC: Dept. of Commerce.

U.S. Department of Health and Human Services Public Health Service (1992). *Healthy people 2000: National health promotion and disease prevention objectives.* Boston: Jones and Bartlett.

Villaruel, A. & Leininger, M. M. (1995). Culture care of Mexican Americans. In M. M. Leininger, *Transcultural nursing: Concepts, theories, research and practices* (pp. 365–382). New York: McGraw-Hill.

Watson, J. (1979). *Nursing: The philosophy and science of caring.* Boston, MA: Little, Brown.

Williams, B. C., Phillips, E. K., Torner, J. C. & Irvine, A. A. (1990). Predicting utilization of home health resources: Important data from routinely collected information. *Medical Care, 28,* 379–391.

Chapter 22

Rituals, Culture, and Tradition: The Puerto Rican Experience

RUBEN D. FERNANDEZ
AND GEORGE J. HEBERT

> *Buen hijo* (good son), you have people everywhere who,
> because they have more, don't remember those who have very
> little. But in Puerto Rico those around you share *la pobreza* (the
> poverty) with you, because only poor people can understand
> poor people. I like *los Estado Unidos,* but it is sometimes a cold
> place to live—not because of the winter and the landlord not
> giving heat, but because of the snow in the hearts of the people.
>
> Piri Thomas in Down These Mean Streets *(Morales-Carrion,*
> *1983)*

PUERTO RICAN CULTURE AND TRADITION

In examining the Puerto Rican perspective as a microcosm of the Hispanic reality in the United States, we must come to understand who the Puerto Ricans are, their *sentimiento* (sentiments), *valores* (values), and *cultura* (culture). Puerto Rico is a society with a national culture tied historically, ethnically, and linguistically to the Latin American culture, universe, and more specifically, to the area of the Spanish-speaking Caribbean. Puerto Ricans are not only resourceful and energetic but are very proud of a tradition of taking the initiative and achieving goals through self-help efforts. In a wide variety of areas, the Puerto Rican works to achieve equality and fair treatment for his fellow countrymen and himself.

The Puerto Rican people comprise almost 6.2 million people who live primarily, but not exclusively, on the island of Puerto Rico and in the northeastern United States.

Lamberty and Garcia (1994) maintain that "one gets to be a Puerto Rican by various means. You are Puerto Rican if you are born in Puerto Rico, although at the same time you are an American because you were born there. You are a Puerto Rican if your parents are Puerto Rican, even if you have never visited the island, have never eaten *arroz con habichuelas* (rice and beans), and have never spoken a word in Spanish." The identification of this concept of *puertoriqueñismo* is further described according to Lamberty and Garcia when you can be a second- and third-generation Puerto Rican of mixed marriage, be highly acculturated to the American culture, but when asked, you say proudly, "I am a Puerto Rican." You can encounter some Puerto Ricans whose world is bicultural, a world where English and Spanish are easily interchanged, where traditional Thanksgiving turkey is followed by *lechon asado* (roasted pig) at Christmas as the main treat, where salsa and bolero are enjoyed with the same passion as rock and roll or the big band sound. As Lamberty and Garcia concluded, being Puerto Rican is a world where various cultures have merged and the historical forces of slavery—and Spanish and American colonialism have left their indelible mark on the collective psyche.

HISTORY

The Puerto Rican culture is shaped and defined through the historical experience of its people. In order to understand better the Puerto Rican community one must look at the major historical events that shaped their view of the world. Puerto Rico was a colony of the Spanish empire from 1493 until 1898 when it became a territory of the United States. American citizenship was awarded to Puerto Ricans in 1917.

The four centuries of Spanish influence can be seen in Puerto Rican folklore, literature, art, music, dance, rituals of life and death, love, and patriotism. But in addition to the Hispanic influence, the Puerto Rican culture is made up of a rich mixture including indigenous peoples, European whites, and African blacks. This richness has proven to be the basic elements defining the ethnic and spiritual structure of the Puerto Rican people. While English is the official language, Spanish predominates in literature, folklore, and formal governmental communications. The vocabulary of the Taino Indians gives flavor and color to the Spanish language of Puerto Ricans by recalling the prehistory of the Caribbean. Words such as *quimbobo* (okra), *Humacao*, and *Coamo* (cities) reaffirm distant roots and a relationship between Spanish and the vernacular of the first inhabitants of the land.

There is religious freedom in Puerto Rico. Although the Roman Catholic religion predominates, there is significant movement toward joining fundamentalist Christian denominations. Supernatural beliefs tied to Catholicism are present in the practice of espiritismo (spiritualism), Santeria, and curanderismo.

Slavery was abolished in 1873. It has been documented that the fight for the freedom of slaves was a struggle without bloodshed, related in ideology to the quest for independence (Morales-Carrion, 1983). The quest for independence remains a crusade that some believe will fulfill the quest for Puerto Rican identity through their independence as a Caribbean Nation. Elections addressing the issue of independence occur regularly.

TODAY

The current sociopolitical changes have had tremendous impact on the structure, values, and beliefs of the Puerto Rican people. Puerto Ricans have a family-oriented culture. They like to celebrate life with vivid color, joyous song, and food. They also love to experience and sustain intimacy in relationships. The family is the most important social unit. Like other Hispanic cultures, the Puerto Rican family is patriarchal, characterized by a dominant and aggressive male, and a passive, dependent female. Traditionally the family has been the source of all emotional support where its members feel free to share their innermost feelings; receive approval for their decisions, and where *consejos* (advice) is given (Bravo, Canino, Rubio, and Serrano, 1991). Social changes in family values and structure have had tremendous impact on the Puerto Rican household. Vasquez (1989) has identified the Puerto Rican home today as a weak and fragile institution affected by the pressures of contemporary society related to its sociopolitical and economic system. The changes include patterns in membership and lifestyle. In 1940, the Puerto Rican household averaged 5.2 members. In 1980, the Puerto Rican household averaged 3.7 members. The number of children has decreased. The composition of the extended family has also decreased. There is an increase in the divorce rate and a significant number of single mothers. Vasquez has identified this pattern as predominantly an urban phenomenon.

Religion, Folklore, and Medicine

The role of religion and belief in the supernatural are part of the care values of the Puerto Rican belief system. For many years the Catholic church has exerted tremendous influence in shaping cultural mores and societal norms by providing educational opportunities at private Catholic schools. The expression of faith by Puerto Rican Catholics is one that is very personal and intimate instead of institutional in nature. Devotion and confiding relationships with Jesus, the Virgin Mary, and the saints are basic to their everyday life with shrines at the entrance of their homes and in the yards. Crucifixes and pictures or statues of saints are decorative elements inside the home. When someone is ill, small pictures of saints called *estampas* (images of saints in relief) are placed under the pillow or at the sick person's bedside. Puerto Ricans tend to make *promesas* or promises of a religious nature in response to illness, stressful situations, and social problems. These *promesas* can be anything from a special prayer, a Mass, a novena, and a pilgrimage to a church or sacred place, to wearing a *habito* or habit/special clothes in honor of a saint that has granted a favor. *Promesas* are used as a bargaining tool for the health of a loved one.

Sources of informal support can come from indigenous traditions of care, including herbs, spiritualism, santeros, and curanderos. These informal social support sources are often more important to Puerto Ricans than traditional medicine.

Santeria is a 300-year-old African-Cuban religious system that combines Roman Catholic elements with ancient Yaruba tribal beliefs and practices. Santeria originated among the Yaruba people of Nigeria who brought their beliefs with them when they arrived to the New World as slaves. As a condition of entry into the West Indies, slaves were required to be baptized as Roman Catholics. In the process of adaptation to their new non-African environment, the slaves altered their beliefs to incorporate those of their predominantly Catholic masters. Thus, Santeria became a product of syncretism between the gods of the slaves and the Catholic saints of their masters (Purnell & Paulanka, 1998). Followers of Santeria believe in the magical and medicinal properties of flowers, herbs, weeds, twigs, and leaves.

Espiritismo or spiritualism is the practice of communication with spiritual forces. Many Puerto Ricans prefer spiritualism as a religion, because while spiritualism is not a total religious system it supplies the need without imposing restrictive obligations on marriage, sex, diversion, or lifestyle. (Steven-Arroyo, 1974). The influence of spiritualism can be seen in individuals carrying protective medals or amulets to keep away evil or as a means to remain healthy and strong.

Curanderismo is a form of folk healing derived from ethnic and historical traditions that have as their goal the amelioration or cure of psychological, spiritual, and physical problems (Lozano, 1995). These health beliefs are based on the notion that healing is an art that includes culturally appropriate methods of treatment delivered by recognized healers in the community who capitalize on a patient's faith and belief system in the treatment process. Lozano states that "curanderismo involves beliefs in natural and supernatural illnesses, a metaphysical connection to the spiritual world, and a view of God's divine will and centrality in all aspects of life." Healing is induced by individuals who have a divine *don* (gift) for healing and who intervene through natural or supernatural means of treatment. Other well-known and respected folk medicine practitioners are *yerberos* (herbalists), *hueseros* and *sobadores* (bone and muscle therapists), and *parteras* (midwives).

Puerto Ricans use traditional medicinal plants in the forms of teas, potions, salves, or poultices. Stores called botanicas sell all varieties of herbs, ointments, oils, powders, incenses, and religious figurines to relieve maladies, bring luck, drive away evil spirits, or break curses. Herbal teas, infusions, and baths may be used to treat common ailments (Purnell & Paulanka, 1998) (Table 22–1). The value of these remedies depends upon who is prescribing them. For example, your grandmother might give you a tea made with *engibre* (ginger) when you are feeling nauseous. She has learned from her mother and grandmother that this is what one takes when they have this problem. The curandero (herbalist) on the other hand frequently has formally or by apprenticeship studied herbs, where to find them, and how they can be used to treat illness. The curandero is often seen as an expert in herbal therapy and his prescriptions carry more status than grandmothers'. However, the santero (spiritualist) is viewed in still a different light. Not only is the santero familiar with herbs and their beneficial powers when treating illness, he is also familiar with their use in treating illness that may have a spiritual foundation or basis, such as *mal de ojo* (evil eye), or if a curse has been wished upon someone else. The spiritual component of illness becomes an important consideration for the santero when developing a treatment plan for any of his clients. Unlike grandmother and the herbalist, the santero will prescribe teas, infusions, baths, or other modalities using herbs to cure illness that is physical in nature, but with a spiritual overlay.

HEALTH ISSUES

Valdez et al. (1993) reports that approximately 35–37 million Americans are uninsured; Hispanics account for approximately 7 million of these uninsured persons. Nationally, more than 7 million Hispanics younger than 65 years are completely uninsured. Children represent nearly two-fifths of all uninsured Hispanics. The best estimates based on the current population survey indicate that 33 percent of Hispanics were uninsured during 1989, compared with 23 percent blacks and 13 percent of whites. In absolute terms, there are more uninsured Hispanics than blacks nationally. In the last ten years, the number of uninsured Hispanics increased by 151 percent, whereas Anglo numbers increased by 32 percent. Many Hispanics, about 20 percent of the insured and

TABLE 22–1
Herbal teas and infusions used to treat common ailments

1. *Cosimiento de Anis* (anise): to relieve stomachache, flatulence, and baby colic
2. *Cosimiento de limon con miel de abeja* (lemon and honey): to relieve cough and respiratory congestion
3. *Cosimiento de calabaza* (pumpkin seed): to treat gastrointestinal worms
4. *Cosimiento de canela* (cinnamon): to relieve cough and menstrual cramps
5. *Cosimiento de manzanilla* (chamomile): to relieve stomachaches
6. *Cosimiento de naranja agria* (sour orange): to relieve respiratory congestion
7. *Cosimiento de savila* (aloe vera): to relieve stomachaches
8. *Cosimiento de yerba buena* (spearmint leaves): to calm the nerves
9. *Chayote* (vegetable): to calm nerves
10. *Sanaoria* (carrots): to help problems with vision
11. *Toronja y ajo* (grapefruit and garlic): to lower blood pressure
12. *Papaya y piña* (papaya and pineapple): to eliminate gastrointestinal parasites
13. *Remolacha* (beets): to treat influenza and anemia
14. *Agua con sal* (salt water): to relieve sore throat
15. *Agua de coco* (coconut water): to relieve kidney problems
16. *Mantequilla* (butter): applied directly on burns to soothe pain
17. *Clara de huevos* (egg whites): applied directly over scalp to promote hair growth
18. *Azabeche* (black stone): placed on infants to protect them from the evil eye
19. *Manito de coral* (coral hand): symbolic of the hand of God protecting a person
20. *Ojos de Santa Lucia* (Eyes of St. Lucy): for prevention of blindness and protection from evil eye

(Purnell & Paulanka, 1998, pp. 208–209)

40 percent of the uninsured, report having no regular source of medical care. Transportation and childcare are serious barriers for Hispanics. Valdez et al. (1993) reported that studies have indicated that 10 percent of Hispanics report lengthy, time-consuming travel to reach a health care facility. Others forego seeking medical care because of household, job, or family responsibilities. He further states in terms of services provided by health care facilities that "Hispanics experience longer periods between appointments, and longer waits in the medical facility than do non-Hispanics."

Hispanics are more likely to have fewer employee benefits (i.e., health benefits) because jobs tend to be in secondary markets like agriculture and manufacturing where salaries are low and working conditions may be harsh, placing workers at risk for occupational disease. They're also less likely to have Medicaid or other, regular sources of medical care available. Therefore, Hispanics are more likely to use emergency rooms/departments of hospitals than preventive health services to meet their primary health care needs (Aguirre-Molina et al., 1993). Experts estimate as few as 50 percent of eligible applicants receive Medicaid coverage (Ashman & Pagnani, 1992). For every ten eligible applicants, four drop out due to enrollment barriers. Ashman and Pagnani identified the barriers as: (1) cumbersome documentation, (2) patient distrust of the welfare system, (3) lack of transportation, (4) the agency employees' lack of incentive to help, (5) patient option to seek emergency room care without insurance, and (6) limited office hours. Furthermore, they documented that for every ten applicants one is erroneously rejected, leaving five to receive Medicaid coverage. Ashman and Pagnani assert that the typical Medicaid sign-up system allows Medicaid-eligible patients to slip through the cracks.

Lack of prenatal care has been cited as a major health care need for Hispanic women. According to the National Center for Health Statistics 13 percent of Hispanic mothers have late or no prenatal care compared to 12 percent of non-Hispanic Black mothers, and 4 percent of non-Hispanic white mothers. Among Puerto Rican mothers, the incidence is as high as 17 percent.

Numerous provider organizations, health service researchers, and advocates have offered recommendations for improving access to care for Hispanics. According to Burciaga-Valdez et al. (1993) these recommendations fall into four main categories: (1) modify governmental and institutional policies, since numerous governmental policies restrict or impede access to care; (2) expand the supply of culturally competent providers to include grants or subsidies in the health professions for the advanced training of Hispanics and others willing to practice in Hispanic communities. Introduce cultural-competency training into professional curricula; (3) restructure incentives to ensure primary care and health services; and (4) enhance services by offering transportation, child care, and weekend and evening services. Promote changes in the institutional culture that reward service to and respect for the client. Burciaga-Valdez, et al. (1993) further postulate considerations for implementation by: (1) developing a strategy targeting states with large Hispanic populations; (2) developing advocacy among national, state, and local officials based on agendas of equity and equal opportunity; and (3) developing national Hispanic images recognizable to the American public.

With Hispanics now the fastest growing minority in the United States, the need to develop culture-specific intervention strategies is of paramount importance. Hispanics have a right to culturally sensitive and competent care that demonstrates an awareness of cultural values, needs, and health care practices and preferences. All institutional services need to be client focused, aimed at meeting the clients' needs. Health promotion and prevention programming materials need to be sensitive to the Hispanic community's health profile and acculturation needs.

Large Hispanic communities exist in practically every major city in the country. In general, Hispanics face financial barriers as well as a barrage of institutional barriers to primary and preventive health care services. Financial barriers may not be easily overcome until federal and state legislation is passed to fund health promotion and prevention strategies aimed at the Hispanic community. There is a dramatic need for personnel to be bilingual and culturally competent. It is worth noting that the need for competent bilingual health care providers will continue to grow as the Hispanic population increases. In March 1996, the Health Resources and Services Administration, Division of Nursing, conducted a National Sample Survey of Registered Nurses and identified that of the 2.5 million registered nurses in the United States only 10% or 246,363 represented minority ethnic groups. An estimated 107,527 (4.2%) were African American; 86,434 (3.4%) were Asian Pacific Islanders with 40,559 (1.6%) Hispanic and 11,843 (0.5%) American Indian/Alaskan Native. In comparison to 1992, Hispanic nurses increased from 1.4% to 1.6%, a negligible increase (Stevens-Arroyo, 1997).

Padilla (1985) cites that for the growing number of Hispanics less desirable occupations have defined and afforded their participation in the institutional life of American society; for these groups, integration has come to mean relegation to economically less productive and increasingly marginal positions in the urban labor force. This form of integration has subjected large portions of the Hispanic population to a distinct configuration of ethnic constraint and social change. He further asserts that Hispanics have been forced to adjust the ways they relate to work, family ties, religion, and in some cases they have had to innovate by creating institutions and cultural symbols that relate to the current circumstances of inequality.

Hispanics are among the largest number of ethnic groups being studied by researchers. Early researchers tended to emphasize cultural differences between Hispanics and whites. Likewise, certain assertions were made about Hispanic subgroups. Hispanics are not a homogeneous group, despite the fact that they share a common language. Hispanics have very different historical and cultural characteristics that are more than the obvious variables of skin pigmentation, country of origin, food preferences, religious beliefs, and folklore. Hispanic ethnicity is then fabricated out of shared cultural and structural similarities and functions. In addition, researchers tended to de-emphasize or ignore other significant variables when studying Hispanics, such as educational, occupational, and economic levels of their subjects. This approach resulted in a long list of cultural characteristics that were then presumed to differentiate Hispanics from whites. Padilla concluded that when research findings did not support the presumed differences, researchers concluded that the results reflected the influence of the acculturation process and then ignored the possibility that the presumed differences may not have existed in the first place.

To conclude, one must reaffirm that the differences that separate and segregate Hispanics from other cultural groups in this society represents a lack of understanding of what it means to be a Latino in American society. It is important to recognize that being Latino is defined within the cultural context of the Latino community, but it is also social and personal and is influenced by one's memberships, affiliations, and extent of acculturation within the non-Hispanic community. Culture represents the symbolic, ritualistic, traditional, and linguistic system within which individual experiences are labeled and acted on. This experience depicts the values and expressions of a people and its linkages between the self and the culture. Puerto Rican culture has wonderful contributions to make to help American culture continue to evolve through sharing its rich heritage, folklore, traditions, rituals, knowledge, and wisdom.

TOMORROW

It is not clear yet what will become the basis of community strength enabling Puerto Ricans to move securely and confidently into full participation in American society. Puerto Ricans must first be able to accept those aspects of their lives which make up this heritage. Abalos (1986) cites the tragedy of the melting pot in that immigrants, at least by the second generation, began to ignore their national and cultural past in their assimilation as Americans.

The Puerto Rican community remains a vital source of strength, hope, and aspiration for its people. As a collective, Puerto Ricans believe that tomorrow things will be better. As a community they have a belief in destiny. This belief provides the incentive to accept failures and disappointments. Puerto Ricans reaffirm their faith in a supreme being that takes care of them and provides for their needs. As a culture, Puerto Ricans continue to enjoy life and love to celebrate religious and civil holidays, weddings, births, *quinceañeras* (girls' social debut at 15 years old), and graduations. They know how to enjoy themselves. They have a keen sense of humor and laugh at the ironies of life. Puerto Ricans are loyal, trustworthy, hard-working people. They take tremendous pride in their accomplishments and the accomplishments and successes of their fellow countrymen. As a group, they have a strong sense of national pride and commitment to maintaining their cultural values and traditions. For them, tradition is grounded in folklore, language, and values transmitted through four hundred years of Spanish rule. Puerto Ricans have a strong commitment to their political ideologies. Politics for Puerto Ricans is a serious business. A national sport, *la politica* (politics), carries with it a strong sense of civic responsibility with a 85–90 percent voter turnout during major elections.

ECONOMICS

Puerto Ricans will continue to be a major force in the economy of the United States. Because of their sheer numbers, this group has developed tremendous political and purchasing power.

By the year 2000, the Hispanic portion of the United States population is expected to increase between 8.6% and 9.6% (Orum, 1986). In March of 1989, the Hispanic population of the United States totaled 20.1 million, and continues to grow rapidly, about five times faster than the rate of non-Hispanics. (Del Pinal and De Navas, 1990). The U.S. Department of Commerce (1990) identified the major Hispanic subgroups in the United States as follows: 62.8% Mexican-Americans, 11.6% Puerto Ricans, 12% Central and South Americans, and 7.8% other Hispanic nationalities. The same report indicated that, as a group, Hispanics are among the poorest people in the United States. In 1988, about one out of every six persons living in poverty in the United States was Hispanic. In addition, Hispanics have a high dropout rate from high school with a resultant low rate of high school completion. Hispanic children comprise over one-third of the Hispanic population of the United States. By the year 2050, it is projected that one in five Americans will be of Hispanic origin (Villarruel, 1996). It is estimated that from 1985 to 2000 there will be 2.4 million more Hispanic children in the United States compared to 66,000 more white non-Hispanic children (De Leon, 1996). The American Academy of Pediatrics has reported that as many as 14 percent of Hispanic children 0–2 years have not been seen by a physician (Secretary's Task Force, 1986; De Leon, 1996). Because of the postulated increasing number of Hispanic youth, it is important that policy makers and health care providers recognize and address the health care problems and barriers to health care confronting this population.

REFERENCES

Abalos, D. T. (1986). *Latinos in the United States*. Notre Dame, Indiana: University of Notre Dame Press.

Aguirre-Molina, M., Ramirez, A. & Ramirez, M. (1993). Health promotion and disease prevention strategies. *Public Health Reports, 108*(5), 559–564.

Ashman, E. & Pagnani, E. (Eds.). (1992). *America's uninsured*. In *Health Care Advisory Board Volume III.* Washington, DC: The Advisory Board Company.

Bravo, M., Canino, G., Rubio-Stipec, M. & Serrano-Garcia, I. (1991). Importancia de la familia como recurso de apoyo social en Puerto Rico. *Puerto Rican Health Science Journal, 10*(3), 149–156.

Burciaga-Valdez, R., Giachello, A., Rodriguez-Trias, H., Gomez, P. & De la Rocha, C. (1993). Improving access to health care in Latino communities. *Public Health Reports, 108*(5), 534–539.

DeLeon, M. L. (1996). Profile of the Hispanic child. In S. Torres (Ed.), *Hispanic voices: Hispanic health educators speak out.* New York: NLN Press, pp. 13–23

Del Pinal, J. & De Navas, C. (1990). *The Hispanic population in the United States:* March 1989 (Series P-20, No. 444). Washington, DC: U.S. Department of Commerce.

Lamberty, G. & Garcia, C. (1994). (Eds.), *Puerto Rican women and children: Issues in health, growth and development.* New York: Plenum Press.

Lozano, S. (1995). Curanderismo: Demystifying the health beliefs and practices of the elderly Mexican Americans. *Health and Social Work, 20*(4), 247–253.

Morales-Carrion, A. (1983). *Puerto Rico: A political and cultural history.* New York: W. W. Norton and Company, Inc.

Orum, L. S. (1986). *The education of Hispanics: Status and implications.* Washington, DC: National Council of La Raza.

Padilla, F. M. (1985). *Latino ethnic consciousness: The case of Mexican Americans and Puerto Ricans in Chicago.* Notre Dame, Indiana: University of Notre Dame Press.

Purnell, L. & Paulanka, B. (1998). *Transcultural health care: A culturally competent approach.* Philadelphia: F. A. Davis Company.

Secretary's Task Force. (1986). *Report of Secretary's Task Force on black and minority health.* Washington, DC: U.S. Department of Health and Human Services.

Stevens-Arroyo, A. M. (1974). *Religion and the Puerto Ricans in New York* (Chapter 14). In E. Mapp (Ed.), *Puerto Rican perspectives.* Metuchen, NJ: The Scarecrow Press Inc. (pp. 119–130). *The Hispanic Nurse.* (1997). 19(2), Second Quarter.

United States Department of Commerce (1990). *The Hispanic population in the United States: March 1989.* Washington, DC: Government Printing Office.

Valdez, R. B., Giachello, A., Rodriguez-Trios, H., Gomez, P. & De la Rocha, C. (1993). Improving access to health care in Latino communities. *Public Health Report, 108*(5).

Vasquez, J. L. (1989). Variantes en la estructura del hogar Puertorriqueño. *Puerto Rican Health Science,* 8(2), 225–230.

Villarruel, A. M. (1996). Health of Hispanic adolescents. In S. Torres (Ed.), *Hispanic voices: Hispanic educators speak out.* New York: NLN Press, pp. 29–48.

Chapter 23

A Challenge to the Puerto Rican Community: An Untold Story of the AIDS Epidemic

GEORGE J. HEBERT
AND RUBEN D. FERNANDEZ

> . . . Small official notices had been just put up about the
> town, though in places where they would not attract much
> attention. It was hard to find in these notices any indication
> that the authorities were facing the situation squarely. The
> measures enjoined were far more Draconian and one had the
> feeling that many concessions had been made to a desire not
> to alarm the public.
>
> *Albert Camus,* The Plague

INTRODUCTION

The ability of individuals within their social and cultural context to recognize problematic behavior, and to change it, is influenced by the community values, perceptions, and options for risk reduction. In the Puerto Rican culture, gender roles, expectations, values, and traditions are important determinants of behavior. The purpose of this chapter is to illustrate those cultural factors that might shed light on high-risk sexual behaviors. Understanding the factors that place a population at risk is necessary if we are going to design effective educational programs aimed at prevention and eradication of the disease.

EL MACHISMO

Even though family is of paramount importance to the Puerto Rican male, a double standard exists in terms of marital commitment. Infidelity among Hispanics, and Puerto Ricans in particular, continues its adherence to the Latino cultural concept of "machismo." Spanish culture tends to accept infidelity as a part of life. A male's infidelity is part and parcel of the Hispanic male/female relationship. Puerto Rican women accept the other women as part of their fate and resign themselves to it just as they saw their mothers do before them.

Wives almost never bring up the issue of infidelity because it is considered by all to be a man's right. At times, the wives blame themselves and try to ignore their emotional pain by dedicating themselves to the family. This is exactly what the male wants because it protects his social, public role as a respected father and husband. Abalos (1993) has cited this behavior as an ill that allowed men to live a double standard and avoid facing their inability to create an intimate, mutual relationship with a woman. This behavior also socializes the children to faithfully carry out their expected gender roles, including the aberrant patterns.

In spite of the "machismo," the social expectation that dictates men displaying physical strength, bravery, and virility, Puerto Rican men have been tremendously affected by the decline in the family structure. Guarniccia, Angel, and Lowe (1989) in their research have demonstrated that Puerto Rican men suffer considerably more than other Hispanic men from unemployment and marital disruptions. This inability to support the family denigrates the male as head of household and family provider, creating a conflict with the macho role and set expectations. The social changes that have occurred in Puerto Rico over the last thirty years have greatly altered the traditional patriarchal role of the Puerto Rican male, causing considerable disruption in the Puerto Rican family and further impacting on the role of males.

SEXUAL PRACTICES

The concept of machismo presents another dimension related to sexual identity, behavior, and roles. Limited data are available on the occurrence of homosexuality among Puerto Rican men, although gay lifestyle would be contradictory to the prevailing machismo orientation. Same-sex couples living together may be alienated from their families, especially among the elderly and those living in rural areas where traditional gender roles and family values are the norm. Given the stigma associated with homosexuality in this culture, a matter-of-fact, non-judgmental approach must be used by health care providers when questioning about sexual orientation and practices. There seems to be more covert practices and a perceived tolerance toward bisexuality and sexual experimentation. Cunningham (1989) reported the preliminary findings of a survey conducted by the University of Puerto Rico on its ten campuses. A total of 3,905 students were questioned regarding anal sex. The report indicated that 39 percent of the males sampled practiced anal sex, and 31 percent of the females sampled had experienced anal sexual relations. Nevertheless, the actual sexual habits or practices of Puerto Ricans are not known due to the lack of research in the area of sexuality and sexual behavior among Puerto Ricans. Little hard data exist discussing issues surrounding bisexuality or how many men engage in bisexual or homosexual sexual practices. However, 15 percent of students who participated in the above survey identified themselves as gay. Human sexuality as a topic for discussion is considered taboo among Puerto Ricans. This cultural perspective inhibits positive and proactive dialogue as well as it impedes discussion of precautionary measures associated with matters of sex and health. Interestingly enough, the survey conducted by the university indicated that 95.2 percent of the students surveyed understood that condom use is a mechanism to help control the spread of AIDS, yet 55 percent of the students that were sexually active used condoms occasionally, and only 11.8 percent used condoms all the time. This disparity between knowledge and practice is closely tied to the cultural perspectives and behavior of Puerto Rican men.

It is common for Puerto Rican males to have more than one female sexual partner. VanOss, Gomez, and Tschann (1993) conducted a survey of Hispanic men ages 18–40 to study predictors of the use of condoms among Hispanic men with secondary female sexual partners. Of a total of 968 Hispanic men surveyed, 37.8 percent reported at least one secondary female sexual partner in the twelve months prior to the interview. The researchers found encouraging levels of condom use with the secondary sexual partners among the Hispanic men with multiple partners. In the study, 60 percent of the men reported "always" using condoms with secondary sexual partners. Because of the large proportion of Hispanic men who have multiple partners and the severity of the sexually transmitted disease epidemic in the Hispanic community, health care providers should recommend Hispanic men carry and use condoms. Condom use should be presented as an important responsible behavior for sexually active males. Since consistent use of condoms is so important to disease prevention and control, we feel promotional campaigns for condom use by Hispanics at risk, which address their beliefs, attitudes, and behaviors need to be developed and implemented.

Hispanics tend to have negative beliefs about condoms. The beliefs include: "the condom might break," "the condom might come off inside your partner," and "you would feel less sexual pleasure using a condom."

During the last decade, studies conducted in the United States exploring obstacles to condom use among men who have sex with men have failed to include sufficient minority participants, especially those of Latin-American origin (Carballo & Dolezal, 1996). Carballo and Dolezel argue that studies on Hispanic sexual behavior have not focused on obstacles to condom use. An exception to this position is discussed in a study conducted by Crandon (1991) who in his survey evaluated 200 men in Puerto Rico, 57 percent of whom self-identified as homosexual or bisexual (Carballo & Dolezal, 1996). Crandon reported that his subjects, when asked about condom use, stated:

- "Condoms ruin sex" (14% of homosexuals/bisexuals and 34% heterosexuals)
- "My partner may think I have AIDS or some other sexually transmitted disease" (9% of homosexuals/bisexuals and 6% heterosexuals)
- "It's embarrassing to buy condoms" (17% of homosexuals/bisexuals and 22% heterosexuals)
- "Condoms are difficult to use" (9% of homosexuals/bisexuals and 6% of heterosexuals)

In his study of inconsistency of condom use, Carballo and Dolezal cite a study by Ford and Norris (1991) in which the authors identify obstacles to condom use by Hispanic men (not restricted to men who have sex with men). The problems identified are: breakage, discomfort in using condoms, decreased pleasure, condoms come off, and that it wasn't manly to use condoms.

It is critical at this point to emphasize that three separate studies (Carballo & Dolezal, 1996; VanOss et al., 1993; Crandon, 1991) with different foci came to similar conclusions regarding condom use. Their findings identified significant attitudes toward condom use by Puerto Rican men, independent of gender preference. Their findings provide cultural contextual rationale for not using condoms. The implications relate to: (1) manliness as best exemplified by machismo attitudes of how men behave; (2) the myth of condom use as it relates to pleasure and manliness; (3) lack of knowledge about correct use of condoms; (4) embarrassment in purchasing condoms due to implications of promiscuity or infection with a communicable disease. An additional obstacle for Puerto Rican men residing on the Island is the expense of purchasing condoms. This doesn't seem to be perceived as an obstacle by Puerto Rican men living on the mainland (Bonilla, 1992).

Another major factor that is culturally problematic for the Puerto Rican community is its difficulty in acknowledging the existence of AIDS in the community, despite of the high incidence of AIDS recorded among Puerto Ricans. Acknowledging the presence of AIDS in the community means acknowledging the existence of homosexuality, bisexuality, IV drug abuse, and extramarital affairs. Making these acknowledgments implies confronting some of the cultural taboos and gender role expectations which are part of the culture's very matrix (Castro, 1990).

It is critical for health care providers to develop an AIDS prevention agenda for the Puerto Rican community. It is imperative to understand the disease and behaviors from a cultural perspective. It becomes crucial to understand and learn more about the behavior and practices of Puerto Rican men. The health education agenda must include a process that is more open to a subject considered taboo. Puerto Rican men must have a better understanding about their bodies, how it works and functions, how to keep it healthy and clean; and how to understand the pleasures that can be derived from it.

Most HIV prevention programs gloss over these issues, as well as the dislike of the use of condoms by Hispanic men. When dealing with condom use, the educational agenda frequently proceeds to emphasize the benefits and techniques of application in terms of how to negotiate condom use with a partner, and refusal of unprotected vaginal, anal, or oral sex. Not enough emphasis is placed on acknowledging the strong rejection of condoms that many men feel (Carballo & Dolezal, 1996).

The machismo norms present in the Hispanic culture (Carballo & Dolezal, 1996) could be used to support HIV prevention: If men's sexual impulses are difficult to control and men are naturally inclined to have many sexual partners, then one or both of the partners involved in a trusting relationship may have other partners, and protection is therefore necessary. Puerto Rican men who have unprotected sex need a personal, emotional experience that will challenge them to engage in safe sex practices. It is necessary to help men associate an emotional experience of support for safer sex behavior with a cognitive awareness of HIV risk.

AIDS is unequally distributed among the Hispanic ethnic subgroups. Puerto Ricans and Cubans rank third and fifth in population size within the Hispanic ethnic group in the United States. Yet, in 1991, Puerto Ricans and Cubans residing in the United States ranked first and second as the Hispanic subgroups with the most AIDS cases (Peragallo & Alba, 1996).

Of the 3,000 children (12 years of age and under) with AIDS reported to the Center for Disease Control as of mid-1991, 53 percent were African American and 25 percent were Hispanic. Nineteen percent of all pediatric cases have been diagnosed in Hispanic children living in the United States; another 6 percent of cases occurred among children in Puerto Rico. New York City has reported almost half of the children with AIDS reported in New York City are Hispanic (Lamberty, 1994, p. 111).

Hispanic men should be encouraged to handle condoms and to practice putting on one before attempting to do so during a sexual encounter. Video presentations or self-instructional approaches should be developed that incorporate modeling of appropriate condom application and removal. Hispanic men reported being embarrassed when buying condoms. Hispanic culture may contribute to high-risk sexual activity. One way is through the common idea that sexuality is embarrassing and not to be discussed either with one's children or with one's sexual partner. The issue of comfort with sexuality needs to be addressed in a culturally appropriate manner by health care providers. VanOss et al. reinforced that the patient's basic information, such as knowing the name for body parts and sexual acts, should not be assumed. A Hispanic man who participated in the survey wondered if oral sex (*sexo oral*) meant "sex by the hour"; another thought a woman's vaginal lubrication means she had "ejaculated," and several believed masturbation causes physical harm. Work is needed on the relationships between the beliefs many Hispanic men hold about what it means to be a man. VanOss et al. identified as issues: low perception of sexual control; associating positive values with sexual behavior; risk taking and the need for multiple sexual partners; and the sexual behaviors that many Hispanic men demonstrate.

Likewise, the beliefs and attitudes of Puerto Rico as they relate to high-risk behavior in HIV/AIDS and the role of women in prevention must be addressed.

Irrizzary (1991) reported that in May 1989, the Latin American Center on Sexuality Transmitted Disease (CLETS) reported having 2.577 cases of the AIDS virus in Puerto Rico with 1.475 deaths. The breakdown of the cases indicated that:

- 19% (90) were people in their teens
- 24% (625) were people 20–29
- 47% (1,210) were people 30–39
- 18% (459) were people 40–49
- 7% (1930) were people over 50

These data place Puerto Rico among the countries with the highest number of diagnosed AIDS cases. The data of Irrizarry's research, which aimed at identifying values, knowledge, beliefs, and attitudes of Puerto Rican youth (13–30 years of age), reported the following findings (see Table 23–1).

The implications of these data to our current strategies, among others, relate to the fact that Puerto Ricans are mobile. There are frequent visits between the mainland and the Island residents. This provides the potential for further spread of infection while hampering programs that may be developed to manage the epidemic.

The role of women in AIDS prevention and exposure becomes a complex issue due to certain cultural imperatives. When dealing with Puerto Rican females, providing AIDS prevention information is too simplistic an answer if it fails to recognize the cultural context within which women must make decisions.

TABLE 23-1
Beliefs About AIDS

- 77% report having some knowledge about the disease.
- 24% report no knowledge of the disease.
- 96% believe that AIDS is predominantly a problem of drug users.
- 12% believe women are immune to the disease.
- 56% believe you can get the disease by eating in a restaurant where the cook has AIDS.
- 64% believe you can get the disease through mouth-to-mouth kissing.
- 57% believe you can get AIDS through a mosquito bite.
- 44% believe sharing plates and silverware is a source of exposure and contagion.
- 49% believe the use of public restrooms is a course to get the disease.
- 50% believe being near a person who sneezes/coughs is a source of contagion.
- 49% believe AIDS patients should be isolated from the rest of society.

Hispanic women, and Puerto Ricans in particular, come from a society with a strong patriarchal family structure, strict cultural norms, and strong church influence. This male-dominated nature has influenced or controlled every aspect of a woman's life—manner of dress, activities, interpersonal relationships, courtship, marriage, and child bearing. It also allowed for the double standard with respect to male promiscuity (Castro, 1990). The use of condoms has been promoted as one of the cornerstones to preventing the spread of AIDS. However, Castro maintains, this is no simple matter for Puerto Rican women to negotiate for safer sex practices. Cultural norms dictate that women appear naïve about sexual matters; a woman prepared for a sexual encounter is considered a loose woman. If married or not in a monogamous relationship, they may consider themselves not at risk. They may fear jeopardizing the relationship by asking for safe sex practices or by asking about previous partners or drug use. They may also fear alienating someone who can provide support, companionship, and protection. Given the lack of marketable skills and the poverty within which some of these women live, they believe that having someone, regardless of his condition, is better than being on their own (Vargas, 1987; Castro, 1990; and Santos-Ortiz, 1990).

Another recommendation to help prevent the spread of HIV infection is for the HIV-positive women to postpone pregnancy or to abort if already pregnant. Neither one of these options may be possible for some Puerto Ricans. They may be due to religious, cultural, or socioeconomic reasons. Asking these women to postpone motherhood negates the role this occurrence plays in their life. It may be the only time they feel special or worthwhile.

Educational interventions must address the needs of Hispanic women within a cultural context. Castro maintains that it is not enough to provide bilingual information. Materials and techniques must demonstrate sensitivity to cultural norms. There is a need for culturally sensitive education programs that will help women to perceive their risks.

The demographics of Puerto Rican women will place the concerns previously postulated as urgent health care priorities. In 1980, it was reported that 201,412 women born in Puerto Rico live in New York City and 258,339 Puerto Rican women were born in the United States of Puerto Rican parents. Living in Puerto Rico that same year were 1,639,793 women who were born in Puerto Rico. In other words, 22 percent of the total Puerto Rican women in Puerto Rico and New York City lived in New York City in 1980 (Menendez, 1990).

In 1987, of a total of 1,682 deaths of Puerto Rican women raised in Puerto Rico but living in New York City, 78 or 57 percent died of AIDS. Puerto Rican women represent the largest group of all races (white, black, Hispanics) or ethnic groups affected by AIDS.

In Conclusion

In the first two quarters of 1996 there were 13% fewer deaths than the estimated number of AIDS deaths in 1995. It is important to note that deaths of males declined 15% but increased 3% in women. In 1985 women accounted for only 7% of newly diagnosed AIDS cases, whereas in 1996 they accounted for 20%. The rate of AIDS in black women is 17% higher than white women. And the AIDS rate is 6% higher for Hispanic women than white women (Phillips, 1997). In 1992, heterosexual-acquired AIDS replaced IV drug abuse (DeCarlo 1996). The trend is frightening. The implications are clear. Prevention programs that are culturally sensitive have to be developed and implemented. Issues that need to be discussed are sexual coercion, abuse, and rape. Methods of prevention need to focus on culture, family, empowerment, self-esteem, and negotiating skills. Preventive measures should include the use of male and female condoms, as well as use of vaginal microbicides when they become available in the United States. Information should be made available in places where women tend to gather (i.e., health clinics, social programs, local churches, schools, apartment buildings, and their homes). Information is power. It can help people decide to change behaviors so as not to be the next victim.

References

Abalos, D. T. (1993). *The Latino family and the politics of transformation*. Westport, Connecticut: Praeger.

Bonilla, L., Porter, J. & Menendez, S. (1992). Condom use in low income island and mainland Puerto Rican population. In International Conference on AIDS. The Netherlands as cited in Carballo-Dieguez and Dolezal, C. (1996). HIV risk behaviors and obstacles to condom use among Puerto Rican Men in New York City who have sex with men. *American Journal of Public Health, 86*(11), 1619–1622.

Carballo-Dieguez, A. & Dolezal, C. (1996). HIV risk behaviors and obstacles to condom use among Puerto Rican men in New York City who have sex with men. *American Journal of Public Health, 86*(11), 1,619–1,622.

Castro, V. (1990). AIDS Prevention Program for Puerto Rican Women. *Puerto Rican Health Science Journal, 9*(1), 37–41.

Crandon, J. E. (1991) Men's health survey: A study concerning AIDS related knowledge, attitudes and behaviors in a sample of Puerto Rican men and its relevance to the epidemiology of HIV in San Juan, Puerto Rico. Hertford, England: Oxford University. Dissertation. As cited in Carballo and Dolezal (1996).

Cunningham, I. (1990). La mujer y el SIDA: Una vision crítica. *Puerto Rican Health Science Journal,* 9(1), 47–50.

De Carlo, P. (1997). What are women's HIV prevention needs? University of California at San Francisco Center for AIDS Prevention Studies.

Guarnaccia, P. J., Angel, R. & Lowe, J. (1989). The factor structure of the CES-D in the Hispanic health and nutrition examination survey: The influence of ethnicity, gender and language. *Social Science and Medicine, 29*(1), 85–94.

Irrizarry, A. (1991). Conocimientos, creencias y actitudes hacia el SIDA en jovenes Puertorriqueños. *Puerto Rican Health Science Journals, 10*(1), 43–46.

Lamberty, G. & Garcia, C. (1994). (Eds), *Puerto Rican women and children: Issues in health, growth and development.* New York: Plenum Press.

Menendez, B. (1990). Mortalidad por SIDA en mujeres Puetorriqueños en la ciudad de Nueva York. *Health and Social Work, 20*(4), 247–253.

Peragallo, N. P. & Alba, M. L. (1996). HIV/AIDS: Risk, factors, incidence and interventions among Latinos in the United States. In S. Torres (Ed.). *Hispanic voices: Hispanic health educators speak out.* New York: NLN Press.

Phillips, P. (1997). No plateau for HIV/AIDS epidemic in U.S. women. *Journal of the American Medical Association, 6*(277), 1,747–1,749.

Santos-Ortiz, M. (1990). La mujer y el SIDA: Sexualidad femenina antes y despues del SIDA. *Puerto Rican Health Science Journal,* 9(1), 33–35. *The Hispanic nurse.* (1997). 19(2), Second Quarter.

VanOss-Marvin, B., Gomez, C. A. & Tschann, J. M. (1993) Condom use among Hispanic men with secondary female sexual partners. *Public Health Reports, 108*(5), 742–750.

Chapter 24

The Asian Indian American Experience: Diversity and Difference

KAREN VERNI-MOOSVI

INTRODUCTION

My association with Asian Indian people began twenty years ago when I worked among so many of them at a hospital in Jersey City, New Jersey. As a second-generation Italian American, I have enjoyed and been frustrated by their culture. I have also been fascinated by how such a nature-loving people have embraced technology.

This chapter is intended to give the reader an overview of the Asian Indian American experience. It contains a brief history of the 5,000-year-old civilization and offers a few images of contemporary Indian life. Many Indians feel India will have significant impact on world affairs as it races toward the millennium.

The Asian Indian religious experience is addressed as the single most powerful influence on the culture. Immigration trends are presented with race issues as explored in the oral history of one family. Family life and assimilation into the mainstream are explored. Finally, links to this community are presented along with my intuitive comments regarding the possible consequences of interventions with this community.

HISTORY

Asian Indians share a 5,000-year cultural heritage and a history characterized as one of conquest and invasion. Originating with the Indus Valley civilization (c. 3000–1550 B.C.E.), it continued through the Aryan invasions (c. 1500–100 B.C.E.), the Greek conquests of Alexander the Great (326 B.C.E.), the Buddhist and Hindu Kingdoms (300 B.C.E.–600 C.E.), the Muslim invasions (900–1200) and the Mogul dynasty (1500–1750). Contact with Europeans began during the seventeenth century when the Dutch, Spanish, Portuguese, French, and English battled and allied to gain control of the Indian subcontinent. England eventually dominated the territory making it a colony of the British Empire. After World War II (1939–1945), British rule ended. India and Pakistan were created in 1947 in response to the differences between the Muslims and the Hindus (Vohra, 1995). Conflicts between the Hindu majority and the Muslim minority have become civic emergencies. Hindu nationalism is at the center of Indian politics. India is now a great democracy with limitless economic potential. India will soon become the world's most populous nation (Jack, 1997).

PHYSICAL CHARACTERISTICS

India is a land of diversity. Its inhabitants number 950 million. Fifteen national languages and 1,652 dialects are spoken in its 25 states and 7 union territories. Its geography and climate are equally as varied. In the north rise the Himalayas, the world's highest peaks. Below them stretch luxuriant valleys, arid deserts, and dense jungles. India's monsoon winds challenge the survival of its inhabitants with a pattern of extremes that sometimes bring floods, and other times bring drought and famine.

The physical characteristics of India's people are as diverse as her ancestry. Descendants from the Aryan and Muslim populations are taller, more solidly built, and lighter skinned. The descendants of the indigenous Dravidians have somewhat deeper skin tones and are of slighter physique (Vohra, 1995).

CULTURE

Indian culture is a composite of the elements of life. Each part has its place in a kaleidoscopic social system that has evolved, despite its seeming rigidity, to accommodate bloody civil unrest, the information age, and political changes.

There are many versions of India. The popular Western perception of India as an impoverished nation with Bombay prostitutes and child laborers is one. However, styles and relationships are changing inside the well-off families living in the big cities (Singh, 1997). India is now like much of the world. Although 40 to 50 percent of the population remains in poverty, it is said even a villager in the remotest part of India knows who Bill Gates is. Popular Western trends reach India over the Internet and via the satellites that cross South Asia (Jack, 1997).

Despite the information age, religion remains the organizing principle of the people. In Indian life, the secular and the sacred are not easily separated. Religion includes the humorous, the erotic, the playful, and the fantastic. The sacred includes the profane (Rao, 1995).

India is the birthplace to two world faiths: Hinduism and Buddhism. India's many religions—Hinduism, Buddhism, Sikhism, Jainism, Islam, Christianity, and Zoroastrianism reflect her racial, linguistic, and cultural diversity. The majority of Indians are Hindu or Muslim. Also, her exploration of spirituality and spiritual techniques—meditation, mandalas, yantras, ecstatic dance, numerology, and the use of mind-expanding herbs and mushrooms have been profound throughout her history (Welch, 1985).

Most Indians are Hindus. Hinduism is different from other major world religions in that it adjusts to time, place, and personality. Without a creed, church, or standardized form of worship, Hinduism is an evolving religious and social system as well as a way of life. Within Hinduism, there is a bewildering diversity based on a common doctrine found in the sacred writings: the four Vedas, the *Upanishads*, and the two great epics, *Ramayana* and *Mahabharata*. From these works the doctrine of birth, rebirth, and reincarnation are founded. The aim of a Hindu is liberation from rebirth and the unity of the soul with the ultimate reality or Brahman. This is achieved with proper conduct and the performance of one's duties. Hindus are guided by their moral duty. One's caste and stage of life determine duty or dharma. The life stages are student, the time of celibacy and learning; householder, the years of marriage, parenthood, and worldly responsibility; and hermit or ascetic, the stage of renunciation when one breaks all ties with the world and prepares one's soul for dissolution or unity with the Ultimate Truth. To the traditional Hindus, life is but illusions. Neither time nor matter is valued as much as in the West. Thus infinite amounts of time and skill may be expended on objects of minor consequence, particularly religious objects (Welch, 1985).

Hinduism structures its social relations into a fourfold caste system that conforms to the laws of spiritual progression. Outside the caste system are the untouchables, who do not have a caste status. As Hinduism came in contact with Western scientific and religious influences, laws evolved outlawing discrimination against the untouchables. Today, popular Hinduism is a practical religion of the masses involving worship and duty. Contemporary Hinduism is often devoid of the abstract philosophy.

Islam means submission to the will of God. It is the religion of 100 million people in India. They compose the largest minority in the world. Islam was developed by Muhammad ibn Abdulla in Arabia in the seventh century. It is based on the Judeo-Christian traditions: the Gospel of Jesus, the Psalms of David and the Torah of Moses. The Qur'an, its sacred book, has the special function of recollecting the messages given in the Holy Bible, the Sacred Vedas, the Gita, in the sayings of Buddha and all the other prophets.

The message of Islam was delivered through Muhammad, the religion's Prophet (Cleary, 1993). The Qur'an relates to the science and religion of Islam. The worship of Allah, the Muslim name for God, in preparation for the Day of Judgment is central to Islamic life. A devout contemporary Muslim is expected to practice the rites: declare one's faith; pray five times a day; give alms; fast during the daytime in the Muslim month of Ramadan; and complete a pilgrimage to Mecca. A Muslim may pray anywhere on virgin land as the earth is considered a sacred mosque. Prayers are offered at sunrise, noon, afternoon, sunset, and at night. Friday is the Sabbath day. These rites are considered essential for the integration of one's health and well-being now and in the afterlife. It is believed Islam came into the world to create a balance between the physical and the spiritual. This equilibrium between the inner and outer world enables a human to understand the Unity, or al-tawhid, that is the goal of human life (Nasr, 1993, 1996).

IMMIGRATION AND RACISM

Since the 1960s, changes in U.S. immigration laws have encouraged large numbers of Asian Indians to leave India for the United States. Their presence has changed the cultural blend of many urban areas. According to the U.S. census, Asian Indian Americans numbered 815,000 in 1990. Seventy-five percent of them were born in India and almost half of these, 44 percent, arrived between 1980 and 1990. Only 25 percent of Asian Indian Americans residing in the United States in 1990 were born there. As with most immigrants, newcomers reside in urban areas. Asian Indians call New York City, Chicago, Los Angeles, and Washington, DC home. They account for 2 percent of the population of New York City and slightly over 2 percent of its neighboring metro Jersey City. Very visible and large suburban communities can also be found in central New Jersey, and California. New York and New Jersey are the states with the highest number of Asian Indian Americans.

As a rule, the first to arrive in the States from India came in the 1960s. Most were male professionals. They were doctors, scientists, and academics. Characteristically, they were married to women who were high school graduates who did not speak English. Their children are now in college or about to start families of their own here in the United States. The second wave of immigration occurred in the 1970s. Unlike the first wave, both the men and women were well educated. Many of these women chose to work outside the home, and typically their children are now college-bound teenagers. This group assimilated easily into the American scene. They have done well financially and academically. Many are comfortably situated in suburban America. Asian Indians have the highest median income for all immigrant groups in the United States.

The most recent wave of Indian immigrants differs in that the professionals who arrive now are not always able to find jobs in their specialty. Also, other new immigrants are less educated and are employed in gas stations, convenience stores, or as cab drivers (Mogelonsky, 1995).

Many find jobs in small family-owned restaurants or motels. The family members work and live together. This is considered desirable and is often preparation for a family member who will later purchase another motel. Members of the Sikh faith, and the people from the states of Punjab and Gujarat in India, are the three largest groups of Indian motel owners. Many of these Gujaratis carry the family name "Patel." They are known throughout India for their industry and business acumen (Matta, 1991).

The Asian Indians generally assimilate easily into the American culture, which one Asian American described as "innately decent" (Rajan, 1995). However, racial incidents have occurred in the New York City area. In neighboring Hoboken and Jersey City there are youth groups called the "Dot-busters." They are named after the dots or bindhis which Indian women wear on their foreheads. These groups have launched daily attacks on over twenty different Asian Indian families. One thirty-year-old man was beaten unconscious by this group and later died. He was a Citicorp manager in Manhattan. In response to this, an Asian Indian living in Jersey City organized his community and started the United Indian American Association. This group succeeded in having the Attorney General's office recommend that the teenage boys responsible for the crime be tried as adults and not as juveniles. There remains some hostility towards Asian Indians on the streets of Jersey City now (Singh, 1991). An eleven-year-old Hindu girl born in the United States and living in Jersey City described to an interviewer how she was tripped by other students who call her a "dirty Hindu." She was chased down the street and forced to run to her aunt's house for safety. She reported that people are jealous of Asian Indians because it is perceived that they own all the stores and have education. Her family was not highly educated and did not own a store (Chawla, 1991).

FAMILY LIFE

The extended family is the womb of Indian culture. Family members often share a residence, eat food prepared in the same kitchen, worship together, and own property together. In general, the family includes several generations and observes seniority. From elder to junior, everyone carries out assigned tasks. While privacy is limited, security and companionship are abundant.

In Canada, interviews with recent Indian immigrant women revealed that leisure or private time, as described by Western women, is not viewed as something positive or desirable. The women in the study described the extended family as a source of friendship and support. Work was also considered an important aspect of these women's lives. Their extended families allowed women to work outside the home with no need for baby-sitters who were not family members. During difficult times, the family offered comfort and support to its members. Such close family arrangements were not considered as constraining by the women. They spoke primarily of the advantages of a close family network. In some situations, the women missed relatives back home and longed for more family members to join them from India (Tirone & Shaw, 1997).

Traditionally, in India, marriage is by arrangement. When a Hindu girl marries she gets the red dot as a symbol of the marriage. Sex is considered a gift from God. When there are problems in the marriage, the relatives get involved and counsel the couple. Problems are not openly discussed with outsiders. There is seldom divorce. A traditional Hindu woman living in Jersey City described her family life to an interviewer. She claims her family works hard and cooks their own food at home to save money. They invest the money and save it for education (Chawla, 1991).

Asian Indians have the lowest divorce rate among foreign-born immigrant groups. However, there are numerous cases of Asian Indian women abandoned by their husbands in New York and Chicago. Domestic violence is a concern. Women have formed community organizations to offer assistance to other women in violent situations. These include Manzi (New Jersey), Sakhi (New York), and Narika (Berkeley) (Mazumdar, 1995). Concern has also been expressed for their higher rates of suicide among all immigrants (Ineichen, 1996).

Americanized Asian Indian children straddle two cultures. Indo-American youth magazines like Masala, Onward, and Hum feature articles on sex and drug use as well as classical Indian music and dance reviews (Mogelonsky, 1995). Children attend cultural activities such as social functions, which offer classical music that is valued for its meditative properties. Their parents, traditions, and religion influence Asian Indian children. Most tend to follow custom with regard to marriage and children. The Americanization of the Asian Indian youth is often a matter of individual desire and educational influences.

Traditionally, women prepare the meals. Religion and the seasons influence dietary choices. Hindus and Sikhs usually do not eat beef. The cow is a sacred animal. Vegetarian dishes are customary, however, nonvegetarian dishes are prepared in contemporary family settings. Muslims do not eat pork, and Orthodox Muslims must eat halal meat, which is meat slaughtered in an Islamic manner. Asian Indians cook rice and curry, and make their own bread.

Food is associated with spiritual values. The use of forks and knives is considered a Western custom and may suggest the adoption of Western values. The use of the right hand is customary and its elegant use conveys one's degree of culture (Bhatia, 1995).

Spicy dishes are prepared for their medicinal properties as well as for enjoyment. The ancient Holy Hindu Scriptures contain Ayurvedic scripts listing the preventive and curative powers of foods. Ayurveda is composed of two words "Ayus" which means "life" or "lifespan," and "Veda" which means "knowledge"(Micozzi, 1996). Americans dining in Indian restaurants have seen this influence in the fennel, cardamom, and cloves that are the Indian substitutes for after-dinner mints, which are known to aid digestion and provide relief from heartburn.

COMMUNICATION

The medium of instruction in India is English, however, because 75 percent of all Asian Indian Americans are foreign born, most families are more comfortable speaking their own language at home. These languages include Punjabi, Bengali, Hindi, Urdu, and Gujarti. One may reach the Asian Indian community through their street festivals, such as Devon Street in Chicago and Jackson Heights in Queens, New York, and their celebration of India Independence Day.

Another key link is through ethnic media. As of 1996, the Asian Indian community had at least twenty weekly newspapers, thirteen magazines, twenty-six television programs, and seventeen radio programs.

At least thirty-five Asian Indian movie theaters show in-language, in-culture films. The Asian Indians are technology savvy. The Internet has over 40,000 India-related Web sites and home pages (DeSouza & Ho, 1996). Both here and abroad, the Asian Indian experience accommodates the seemingly disparate aspects of life as the information age advances.

Professionals outside the Asian Indian culture may gain easy access to individuals from India and their descendants at work, in their communities, and in educational, cultural, and health care settings. Perhaps the most curious aspect of mingling with the Asian Indians is their readiness to be polite and accommodating.

An Asian Indian in his early twenties explained to me that he saw the Asian Indian man as a "frog in a well." A man with some money and status in his community back home arrives in America with little social status and must cultivate acquaintances in the hopes of establishing himself in the greater American society. In general, every effort is made to be law abiding and accommodating in the hopes of an easy and prosperous assimilation into the mainstream. This agreeable, accommodating demeanor, in my opinion should not be confused with feebleness or subservience. Underlying a reserved manner is often clarity of purpose that propels the individual in the desired direction socially.

If our intentions are to change behavior or thought patterns, then we need to be highly sensitive to the cultural variations within and without the culture. We need to explore the underlying assumptions our intentions hold, and the impact of the intention on the family system. Do we assume that self-reliance and individual initiative are desired qualities in this population?

Further qualitative research is needed to assess not only whether these characteristics are desirable, but also in how to increase social support from within the Asian Indian family and lessen the potential for poor crisis resolution in a new land. Attention to particular outcomes without consideration of the family process is particularly insensitive when working with the Asian Indian family. For example, the junior woman in an extended family often has the lowest status in the extended family. If she wishes to reach out into the community but does not have the support of her family, feelings of isolation and helplessness may arise or be heightened by the attempted interventions.

When studies or programs are designed, interviewers may wish to get the name and phone number of a potential participants' temple or mosque. If the participant does not receive the support of the program for whatever reason, follow-up social support could be given through the religious community. Such communities can be invited to join in partnership with the health or social program in development. A study of Indo-Canadian women and prenatal classes (Dhari et al., 1997), indicated that effective prenatal education could take place under certain conditions: program participation by a grass-roots organization from the target culture, local health professional support of the program, and the delivery of ongoing encouragement, support, and useful information from the project staff.

During a recent visit to a storefront Hindu temple in Jersey City, I spoke with two local Hindu men and a woman. The men explained to me that Hindus without insurance could receive free medical care on a regular basis at the temple. Two Hindu physicians regularly visit the temple and use it as a clinic. Anyone in need of help could receive it there. The woman, a biotechnician with a local pharmaceutical company, was at the temple to have her palm read before a five-week visit to India. She explained she would like to help the people of the Indian community in Jersey City but she would not know how to go about it.

As the numbers of Asian Indians without employment and health insurance increase in our communities, we will need to join forces with the more advantaged Asian Indians and their religious communities. Culturally relevant interventions are the responsibility of us all. Certainly much can be gained in the area of primary prevention from a continued exploration of the spiritual dimensions of Asian Indian lifestyles.

REFERENCES

Bhatia, S. K. (1995). Indian restaurants and cuisine. In F. Ng (Ed.), *Asian American encyclopedia* (pp. 670–674). New York: Marshall Cavendish.

Chawla, M. S. (1992). Racial hatred. In J. F. J. Lee (Ed.), *Asian Americans.* (pp. 116–117). New York: The New Press.

Chawla, S. S. (1992). Different By Choice. In J. F. J. Lee (Ed.) *Asian Americans* (pp. 118–120). New York: The New Press.

Cleary, T. (1994). *The essential Koran: The heart of Islam.* New York: Harper Collins.

DeSouza, P. & Ho, S. (1996, October). *Targeting the upscale Asian Indian market.* Presentation at the meeting of the New York American Management Association, Ethnic Marketing Leadership Council New York, NY.

Dhari, R., Patel, I., Fryer, M., Dhari, M., Bilku, S. & Bains, S. (1997). Creating a supportive environment for Indo-Canadian Women. *The Canadian Nurse,* March, 27–31.

Ineichen, B. (1996). Suicide and Hinduism. *Psychiatric Services, 17,* (10), 1,128.

Jack, I. (1997, Spring). Introduction. *Granta,* 7–12.

Matta, W. (1995). Asian Indians in the motel/hotel business. In F. Ng (Ed.), *Asian American encyclopedia* (pp. 92–93). New York: Marshall Cavendish.

Mazumdar, S. (1995). Asian Indian Women in the United States. In F. Ng (Ed.), *Asian American encyclopedia.* (pp. 87–91). New York: Marshall Cavendish.

Mogelonsky, M. (1995). Asian-Indian Americans. *American demographics, 17,* (8), 32–39.

Nasr, S. H. (1993). Islam. In A. Sharma (Ed.), *Our religions,* (pp. 427–523). New York: HarperSanFrancisco.

Nasr, S. H. (1996). *Religion and the order of Islam.* New York: Oxford University Press.

Rao, A. (1995). Immortal Picture Stories: Comic art in early India Art. In J. A. Lent (Ed.), *Asian popular culture* (pp. 237–240). Boulder, Colo.: Westview Press.

Rhajan, T. V. (1995). One immigrant's view: Racism in America. *Connecticut Medicine, 59* (7), 421–422.

Sharma, A. (1993). Hinduism, In A. Sharma (Ed.), *Our religions* (pp. 1–67). New York: HarperSanFrancisco.

Sharma, H. M. (1996). Maharishi Ayurveda. In M. Micozzi (Ed.), *Fundamentals of complementary and alternative medicine,* (pp. 243–244). New York: Churchill Livingstone.

Singh, D. (1997, Spring). Mother India. *Granta,* 221–233.

Singh, H. (1992). Being Indian in Jersey City. In J. F. J. Lee (Ed.), *Asian Americans* (pp.113–115).

Tirone, S. C. & Ho, S. (1997, Second Quarter). At the center of their lives: Indo Canadian women their families and leisure. *Journal of Leisure Research, 29* (2), 225–224.

Vohra, I. (1995). Republic of India. In F. Ng. (Ed.), *Asian American encyclopedia.* (pp. 656–660).

Welch, S. (1985). *India: Art and culture 1300–1900.* New York: Holt, Rinehart, and Winston.

Chapter 25

Profile of a Church-Based Tutorial/ Enrichment Program

Betty W. Barber

INTRODUCTION

It is an established fact that there are very serious problems in our urban educational system. Too many of our youth, particularly African American children, are poorly motivated, lack self-esteem, and have difficulty mastering the basic skills in reading, writing, and mathematics. In addition, they demonstrate weakness in higher level skills of critical thinking, reasoning, and problem solving. Population shifts have also contributed much to the shortcomings of urban education. The increasing flight to the suburbs, the demographic redistribution of the white middle class, and the desire on the part of teachers to seek both safety and the ease of suburban teaching have left the schools of the inner city, for the most part, academically, culturally, and economically disadvantaged.

The question is what can be done to rectify some of these ills, and who is responsible for initiating change? Many may feel that this problem is solely the responsibility of the school board and our many competent professional educators. However, a more realistic answer is that each of us as parents and/or as citizens of this great society is responsible. The challenge is ours, each of us, to make a difference by utilizing whatever constructive resources are available to us to improve our educational system and to ensure that every child, whether he resides in the inner city or in suburbia, receives a decent education. The following chapter is a report of how one concerned institution, the First Baptist Church of Lincoln Gardens, in Somerset, New Jersey, attempted to meet the challenges of our urban schools by organizing a Tutorial/Enrichment Program for its members and neighboring children on a free voluntary basis.

THE INCEPTION OF FIRST BAPTIST CHURCH TUTORIAL/ENRICHMENT PROGRAM

The First Baptist Church of Lincoln Gardens is the largest predominantly black Baptist Church in Central Jersey. The rapidly growing congregation of more than 3,000 members consists of a large population of youth and teenagers who attend the public schools of Somerset County where the church is located. Several low-income housing projects are in close proximity to the church. The dynamic pastor of First Baptist Church, Reverend Dr. DeForest B. Soaries, is very committed to the service aspect of Christian responsibility. On many occasions he has expressed to the congregation his belief that the church is not only responsible for meeting the spiritual needs of people, but it is also the responsibility of the church-community to help alleviate some of the social ills of our society. The pastor has a particular interest in supporting the educational process of our youth.

As a member of the church and a nurse educator, I was very inspired by Pastor Soaries' position on the expanded role of the church in supporting the educational process of our children. It has been my philosophy for many years that the Black Church can and should play a vital role in the education of our youth. Building partnerships with school, church, and home is an effective way of providing an educational support system that brings school, family, and community together to counteract negative influences on our youth and encourage them to pursue successful educational goals. It was, therefore, with great honor and pleasure for me to accept Pastor Soaries' request that I serve as coordinator for developing the First Baptist Church Tutorial/Enrichment Program.

GOALS AND OBJECTIVES

One of the critical elements necessary for the organization and development of any successful program is the establishment of clearly stated goals and objectives. During the summer of 1991, the educational planning committee, which included teachers and guidance counselors from the local schools, met for many hours over several weeks to discuss the nature and scope of the program to be implemented. As a committee, we were cognizant of the fact that we needed to affirm our own commitment. We agreed that it was our hope that the program would benefit all of the children who chose to participate. To achieve this, we all acknowledged that the nature of the program should be designed to emphasize the positive attributes of all participants, while recognizing human diversity and individual differences; capitalizing on strengths while accepting and remediating those weaknesses that could be corrected. Further, we believed it was important to emphasize that it was not the intent of the tutorial program to replace the role of the parents or to displace the school as the chief means of academic learning. In fact, we were firmly committed to a program that focused on the ideas of family life, extended family, and to the process of formal education supported by the church.

TUTORIAL/ENRICHMENT PROGRAM

It took several weeks of devoted work by the planning committee before the First Baptist Church Tutorial/Enrichment Program became a reality. The first classes began in October of 1991. Our primary objective was to fill the void in the educational experience of students with serious educational deficiencies. More specifically, the objectives were individualized based upon assessed needs and included the following:

1. To increase students' performance on the high school proficiency exam
2. To assist students and parents in assuming more responsibility for the student's academic development
3. To increase the student's knowledge of how to study efficiently and effectively

I wish to point out that most of the students demonstrated a need for objective no. three. We have, therefore, devoted a special section later in this chapter describing how the *Learning to Learn* (1993) concept was utilized in the program to enhance academic achievement.

ABOUT THE PROGRAM

The response from the church congregation to the program was very favorable. More than fifty students signed up for the initial program. The students represented grade levels from grade 1 through 12.

The academic component of the program was designed to provide support to the existing curriculum of the various schools in which the students were enrolled. As stated earlier, it was not our intent to displace the school as the primary source of academic learning. Accordingly, we worked collaboratively with the designated curriculum personnel in each school to design the academic component of the church tutorial program. Our goal was to provide a source of support to the enhancement of the academic programs in the schools and to ultimately improve the retention and graduation success rate of the students enrolled in our church program.

Discipline-specific tutorial sessions were developed in a broad range of courses including basic arithmetic and advanced mathematics, general and advance sciences, reading, spelling, vocabulary building, and foreign languages. We also offered "crash" study courses to students preparing to take the General Equivalency Diploma (GED) test.

Consistent with the approach that learning can be fun, we used many educational games as an integral part of our teaching methodology. This strategy proved to be particularly useful for the elementary and middle school age groups. Most of the educational games, which included math facts of different levels, vocabulary building, and spelling, had pre-tests and post-tests. The pre-tests were used, when available, to determine the educational level of the student prior to participating in the learning activity. This was a valuable aid to the tutor in guiding the student through the activity. Likewise, the post-test serves as a means of evaluating the progress or lack of progress of the student after completing the activity.

At this point, let me share that an analysis of the data gathered by the educational planning committee in assessing the need for this program was done. Results indicated a particular need to evaluate and enhance the learning styles and the learning process utilized by the students. Research has shown that many minority students are at risk academically because they have not developed the skills necessary to engage in effective study and learning. Knowing how to apply oneself and negotiate the learning process is essential to academic success.

It was decided that *Learning to Learn* would be one of the components of the Church Tutorial/Enrichment Program. However, since most of the tutors were not familiar with the *Learning to Learn* concept, it was necessary to provide training for the tutors in this area. As coordinator of the program, and as a faculty/administrator at Kean College, I was fortunate to have access to faculty at the college with expertise in this area. I arranged for one of the faculty from Kean College, Dr. Bailey Baker, to provide a presentation on the concept of *Learning to Learn* to the tutors and the students. I was also able to acquire materials on this concept to be used by the tutors. Our goal was to integrate the concept of *Learning to Learn* in all of the subject areas as appropriate by the end of the first academic year of the program.

THE FOURSOME RECIPE: STUDENT-PARENT-TUTOR-SCHOOL

The four ingredients that were unique to the effectiveness of the Church Tutorial/Enrichment Program were the student, the parent, the tutor, and the school. The collaborative partnership that evolved between these four entities provided the cornerstone for our program. The students and their parents were required to participate in a very comprehensive orientation session. At the general orientation session, all of the students and their parents met with the tutors. Each was provided a handbook which contained basic information about the program including student and parent expectations. The motto adopted for the students was, "Knowledge Is Power." They were instructed to repeat the motto aloud several times which produced a beautiful resounding echo. We encouraged the students to internalize the principle of this motto by not only repeating the slogan regularly, but more important, by committing themselves to the program expectations. Some of the expectations stressed during the session were regular attendance, being on time, sharing their specific tutoring program goals with their parents, reviewing and/or completing homework assignments from school prior to their tutoring session, and to come to each tutoring session prepared to ask their assigned tutor questions about their homework or school activities. Each student was assigned to a specific tutor based upon the subject they had identified as being very difficult for the student to understand.

A special orientation session was also scheduled for just the parents and tutors. Since the parents were expected to play a key role in their child's learning process, it was very important that they get to know the assigned tutor. Also, because of the privacy law regarding the confidentiality of students' records, it was often necessary for the parent to serve as the liaison between the church program and the school in order for the tutor to gain access to certain information necessary to assist the student. We also expected the parents to work with and assist their children in establishing scheduled time at home to study and/or do homework assignments.

The majority of the tutors were members of First Baptist Church, including some local college students, who had expertise in a variety of academic subject areas. Also some individuals who were not members of our church volunteered to serve as tutors because they believed so deeply in what we were doing. In addition, a number of high school students with strengths in particular academic subjects participated as Peer Tutors.

MY INSPIRATION

How inspiring it was to work with a staff of individuals who willingly responded to a need by volunteering their services in assisting in the academic development of our young people.

The philosophy adopted by the tutors, which expressed their commitment to the students, is reflected in the statement:

> The student is the most important person in the program. Without the students there would be no need for this program. We do not believe the student is an interruption of our work, but the purpose of it. We are not doing them a favor by serving them. They are doing us a favor by giving us the opportunity to do so.

Tutoring for selected subjects was offered every week night, except Wednesday, from 5:00 p.m. to 9:00 p.m., Saturdays and Sundays were also available by special appointments. Each tutor was assigned one or more students. There were arrangements for one-on-one as well as group sessions. However, even when the tutors scheduled small group sessions, students received individualized support based upon their assessed needs.

The tutors worked with each student to establish individualized short-term goals which included projected time lines as appropriate. These goals were listed on a form, which required the signature of the student, the tutor, and the parent or guardian. In addition each tutor was expected to complete a monthly student progress report consistent with the established goals (Table 25–1). These reports were shared with the students and the parents/guardians.

THE PROCESSES

All of the students were expected to bring their report card to the church for each grading period. Pastor Soaries was very actively involved in this aspect of the program. The students had come to expect, sometimes with a little apprehension, the "call for report cards" by Pastor Soaries from the pulpit during the regular Sunday morning worship services. Pastor Soaries insisted that students bring their report card to him each grading period. After reviewing them, he passed them on to me for distribution to the appropriate tutors.

An invaluable component of the Tutorial Program involved exposing the students to enrichment activities as well as assisting them with academic subjects. In response to the First Baptist Church Vision 2000—Strategic Plan, a number of committees and groups evolved. Many of them are primarily responsible for administering various types of educational and cultural development activities. A subcommittee of our Tutorial Enrichment Program serves as a liaison to the groups who are responsible for these activities. In consultation with these groups, arrangements are made for tutorial students to take full advantage of these planned enrichment activities. Such activities often include educational and social camping retreats, and field trips to corporations such as AT&T, Pharmaceutical Companies, museums, art galleries, and various stage and film productions in New York City and Philadelphia. There is also a Mentoring Program sponsored by the Men's Fellowship of the church. In this program, adult men of the church are assigned to boys and young men to serve as role models and mentors.

TABLE 25–1
First Baptist Church of Lincoln Gardens Tutoring Program
Monthly Student Progress Report

Name of student_____
Last name, first name

Name of tutor_____
Last name, first name

1. Assessment period: ___/___/___ to ___/___/___

2. Number of missed tutoring sessions: ____

   Follow-up phone call made to parent: ___ yes ___ no

3. Number of late arrivals to tutoring sessions: ____

   Parent notified: ___ yes ___ no

Level of Student's Progress Toward Achievement of Goals

Goal #1	1	2	3	4	5
	minimal progress		average progress		goal accomplished
Goal #2	1	2	3	4	5
Goal #3	1	2	3	4	5
Goal #4	1	2	3	4	5

Comments: 10/15/91

Finally, the school. There is no question that the level of success we have experienced thus far with the tutorial program is in large measure due to the interest, support, and cooperation we have received from the participating school districts. A very healthy rapport has developed over the years between the educational staff at the church and the teachers and guidance counselors from the participating schools. Over the past two years, the tutorial program has outgrown the space available at the church. We are thankful and very fortunate that an arrangement for additional space has been made available in one of the local elementary schools located in close proximity to the church.

THE OUTCOMES

One of the most important components of any educational program is a built-in functional evaluation system. The evaluation tool that was designed for our program is illustrated in Table 25–2. Unfortunately, this was one of the weakest areas of the program. First of all, notwithstanding the numerous learning experiences offered, the program experienced difficulty in integrating a systematic, structured evaluation system for assessing the level of student readiness and measuring their level of achievement as they entered and progressed through the program.

TABLE 25–2
The First Baptist Church of Lincoln Gardens Learning to Learn Tutorial Program Evaluation Form

Name of Tutor:

<u>Student(s) Tutored</u>   <u>Subject(s)</u>

  1.

  2.

I.   Please indicate the number of hours you spent with the student(s) per week: _____hrs.

II.   The amount of time spent tutoring the student was:

    1. Adequate_____   2. Not Adequate_____   3. Comment:

III. Were you able to accomplish the goals that were established for your student(s)? Please comment:

IV. Were you provided with adequate resources to do your job effectively? Comment:

V.   How would you rate the level of parent support:

    1. Adequate_____   2. Not Adequate_____   3. Comment:

VI. Did the students or parents indicate an improvement in the student's report card grades?

    Yes_____   No_____

    Comment:

VII. Please list your suggestions for improvement of the Tutoring Program.

10/15/91

For various reasons, many of the tutors were inconsistent in keeping up-to-date records of their students' progress. Consequently, it was extremely difficult to document how much new learning, if any, had occurred. During the first year of the program, the enrollment of students grew at a much faster rate than the recruitment of tutors. This was particularly evident for mathematics and science disciplines. We were significantly understaffed for mathematics and science tutors, which resulted in a higher student/tutor ratio for these disciplines.

On the positive side, it was obvious that all of the students were interested and motivated to develop their potential. This was evidenced by nearly one hundred percent attendance each week. Also, there was a lot of interaction between tutors and students, and between the students themselves. Our students were exposed to many varied and valuable academic learning and culturally enriching activities.

The following summarizes some of the comments from the evaluation form.

Comments

1. Comments regarding support from parents were very positive in most instances.
2. There was a general feeling among the tutors that the one-hour tutoring sessions were adequate. However, several tutors expressed a desire for flexibility in extending the time allotted under special circumstances.
3. There was unanimity among the tutors regarding the need for them to have desk copies of the textbooks used by the students in their respective schools.
4. The rapport between the tutors and teachers from the participating schools was rated as very high.
5. The need for an improved system for tracking the progress of students and to computerize the program was identified.
6. There was a number of suggestions to strengthen the *Learning to Learn* component by offering *Learning to Learn* training for all tutors on a regular basis.

CONCLUSION

The First Baptist Church Tutorial Program clearly demonstrates the need and value of church-based educational and cultural enrichment programs as an integral part of the traditional educational process of our youth. We strongly advocate that church organizations develop similar programs and utilize the talents and skills within their memberships to staff and administer these educational support initiatives. With the public school systems under daily assault from nearly all segments of our society, the role of the church, with its financial and membership resources, has become increasingly important.

REFERENCES

Claxton, C. S. & M. P. (1987). Learning styles: Implications for improving educational practices. *Higher Education Research Report*, 4. ASHE-ERIC Clearinghouse. Washington, DC.

Cole, C. G. Jr. (1982). Improving instruction: Issues and alternatives for higher education. *Higher Education Research Report*, 4. AAHE-ERIC Clearinghouse. Washington, DC.

Heiman, M. & Slomianko, J. (1993). *Success in college and beyond.* Cambridge, MA: Learning to Learn, Inc.

Riley, R. W. (1993). Will blacks rally to Riley's education reforms?: An interview with Secretary of Education Richard W. Riley. *The Journal of Blacks in Higher Education* (No. 1), pp. 83–87.

Soaries, D. B. (1995). *What every member should know about Christian duty: Social action and civic responsibility evangelism manual,* First Baptist Church of Lincoln Gardens.

Chapter 26

Minority Men's Health: A Review of the Literature with Special Emphasis on African American Men

DAVID ANTHONY FORRESTER

This chapter provides a review of contemporary literature focusing on: (1) minority men's health—general background; (2) Hispanic and African American men's health promotion—beliefs and behaviors; (3) African American men's family and parenting patterns, including both father-absent and father-present homes; (4) African American men's religious involvement; (5) minority men and assaultive violence; (6) African American men and incarceration; and (7) minority men and occupational and environmental hazards. In an effort to provide a context for better understanding of recent research studies, the historical evolution of minority men's health issues is described where appropriate. Finally, implications for future research and education regarding minority men's health are identified; and recommendations are made for the investigation of men's health topics in addition to those discussed in this chapter.

MINORITY MEN'S HEALTH— GENERAL BACKGROUND

While the health of the U.S. population as a whole has steadily improved each year, it continues to decline for minority populations (Weitzel, Hudak, Becker, Waller, & Stuifbergen, 1994). The growth of minority populations is increasing; thus, the U.S. is rapidly becoming populated by a "majority of minorities" (Pahnos, 1992, p. 24). By the year 2000, more than 25% of the United States population will consist of ethnic minorities, and by 2080 approximately 51% of the population will be minorities (Andrews, 1992).

Most of the research regarding the health of racial and ethnic minorities highlights the disparity in morbidity and mortality rates between minority and nonminority populations (U.S. Department of Health and Human Services [DHHS], 1985, 1990). Approximately 60,000 excess deaths occur annually among minority populations. The mortality rates among African Americans are the highest of the minority groups and are approximately 50% higher than whites. The health of Hispanics, in the aggregate, is more similar to that of the white population than the African American population, even though the income levels of Hispanics and African Americans are more similar (Nickens, 1990).

On numerous indicators of morbidity and mortality, the health status of African American men ranks significantly lower than that other segments of the U.S. population: (1) the average life expectancy at birth for African American males is lower than that of white males, African American females, or white females by 2.1, 10, and 8.4 years, respectively (U.S. DHHS, 1991); (2) African American men tend to have greater exposure to hazardous occupations, have higher rates of hypertension, and have greater morbidity from selected cancers than their white counterparts (National Center for Health Statistics [NCHS], 1991); and (3) African American men's age-adjusted mortality rates for cardiovascular disease, diabetes, and cirrhosis of the liver exceed rates for other segments of the U.S. population (U.S. DHHS, 1991).

HISPANIC AND AFRICAN AMERICAN MEN'S HEALTH PROMOTION: BELIEFS AND BEHAVIORS

To determine the differences in health beliefs and behaviors among white, Hispanic, and African American men, Weitzel and others (1994) studied 1,033 men and found: (1) whites may have a more internal locus of control regarding health outcomes than do Hispanics or African Americans, likewise, Hispanics more than African Americans; (2) whites tend to score higher on measures of health promotion than Hispanics and African Americans; and (3) whites, therefore, tend to perform more self-initiated health-promoting behaviors than either the Hispanic or African American groups. These investigators contend that these findings may help to explain lower morbidity and mortality rates among the white population. The health and behavior patterns of Hispanics and African Americans were found generally not to be similar: (1) Hispanics may have a greater need for intervention strategies that emphasize health responsibility and self-actualizing behaviors; and (2) African Americans may have greater need for strategies emphasizing interpersonal support and stress management. These findings support Weitzel and Waller's (1990) conclusion that "combining data from different minority samples to produce a mixed minority sample may be a questionable practice in research" (p. 32).

Weitzel and others (1994) recommended that other factors potentially influencing Hispanic and African American men's health beliefs and behaviors be studied. Among these factors, they suggest: (1) social support; (2) environmental stressors; (3) knowledge regarding healthy lifestyles; (4) availability of resources; and (5) cultural practices, especially regarding diet.

Porter and Villarruel (1993) recommend that researchers identify the various subgroups within ethnic groups because homogeneity of minorities should not be assumed. "For example, persons of Mexican American, Puerto Rican, and Cuban descent are often designated as Hispanic, even though they each have unique cultural characteristics that may distinctively influence their health beliefs and behaviors" (Weitzel et al., 1994, p. 32).

AFRICAN AMERICAN MEN'S FAMILY AND PARENTING PATTERNS

African American families in the United States currently number 7,854,800 (U.S. Census Bureau, 1992). Little has been written about the strengths of African American parents (Hale-Benson, 1986; McAdoo, 1988). "The majority of studies on African American fathers focus on the pathological consequences of fathers' absence from the family or on the dysfunctional lower-class single-parent household and the 'black matriarchy.'" (Wade, 1994, p. 561).

The communal nature of African American parenting has been noted by numerous authors (Boyd-Franklin & Franklin, 1985; Manns, 1988). Much has been written in the past two decades documenting that many African American families are embedded in a complex kinship network of blood-related and non-blood kin (Gray & Nybell, 1990; Martin & Martin, 1978, 1985; Sudarkasa, 1988). Within such African American kinship networks, child care responsibilities are often shared by nieces, nephews, and/or grandchildren. According to Gray and Nybell (1990), "this kinship system, with its strong helping tradition, is rooted in West African culture and enabled African Americans to survive slavery and the continued oppression of the post-slavery eras" (p. 515).

A modest body of literature describes the strengths of African American families in fulfilling their socially appointed roles and functions (Billingsley, 1968; Billingsley, 1992; Hale-Benson, 1986; Hill, 1972; Lum 1992; McAdoo, 1988; Royse & Turner, 1980; Smith, 1992; Washington & LaPoint, 1988). By 1903, scholars such as W. E. B. Dubois had begun to describe the talents and abilities of African American families. It was not until after the social activism of the civil-rights movement of the late 1950s and early 1960s, however, that a new group of scholars, including Billingsley (1968) and Hill (1972), returned to chronicling the strengths rather than the deficits of African American families.

Hill (1972) described five major competencies of African American families: (1) strong kinship bonds; (2) strong work orientation; (3) adaptability of family roles; (4) high achievement orientation; and (5) strong religious orientation. Subsequent researchers have substantiated and expanded Hill's work. Royse and Turner (1980) found that African American subjects believed that Hill's list of African American family attributes accurately described them. Peters (1988) found that African American parents placed a high priority on developing the self-esteem of their children and that they sought to instill the values of love, respect, personal uniqueness, and desire for educational achievement in their children; and, that African American parents sought to prepare their children for survival in a racist society. In their list of African American family values, Washington and LaPoint (1988) included: (1) work and persistence; (2) ethnic pride; (3) religion; (4) caring; and (5) regard for achievement in children. Billingsley (1968, 1992) identified traditional values currently held by African Americans including: (1) love of learning; (2) deep-rooted spirituality; (3) desire for self-governance; and (4) commitment to serving others.

Building on a model of family competence, Hurd, Moore, and Rogers (1995) examined the strengths among fifty-three African American parents. These parents were asked to describe the values and behaviors they imparted to their children. By analyzing the statements of these respondents, Hurd and others (1995) identified three trends and eight themes. Trends, which were these African Americans' parenting patterns that were based on quantifiable data, included: (1) substantial parental involvement in the lives of their children; (2) plentiful support for parenting from external adult care givers; and (3) considerable involvement and high frequency of positive role modeling by African American men. Themes, which were based on these African Americans' self-reported narrative comments regarding their self-perceived family values and behaviors, included: (1) connection with their families; (2) emphasis on achievement and effort; (3) recognition of the importance of respect for others; (4) cultivation of spirituality; (5) ability to foster self-reliance; (6) recognition of the importance of education; (7) acceptance of life's pain and instruction in coping skills; and (8) recognition of the importance of self-respect and racial pride.

Prior to the 1970s, fathers in general appeared only in research regarding boys' sex-role identity. Studies of delinquent boys in the 1950s and 1960s suggested that paternal absence, especially common in African American families, induced a type of hyper masculinity resulting in delinquent styles and behavior (Segal, 1990). Studies in the 1970s contradicted these findings (e.g., Badaines, 1976; Davis, 1974; Hunt & Hunt, 1975; Longabaugh, 1973; Rubin, 1974; Wilkinson & O'Connor, 1977). Rarely are African American fathers used as direct participants in research regarding African American parenting (McAdoo, 1988).

In the late 1970s and early 1980s, research on father-present, middle-class families focusing on the strengths of African American families began to challenge the prevailing view of African American families as disorganized and unstable (Wade, 1994). "Absenteeism of males, combined with matrifocal homes," however, "is suggested by the literature and accepted by society at large as the primary type of African American family household in the United States today" (Connor, 1988, p. 191). Recent studies demonstrate that African American fathers are generally very concerned about being "good" fathers and that taking responsibility for and interest in their children's lives and that having an adequate and secure economic status facilitates their fathering roles (Cazenave, 1984; McAdoo, 1986).

According to Eshleman (1985), African American families have three distinct patterns: (1) matriarchal-matricentric families usually headed by a single parent, although some may include fathers who cannot support a family or who cannot exercise parental authority; (2) egalitarian two-parent families that are primarily middle class; and (3) affluent patriarchal two-parent families.

FATHER-ABSENT HOMES

In the late 1960s, the cumulative effects of poverty, racism, and segregation peaked, the country's economic progress began to deteriorate, the economy began to shift away from unskilled labor, and the social programs of the Great Society began to have an impact on the poor (Murray, 1984). The two-parent structure of African American families began to deteriorate (Connor, 1988). In 1950, only 9% of African American families were headed by one parent. By 1970, this number grew to 33.3%; by 1980, 45.8% of African American families were single-parent households (Glick, 1981).

According to Wade (1994, p. 564), "the African American single-parent family can be viewed as an adaptation to the forces of racial oppression and economics—a by-product of and response to modern capitalism." Madhubuti (1990) contends that fatherhood may increase a man's sense of failure and vulnerability if he knows or fears that he cannot provide for his family. Such men may react negatively by: (1) withdrawing from or abusing their families; (2) resorting to crime; (3) developing outside relationships with other women; (4) and/or resorting to self-destructive behavior such as suicide and substance abuse.

According to Campbell, Converse, and Rodgers (1976) and Voydanoff (1983) the perception of not being able to provide for their families is a great source of stress for African American men and contributes to their having a marginal position within the family. "The highly valued role of father/provider has implications for absent fathers. A father who is unable to provide financial resources may feel, and therefore, behave, as if he no longer has a role in the family" (Wade, 1994, p. 565). Unemployment has been found to inhibit African American men's attractiveness as a role model for their sons (Ray & McLoyd, 1986) and is related to fathers feeling less positively about their children (Sheldon & Fox, 1983).

Studies of African American adolescent fathers have found that these fathers are concerned primarily with financial responsibilities to their children, parenting skills, continuing their education, problems with the mother's parents, and their own futures (Brown, 1983; Hendricks, 1981). In their study of fifty African American teenage mothers, Massey (1991) found that 58% of these mothers reported receiving some marginal financial support from their baby's father and 42% felt that the father was a good or excellent provider.

Minority men reared in father-absent homes generally have problems with: (1) sex-role and gender identification; (2) school performance; (3) psychosocial development and adjustment; and (4) controlling aggression (Lamb, 1986). Connor (1988) contends that such depictions of the effects of father absence are not generally representative of African American families since such portrayals fail to take into account such factors as: (1) supportive extended-family networks; (2) institutional racism; and (3) the effects of discrimination. According to Wade (1994), "These studies tend to be biased toward traditional Western family norms and values and lack a comparison group of African American families in which mother and father are present or in which the single-parent family is economically sufficient" (p. 561). Wade (1994) further contends that, "these studies are easily accepted as representative of African American male psychology because they fit well with stereotypes and myths cultivated by a historically racist and sexist society" (pp. 561–562).

Contrary to much of the literature, Earl and Lohmann (1978) found that many African American male children from father-absent homes actually saw their fathers frequently, and all of the boys in their study had access to an African American male who could potentially serve as a role model. When asked to whom these boys would go for advice that "only a man could help me with," 37% (N = 53) said they would go to their biological father. When the mothers were asked the same question about their sons, however, only 5% thought that their sons would seek their father's help. The father-son relationship, therefore, appeared to be more important to these boys than many of their mothers realized.

FATHER-PRESENT HOMES

In general, middle-income African American fathers have been found to exhibit the same range of attitudes, behaviors, and beliefs as do fathers from other ethnic groups in American culture (McAdoo, 1981). They consider themselves effective, active participants in the care and upbringing of their children (Harrison, 1981).

In a study of family interpersonal dynamics and adolescent male outcomes among 100 middle-class families, Allen (1981) found interesting differences between African American and white parents: (1) African American wives rated their husbands' involvement in childcare and child rearing slightly higher than did white wives; (2) 63% of the African American mothers versus 47% of white mothers perceived their husbands as providing more help than the "average" husband in rearing their sons; and (3) African American fathers gave material rewards to their sons significantly more often than white fathers who were the least likely to reward their sons materially. According to the adolescents in this study: (1) African American mothers and white fathers shared significantly more activities with their sons than did white mothers and African American fathers, even though African American parents apparently spent approximately the same amount of time in shared activities with their sons; (2) 60% of the African American adolescents reported above-average closeness with their parents, whereas only 47% of the white adolescents claimed above-average closeness with their parents; and (3) African American sons were significantly more likely than white sons to identify more closely with their mothers than with their fathers.

Connor (1986) studied the parenting attitudes of 136 young African American men and found that these men perceived themselves as actively involved with their children; and in a follow-up study of 138 African American women (1988), found that these women also perceived African American men to be meaningfully involved with their children. Hyde and Texidor (1988) found that African American fathers ($N = 135$) generally perceived the experience of fatherhood positively and that the majority of these fathers viewed childcare as a responsibility to be shared by both parents, including such activities as diapering, feeding, bathing, and dressing their children. Seventy-three percent of these fathers believed that direct daily contact with their children was needed; 90% indicated that they would like to spend more time with their children. Although African American and white fathers have been found to be more similar than dissimilar in their participation in and attitudes toward their roles as fathers, African American fathers have been found to be more expressive and affectionate with their children than their white counterparts (Price-Bonham & Skeen, 1979).

AFRICAN AMERICAN MEN'S RELIGIOUS INVOLVEMENT

Religion and religious activities have long been an integral part of African American communities (Dubois, 1903; Frazier, 1964). "For the most part, the distinctiveness of religious involvement among African Americans is manifested in the form of the black church. As enduring, uniquely African American institutions, black churches have played a major role in the development and survival of African American communities" (Brown & Gary, 1994, p. 825). In recent years, black churches have become the focus sites of numerous health-related interventions for hypertension, smoking cessation, and heart disease, etc. (Robbins, 1991; Hatch & Voorhorst, 1992).

Several studies have found that African American men tend to participate less in formal religious organizations than do African American women; African American men comprise only 33% to 40% of black churches' congregations (Walters & Brown, 1979; Lincoln & Mamiya, 1990; Billingsley, Caldwell, Hill & Rouse, 1991). Other studies have found a positive relationship between religious involvement and physical and mental health (Mullen, 1990; Levin & Vanderpool, 1987). "Few studies of religious variables and health have focused on males (or even on gender differences), and even fewer have included black male respondents" (Brown & Gary, 1994, p. 826).

In a study of men 55 years of age or older, Larson and others (1989) found that religious commitment (i.e., the importance of religion more so than church attendance) was related to lower systolic and diastolic blood pressure. Levin, Jenkins, and Rose (1988) obtained mixed results in their study of the effect of religious variables on several health outcomes including hypertension and alcohol use in a sample of men. In a study of religious factors and physical health that included African American men, Livingston, Levine, and Moore (1991) found that having a church affiliation was related to lower systolic and diastolic blood pressure.

Studies that have included African American samples indicate that religious involvement tends to buffer the effect of stressful life events on mental health (Neff & Husaini, 1982; Williams, Larson, Buckler, Heckman, & Pyle, 1991). Schoenbach and others (1986) found that participation in church activities was associated with lower mortality for persons 60 years of age, except for African American men. Brown and others (1990) found that religious involvement tended to reduce depressive symptoms among African American males with personal injuries.

In a study of 537 urban African American men, Brown & Gary (1994) found: (1) religious involvement was not significantly related to physical health status or hypertension (i.e., neither religiosity, frequency of church attendance, nor denominational affiliation was associated with overall self-appraisal of physical health status nor the presence or absence of hypertension); (2) African American men who had an overall moderate to high level of religiosity, who attended church regularly, and who saw themselves as being affiliated with a denomination had significantly lower depressive symptom scores; (3) religiosity, church attendance, and denominational affiliation all had significant inverse associations with current smoking behaviors (e.g., among those men who attended church once a week, only 27.2% were current smokers compared with 64.3% of those who never attended church); and (4) African American men who reported moderate to high levels of religiosity, attended church at least a few times a month, and were affiliated with a denomination were significantly less likely to drink alcohol on a daily basis.

MINORITY MEN
AND ASSAULTIVE VIOLENCE

"African American male adolescents face disproportionate risk for death or injury resulting from assaultive violence" (Hammond & Yung, 1993, p. 142). Current levels of funding for research and for the creation of new prevention programs are not commensurate with the epidemic proportions of the problem. African American adolescents are more likely to die of injuries received from a gun wielded by a friend or acquaintance than from any other cause (Fingerhut, Ingram, & Feldman, 1992; Humphrey & Palmer, 1986; Mercy et al., 1986; NCHS, 1990; Wilbanks, 1986).

Homicide now stands as the second leading cause of death among children and adolescents across all ethnic groups and ages in the United States (Rodriguez, 1990). Teen-agers are approximately two and a half times as likely to be victims of violent crime than are persons over 20 years of age (U.S. Department of Justice, 1991a).

In a national survey conducted by the American School Health Association (1988), nearly one half the boys and one fourth of the girls reported having been involved in at least one fight during the past year. Twenty-three percent of the boys reported carrying a knife to school; 3% reported carrying a gun. The Youth Risk Behavior Surveillance Survey (Centers for Disease Control [CDC], 1991b) found that one in five high school students carried a weapon of some kind during the thirty days preceding the survey; one in three specifically admitted carrying a gun.

The nature and sources of risk from assaultive violence vary by age. Infants and young children are most frequently victims of fatal abuse by a parent or caretaker; adolescents are more likely to be victimized by friends or acquaintances (Christoffel, 1990). Homicide risk increases dramatically in adolescence, with the most vulnerable group being older African American adolescents and young adults, ages 15 to 24 (Rodriguez, 1990).

Male youth receive injuries from assault more frequently than female youth and their injuries are more likely to be serious (Hammond & Yung, 1993; Harlow, 1989). Males 12–19 years old experience violent crime at a rate of 80 per 1,000, nearly double that of female rates (Christoffel, 1990). Males are also much more prone to engage in risky behavior such as carrying weapons. In fact, the male rate of carrying weapons has been found to be more than three times the female rate (U.S. Department of Justice, 1991a).

Adolescents of specific ethnic groups face greater risk than white youth of being victims of violent assault (Hammond & Yung, 1993). National data on the homicide victimization rates for Latinos, American Indians, Alaska Natives, and Asian Americans are less accurate than figures for African Americans (U.S. DHHS, 1990; Prothrow-Smith, 1991; Smith, Mercy, & Rosenberg, 1986). The incidence of fatal violence for young Latino men is approximately three to four times greater than that for young white men of the same age (Smith et al., 1986; Tardiff and Gross, 1986) and for American Indians and Alaska Natives more than twice that for all Americans (Indian Health Service, 1990).

Homicide victimization statistics for African American youth show a risk far exceeding that of the white population and all other ethnic groups. Homicide is the leading cause of death for both male and female African Americans aged 15 to 34 (NCHS, 1990, 1992). Murders of young African American men account for some 42% of all deaths for those 15 to 24 years of age, making this age, gender, and ethnic group the subpopulation at greatest risk. Mortality rates of men between these ages indicate that African Americans are homicide victims at an annual rate of 101.8 per 100,000, compared with a rate of 11.5 for white men the same age (NCHS, 1992). Homicide victimization rates for African American males 10 to 14 years of age and for African American females between 10 and 19 are approximately four times that of their white counterparts (NCHS, 1992). A survey of gun-related violence around inner-city schools (in which the sample was 75% African American) found that 20% of the students had been threatened with a gun and 12% had been shot at, with male rates exceeding female victimization by a 3 to 1 ratio (Sheley, McGee & Wright, 1992).

All youth are at greatest risk for assaults or murders involving loss of control between family, friends, or acquaintances (Hammond & Yung, 1993). Assaultive violence among adolescents often erupts from an escalating argument, with the victim-perpetrator outcome resting in variations in physical strength and/or the availability of a weapon (Hawkins, 1986; Prothrow-Stith, 1991).

Both white and non-white young men and women are most likely to be assaulted or murdered by men (Harlow, 1991). African American women are most likely to be murdered by a family member or intimate partner; in the case of adolescents, the perpetrator is usually a boyfriend (Harlow, 1991; Humphrey & Palmer, 1986; Mercy et al., 1986). Both male and female African Americans are usually killed at home; for men, the most common weapon of death is a handgun (Mercy et al., 1986). Virtually all published reports regarding youth homicide and assaultive violence have concluded that late adolescent/young adult African American men from inner cities and low-income families are the most vulnerable group for death or injury from assaultive violence, with Latino men of similar age and circumstances being the second highest risk group (Christoffel, 1990; Harlow, 1989, 1991; Sumner, Mintz, & Brown, 1986).

The incidence of primary relationship between victims and offenders is higher for African Americans than for whites (Humphrey & Palmer, 1986; Mercy et al., 1986; O'Carroll & Mercy, 1986; Parker, 1989; Wilbanks, 1986). In fact, Wilbanks (1986) found that African American male youth had a rate of friend/acquaintance homicide that was six times higher than that of white male teenagers.

Young Latino men have been found to have higher rates of family/friend/acquaintance homicide than young white men, but slightly lower rates than African Americans; as well as the highest rates of death by gang-related violence of all ethnic groups (Loya et al., 1986). Young Latino men are killed more often in the street and are more frequently the victims of stabbings than are other ethnic groups (CDC, 1991a; Loya et al., 1986; Mercy et al., 1986; U.S. Department of Justice, 1991). Asian Americans have been found to have very low rates of primary homicide but the most likely group to be victimized by strangers, usually in crime-related incidents such as mugging or burglary (Loya et al., 1986).

African American victims and their assailants are likely to be of the same ethnicity (Hammond & Yung, 1993). More than 90% of both male and female African American murder victims of all age groups are slain by other African Americans (Federal Bureau of Investigation [FBI], 1987, 1989). In addition to ethnicity, African American men involved in assaultive violence are likely to have other characteristics in common such as: (1) low socioeconomic status; (2) residence in the same neighborhood; (3) similarity in age; and (4) histories of frequent fighting (Prothrow-Stith, 1991).

Wilson and Daly (1985) found that the three most frequent correlates of fatal assaultive violence were: (1) retaliation for previous verbal or physical abuse (46%); (2) escalating showing-off contests (16%); and (3) jealously conflicts (12%). Agnew (1990) found that the most common explanation for violent offenses was "retaliation-revenge."

Poverty and inner-city residence have been identified as the environmental risk correlates most strongly associated with violence victimization among all adolescents (Fingerhut et al., 1992). Urban adolescents of low socioeconomic status have been found to fight, carry weapons, and witness violence more frequently than national youth samples (Menacker, Weldon, & Hurwitz, 1990; Shakoor & Chalmers, 1991). In fact, Shakoor and Chalmers (1991) studied African American eighth graders living in an extremely violent low-income neighborhood in Chicago and found that 55% of the boys and 45% of the girls in their sample had actually witnessed someone being shot.

Low socioeconomic status is not, in itself, thought to account for the high rates of violence in urban neighborhoods. Rather, investigators have implicated a number of factors closely associated with poverty such as: (1) community disorganization; (2) joblessness; (3) mobility; (4) family dysfunction; and (5) high population density/crowding (Messner & Sampson, 1991; Patterson, 1991; Sampson, 1987).

There is continuing debate over the exact role of ethnicity as a predictor of assaultive violence. Some investigators have found that ethnic effects remain even when poverty is taken into account (e.g., Balkwell, 1990; Rosenfeld, 1986). Others contend that extreme poverty is a stronger predictor of homicide than ethnicity (e.g., Huff-Corzine, Corzine, & Moore, 1991; Loftin & Parker, 1985, 1985; Messner & Tardiff, 1986).

Certain cultural values held by African American men may contribute to violent aggression (Oliver, 1989a, 1989b; Roberts, 1990). Carmichael (1990) conducted an exploratory study of attitudes about crime among male African American delinquents in custody and found that respondents indicated they held high respect for assailants (80%), drug dealers (65%), and murderers (60%).

AFRICAN AMERICAN MEN
AND INCARCERATION

Since statistics on prison inmates have been recorded, African American men have constituted a disproportionate percentage of state inmate populations (Cahalan, 1979). In 1880, when African Americans were 13.1% of the U.S. population, 28.6% of all prisoners in state correctional institutions were African American men (Cahalan, 1970). By 1989, African Americans made up 12% of the U.S. population and African American men less than 6% of the population; the number of African American men confined to state prisons had grown to 48% of the total prison population (U.S. Department of Justice, 1989, 1991b). In the northeastern and southern regions of the United States, African American men make up 50% and 58% of state prison inmates, respectively (U.S. Department of Justice 1989, 1991b).

At the current annual cost of $20,000 per inmate, the United States spends approximately $7.6 billion per year to warehouse roughly 370,000 African American men in prisons (Brazaitis, 1991). In 1990, approximately 525,000 African American men were confined to jails or state or federal prisons (U.S. Department of Justice, 1991c, 1991d). In that same year, fewer than 480,000 African American men were enrolled in U.S. colleges or universities (Evangelauf, 1992). According to King (1993), "at the current pace of African American male incarceration, by the year 2000 nearly 60% of the total U.S. prison population, or roughly 900,000 African American men, will be locked behind prison walls" (p. 146).

Some have contended that the disproportionate percentage of African American men in state prisons is the result of the disproportionate number of serious crimes that African American men commit (*Furman v. Georgia,* 1972; Hagan, 1974; Blumstein, 1982). Others have argued that race and class discrimination in arrest, conviction, and sentencing practices is responsible for this phenomenon (Adamson, 1983; Christianson, 1981; Dunbaugh, 1979; Hawkins & Jones, 1989; Lichtenstein & Kroll, 1990; Nagel, 1977; Petersilia, 1983; Zatz, 1987). This position finds merit in the fact that African American men are convicted of serious crimes at a rate that is more than eight times the proportion of their representation in the U.S. population (U.S. Department of Justice, 1989, 1991b).

Recognizing that African American men constitute the largest group of men in the nation's state correctional systems, King (1993) advocates that social service agencies and correctional institutions develop and implement five types of programs or services to meet the needs of incarcerated African American men and their families, including: (1) culturally appropriate family-support groups; (2) psychiatric/psychological and social clinical services; (3) community-based family life education programs; (4) family life education programs in correctional institutions; and (5) family case-management services.

MINORITY MEN AND OCCUPATIONAL AND ENVIRONMENTAL HAZARDS

Occupational illnesses and injuries in minority groups are under-reported and under-diagnosed. Although African Americans are more likely to suffer work-related injuries and disabilities, they are less likely than their white counterparts to report this information (Davis, 1983).

OCCUPATIONAL HAZARDS

"Since whites colonized the Americas, occupation has been a risk factor for people of color in the United States" (Dula et al., 1993, p. 181). "People of color have historically had the lowest paid, lowest mobility, and most unpleasant jobs in the work force" (Dula et al., 1993, p. 182).

During the nineteenth century, large numbers of slaves suffered from such diseases as anthrax contracted from animals and nicotine poisoning from tobacco plants with which they worked (Savitt, 1978). In the 1930s, of 5,000 African Americans recruited to tunnel through a mountain in West Virginia, almost 500 died of silicosis (Dula et al., 1993). In the 1950s, African Americans employed in the chromite industry were found to have 80 times the expected number of lung cancers (Dula et al., 1993). During the 1960s and 1970s, African Americans in the textile industry were concentrated in high-dust areas and were, therefore, placed at greater risk of developing byssinosis (Davis & Rowland, 1983).

For poor people and people of color, occupational hazards are not the only issue. For many poor people, employment must take precedence over occupational hazards. In addition, due to limits in education and access to information, they may not be fully aware of the dire health consequences of their jobs" (Dula et al., 1993, p. 185). Ciesielski and others (1991) reported that among migrant farm workers in North Carolina: 37% of Hispanics, 62% of African Americans, and 76% of Haitians were infected with tuberculosis. Kippen (1991) reported that of 116 epidemiological occupational cancer studies, only 14 made any reference at all to nonwhites.

ENVIRONMENTAL HAZARDS

According to Dula and others (1993), "people of color are subjected to disproportionately large amounts of pollution, not only in their workplaces, but also in their communities" (p. 184). Three out of four federally designated hazardous waste sites are located in communities of color (Durning, 1991). The nation's largest hazardous waste landfill is in Emelle, Alabama, where the population is nearly 80% African American (Bullard, 1990). The Center for Third World Organizing reported that 2 million tons of radioactive uranium tailings were dumped on Native American lands (Environmental Services Coordination Office [ESCO], 1991), while a U.S. Environmental Protection

Agency (EPA) study found that people living within a half mile of uranium tailings were twice as likely to die of lung cancers as the rest of the population (Freudenberg, 1984). Using National Health and Nutrition Survey data, Mushak and Crocetti (1989) estimate that 3 to 4 million children are exposed to toxic levels of lead in the United States. Most of these lead-poisoned children are African American and Latino (Russell, 1989).

Dula and others (1993) advocate that educators, environmental activists, and health professionals coordinate their efforts to address the inequities confronting minorities in employment opportunities and in exposure to occupational and environmental hazards. These authors recommend: (1) effectively involving community organizations and using other community resources to communicate culturally sensitive health information; (2) establishing a national clearinghouse for occupational and environmental health education materials; and (3) encouraging minority empowerment by supporting the development of a generation of young health researchers, educators, and practitioners of color.

IMPLICATIONS AND RECOMMENDATIONS

The implications of these studies for future research and education regarding minority men's health are clear: (1) numerous factors influencing minority men's health are in need of further study (e.g., social support, environmental stressors, knowledge regarding healthy lifestyles, availability of resources, and cultural practices); (2) assumptions of homogeneity of minorities should be challenged (i.e., various subgroups within ethnic groups should be studied individually and comparatively); (3) future studies should continue to examine the strengths rather than the deficits of minority families; (4) the role of religion, particularly black churches, regarding minority men's health should be further examined (e.g., strategies to engage and further involve minority men in religion should be identified and disseminated; the potential health outcomes of religious involvement of minority men should be further documented); (5) initiatives to explicate and eradicate violence among minorities, especially minority men, should be undertaken; (6) community-based family life education programs should be developed and implemented both in the community and in correctional institutions; (7) community-based psychiatric and social services for minority men should be enhanced and should include culturally appropriate family case-management services; and (8) a coordinated effort should be made by educators, community and environmental activists, and health professionals to address the inequities experienced by minorities in employment opportunities and exposure to occupational/environmental hazards.

In addition to the topics discussed in this chapter, it is recommended that future investigation of minority men's health continue to address such important topics as: (1) substance abuse (e.g., tobacco, alcohol, opiates, cocaine, etc.); (2) HIV/AIDS; (3) geriatric issues specific to minority men (e.g., psychological depression, heart disease, prostate cancer, etc.); (4) homelessness and its implications for minority men's health; and (5) gay and bisexual minority men's health (e.g., high-risk sexual behavior, victimization/violence, etc.).

REFERENCES

Adamson, K. (1983). Punishment after slavery: Southern state penal systems, 1865–1890. *Social Problems, 30*: 555–569.

Agnew, R. (1990). The origins of delinquent events: An examination of offender accounts. *Journal of Research in Crime and Delinquency, 27*: 267–294.

Allen, W. R. (1981). Moms, dads, and boys: Race and sex differences in the socialization of male children. In L. E. Gary (Ed.), *Black men* (pp. 99–114). Beverly Hills, CA: Sage Publications.

American School Health Association. (1988). *National adolescent student health survey.* Washington, DC: Author.

Andrews, M. M. (1992). Cultural perspectives on nursing in the 21st century. *Journal of Professional Nursing, 8*: 7–15.

Badaines, J. (1976). Identification, imitation, and sex-role preference in father-present and father-absent black and Chicano boys. *Journal of Psychology, 92*: 15–24.

Balkwell, J. (1990). Ethnic inequality and the rate of homicide. *Social Forces, 69*: 53–70.

Billingsley, A. (1968). *Black families in white America.* Englewood Cliffs, NJ: Prentice-Hall.

Billingsley, A. (1992). *Climbing Jacob's ladder: The enduring legacy of African-American families.* New York: Simon & Schuster.

Billingsley, A., Caldwell, C. S., Hill, R. B. & Rouse, W. V. (1991). *Black churches and family-oriented community outreach programs.* College Park, MD: University of Maryland, School of Human Ecology.

Blumstein, A. (1982). On the racial disproportionality of United States' prison populations. *Journal of Criminal Law and Criminology, 73*: 1259–1282.

Boyd-Franklin, A. & Franklin, N. (1985). A psycho educational perspective on black parenting. In J. McAdoo & H. McAdoo (Eds.), *Black children.* Beverly Hills, CA: Sage Publications.

Brazaitis, T. (1991, January 4). U.S. is the world's top jailer with high crime, tough laws. *Cleveland Plain Dealer*, pp. 1-A, 11-A.

Brown, D. R. & Gary, L. E. (1994). Religious involvement and health status among African-American males. *Journal of the National Medical Association, 86*(11): 825–831.

Brown, D. R., Ndubuisi, S. C. & Gary, L. E. (1990). Religiosity and psychological distress among blacks. *Journal of Religion and Health, 29*: 55–68.

Brown, S. V. (1983). The commitment and concerns of black adolescent parents. *Social Work Research, 19*(4): 27–34.

Bullard, R. (1990). *Dumping in Dixie: Race, class, and environmental quality.* Boulder, CO: Westview Press.

Cahalan, M. (1979). Trends in the incarceration in the United States since 1880: A summary of reported rates and the distribution of offenses. *Crime and Delinquency, 23*: 9–41.

Campbell, A., Converse, P. & Rodgers, W. (1976). *The quality of American life*. New York: Russel Sage Foundation.

Carmichael, B. (1990). An exploratory study of values and attitudes of black delinquents in custody. *Journal of Crime and Justice, 13*: 66–85.

Cazenave, N. A. (1984). Race, socioeconomic status, and age: The context of American masculinity. *Sex Roles, 11*: 639–656.

Centers for Disease Control. (1990). Homicide among young black males—United States, 1978–1987. *Morbidity and Mortality Weekly Report, 39*: 869–873.

Centers for Disease Control. (1991a). Forum on youth violence in minority communities: Setting the agenda for prevention. *Public Health Reports, 106*: 225–253.

Centers for Disease Control. (1991b). Weapon-carrying among high school students. *Journal of the American Medical Association, 266*: 2342.

Christianson, S. (1981). Our black prisons. *Crime and Delinquency, 25*: 365–375.

Ciesielski, S. D., Seed, J. R., Esposito, D. H. & Hunter, N. (1991). The epidemiology of tuberculosis among North Carolina migrant farm workers. *Journal of the American Medical Association, 265*: 1715–1719.

Connor, M. E. (1986). Some parenting attitudes of young black fathers. In R. A. Lewis & R. E. Salt (Eds.), *Men in families* (pp. 159–168). Beverly Hills, CA: Sage Publications.

Connor, M. E. (1988). Teenage fatherhood: Issues confronting young black males. In J. T. Gibbs (Ed.), *Young, black, and male in America: An endangered species* (pp. 188–218). New York: Auburn House.

Davis, J. A. (1974). Justification for no obligation: Views of black males toward crime and the criminal law. *Issues in Criminology, 9*: 69–87.

Davis, M. E. & Rowland, A. (1983). Problems faced by minority workers. In B. S. Levy & D. H. Wegman (Eds.), *Occupational health: Recognizing and preventing work-related disease*. Boston, MA: Little, Brown and Company.

Dubois, W. E. B. (1903). *The Negro church*. Atlanta, GA: Atlanta University Press.

Dula, A., Kurtz, S. & Samper, M. (1993). Occupational and environmental reproductive hazards education and resources for communities of color. *Environmental Health Perspectives Supplements, 101*(Supplement 2.): 181–189.

Dunbaugh, F. M. (1979). Racially disproportionate rates of incarceration in the United States. *Prison Law Monitor, 1*(9): 219–220.

Durning, A. B. (1991). *Poverty and the environment: Reversing the downward spiral*. Washington, DC: Watchworld Institute.

Earl, L. & Lohmann, N. (1978). Absent fathers and black male children. *Social Work, 23*: 413–415.

Environmental Services Coordination Office. (1991). *Race, poverty, and the environment*. Ann Arbor, MI: Author.

Eshleman, J. R. (1985). *The family: An introduction* (5th ed.). Boston, MA: Allyn and Bacon.

Evangelauf, J. (1992, January 22). Minority-group enrollment at colleges rose 10% from 1988 to 1990, reaching record levels. *Chronicle of Higher Education*, pp. A33, A37.

Federal Bureau of Investigation. (1987). *Crime in the United States: 1986*. Washington, DC: U.S. Department of Justice.

Federal Bureau of Investigation. (1989). *Uniform crime reports for the United States*. Washington, DC: U.S. Department of Justice.

Fingerhut, L., Ingram, D. & Feldman, J. (1992). Firearm and nonfirearm homicide among persons 15 through 19 years of age. *Journal of the American Medical Association, 267*: 3048–3053.

Frazier, E. F. (1964). *The Negro church in America*. New York: Schocken Books.

Freudenberg, N. (1984). *Not in our backyards*. New York: Monthly Review Press.

Furman v. Georgia, 408 U.S. 238, 399, 405 (1972). (Burger, C. J. dissenting).

Glick, P. C. (1981). A demographic picture of black families. In H. P. McAdoo (Ed.), *Black families* (pp. 106–126). Beverly Hills, CA: Sage Publications.

Gray, S. S. & Nybell, L. M. (1990). Issues in African-American family preservation. *Child Welfare, 69*(6): 513–523.

Hagan, J. (1974). Extra-legal attributes and criminal sentencing. *Law and Society Review, 8*: 357–383.

Hale-Benson, J. (1986). *Black children*. Baltimore, MD: Johns Hopkins University Press.

Hammond, W. R. & Yung, B. (1993). Psychology's role in the public health response to assaultive violence among young African-American men. *American Psychologist, 48*(2): 142–154.

Harlow, C. (1989). *Injuries from crime* (Bureau of Justice Statistics, Special Report No. NCJ-116811). Washington, DC: US Department of Justice.

Harlow, C. (1991). *Female victims of violent crime* (Bureau of Justice Statistics, Special Report No. NCJ-126826). Washington, DC: U.S. Department of Justice.

Harrison, A. (1981). Attitudes toward procreation among black adults. In H. P. McAdoo (Ed.), *Black families* (pp. 199–208). Beverly Hills, CA: Sage Publications.

Hatch, J. W. & Voorhorst, S. (1992). The church as a resource for health promotion activities in the black community. In D. M. Becker, D. R. Hill, J. S. Jackson, D. M. Levine, F. A. Stillman, & S. M. Weiss (Eds.), *Proceedings from workshop on health behavior research in minority populations: Access, design, and application* (NIH Publication 92-2965) (pp. 30–34). Washington, DC: National Institutes of Health.

Hawkins, D. F. & Jones, N. E. (1989). Black adolescents and the criminal justice system. In R. L. Jones (Ed.), *Black adolescents* (pp. 403–425). Berkeley, CA: Cobb & Henry.

Hendricks, L. E. (1981). Black unwed adolescent fathers. In L. E. Gary (Ed.), *Black men* (pp. 131–138). Beverly Hills, CA: Sage Publications.

Hill, R. (1972). *The strengths of black families.* New York: National Urban League.

Huff-Corzine, L., Corzine, J. & Moore, D. (1991). Deadly connections: Culture, Poverty, and the direction of lethal violence. *Social Forces, 69*: 715–732.

Humphrey, J. & Palmer, S. (1986). Race, sex, and criminal homicide: Offender-victim relationships. In D. Hawkins (Ed.), *Homicide among black Americans* (pp. 57–68). Lanham, MD: University Press of America.

Hunt, L. L. & Hunt, J. G. (1975). Race and the father-son correlation: The conditional relevance of father absence for the orientations and identities of adolescent boys. *Social Problems.* 35–52.

Hurd, E. P., Moore, C. & Rogers, R. (1995). Quiet success: Parenting strengths among African Americans. *Families in Society, 76*(7): 434–443.

Hyde, B. L. & Texidor, M. S. (1988). A description of the fathering experience among black fathers. *Journal of National Black Nurses' Association, 2*: 67–78.

Indian Health Service. (1990). *Injuries among American Indians and Alaskan Natives, 1990.* Rockville, MD: Public Health Service.

King, A. E. O. (1993). The impact of incarceration on African American families: Implications for practice. *Families in Society, 74*(3): 145–153.

Kippen, H. M. (1991). Are nonwhites at greater risk of occupational cancer? *American Journal of Indian Medicine, 19*: 67–74.

Lamb, M. E. (1986). *The father's role: Applied perspectives.* New York: Wiley Interscience.

Larson, D. B., Koenig, H. G., Kaplan, B. H., Greenberg, R. S., Logue, E. & Tyroler, H. A. (1989). *Journal of Religion and Health, 28*: 265–278.

Levin, J., Jenkins, D. & Rose, R. M. (1988). Religion, type A behavior and health. *Journal of Religion and Health, 27*: 267–278.

Levin, J. & Vanderpool, H. Y. (1987). Is frequent religious attendance really conducive to better health? Toward an epidemiology religion. *Social Science and Medicine, 24*: 589–600.

Lichtenstein, A. C. & Kroll, M. A. (1990). *The fortress economy: The economic role of the U.S. prison system.* Philadelphia, PA: American Friends Service Committee.

Lincoln, C. E. & Mamiya, L. H. (1990). *The black church in the African-American experience.* Durham, NC: Duke University Press.

Livingston, I., Levine, D. M. & Moore, R. (1991). Social integration and black intraracial variation in blood pressure. *Ethnicity and Disease, 1*: 135–149.

Longabaugh, R. (1973). Mother behavior as a variable moderating the effects of father absence. *Ethos, 1*: 456–465.

Loya, C., Garcia, P., Sullivan, J., Vargas, L., Mercy, J. & Allen, N. (1986). Conditional risks of homicide among Anglo, Hispanic, Black, and Asian victims in Los Angeles, 1970–1979. In *Report of the Secretary's Task Force on Black and Minority Health* (Vol. 5, pp. 137–144). Washington, DC: US Department of Health and Human Services.

Lum, D. (1992). *Social work practice and people of color.* Pacific Grove, CA: Brooks/Cole.

Madhubuti, R. (1990). *Black men: Obsolete, single, dangerous?* Chicago, IL: Third World Press.

Manns, W. (1988). Supportive roles of significant others in black families. In H. McAdoo (Ed.), *Black families.* Newbury Park, CA: Sage Publications.

Martin, E. P. & Martin, J. M. (1978). *The black extended family.* Chicago, IL: University of Chicago Press.

Martin, J. M. & Martin, E. P. (1985). *The helping tradition in the black family and community.* Silver Spring, MD: National Association of Social Workers.

Massey, G. (1991). The flip side of teen mothers: A look at teen fathers. In B. P. Bowser (Ed.), *Black male adolescents: Parenting and education in community context* (pp. 117–128). Lanham, MD: University Press of America.

McAdoo, J. L. (1981). Black father and child interactions. In L. E. Gary (Ed.), *Black men* (pp. 115–130). Beverly Hills, CA: Sage Publications.

McAdoo, J. L. (1986). A black perspective on the father's role in child development. *Marriage and Family Review, 9*: 117–133.

McAdoo, J. L. (1988). The roles of black fathers in the socialization of black children. In H. McAdoo (Ed.), *Black families.* Newbury Park, CA: Sage Publications.

Mercy, J., Goodman, R., Rosenberg, M., Allen, N., Loya, F., Smith, J. & Vargas, L. (1986). Patterns of homicide victimization in the city of Los Angeles, 1970–1979. *Bulletin of the New York Academy of Medicine, 62*: 427–445.

Messner, S. & Sampson, R. (1991). The sex ratio, family distribution, and rates of violent crime: The paradox of demographic structure. *Social Forces, 69*: 693–713.

Messner, S. & Tardiff, K. (1986). Economic inequality and levels of homicide: An analysis of urban neighborhoods. *Criminology, 24*: 297–315.

Mullen, K. (1990). Religion and health: A review of the literature. *Journal of Sociology and Social Policy, 10*: 85–96.

Murray, C. (1984). *Loosing ground: American social policy, 1950–1980.* New York: Basic Books.

Mushak, P. & Crocetti, A. R. (1989). *Determination of number of lead-exposed American children as a function of lead source.* Integrated summary of a Report to the U.S. Congress on Childhood Lead Poisoning. London: Academic Press.

Nagel, W. G. (1977). On behalf of a moratorium on prison construction. *Crime and Delinquency, 23*: 154–172.

National Center for Health Statistics. (1990). *Prevention profile: Health, United States, 1989* (DHHS Publication No. PHS 90-1232). Hyattsville, MD: US Department of Health and Human Services.

National Center for Health Statistics. (1991). *Current Estimates from the National Health Interview Survey, 1991.* Washington, DC: US Government Printing Office.

Neff, J. A. & Husaini, B. A. (1982). Life events, drinking patterns and depressive symptomatology: The stress-buffering role of alcohol consumption. *Journal of Studies of Alcohol, 43*: 301–317.

Nickens, H. W. (1990). Health promotion and disease prevention among minorities. *Health Affairs, 9*(2): 133–143.

Nobles, W. (1988). African American family life. In H. McAdoo (Ed.), *Black families.* Newbury Park, CA: Sage Publications.

O'Caroll, P. W. & Mercy, J. A. (1986). Patterns and trends in Black homicide. In D. Hawkins (Ed.), *Homicide among black Americans* (pp. 29–42). Lanham, MD: University Press of America.

Oliver, W. (1989a). Black males and social problems: Prevention through Afrocentric socialization. *Journal of Black Studies, 20*: 15–39.

Oliver, W. (1989b). Sexual conquest and patterns of black-on-black violence: A structural-cultural perspective. *Violence and Victims, 4*: 257–271.

Pahnos, M. L. (1992). The continuing challenge of multi cultural health education. *Journal of School Health, 62*: 24–26.

Patterson, B. (1991). Poverty, income inequality, and community crime rates. *Criminology, 29*: 755–776.

Peters, M. (1988). Parenting in black families with young children. In H. McAdoo (Ed.), *Black families.* Newbury Park, CA: Sage Publications.

Petersilia, J. (1983). *Racial disparities in the criminal justice system.* Santa Monica, CA: Rand Corporation.

Porter, C. P. & Villarruel, A. M. (1993). Nursing research with African American and Hispanic people: Guidelines for action. *Nursing Outlook, 41*: 59–67.

Price-Bonham, S. & Skeen, P. (1979). A comparison of black and white fathers with implications for parent education. *Family Coordination, 28*: 53–59.

Prothrow-Stith, D. (1991). *Deadly consequences: How violence is destroying our teenage population and a plan to begin solving the problem.* New York: Harper Collins.

Ray, S. A. & McLoyd, V. C. (1986). Fathers in hard times: The impact of unemployment and poverty on parental and marital relations. In M. E. Lamb (Ed.), *The father's role: Applied perspectives* (pp. 339–383). New York: John Wiley.

Roberts, S. (1990). Murder, mayhem, and other joys of youth. *The Journal of NIH Research, 2*: 67–72.

Robbins, K. (1991). Heart, body, and soul: The gospel of good health. *Hopkins Medical News, 14*(3): 28–33.

Rodriguez, J. S. (1990). Childhood injuries in the United States. *American Journal of Diseases of Childhood, 144*: 627–646.

Rosenfeld, R. (1986). Urban crime rates: Effects of inequality, welfare dependency, region, and race. In J. Byrne & R. Sampson (Eds.), *The social ecology of crime* (pp. 116–130). New York: Springer-Verlag.

Royse, D. & Turner, G. (1980). Strengths of black families: A black community's perspective. *Social Work, 25*: 407–409.

Rubin, R. H. (1974). Adult male absence and the self-attitudes of black children. *Child Study Journal, 4*: 33–46.

Russell, D. (1989, Summer). Environmental racism. *Amicus Journal*: 22–32.

Sampson, R. (1987). Urban black violence: The effect of male joblessness and family disruption. *American Journal of Sociology, 93*: 348–405.

Savitt, T. L. (1978). *The diseases and health care of blacks in antebellum Virginia.* Urbana, IL: University of Illinois Press.

Schoenbach, V. J., Kaplan, B. H., Fredman, L. & Kleinbaum, D. G. (1986). Social ties and mortality in Evans County, Georgia. *American Journal of Epidemiology, 23*: 577–590.

Segal, L. (1990). *Slow motion: Changing masculinities, changing men.* New Brunswick, NJ: Rutgers University Press.

Shakoor, B. & Chalmers, D. (1991). Co-victimization of African American children who witness violence: Effects on cognitive, emotional, and behavioral development. *Journal of the National Medical Association, 83*: 233–237.

Sheldon, A. & Fox, G. L. (1983). *The impact of economic uncertainty on children's roles within the family.* Paper presented at the meeting of the Society for Study of Social Problems, Detroit, MI.

Sheley, J., McGee, Z. & Wright, J. (1992). Gun-related violence in and around inner-city schools. *American Journal of Diseases of Childhood, 146*: 677–682.

Smith, J., Mercy, J. & Rosenberg, M. (1986). Suicide and homicide among Hispanics in the Southwest. *Public Health Reports, 101*: 265–270.

Sudarkasa, N. (1988, January). Reassessing the black family: Dispelling the myths, reaffirming the values. *Sisters, 1*: 22–23, 38–39.

Sumner, B., Mintz, E. & Brown, P. (1986). Interviewing persons hospitalized with interpersonal violence-related injuries: A pilot study. In *Report of the Secretary's Task Force on Black and Minority Health* (Vol. 5, pp. 267–311). Washington, DC: US Department of Health and Human Services.

Tardiff, K. & Gross, E. (1986). Homicide in New York City. *Bulletin of the New York Academy of Medicine, 62*: 413–426.

U.S. Census Bureau. (1992). *Current population reports.* Washington, DC: U.S. Government Printing Office.

U.S. Department of Health and Human Services. (1985). *Report on the Secretary's Task Force on Black and Minority Health.* Washington, DC: U.S. Government Printing Office.

U.S. Department of Health and Human Services, Public Health Service. (1990). *Healthy people 2000: National health promotion and disease prevention objectives* (Report No. PHS 91-50212). Washington, DC: U.S. Government Printing Office.

U.S. Department of Health and Human Services. (1991). *Health status of minorities and low-income groups* (3rd ed.). Washington, DC: U.S. Government Printing Office.

U.S. Department of Justice. (1989). *Correctional populations in the United States, 1989.* Office of Justice Programs, Bureau of Justice Statistics (NCJ-111611). Washington, DC: U.S. Government Printing Office.

U.S. Department of Justice. (1991a). *Criminal victimization, 1990.* Office of Justice Programs, Bureau of Justice Statistics (Special Report No. NCJ-122743). Washington, DC: U.S. Government Printing Office.

U.S. Department of Justice. (1991b). *Correctional populations in the United States, 1989.* Office of Justice Programs, Bureau of Justice Statistics (NCJ-130-445). Washington, DC: U.S. Government Printing Office.

U.S. Department of Justice. (1991c). *Jail inmates, 1990.* Office of Justice Programs, Bureau of Justice Statistics (NCJ-129756). Washington, DC: U.S. Government Printing Office.

U.S. Department of Justice. (1991d). *Prisoners in 1990.* Office of Justice Programs, Bureau of Justice Statistics (NCJ-129198). Washington, DC: U.S. Government Printing Office.

Voydanoff, P. (1983). Unemployment and family stress. In H. Z. Lopata & J. H. Pleck (Eds.), *Research in the interweave of social roles: Vol. 3. Families and jobs* (pp. 239–250). Greenwich, CT: JAI Press.

Wade, J. C. (1994). African American fathers and sons: Social, historical, and psychological considerations. *Families in society, 75*(9): 561–570.

Walters, R. W. & Brown, D. R. (1979). *Exploring the role of the black church in the community (Final Report).* Washington, DC: Institute for Urban Affairs and Research, Mental Health Research and Development Center, Howard University.

Washington, V. & LaPoint, V. (1988). *Black children and American institutions.* New York: Garland Publishing.

Weitzel, M. H. & Waller, P. R. (1990). Predicative factors for health-promotive behaviors in white, Hispanic, and black blue-collar workers. *Family and Community Health, 13*(1): 23–24.

Weitzel, M. H., Hudak, J. L., Becker, H. A., Waller, P. R. & Stuifbergen, A. K. (1994). An exploratory analysis of health-promotion beliefs and behaviors among white, Hispanic, and black males. *Family and Community Health, 17*(3): 23–34.

Wilbanks, W. (1986). Criminal homicide offenders in the U.S.: Black vs. white. In D. Hawkins (Ed.), *Homicide among black Americans* (pp. 43–56). Lanham, MD: University Press of America.

Wilkinson, C. B. & O'Connor, W. A. (1977). Growing up male in a black single-parent family. *Psychiatric Annals, 7*(7): 50–59.

Williams, D., Larson, D. B., Buckler, R. E., Heckman, R. C. & Pyle, C. M. (1991). Religion and psychological distress among blacks. *Social Science and Medicine, 32*: 1257–1262.

Wilson, D. & Daly, M. (1985). Competitiveness, risk taking, and violence: The young male syndrome. *Ethology and Sociobiology, 6*: 59–73.

Zatz, M. S. (1987). The changing forms of racial/ethnic biases in sentencing. *Journal of Research in Crime and Delinquency, 24*: 69–92.

Chapter 27

Adolescents with Cancer: A Struggle to Understand a New Way of Living

KATHLEEN NEVILLE

Adolescence is a distinctive period of life characterized by change and transition. As a subculture, commensurate with the developmental tasks of this age group, developmental concerns pertain to identity formation, career goals, peer relations, and emancipation from family. Adolescents with cancer represent a unique subculture of individuals who have special needs and concerns. The issues of living with uncertainty, the use of adaptive denial, and the important role of pediatric cancer nurses in meeting the needs of these seriously ill adolescents are addressed.

The period of adolescence is a remarkable and distinctive time of life characterized by rapid change. It is a unique developmental timespan. Adolescents are beyond childhood, but they are not yet adults. Adolescence is a transitional time marked by physical, psychological, and social uncertainty; and physical and physiological changes. The evolution of new relationships with family and peers often produce great uncertainly and distress.

THE CULTURE OF ADOLESCENCE

A culture is defined as a group of individuals who share common beliefs, attitudes, and behaviors (Fitzsimons & Kelley, 1996). The period of adolescence, from approximately 14 to 22 years of age (Scipien, Barnard, Chard, Howe, & Phillips, 1986), can be viewed from a cultural perspective as a developmentally unique group of individuals who share common behaviors, beliefs, and attitudes. The characteristic behaviors, beliefs, and attitudes of adolescence revolve around the acquisition of the development tasks of this age group. The main developmental tasks in adolescence are identity formation, emancipation from family and parents, acquiring independence, intense peer relationships, and career development.

A common misconception regarding the culture of adolescence is the belief that during these years, adolescents experience life and living with a care-free attitude and approach, with few worries. Adolescence may be erroneously viewed as an exclusively fun-filled time of dating, parties, and social activities.

While these activities do exist and are vital to the acquisition of developmental tasks during this period, there exists much turmoil in these developing individuals. In reality, adolescence is one of the most stressful and complicated times of life, one filled with "Sturm and Drang" (Blos, 1962).

There is substantial growth occurring during this life period. It encompasses not only somatic and physiological maturation, but also accompanying cognitive, emotional, and social development as well. Adolescence is usually hallmarked by the onset of puberty for both males and females, but far less clear is division between the boundaries of adolescence and young adulthood. If the developmental tasks of adolescence are successfully achieved, the adolescent will emerge from this phase of life with an adequate self-esteem, a comfortable body image, identity formation, economic independence, and a realistic goal orientation toward the future (Blumberg, Lewis, & Susman, 1984). In recent years, however, due to increased difficulties in achieving financial independence, many individuals remain in adolescence for a prolonged period of time.

During adolescence, there is an intense concern with the body, and particular concern is focused on how other peers view the teenager and the degree of sameness. There is, in general an intolerance of differences. Classic evidence of this cultural belief is witnessed by an uniformity of dress and style, mannerisms, speech, and music. In terms of bodily concerns, overmaturation, or undermaturation in comparison to peers can be very problematic to teens. Partial answers to the characteristic question of this time period, "Who am I?" can best be facilitated by identifying with a peer group. Sexual identity is a key task of this period and the pursuit of romantic experiences and sexual experimentation facilitate the acquisition of this important task.

As a component of the first adolescent question, "Who am I?" the additional question of "Whom will I become?" must be addressed during this developmental period. The adolescent must develop an orientation toward the future with specific goals and objectives for vocational, career, and life interests. Attainment of the task of independence from parents and family must be established. Often this occurs when adolescents attend a distant college or move away from home to start a new life. While financial emancipation may not be fully achieved at the end of adolescence, plans are usually underway for the attainment of financial independence in the future.

CANCER: A SUBCULTURE OF ADOLESCENCE

A potentially life-threatening disease such as cancer profoundly impacts on an adolescent's life. Adolescents with cancer represent a subculture of adolescence by virtue of their illness and the treatment modalities associated with it (Neville, 1996). Adolescents with cancer share common beliefs, attitudes, and actions which are unique to their experiences and phenomena related to age and cancer. These seriously ill teenagers experience many additional stressors which are superimposed upon the normal physical and psychosocial stresses associated with the age period (Baum & Baum, 1990). Normal body image concerns become dramatically altered in the face of cancer treatment far beyond the typical concerns of bodily sameness of normal adolescence. Irrespective of age, the effects of treatment such as alopecia, pallor, a steroid induced cushnoid appearance, and disability are generally viewed as anomalous to most individuals outside of a hospital setting. In consideration, however, of the major development task of achieving a comfortable body image and identity in adolescence, an altered appearance from cancer treatment can be particularly traumatic to both male and female adolescents alike.

Alterations in peer relations inevitably occur as a result of the multiple absences or exclusions from everyday, normal adolescent social and academic activities afforded to well teenagers. Many adolescents report the isolation from peers as more disturbing than the actual disease. Parental dependency needs reemerge in the form of necessary social support and clinical decision-making regarding treatment choices. As a unique subgroup, adolescents have special needs and concerns, which often differ from the physical and psychosocial problems of adults with cancer (Cohen & Klopovich, 1986). In addition to the disruption in the achievement of developmental tasks, concerns regarding the management of living with uncertainty and protecting parents from additional fears and worries are paramount to this cultural subgroup.

UNCERTAINTY IN CANCER

Uncertainty has been identified as the most striking feature of cancer in children and adolescents (Van Dongen-Melman Pruyn, Van Zanen, & Sanders-Woudstra, 1986) and a major concern in adolescents with cancer (Bearison & Pacifici, 1984; Brunquell & Hall, 1982).

Uncertainty is the inability to determine the meaning of events, to assign definite values to objects and events, and/or accurately predict outcomes (Mishel & Braden, 1988, p. 98). Koocher and O'Malley (1981) describe uncertainty in pediatric cancer as the Damocles Syndrome, named for a courtier in ancient Syracuse whose king invited him to a lavish banquet, but arranged his seat directly below a sword suspended by a single thread. Although scientific progress has created realistic hopes, the ultimate fate of any adolescent with cancer remains unknown.

Living with uncertainty becomes a reality for adolescents diagnosed with cancer. This uncertainty may be more difficult for the adolescent who is experiencing rapid developmental changes than for an adult with cancer who has attained a relatively stable life-style (Koocher, 1985). Like Damocles, these adolescents are never free from worry about their health. The fears, anxieties, preoccupation with bodily function, and obsessive concern about progression of disease are symptomatic of the Damocles Syndrome.

ADAPTIVE DENIAL

Despite the cognitive ability of adolescents to think logically and to appreciate the implications of having cancer, research has identified that adolescents with cancer do not score significantly different from healthy adolescents who were evaluated for psychological distress (Neville, 1993). Koocher and O'Malley (1981) in a long-term follow-up study of survivors of childhood cancer reported that these children reacted to the stress of cancer in three ways: one group manifested high anxiety and other psychological adjustment problems as a result of being preoccupied with the fear that their malignancy would return; another group falsely believed they had gained immunity to cancer as a result of their treatment; and a third group developed an approach of not thinking about it. Other investigators have found that adolescents with cancer tend to function by attending to day-to-day tasks such as school events, social activities with peers, and school work (Zeltzer, LeBaron, & Zeltzer, 1984). Both the attitude of not worrying about cancer and the attempt to normalize their lives have been identified as a form of adaptive denial (Katz, Kellerman, & Siegal, 1980; Zeltzer et al., 1984). Koocher (1995) reported that adolescents who believe they are immune to cancer and those who do not think about it are using adaptive denial to cope with the uncertainty about cancer. Poignant displays of adaptive denial were observed while interviewing adolescents recently diagnosed with cancer (Neville, 1993). Two examples follow.

While participating in a brief interview, one 20–year-old male with advanced testicular cancer became visibly upset when describing his liver and pulmonary metastasis to the researcher. In response to one item on a scale measuring seriousness of illness, he looked over at his father and sincerely said, "Dad, this question—the seriousness of my illness has been determined—I don't think my disease is serious at all." In another example which highlights the attempt of adolescence to normalize their lives, an 18-year-old boy who was receiving his first chemotherapy treatment maintained a nonchalant conversation in which only the upcoming prom was discussed. Other participants spoke of future events, such as becoming engaged, or planning for marriage in the next few years. Although these plans were certainly not impossible for many of these adolescents, for others they did not seem likely, given the severity of their disease.

Many adolescents demonstrated the strong belief that everything would turn out fine. Elkind (1985) refers to this as a personal fable, a mental construction or story which may not be true, but enables one to go about everyday life without worrying about real dangers. Martinson (1976) identified that adolescent concerns about death are frequently masked by airs of bravado to cover up those anxieties such as defiant risk-taking behaviors and jokes about death.

HIGHER ORDER OF LIFE

Although uncertainty about one's diagnosis, prognosis, and treatment is generally viewed as a stressful, negative outcome at the time of diagnosis, reconceptualization of the uncertainty in illness theory (Mishel, 1990) provides new insight about the appraisal of uncertainty. With time, an acceptance or tolerance for longstanding chronic uncertainty may develop, and the initial appraisal of uncertainty as a danger may evolve into an appraisal of this as an opportunity. Based on a framework of chaos theory (Priginine & Stengers, 1984) as uncertainty increases, it can exceed a person's tolerance level, and shifts the person from one perspective of life to a new, higher order of life. This new view of life allows the evaluation of uncertainty to be changed from an aversive event to a positive experience. Examples of this new orientation to life among people with cancer may be evidenced by the reevaluation of what is seen as important in life, and an appreciation of the fragility and impermanence in life (Mishel, 1990). One adolescent male commented to the researcher:

> Since I've been sick, things are different, I know what is important and what is not.

Comaroff and Maguire (1981) describe a common approach used by health professionals in presenting cancer and its treatment to children and their families.

In order to redirect focus from long-term and existential issues, a "let's take it day to day" approach is commonly employed. Adolescents and their families learn very early in the cancer experience that there are relatively few certainties, and a newer, more complex orientation toward life evolves (Comaroff & Maguire, 1981). Whereas uncertainty in the early illness creates fluctuation and disruption, later uncertainty becomes the foundation in which a new order is constructed (Mishel, 1990). Possible support for the beginning tolerance or acceptance of uncertainty and a new order was evidenced by one 22-year-old now deceased male who responded to the investigator when asked how he was doing:

> I'm doing okay; I worry about today, getting here on time, getting chemo, and going home. I can't worry about tomorrow.

PROTECTING PARENTS

Adolescents with cancer also exhibit protectiveness toward their parents in attempts to shield them from additional pain and worries. One example was described by an 18-year-old male with testicular cancer:

> I hear my mother on the phone. She is so upset, she gets me crazy, so I try to make it easy for her.

Another adolescent, a 19-year-old college student with Hodgkin's Lymphoma reported:

> I don't want to stress my mother. I have an aunt who really helps me. She gives me money and everything. When I can't sleep at night, I call my boyfriend.

These findings of protective or inhibited communication between parents and their children is consistent with previous research using participant-observation in younger children with leukemia. Bluebond-Langer (1978) found that children avoided open discussions with parents in order to protect their parents from knowledge about dying. Beginning with the suspicion of a life-threatening illness, Bluebond-Langner observed an interaction pattern of mutual pretense, in which children concealed awareness of their prognosis and avoided discussions of death with parents. Similar findings of the societal avoidance of death were described in a descriptive research program on home care for eight terminally ill children and adolescents (Martison, 1976), in which parents avoided the subject of death, and children and adolescents subsequently ceased seeking information. Martison (1976) in her work with dying children found that children expressed a preference for open communication rather than a protected communication style of secrecy.

Few experiences in nursing exceed the challenges of caring for a child with cancer (Wong, 1995). The physiological challenges of cancer and its treatment coupled with the intense emotional, social, and real existential issues facing these adolescents demand a resilient professional stamina and true hardiness to provide sensitive, compassionate, and humanistic care to these unique individuals and their families. In many cases, the nurse is the one available person to channel and express personal fears and concerns. It is the nurse who has continuous contact with the child or adolescent, and by virtue of his or her education and knowledge, can assist in coping and facilitating management of this difficult disease.

In my experience as a pediatric nurse and nurse educator in various cancer centers for children, I have observed several findings about pediatric cancer nurses. While not empirically tested, anecdotal data of colleagues has revealed that most nurses did not plan to specialize in pediatric oncology, but rather "fell in love with the specialization once exposed to it on a clinical rotation during school." As taxing as the specialty is, most nurses agree that few clinical experiences provide more meaning in their lives and purpose to what they do and who they are. While many nurses may initially desire to engage in pediatric nursing practice, there is indeed a specialty in working with children with potentially life-threatening malignancies.

THE ROLE OF EDUCATION

As educators, the question can be asked, "How do we best prepare nurses for such a specialization?" Responses from colleagues consistently report that role-modeling and mentoring are the most important components to their selecting this specialty as their practice arena. Having supportive others to introduce and guide them in this unique practice facilitates acquisition of the many psychomotor, affective, and cognitive domains of learning necessary for excellence in practice. An ongoing, open exchange of values, beliefs, and feelings between experienced and neophyte nurses, as well as other staff members, is necessary to provide the most comprehensive, humanistic care to adolescents and families dealing with undoubtedly one of life's most stressful and difficult events.

REFERENCES

Baum, B. & Baum C. (1990). Psychosocial challenges of childhood cancer. *Journal of Psychosocial Oncology, 7*, 119–129.

Bearison, D. & Pacifici, C. (1984). Psychological studies of children who have cancer. *Journal of Applied Developmental Psychology, 5*, 263–280.

Blos, P. (1962). *On adolescence.* New York: Macmillan.

Blumberg, B., Lewis, M. & Susman (1984). Adolescence: A time of transition. In M. Eisenber, L. Stukin, & M. Jansen (Eds.), *Chronic illness and disability through the lifespan: Effects on self and family* (pp. 133–149). New York: Springer.

Brunquell, D. & Hall, M. (1982). Issues in the psychological care of pediatric oncology patients. *American Journal of Orthopsychiatry, 50,* 32–44.

Cohen, D. & Klopovich, P. (1986). Editorial introduction. *Seminars in Oncology Nursing, 2,* 73–74.

Comaroff, J. & Maguire, P. (1981). Ambiguity and the search for meaning: Childhood leukemia in the modern clinical context. *Social Science & Medicine, 158,* 115–123.

Elkind, D. (1984). Cognitive development and adolescent disabilities. *Journal of Adolescent Health Care, 6,* 84–89.

Fitzsimons, V. & Kelley, M. (1996). *The culture of learning: Access, retention, and mobility of minority students in nursing.* New York: NLN Press.

Katz, E., Kellerman, J. & Siegal, S. (1980). Behavioral distress in children with cancer undergoing medical procedures: Developmental consideration. *Journal of Consulting and Clinical and Psychology, 3,* 356–365.

Koocher, G. (1985, March/April). Psychosocial care of the child cured of cancer. *Pediatric Nursing,* 91–93.

Koocher, G. & Malley, J. (1981). *The Damocles Syndrome: Psychological consequences of surviving childhood cancer.* New York: McGraw-Hill.

Martinson, I. (1976). *Home care of the dying child: Professional and family perspectives.* Norwalk: Appleton-Century-Crofts.

Mishel, M. (1990). Reconceptualization of the uncertainty in illness theory. *Image, 22,* 256–262.

Mishel, M. & Braden, C. (1988). Finding meaning: Antecedents of uncertainty in illness. *Nursing Research, 37,* 98–103, 127.

Neville, K. (1996). Psychological distress in adolescents with cancer. *Journal of Pediatric Nursing, 11,* 243–251.

Neville, K. (1993). The relationships among perceived social support, uncertainty, and psychological distress of adolescents recently diagnosed with cancer. Unpublished doctoral dissertation, New York University, New York, New York.

Prigogine, I. & Stenger, I. (1984). *Order out of chaos: Man's new dialogue with nature.* New York: Bantam Books.

Rait, P. & Holland, J. (1986). Pediatric cancer psychosocial issues and aproaches. *Mediguide to Oncology, 6,* 1–6.

Scipien, G., Barnard, M., Chard, M., Howe., J. & Phillips, P. (1986). *Comprehensive pediatric nursing* (3rd ed.). New York: McGraw-Hill.

Van Dongen-Melman, J., Pruyn, J., Van Zanen, G. & Sanders-Woudstra, J. (1986). Coping with childhood cancer: A conceptual view. *Journal of Psychosocial Oncology, 4,* 147–161.

Wong, D. (1995). *Whaley & Wong's nursing care of infants and children* (5th ed.). St. Louis: C. V. Mosby.

Zeltzer, L., Lebaron, S. & Zeltzer, P. (1984). The adolescents with cancer. In R. W. Blum (Ed.), *Chronic illness and disabilities in childhood and adolescence* (pp. 375–395). New York: Grune & Startton.

Chapter 28

The Married Couple:
In Loss, Grief, and Transition

ROBERT T. TOBIN

The community is the primary vehicle for cultural norms and the individual family unit is central to the transmittal of those norms. The married dyad, the couple, is the foundation of the family. This essay relates the experience of such a couple, 31 years married, who faced a life-taking illness. It is told by the husband/widower as he lives out the grief and pain of his enormous loss only three months prior. And it demonstrates how pivitol common community cultural norms and support are to the well-being, humanistic care, and support of individuals and family units.

HE BEGINS

This is a history for our children while my memory is fresh and before the data gets lost. First, let me describe my wife Rita so that some of what follows will make more sense. She was a warm energetic woman with a great smile—very sparkly, if there is such a word. A Boston Irish Catholic who loved life and had a great sense of humor. She combined this with style, grace, and humility. Whoever she met, she made feel comfortable, and they became her friends.

She touched a lot of people. I used to say she could have been a politician but she had her own priorities. Her family, her church, her belief in helping others, all were centered around her deep faith in God. People may think all of this is an exaggeration, but this was who she was from the day I met her until the day she died.

REMINISCENCE

This is the time of the year it all began. I see two phases, one is coming out of the death, burial, and grieving. I am experiencing the grieving now. And, at the same time it is as if I am experiencing a video tape replay of the illness. It is as if I am taking a video tape and through the replay of the tape experiencing it all over again.

It is as if I am playing the video tape of our marriage and these are two chapters in it. This fall-like weekend reminds me of the weekend last year, with the same change of season, that we found out that Rita had cancer. She had had trouble with her stomach for a long time. It was a weak spot for her. When she got nervous her stomach acted up. It had been trouble for all of her life.

In July of last year, we had taken a trip to Turkey and when we came back it all began. During the trip, we stopped in Germany for a few days and while we were in Germany, she had four or five terrible days with her stomach. All through July and August it continued to bother her. She made several trips to the doctor where they suspected she had picked up a bug or parasite from Turkey or had an ulcer. Finally, after weeks of difficulty, she went for a sonogram looking for ulcers. This would have been in November.

That weekend, I went up to Lake George (New York). It was a long-planned law school reunion with some buddies of mine. Rita stayed home and saw her sonogram results that Friday. She had peeked at them and saw the word ascites. At an engagement party that Sunday, she saw a good friend of ours, a surgeon, and he asked her, "How are you?" She responded, "Do you want to know now or in your office?" She told him of the sonogram of her stomach and that the report said "ascites." He almost dropped his glass. He suggested that a CAT scan be done as soon as possible the following week. While I was driving home on Sunday, I called and heard the story. I knew then that we were in trouble.

We arranged for the CAT scan early that week and I went with Rita. I was to get the results. The surgeon called me two days later, on the following Friday, and told me that it was ovarian cancer.

Rita asked me did I know the results and, I don't know how I did it, but I finessed it. I had never lied to her. I said that the doctor didn't know the definite results because he was not a radiologist and I had not talked to the radiologist. I didn't want to spoil things. This was Friday. We were on our way out to dinner and we had a full weekend planned. Saturday, we went to a wedding. I wanted to protect her and let her enjoy the wedding. I almost exploded.

Later that weekend, on Sunday, we moved furniture to our youngest daughter, Katie, in Boston. My oldest daughter, Beth, was also there and I told her what was going on. I just had to talk to someone.

On Monday, three days after I had heard from the surgeon, all hell broke loose. After we saw Rita's regular doctor we went to the oncologist. He confirmed the results. We went from there to the gynecological surgeon and within two days she was scheduled for surgery the following week, right after Thanksgiving. Everyone was positive. There was no doubt that it was needed.

The surgery was completed. The doctors told us they got 95 percent of it out, but they couldn't get the last 5 percent. The hospital stay was difficult. There was an infection and it was treated with antibiotics. She couldn't take food. It was the pits. She looked terrible and had no energy. She finally got Total Parenteral Nutrition (TPN) and responded. All of this caused a delay in getting her on chemotherapy.

Recovery from the operation was long and difficult. We were optimistic though, we thought that she would be on chemotherapy for two months and then have stem cell therapy when the cancer was under control. The CA125 would have to be under 25 to do it. I then got involved in trying to understand the disease and the treatments. I checked Hackensack Hospital and Sloan Kettering Medical Centers for information on stem cell transplant.

We stayed here in New Jersey for the treatments. It was Rita's wish. She felt that she would get lost in New York City. That is what happened when she went in for the chemotherapy (for breast cancer) in 1978. She wanted to be close this time, and it was the right choice. Our friends were here. We knew the doctors. We had the support of our community.

The doctors looked at her history and admitted her to the stem cell program. Although we had an executive level health insurance plan, no stem cell replacement was permitted on this plan because it is considered experimental.

I made many, many calls inquiring how to overrule this decision. So did the doctors. Finally, a health insurance nurse found a Stage Three clinical trial and so we were on track for that. They would pay for the treatment.

The chemotherapy started. It was Taxol and Cisplatnin and so this meant all day in the hospital, a full eight hours to monitor Rita and see how she did. There was no problem and she tolerated it well. Rita had no nausea or vomiting. Then, three weeks later, she went to the doctor's for the next series.

CRISIS

Then we hit bottom. It was a real downer. After the third series, the doctor was concerned because the CA 125 was going up instead of down. I researched and knew that CA 125 levels should be below 25 and Rita's was at 200 to 400. The doctor said that the high numbers weren't as much of a concern as was the trend which should be going down. I knew what we were looking at.

We both figured out what was going on. We had our roles defined. We both knew what was happening. I was the cheerleader. I knew what the odds were for Rita. But even knowing things, sometimes you ignore the information. For example, at the special stem cell program, we were told that she had a 30 percent chance of survival even with the stem cell treatment. It's funny how it all works. Somehow, I missed that information, or ignored it. Rita heard it, told me, but I denied it. I said, "It *will* work."

We kept up a public side. Rita felt good and she was outwardly positive. I scrambled around for information. It was apparent that the Taxol chemotherapy was not working. I had my office computer people research abstracts of the National Institutes for Health (NIH) protocols. The more I read the more I was convinced that nothing was going in the right direction and the odds were bad. They increased the chemo to another two rounds. Originally, it was to be three and then the stem cell. This was out and we went for two more rounds of the Taxol instead.

Rita used me as a buffer against what the doctor said. I was her cheerleader. I gave her support as best I could. I talked to the doctors and she never really directly asked what was happening. It was down to the basics. We both knew what we were dealing with.

MY COMMUNITIES

I'm a lawyer, a partner in the best law firm in the country in my specialization. I have been there all my professional life. My partners, the staff, and everyone were great. I went with her to the doctor's appointments. I could keep going because of the support of my partners who encouraged me and let me do whatever I had to do for Rita.

We truly had the support of the community. Her friends would bring her to and from the chemotherapy visits and stay with her through the day at the doctor's office. The community and her friends were fantastic. They showed up for her. They prayed with and for her. They arranged a time schedule to bring us meals all of the time. We received phone calls. There was a tremendous outpouring by people. There were always cards. There is still a foot high stack of cards and letters at home.

All of this really spoke to the person Rita was and her uniqueness. She had a whole collection of friends. I had issues with some of them and she would say, "Oh, they mean well." There was no one who met her who disliked her.

The letters would knock your socks off. The messages all testified to the ability of people to be friends and to help. Everyone came through, our family, our kids. Everyone stepped up and supported us.

THE TAPE CONTINUES

Back to the medical part. The Taxol and Cisplatnin were not working. Stem cell therapy was out of the question. We got in touch with all sorts of doctors. We contacted Sloan Kettering in New York and had a second opinion in there. Nothing changed. They had no new approaches.

From a super kind woman who I knew at my law school's development office, I got in touch with her brother-in-law who was an MD at the NIH doing research and in charge of the breast cancer unit. He went to the head of NIH ovarian cancer project. Both of these physicians actually called me back themselves! He told us about an experimental drug which was not yet approved but was to be used for those who had not responded to Taxol. At the same time our doctor found out about it too. Through the NIH doctor, we got an NIH compassionate release for the then experimental new drug Topetecan.

Once again, our hopes were up. There was a high response rate to this drug, and after the paperwork delay, we got approval in June. Rita's general health was good and she had minimum pain. We assumed that everything would be OK. I knew the odds and she did too. But we went into the program with our hopes up, at least to each other and to the world. Our private thoughts were our own.

US

Topetecan didn't work. We both became intense about what was happening. I was reading about Cardinal Bernardin (of Chicago) recently and how serene he was through his illness. Rita was the same.

We cried at night. That's where we were. Basically, her wish was to continue to go to St. Rose's Elementary School in Newark where she volunteered as a teacher to help the kids there.

All we wanted was to be together and to see our kids grow up and be at their weddings and see the grandkids. Rita's grief was that I would be alone and lonely.

Her mom was widowed and my father was also. She remembered the loneliness and she didn't want that to happen to me. Rita was more concerned about me.

I can speak about love. It was an intense time in our marriage. We didn't know how much time we had, but we knew that it was not much time. She always used to chide me about my impatience and now she marveled at my patience. We laughed about it.

We had intense love for each other during this time. In a weird way, it was one of the best years of our marriage. If only it could have continued.

In June, the pain escalated considerably. Our son had gone to Cape Cod to work and was in our house up there. Rita, for years as the kids were in college, would go there for June, July, and August. I would be there in August. We have had our place for ten years. The kids all worked summers there. The plan this year was that our son would be there, Beth, with our granddaughter Rose, Katie and Meg would come there on weekends. We would all spend time together.

The last time we went there together, it was a tough trip. It was for a long weekend and we had to stop and rest twice going up and coming back. The pain was coming on. When we were there, we were saying good-bye to the Cape. Rita had her flowers and I had my herb garden. We planted flowers that weekend, but she basically knew that it was the last time we would do this together. We cried together without saying anything about it.

I had a trial in Delaware in 1994 with a decision in 1995. It was being appealed in July, and on July 7, I was to present the oral argument in Washington, DC. I spent the July Fourth weekend preparing for it. But in the middle of the weekend we had a crisis. Rita began to try the macrobiotic diet, but it was beyond what any diet could help. In the middle of the weekend, I had to take her to the emergency room to keep the colostomy working. I did not want to go to Washington. Rita said, "Go."

I went to Washington, DC, to argue the case and it was touch and go as to whether I could do it. My partners said, "Don't worry, Bob will do it." You do what you have to do because you are a professional. But it was a *major* conflict. I went down on Monday and argued the case. And I said, "This one is for you Rita with all of my heart."

But having spent all of July Fourth weekend preparing, it was the most prepared that I ever have been. It was a piece of cake. I knew it all. Within a week there was a decision in our favor. It was a major coup. Rita and I celebrated our victory. It was a crowning point of my professional career and we were together.

THE ENDING

The pain increased and we knew that the new chemo wasn't working. Our doctor suggested one more round of chemo, a "nuclear bomb." I had questions as to whether it should be done or not. Rita's quality of life really was my deepest concern. I helped her make the decision. There were tricky issues: quality of life versus whether it will work. We had doubts but she wanted to do it. So, we went off to do it.

We are now in August and it all collapses here. There was a CAT scan needed for the new chemo. Rita was in moderate pain taking Tylenol for relief. Her concept was that as long as she was only on Tylenol things were stable. But with higher pain killers, in her view, things were escalating. Now she had to take increased pain killers.

The CAT scan was read by the MD and they had us wait. He wanted to admit her to the hospital. But the oncologist said no. She was scheduled for more chemo, so she should wait before coming into the hospital. We were both worried.

A clot in her leg had formed and we all were concerned. It was an emboli and needed immediate treatment. A filter had to be put in and the prep was done. Ultimately, the doctors couldn't do the procedure for technical reasons so the operation was not done. At this point, the cancer had grown big enough to begin to block her GI tract. We went ahead with the chemo.

My head told me that whether or not this round of chemo worked or not, we had only three to six months left together.

OUR FAMILY

Our kids were great throughout all of this. As you raise them you go through all sorts of different experiences with them, each unique to each kid. You don't know where it is all going and how they will turn out. But, when they all respond so positively at a time like this, it is truly rewarding. Their support was remarkable. One of our daughters, Meg, lived with us and was always there to help, doing whatever was needed. We had calls from the kids who lived away. They came home any chance they had, on all their time off. They organized and supported our life. For example, the kids organized a calendar so that there would be someone home to work with us at all times. One of my daughter's was at home as I said, but the others all chipped in. Our daughter Beth has a young baby, Rose, and a great husband, John, who supported us completely. She had the most flexibility and could cover weekdays freely. Katie had an understanding boss who gave her time off to come home from Boston to cover also. They alternated weekends. Our son, Robert, came home on his time off. I look at the calendar now and see coverage through October (two months after she died).

It didn't really dawn on me what was actually, in reality, happening. Rita went into the hospital for the chemo treatment and all that I knew was that I did not want any more hospital. My only question was, "How could we get her home?" I didn't care regarding the cost. The end seems crazy, surreal, out of control. Thursday, Katie was home with me. That weekend was the last crunch in the chemo cycle. She was at the bottom of the chemo cycle. The MD was saying that at most, Rita had a month to live. Everything collapsed. Everything became difficult. The pain escalated. Meg, Katie, and I were there. Katie and I slept in the room with Rita. She had much pain and needed morphine.

It was entirely clear where we were heading. Our fears increased. Rita's pain increased. The colostomy was obstructed and backed up. We had a discussion with the MD and she needed a naso-gastric tube to keep her bowel decompressed and the colostomy going. By Friday evening, all signs indicated that things were very bad. Katie and I talked to her and tried to help.

The doctor and the staff were there and supportive. By Saturday morning, Rita needed increasingly higher doses of morphine to relieve the pain. Early that morning, I called Beth in Boston and Robert on the Cape, and told them to get home. They both came down. Meg came over and we were all at the hospital on Saturday afternoon. All the kids were there with me.

Rita responded. We talked with her and reassured her that it was OK. It was alright to go ahead and take the morphine to relieve her pain. But still she got worse, and lost consciousness.

I saw what was missing. I needed to call the priest for her now. I called the rectory but at first, nobody was there to answer the phone. But then the priest arrived by 10:30 p.m. He had just been ordained and was brand new to our parish. This was a first for him. His hands were shaking as he gave her the last rites. But he was very warm and caring. He was sincere and honest, as the kids said.

My Rita slipped away. The kids were there. I was there. We all prayed. It was beautiful.

REFLECTION

That was the end of Phase I of our grief, finished. The end of that video tape. The script was not as we wanted it. Let me backtrack. During all this struggle, we had support, prayers, spiritual bouquets, crosses, Masses, and Lourdes and Fatima water. Again, people are fundamentally good. They responded in whatever way they could. One night I came home and here were chocolate chip cookies at the back door with a note, "Thought you could use these." Cynics would say, "What good were all the prayers?" Then I think of Cardinal Bernardin and the serenity of the whole thing.

We had no cure. The odds were low. But we had the ability to handle it. This was the answer. This was the answer to all of the prayers. We had little doubt as to what we were doing. We had little anger as to what was happening. Rita had tremendous courage. We felt mellow, rather serene. The prayers gave me the control to be the cheerleader and not to panic, to be there entirely for her, to see what had to be done, and to call the shots for her. All of the prayers were answered in this way.

TRANSITION

Phase II, this was probably the far more difficult phase. *Grief and mourning.* It is described as shock, disbelief, denial, and then realization. This is the description of grief and then healing and then moving on. It's like surgery. Shock, bleeding, healing, scarring.

It is all true. The shock is dramatic and incredible. It was the first close loss for the kids. I had lost a brother, father, mother, and Rita's mother. But this does not compare, it does not make it easier. This was the most intense.

I went on automatic pilot. I did what I had to do. I made choices. There is stress in my professional life and I have dealt with stress in the past. But not like this.

I got us together. The kids were once again tremendous. They raised questions and issues. We planned everything together. Made decisions together.

Weird things made a difference. The undertaker was a good source of support. We made the necessary calls. We planned the Mass. I had gone to funerals before and knew what Rita would have liked. I knew a nun who assisted us to prepare a funeral Mass that Rita would have liked. We tried to find her.

Rita liked certain hymns and so I knew the direction that she would want. Then the nun called and said she heard we needed her. We gave her the songs and readings we wanted. She showed up the day of the funeral with 200 copies of the Mass program. Everything was done.

UNBELIEVABLE

We have a very close friend who is a Jesuit priest, whom I had known from high school. He has known Rita since we were married. We both went to his first Mass. Our kids grew up with him. I asked him to come and to do the eulogy. He had been thinking of it. He is such a good friend, a part of our family. He has spent weekends with us here and at the Cape. He loved us both. His eulogy was fantastic. He captured the spirit of Rita's love for God, family, and others.

One hymn we selected was, "Lift High the Cross." It had a special history for us and our family. When Beth, our daughter, went to college, they played this in the chapel with horns and a choir and it was one of our favorite hymns. Rita said that she wanted to be able to sing, "Lift High the Cross" when our priest friend marched down the aisle at his inauguration as president of his college. And she did this when he was inaugurated. It was Rita's song. And it was the last hymn of the funeral service, "Lift High the Cross." Other hymns were one's Rita loved:

"Here I Am, Lord,"
"On Eagles' Wings,"
"City of God,"
"I Am the Bread of Life," and
"Precious Lord, Take My Hand."

This last one is a spiritual that they played at a mission Rita and I went to during the last year. She said it was a great hymn to play at her funeral.

THE LAST GOODBYE

The funeral was phenomenal. It was standing room only in the church. I couldn't believe all of the people who attended and came back to the house and gave us their support. This was incredibly important for us. It helped us through the shock. Then that was over. We all went off to the Cape together and talked while a near-miss hurricane went by. Rita's birthday was then and we passed that together. All of this gives me a deeper appreciation for the need to help people who are grieving. I see in particular the need to support the caregivers. Yes, support for the caregivers.

WHEN THE SILENCE COMES IN

People all try to help but they can't keep the intensity up. They begin to go about their own business again. But for us, it is a continuum of grief. It is now the realization phase of the grief. It is the beginning of the mourning process.

I am analytical. I think more about things than I feel or emotionally react to things. I didn't understand the process. I read books. I was able to take out of them information on what was the process of grief.

Serendipitous or divine intervention? From a friend of ours, I was referred to bereavement sessions at a Catholic hospice center. It was a six-part series on bereavement. I also listened to the tapes in my car as I commuted.

I am in an agitated state. I feel like a waterbug flitting around from subject to subject. The weekends are horrendous. When we were together the weekends were our time together. Friday through Sunday was our time. Monday to Friday was my work and Rita's projects. Her volunteering, working with the kids, and other projects. Her two-day a week job. But Friday to Sunday, then she and I had time together.

I had never been alone. I was alone. I cried. I did a lot of things. I listened to the tapes. I learned what grief was about. Was I angry? No. Second guessing? No. Did I feel guilty that we should have done more? No.

The priest at the hospice spelled out the process, like a surgical operation:

amputation,
shock,
bleeding,
healing, and
scarring.

You have to move on. It is a journey through grief. Pass through the emotions, through sorrow, to survival. I bought the tapes of the grief sessions and gave them to the kids. The books, the counseling, and others all say crying is therapeutic. It is necessary. Don't bottle up the tears. All this leads to conflicting emotions. "What control you had," people told me. "You were magnificent." I sure had emotions. I'd smile. I now understand the process. They did not know what I was going through.

THE WORST PAIN

Phase II is the worst. It is like falling out of love. Unfulfilled wishes. Loneliness. Love does not accept death quickly. Am I angry at God? At the doctors? I am frustrated that I am where I am at this point of my life, but not angry. Guilt—she and I had a great life. You sort of look at what we did together. I am so proud of my wife's accomplishments. She was an incredible woman. Pride—I was the guy who gave her the security to go out and do her work. She had no financial worries. The kids realize now what a mother they had.

Rita and I travelled. We had such good times. It was so good while it lasted. But it did not last long enough.

I step out. Then I fall back. At times, I feel utterly blindsided. I am rolled back. Back to point zero. And I relive the whole experience again. The video tapes play.

There is a double aspect to it at this point. It is as if we are acting out a video replay of the whole experience; grief coming out of the death; reliving the experience of the death and burial; and at the same time reliving the experience of the illness.

The issues are clear. There is a need for family support. I can't conceive of having to go through the whole process alone. Yet, I have the children, relatives, friends, and a tremendous community of people. The support of the community for our family is and was so comforting. The disintegration of family life must have an incredible impact on how people deal with this. They were essential parts of the process for us. Without them I cannot imagine how much more painful it would have been.

Again, I have to say that it is an attestation to Rita's impact on our community. In the professional world, I was Bob Tobin. Here, in our community, I was "Rita's husband." I liked that and got a kick out of it.

A BEGINNING

So here we are and we must continue. We are born, we live our lives, marry, make our careers. We are born and die. Some die before others. But we who survive must continue. We, for whatever reasons, survived. We must learn by our experiences. Take the best of what we witnessed and continue on.

That is where I am now.

REFERENCE

Fitzgerald, H. (1994). *The mourning handbook.* A Fireside Book. New York: Simon & Schuster.

Chapter 29

Aging:
A Culture of Changes and Growth

VIRGINIA M. FITZSIMONS

A memorable scene: A few months ago, as a 93-year-old woman lay in her hospital room after a hip repair, she asked that "the children" come and visit with her. Her two sons were in their 70s, their children were mature, 50-year-old adults with their own children and grandchildren. It sounded strange that "the baby" of the family was a 70-year-old uncle.

I was looking at the new century family. Every five minutes, a "baby boomer" turns 50-years-old. By 2015, those baby boomers turn 65. One in four persons will be over 50 years old. For the first time in human history, the five generational family will be commonplace. The parents will be 90+, the children 70+, the grandchildren 50+, the great-grandchildren 30+, and the great-great grandchildren will be under 30 years old.

We now understand that "aging" is not a title for the over 65-year-old set. But in fact, all of the time everyone is aging. So the aging process is a life-long phenomenon. Each generation is, in fact, a cultural subgroup having unique attitudes, beliefs, and behaviors common to that age group.

INTRA-FAMILIAL CULTURAL DIVERSITY

The spread of cultural diversity within the intergenerational family will be unprecedented. If it is an immigrant family, as many families in the United States are, then that family will have an aggregate of living members from the original country of cultural heritage. The first and second generations are pressed to accomplish acculturation/assimilation tasks. Later generations often intermarry outside the culture of origin. The immigrant experience, and its demands for change, is a dramatic stressor with change, loss, and lifestyle and values challenges to each individual.

INTRA-FAMILIAL DEVELOPMENTAL DIVERSITY

The new century family, a middle-aged and an older unit, face unprecedented challenges. Developmentally, the older family members face the task of accepting the shift in traditional generational roles. The individuals maintain couple (or single) role functioning and interests in face of physiological changes. They explore new family and social role options and support a more central role for the middle, younger generation. This younger family member experiences the assets and limitations of making room for wisdom and traditions through support of the older generation.

The older family member prepares to face losses of a spouse, siblings, and other peers and prepares for a personal life review and integration. Inherent in these tasks are the necessities of renegotiation of the marital relationship, development of adult-to-adult relationships with grown children, realignment of relationships to include in-laws, mature children and new members subsequent to divorces and new marriages, and maintaining one and/or couple functioning.

Dramatic changes in the Social Security retirement ages have considerable impact in the new century. The standard retirement age of 65 is obsolete. A progressive retirement age from 66 to 72 years of age now moves the bulk of retirement age forward for some of the baby boomers by almost ten years.

THE LONGEVITY REVOLUTION I AND II

Our industrialized society has gained twenty-five years of added life expectancy over this century. These added years of longevity increased because of the rise of basic scientific cell research, public health gains in maternal and child health, and more stable economic, and thus nutritional and social, conditions.

Current research targets in human development and further biotechnological and genetic information gains will focus on middle-age health issues, the stabilization and prevention of chronic diseases, primary and secondary prevention strategies, traditional public health and the application of new scientific findings to the quality of life to the old-old (over 90-year-old) population.

The Longevity Revolution Stage II is witnessed in the maintenance and restoration of biological functioning. Estrogen replacement therapy prevents the onset of osteoporosis, cardiovascular deterioration, and Alzheimer's disease. Genetic research and application to clinical practice is a fast-moving new frontier. Organ transplant, new organ growth from stem cells, cadaver tissue donation and reconstructive surgery provide added years of life to persons with non-functioning hearts, livers, corneas, lungs, pancreases, cartilage, teeth, and bones.

With added understanding of the complex, multiple, interacting acute and chronic psychological and physical conditions attendant to an aging population, focus on the coping and adaptation mechanisms of our society is warranted. Science has moved from the narrow view of aging as a disease and biological inevitability to a broad view of healthy aging, and healthy living as a matrix of nutritional, physical, social, psychological/emotional, and behavioral needs.

THE LIFE SPAN

Common life events for older families span retirement, bereavement, sexuality, and cultural norms and are being addressed as legitimate research issues. The addition of added years of life expectancy dramatizes shifting societal objectives. The one variable of added years challenges us to explore ways for older individuals to remain active, productive members of their families and communities.

Family role research and application supporting the quality of life for the older member span a full spectrum of health stabilization goals using self-care, socialization within the family and the community, economic stability, safety, living accommodations, leisure activities and lifestyle, and personality characteristics. An ability to cope with change, new stressors, understanding of physical and emotional changes, developmental tasks and attitudes toward aging are needed skills for all family members. Flexibility is essential. Goals to retain independence and vigor are essential in order to stabilize chronic illness and extend tertiary care norms. The family provides the health care, social and physical environments to support ongoing physical, social activity, and emotional growth. Added knowledge about these functions supports an adequate family life.

AGE AND CONDITION

There is a wide range of health and functioning levels of persons of the same age. For example, in the presence of identical X-rays of arthritic hips, two older women can have vastly differing lifestyles. One can be wheelchair-bound and the other can be an active traveler and community volunteer. The differential variables lie in perceived world views, blood seratonin levels, individual pain thresholds, and an ability to manage stressors.

It is the family unit that determines the environmental and social variables that define the impact of acute and chronic diseases and their outcomes. The individual's self-care level supports social status, independence, and empowerment. The family modifies stress by offering social support, expressions of love, connectiveness, stability, financial assistance, and behavioral skills that foster feelings of well-being.

INTO THE NEW CENTURY

End of the twentieth century trends are predictors of the emerging potential family stressors. These stressors of changes in current family roles, the implementation of contemporary science findings, and increasing family geographical mobility. Understanding that family units will be older and knowing what stressors and adaptations are needed for a healthy older family life benefits the entire society looking for reality-based planning and living. The new century demands vigorous research into the central nervous system physiology, energy, and spirit of the older human.

GRANDPARENTS AS PARENTS

Three million infants and school-aged children currently are being raised by their grandparents, a 50 percent increase in occurrence the last decade. In many of the homes, neither biological parent is physically present because of chemical addictions, economics, or emotional illness issues. Their own children's emotional immaturity, addictive behaviors, divorces, financial difficulties, and the time and physical demand of two-career marriages lead to the relegation of the parental duties to the grandparents, the middle-aged couple.

Historically, multigenerational households are not an uncommon phenomenon in ethnic and working-class communities, and now increasingly, includes the full landscape of all social and economic groups. These middle-class grandparents who planned to have freedom and independence in their retirement years are providing increasing amounts of child rearing and full-time care. These grandparents report that assuming parenting responsibilities again is not a first choice, but a measure of last resort for the family. Social scientists had predicted that grandparents would have more retirement alternatives than in past years: new areas or work, travel, hobbies, and sports. These middle-aged grandparents express their view that they have given their lives to child-rearing and it should be time for them to be free of responsibilities.

Instead of new freedom, these grandparents serve as parents to young children, and experience considerable stress and resentment. Emotional, financial, and legal pressures of their unplanned-for status as caregivers can be overwhelming. While middle-class grandparents feel the added expenses are a burden, those on fixed incomes are particularly distressed. Many of the caregivers are widows and serve as parents as well as grandmom and granddad.

Grandparents frequently report the experience to be frustrating and exhausting and, as with all new parents, they experience the social isolation of being at home all day. Support groups provide these grandparents/parents a forum to express their anger toward their own children for having forfeited their parental responsibilities. Support groups also provide a network for child-care information such as medical care and educational opportunities.

Some grandparents report being so frustrated that they close the door to more child-rearing experiences. Most grandparents, however, dig in for the formidable task of ten to twenty additional years of caretaking. They, sometimes and reluctantly, set aside their retirement plans and do what they are asked to do with a sense of responsibility. New century research in these evolving roles and relationships will enable these families to cope and adapt.

A biological footnote: Anthropologists hypothesize that female longevity over males is an evolutionary variable. Grandmothers' child caretaking roles and skills for the next generation gives the woman added value and purpose and thus added years of life.

CENTENARIANS FOR THE NEW CENTURY

The single, fastest growing segment of our population is the over 90-year-old group: 1.7 million Americans turn 100 as the new century begins, the greatest number in human history. (Turning 100 no longer warrants special recognition on national television news programs. Too many centenarians to make news! A person must turn 104 to be recognized as unique.) These hearty old-old persons attribute their long lives to the choice of the right occupation, right diet, good genes, and their faith in God. Ninety-five percent of the centenarians are nonsmokers. They have common personality traits. Common characteristic behaviors in the well old-old person are an assertive pursuit of their needs and hearty appetites. That passive individuals have long succumbed to illness gives evidence to the benefit of assertiveness training and nutritional research.

MEN OF A CERTAIN AGE

Hormone replacement therapy for older people is an ongoing field of research. Estrogen replacement for women has received wide acceptance as a routine perimenopausal prescription. Research is active in studies on human growth recombinant hormone in climacteric men. Increased male lean muscle mass, thickened skin, improved appetite, greater cardiac stroke volume, and respiratory tidal volume are supported by DHEA supplements. The improved weight gain and general improvement in fitness are the best short-term treatment for the frail, malnourished, those older persons with poor wound healing and who are prone to falls.

Research continues on testosterone precursor replacement in elderly men. Hypogonadal males are more than six times more likely to break a hip during a fall than those with normal testosterone levels. The men like the feeling of well-being the testosterone replacement provides.

Exercise plays a critical part in the hormone replacement question. It is likely that exercise increases the natural production of the growth hormone and the development of the receptor sites.

Two questions regarding female and male hormone replacement therapy move into the new century: What effect will long-term replacement have on the nests of slow-growing breast and prostate cancer cells found in almost all elderly women and men? And what is the appropriate age for intervention? Should men begin hormone replacement at age 40 or 50 years to prevent problems later in life?

YOU ARE WHAT YOU EAT

Nutritional surveys indicate that up to one in four elderly persons have clinical malnutrition. Even the persons who are well educated and financially comfortable may be seriously malnourished.

Good nutrition is the essential ingredient of good health. Poor nutrition aggravates chronic ailments such as heart disease and hypertension. It becomes a vicious cycle. Chronic illnesses such as arthritis, diabetes, depression, and strokes can greatly diminish appetite and the ability of the individual to physically perform the act of eating. Poor dental health, broken, decayed or missing teeth also make it difficult to chew. Meal taking with others is a primary occasion of social interaction in our society.

Reasons for malnutrition include: unhealthy choices such as excessive alcoholic intake, low nutritional dense foods ("junk foods"), inadequate amounts of meats, fruits, and vegetables, and skipping meals altogether; poverty leading to insufficient food budget; social isolation by living alone; and drug interactions and side effects that diminish the appetite.

"Senior" vitamins, protein drink supplements, prepared meals delivered to homes, and communal dining rooms showcase the new century management of health maintenance and disease prevention through micronutrient approaches. Multivitamin and multimineral regimens significantly increase immune functions and decrease the frequency of infections in the older adult. The addition of baseline levels of vitamins and minerals improve immunocompetence and reduce infection-related diseases by 50 percent in persons over 70 years of age.

Aging is generally associated with impaired immune responses and the subsequent increase in infections, particularly respiratory diseases such as bronchitis and pneumonia. Pneumonia remains the fourth most common cause of death in the elderly. Deficiency in protein leads to muscle wasting and impaired immune responses. Subsequent feelings of fatigue and lethargy create a downward spiral of inactivity and further disuse atrophy.

Blood samples taken before beginning the vitamin therapy showed many deficient levels of vitamins in the bodies of the senior subjects. After one year of vitamin therapy, blood samples demonstrated significant uniform improvement in all areas of nutritional measures. Even in apparently healthy older persons there are dangerous deficiencies of essential nutrients are improved by base-line doses. Megadoses of vitamin and mineral supplements were not required to effect a change.

All people, older people included, find it impossible to alter the food habits of a lifetime. Nutrition teaching and better eating patterns are the keys to better health. Major chronic diseases such as diabetes, cancer, and respiratory and heart disease are diet related and respond to alterations in particular food groups. Disease promotion through a positive, proactive, contemporary approach to nutrition is the new century approach to high level wellness.

FITNESS COUNTS

For every member of the family, from the pregnant woman to the old-old man, physical fitness is vital to health promotion, a longer life and higher levels of cognitive and affective functioning.

A less active and more dependent approach to life places the older adult at particular risk for depression and physical dependency. Bodybuilding, with weight training and aerobic exercise, is most effective and recommended even into the late 90s. Weight bearing activities reduce the risk of hypertension, diabetes, osteoporosis, osteoarthritis, heart disease, and the fatigue of muscle atrophy and weakness.

Even centenarians improve their physical capabilities with exercise. Weight-bearing exercises hold calcium in the bone and increase the fluid in intervertebral disks diminishing the loss of height, improve the blood supply to muscles, improve tissue elasticity, and muscle mass and strength. Within two weeks of moderate exercise benefits can be measured. Vitality, energy, and strength contribute to feelings of greater well-being.

VACCINATION FOR THE YOUNG AND OLD

Vaccination schedules for the young members of a family are well-known. Immunizations are crucial for the older adult also. Men 65 years or older have a greater risk than older women of dying from pneumonia. Impaired physical and mental ability increases this risk. Pneumonia and influenza vaccines serve as important health resources for the elderly, especially older disabled men.

The influenza vaccination not only prevents viral infection, but if taken each year by the over 60-year-old family members, it can enhance the immune system so that it is just as functional as a younger person's immune system. The vaccine energizes the immune system's helper T-cells' memory for many different flu strains. The cells are remains from the initial response to the virus when the body originally responded to it as a younger person. T-cells circulate in the blood and still have a memory of the virus, though that memory is not sharp. Vaccination assists the aging immune system to remember the virus and protective T-cells can respond more quickly and with more robust energy when that virus reenters the body. Consequently, the pneumonia or the flu is of shorter duration and with far less serious presenting symptoms and sequeli.

ATTITUDE, SELF-CONCEPT, AND HIGH-LEVEL WELLNESS

The new century family monitors its unique attitude toward itself and its approach to living. Attitudes count. Older family members who attribute deteriorating health status to the aging process have a far greater, up to 78 percent greater, risk of dying. When faced with problems in typical activities of daily living, older adults who identified only with a negative self-concept regarding aging have a far greater risk of dying that those adults who could give specific, self-affirming, non-aging reasons for the limitations. When perceived powerlessness over physical and emotional problems is attributed to old age, the individual becomes resigned to believing that it is not treatable or preventable and delays or omits getting care. The individual gives up and becomes less self-directed and powerful.

Wellness promotion is not merely good nutrition or fitness or rest. Wellness is essentially a mental approach to life. Optimism actually increases the potential for a full lifespan. It has a placebo effect. An optimistic outlook on life is a vital component of a high level of wellness life.

MAKING WHOOPEE

Well older adults have active sex lives. In fact, in the new century five generational family, the older adults are very likely to be having the most satisfactory sex life.

Just as teen-agers cannot believe that their parents ever have a sexual life, many 50-year-old adults are surprised at the activity of the healthy adults in their 60s, 70s, and 80s. It is a myth, and only a myth, that older people are not sexual. Older people have active sexual lives. Until recently, sex researchers have not studied the 60- to 90-year-old age group. It was assumed that not much sex was going on, so it was not studied carefully. The classic Kinsey report on male sexuality devoted only a few passing comments on sex after 60. There is now mounting evidence that the older members of families are not at all celibate. Women in particular remain multiorgasmic. What is needed is generally good health, a partner, or masturbation and privacy.

When the general health is good, sexual activity in adults over 60 is very active. Four out of five women reported themselves as sexually active, and 65 percent at age 70 and over. Ninety-one percent of men reported that they were still sexually active at 60 and 79 percent after 70 years old.

Poor health and widow/widowerhood diminish sexual desire and sexual availability. However, more than half of all seniors desire sexual orgasm well into their 90s if a partner or masturbation opportunities are available.

Levels of older adult sexual satisfaction is greater than a younger person might predict. Older persons who reported that sex and sexual satisfaction was important in their 40s still found satisfaction at the same and even better than in younger years. Such data have serious implications for persons in their middle-age to take pleasure in sexual activities.

In what is reported in the research, it is clear that like heterosexual couples, male homosexuals report sexually active lives after 60. There are no studies of older lesbians.

Normal aging alters some sexual responses for both the male and the female. When men produce less testosterone, reducing the sexual desire and decreased sensitivity with diminished peripheral neuron sensory fibers. Longer and more direct stimulation of the penis is needed. This may not be a bad thing vis à vis intimacy. At 18 to 30 years old, sexual intercourse can be a quick response requiring little attention. However, older men require more stimulation in order to keep an erection, and even in the absence of ejaculation, orgasm is possible. As with any age group, sexual fantasy continues and increased potency is possible with a desirable partner.

The drop in estrogen level in women accompanies the proportional inverse action of the natural testosterone in her body previously overshadowed by the estrogen. Many women experience an increase in libido. Hormone replacement therapy overrides this effect of the testosterone and the status quo is maintained. The use of estrogen creams avoids discomfort during intercourse and improves the diminished vaginal lubrication and vaginal elasticity. Women can remain multiorgasmic well into their 90s.

A classic example of sexuality in the older adult is seen on nursing units in a long-term facility or community senior housing unit. Admit a male to a unit including women and there is a marked increase in the women's hygiene and dressing behaviors. Female flirting and attention-getting behaviors become flagrant. Gender awareness in all of us remains strong even into the ninth decade.

The sexual needs and potential of the family's older members should be recognized, understood, and respected. Social freedom for outward displays of affection, such as hugging, kissing, and cuddling is fundamental. Negative sanctions by younger generations in the family are values best left behind as archaic.

Partners over 60 years of age have an opportunity to enjoy biological and emotional synchrony unparalleled at any other age. The male's tendency to reach orgasm more slowly is well suited to the longer time a woman needs to become aroused. Birth control hassles are finished, children no longer need their immediate attention, and both partners have the leisure time to enjoy the physical intimacy.

Prescription and over the counter drugs taken by older persons for hypertension, anxiety, and digestive and infectious conditions can dampen libido and cause impotency. Pharmaceutical companies, aware of the impact, are developing second- and third-generation drugs with a target of decreasing these life changing side effects.

However, and it is a big however, sexual function is dependent on a state of good, or at least, adequate health. After a heart attack, the fear of death is associated with sexual activity. Will it cause too much of a strain on the heart, will it raise the blood pressure? Physicians recommend that sex can be resumed when the person can tolerate an exercise stress test level heart rate of 120. In the presence of angina, nitroglycerin shortly before making love eases the potential for chest pain.

The new century promises enormous growth in surgical techniques such as laser and microscope mincroscopic instruments. These high-tech devices spare tissue trauma and decrease the damage to neurons. Today, far fewer colostomies and mastectomies will be needed and changes in body image mutilation are history only.

MONEY MATTERS

Whether living in their own home or in senior housing agencies, 97 percent of older families have as a major source of income some federal assistance (Social Security, Medicare). Medicare itself will account for 18 percent of the federal budget by 2020. The financial aspects of caring for the elder members of the family are matched with the emotional aspects in importance and priority. When parents age, their role in the family unit is altered. It is predicted that all generations of the family will be expected to contribute financially to the care of the elders.

COMMUNICATION AND DECISION MAKING

Successful multigenerational family communications stress reviewing options for living ten to twenty years before decisions must be made. Experts recommend that discussions be held openly and that each generation be a part of the decision-making process.

For example, on a par of importance to availability to health care is the decision regarding retirement living. The new, more mobile culture offers many more alternatives to retirement housing.

Reverse-mortgage loans convert the equity in the family home into a monthly income. This innovative program means the family members will be able to maintain their standard of living and not be plunged into house-rich but cash-poor poverty. Little or no money is left for the children, and this can be a source of intergenerational conflict.

Unknown ten years ago, now thousands of reverse mortgages are given each year. Reverse mortgages provide a steady income to elderly homeowners.

A reverse mortgage is a loan that does not have to be repaid until the property is sold. Additional equity, above the amount loaned, belongs to the home-owner. Federal support for this innovation is seen in such programs as the Federal Housing Administration and the Federal National Mortgage Association (Fannie Mae) mortgages.

The seniors, having worked hard for their homes, let the homes be a source of investment income and yet can remain in the home or condominium. Credit lines or lump-sum payments are additional payment options for those who have only an occasional or one time only cash advance.

MORE MONEY

Over the next 15 years, $50 trillion will change hands from one generation to the next, as the baby boomer generation prepares to retire. Never before in human history has so much capital been moved across so many families. This transfer of capital is in the form of stocks, bonds, and mutual funds in retirement accounts and in the equity of the homes bought and paid for by the working and middle classes in America. It is the beginning of this transfer that is one cause of the enormous rise in the New York Stock Exchange to over 8500 points in the last few years.

Intergenerational planning facilitates decisions regarding lifestyle, place of residence, sources of income, health care, and financial planning for all members during schooling, working, and retirement periods. Planning insures the proper protection of the family's monetary base and enables the family to remain flexible to market changes. Family assets are protected.

WORK AND LONGEVITY

Anticipating adult family member's needs for the new century includes aspects of the work world and added life expectancy. Work opportunity strategies target education for a full scope of jobs, promoting health maintenance behaviors, developing new interests and abilities, diminishing stressors related to work and adjusting work, assignments to accommodate changes in aging.

Bismark set retirement at 65 years old in the early 1900s. The new century will have later specific retirement age. The interests, needs, and stamina of the worker will determine career paths. For the middle- and older-aged person, continued work will mean a new partnership with the company and mutual planning.

Having five careers in a lifetime becomes the norm. As a result, career development must incorporate variables such as: broader career options, with ongoing on-the-job education; attention to self-presentation; maintenance of workplace safety; continued professional and personal development to keep current work skills and friendship networks; and appropriate workload management for the older worker.

Overall, the longer-lived U.S. population results in substantial increases in the numbers of older workers. Their valued critical skills and expertise will be critical to businesses aiming to meet higher production targets. Challenged to learn new skills and to communicate those knowledges and skills through new technological developments, seniors' cognitive and psychomotor competencies continue to grow.

Increased worker longevity is an artifact of continued job satisfaction and organizational commitments are the variables inherent in worker longevity. Older workers are more committed to their employers than younger workers. Workforce downsizing, therefore, has dramatic emotional implications for the middle-aged and older worker.

Studies predict that most workers will consider employment in smaller companies. Small business owners encounter difficulties in staffing, finding, and retaining competent employees. Small business owners face an increasing need to improve productivity and company commitment. Given the high correlation of older workers' organizational commitment and the need for small companies for such a characteristic, it is predicted that older workers will be more likely to hold positions in smaller companies.

The U.S. Small Business Administration projects some new century trends. Changing demographics (the aging of the population, fewer numbers of younger persons) makes the senior worker quite desirable. The older worker's favorable attitude toward work, years of experience, and high level of commitment and job satisfaction makes this category of worker very employable.

MARKETING TRENDS

Advertising firms now understand that many popular perceptions of older adults stereotypes are not based on reality. These misperceptions are perpetuated in the attitudes of both the young and the old. Advertisers are improving in their success in portraying older consumers in a positive and representative way. Multigenerational families now are a common part of both television and print ads. The new century trends in advertising will include far more families interacting in an intergenerational manner, demonstrating the family roles each generation plays in the development of the other.

REALITY

The twenty-first century dawns on a thriving population with a life span potential of 100 years of age. Widespread health standards and the application of research will enable these new century persons to have a full and fulfilling living experience.

REFERENCES

Abeles, R. (1994). *Springer series on life styles and issues in aging.* New York: Springer Publications.

Butler, R. N. (1994). *Historical perspective on aging and the quality of life.* In *Aging and the quality of life.* New York: Saunders Publications

Curry, M. (1998). Vitamins for the elderly: Disease prevention through the use of micronutrient. *Medical World News, 33*(12), 32.

Gutfeld, G. & Rao, L. (1992). Healthy aging. *Prevention. 44*(12), 10.

Smith, P. and Hoy, F. (1992, October). Job satisfaction and commitment of older workers in small businesses. *Journal of Small Business Management, 30*(4), 106.

Smolowe, J. (1990, November 5). To grandma's house we go: More and more senior citizens are missing out on retirement while they serve as surrogate parents for their grandchildren. *Time*, p. 86.

Chapter 30

Our New Century Leaders: A Culture of Learning

KATHERINE MACKEN

This chapter is a peek into the new century. It is a conversation between a young teacher, the granddaughter of Irish immigrants, in her first year of teaching high school English. This transcript shares with us her interactions with two teen-aged boys. These two new students are in the United States from Brazil barely one month. As these three human beings struggle to adjust to each other and to the demands of a high school curriculum, we get a sense of the twenty-first century: its culture, its curriculum, and its people. We are viewing our new citizens and leaders.

Kathy Macken, teacher:

The following is a transcription of a conversation I had with two of my students from Brazil—Ricki and Orlando. At the time of the interview, the students had been in the United States for approximately twenty-three days. They are attending a high school in Georgia and have a schedule of standard high school classes.

Ricki is more English-proficient than Orlando, as reflected in the following transcription. Ricki was in my American Literature class for the first three weeks of school. Fortunately, I was able to have him transferred into my Applied Communications course (more hands-on, slower paced course with less writing).

The conversation begins:

Kathy:	First tell me—what is going on in your classes? How are they working out?
Ricki:	How am I? I am better now. Since I have changed class, I am better . . . I wasn't . . . able last class . . . now, I feel better.
Kathy:	Changing to the Applied Communications class made it better for you?
Ricki:	I am able to understand more.
Kathy:	How about you Orlando, what class were you in?
Orlando:	Ah, English.
Kathy:	O.K. What English class? College prep?
Orlando:	Yes, with Ms. Cannon.
Ricki:	What is he doing?
Kathy:	He's in the same class as you. . . . Did you two know each other when you got here?
Ricki:	Ah, we met in the plane.
Kathy:	So are you from the same place in Brazil?
Ricki:	No. . . . I live here, he lives in Arkansas!
Kathy:	Oh, Arkansas, comparing the distance?
Ricki:	. . . it's far.
Kathy:	How was it when you first came here? What kind of expectations did you have? What did you expect when you came here? Was it different?
Ricki:	. . . yea, a little different because . . . my expect . . . my expectations before I came was worse.

	. . . I am liking the way . . . the way of the things . . . the things are happening.
Kathy (to Orlando):	What did you think would happen?
Orlando:	I don't know.
Ricki:	Different . . . a lot of work . . . we . . . people are different . . . the way of the people are different.
Kathy:	Are the teachers different?
Ricki:	No, no . . . the teachers are the same.
Kathy:	Okay, how are the students different?
Ricki:	I thought . . . my cousin came to the United States and he said . . . some people in the United States are very . . . cold . . . very cold.
Kathy:	Really? Have you found that people here are cold?
Ricki:	Ahh . . .
Kathy:	Some people?
Ricki:	Some . . . some people are *abuhabdo* . . .
Kathy:	What does that mean?
Ricki:	It's *[gives a sign for a snob]*.
Kathy:	Oh, snobby! Do you think they are judging you because you're from somewhere else?
Ricki:	. . . and some people say "Hello" . . . and later you pass and he looks like he don't know you.
Kathy:	Have you two become better friends now at all?
Ricki:	Uh?
Kathy:	Do you talk more now, or no?
Ricki:	Yea.
Kathy:	You do . . . You both speak Portuguese right?
Orlando and Ricki:	Yes.
Kathy:	You've been here how long, four weeks?
Ricki:	No, two weeks . . . no twenty-three days.
Kathy:	So, has the language gotten easier?
Ricki:	What English? . . . I do not think so . . . it is hard . . . because I am here two weeks . . . twenty-three days . . . and I am . . . I am . . . going well . . . If American goes to Brazil . . . he will have more difficulty than me.
Kathy:	Do you ever talk to your friends at home (in Brazil)?
Ricki:	Yes.
Kathy (to Orlando):	Do you?
Orlando:	Yes.
Kathy:	How often?
Ricki:	. . . miss . . . miss and miss and miss.
Kathy:	So you miss them?

Ricki:	Uh, uh . . . Some time I thought what . . . I was . . . I was . . . would doing in Brazil . . . like this time I thought . . . what are . . . what are was I would doing . . . would doing?
Kathy:	What you would be doing?
Ricki:	Yes, in Brazil.

Orlando and Ricki converse in Portuguese.

Kathy:	Now I know how you feel! Okay . . .
Ricki:	That's it.
Orlando:	Ricki . . .
Ricki:	I am adapting . . . adapting . . . adapted.
Orlando:	Yea, Ricki . . .
Kathy:	Oh, you have adapted?
Orlando:	Ricki has . . . *[talks to Ricki]* . . . more facility . . . he knows better English . . . my English . . .
Kathy:	It's not as . . . *nods* . . . I think it will get better though, when you are here a whole year. Don't you?
Orlando:	Yea.
Kathy:	So think about this time three months from now. I think it will be a lot better.

They laugh.

Ricki:	Ah, three months!
Orlando:	I hope so!
Ricki:	The most . . . began . . . speaking English better . . . three months . . . but we came to the United States knowing . . . the first three months would be . . . hard.
Kathy:	Right.
Ricki:	Five months sounds wonderful.
Kathy:	Yea, it's adjusting, the language, meeting new friends, being away from home . . .
Kathy:	Orlando, what did you think, when you were in Brazil before you came to America. What did you think it would be like?
Orlando:	. . . ahh . . . *[talks to Ricki]* . . . for a while not . . . not.
Kathy:	So you didn't think about it.
Orlando:	Yes . . . but I don't know it!!
Kathy:	So you didn't know . . . you didn't know what to expect?
Orlando:	Yes.

Kathy:	You didn't know what to expect . . . .but it is different?
Orlando:	Yes.
Kathy:	How are the students different? I don't understand . . . they're colder?
Ricki:	Yes, much . . .
Kathy:	How about when you are in class school? Is school different?
Orlando and Ricki:	Yes!
Ricki:	In Brazil the teacher moves (from class to class) and the students stay.
Kathy:	Oh, really?
Ricki:	Yes, very better.
Kathy:	Why did you like that better?
Ricki:	It's less work . . . the teachers . . . it isn't confusing . . . it's more simple.
Kathy:	It's harder for the teachers! I wouldn't want to do that! . . . that's good though . . . so are things going OK? You are doing OK in your classes?
Ricki:	In Brazil, the teacher don't have class, like you do . . . this class, is it all you? Is Brazil harder?
Kathy:	Yes, this is my classroom, I'm here all day . . . What about the learning? Is Brazil harder?
Ricki:	Yes, harder, very harder.
Kathy:	Really.
Orlando and Ricki:	Yea, yea.
Kathy:	More work?
Ricki:	. . . it's . . . cause in Brazil . . . for graduate it's different for graduate here . . . cause in Brazil you have to make-up test . . . a lot of test . . . chemistry . . . a lot of subjects . . . with thousands of peoples . . . there is only . . . there is thousands peoples . . . only a hundred pass . . .
Kathy:	So what happens if you don't pass?
Ricki:	You try again . . . and you try, try, try, if you fail you try again . . . and it's hard . . . like algebra, I learned it . . . I have learned it in Brazil.
Kathy:	So you're in Algebra? What grade of students are you with?
Ricki:	Here? Twelfth grade.
Kathy:	You are with twelfth grade students and you're doing Algebra? Is it senior math?
Ricki:	. . . in Brazil, I was eleventh grade . . .
Kathy:	When I was in high school, my junior year, I took trig and I took calculus my senior year . . .

	but I didn't go to school here . . . I went to school in Atlanta . . . Have you been to Atlanta yet? The city?
Orlando:	Yea, yea . . . I went . . . game . . . Braves . . .
Kathy:	Oh, yea that's good! Okay, will you let me know if there's anything you need? You can still come on Wednesday . . . I can help you with work or whatever . . . because even just to talk—conversation—is good . . . and then if you have problems like we swapped you out of this class and put you in the other class . . . American Lit to Applied Communication.
Ricki:	. . . now this subject is . . . much better . . .
Kathy:	This class (Applied Communication) is better than American Lit?
Ricki:	I'm doing better here.
Kathy:	So you let me know what you need.
Orlando:	What is the PSAT *(They have just received a newsletter for their parents informing them about the PSAT.)*.
Kathy:	Do you know what the SATs are?
Orlando:	No.
Kathy:	You may want to talk to Mrs. Welch about it because if you are planning to go to college you will have to prepare for the SAT. The SAT is a test to get into college and the PSAT prepares you for the SATs. You will want to go to college won't you?
Orlando and Ricki:	No!!
Kathy:	Why not?
Orlando:	The colleges in America is very . . . very . . . very . . . complicated . . . many papers . . . in Brazil . . . need money! Just money!
Kathy:	It's like that a lot here too!!!

[And they laugh together.]

This is the end of the conversation. And it is the beginning of the new world and the new century for these three young adults. As they grow and learn, change and plan, each moves deeper into the American culture. Each brings the beauty, strengths, and traditions from their families' cultural heritage. Each is an American.

Part Four

ADMINISTRATIVE METAPHORS: TUGBOATS REVISITED

Chapter 31

Of Tugboats, Transitions, and Time

MARY L. KELLEY AND
VIRGINIA M. FITZSIMONS

CHANGE

As we closed the *Culture of Learning*, the last chapter addressed our perspectives regarding moving large educational agencies into new ways of thinking, teaching, and measuring program outcomes. The analogy of tugboats seemed most appropriate. We had grown up in port cities, and we understood how these mighty little movers know where they are going and how to get there. The amount of energy expended and exchanged by these little tugboats enable huge vessels to move sleekly into narrow port slips.

Our project groups comprised four distinct educational units, and each school had its own mission, experiences, organization, communication network, norms, and personnel. Our administrators, faculty, students, and patients represented then, and now, the vast diversity of persons from around the world representing thirty-two countries. We serve one of the highest number of minority student populations in New Jersey.

As administrative "tugboats," we have witnessed the change over time: changes in attitudes, changes in understanding, and changes in responses. People change, transitions are made, and new organizational cultures are developed and each aspect takes considerable time. While the norm for sociological change is said to be thirty years, we believe that the press of today's pace of living and complexity of lifestyles is compressing that usual slower pace into a more rapid evolution.

SCHOLARLINESS AS COMPASS

Initial attempts to address personnel diversity topics left our groups filled with considerable dissonance. Discussions aimed at reducing prejudice actually increased feelings of misunderstanding and insensitivity. An analysis indicated that the discussions centered on ethnic cultures only and it appeared that each person used his or her own individual experience, that is an N of 1, as the depth of experience and attitude development. There were some rather heated discussions centered on which ethnic group suffered more or had been subject to historic prejudice. What was missing centered on both a lack of breadth and depth of knowledge regarding the concept of culture itself and an authentic understanding of similarities and differences in human experiences. A scholarly approach was chosen in order that we might seek rational rather than emotional solutions.

A scholar defines his/her terms. The disciplines of sociology and anthropology define a culture as a group of persons who share similar beliefs, attitudes, and behaviors. Values are behavioral patterns that consistently reoccurred in an individual or group.

Even this first step of defining our terms was very helpful. It moved our discussions from the affective to the cognitive domain. Whereas feelings are neither right nor wrong they just are, thinking connotes data collection and problem solving. Inherent in this process is the weighing of facts and evidence. There can be demonstrable validity to various positions and reliability measurements in reoccurring situations.

Our agencies decided to adopt the common anthropological understanding of cultures and subcultures and so we expanded our view of cultures beyond merely ethnicity to encompass also subgroups such as age-related (e.g., school-age, adolescence, middle-age, elderly), socioeconomic class, chronic disease, and religion, as common examples. Group discussions moved from particular ethnic group experiences to the complexity of reality. Each person actually is invested in any number of subcultures, each subculture giving that person role responsibilities, perspectives on various issues, and a broad range of skills, beliefs, and behaviors.

This was a breakthrough for us as we struggled to address the needs of students and faculty from widely diverse ethnic groups. There are differences in understanding world perspectives. However, the culture constant to all was the mission of the health care agency, the educational program and the needs of the individual patients that we serve. The common denominator became the development of proficiency in the professional culture of nursing with all of the attendant beliefs, attitudes, and behaviors implicit in safe and effective nursing practice. Ethnic differences blur when patient therapeutics, protection, and comfort are the agreed to priorities. Communication goals are clarified when posed in terms of professional expectations and outcomes. Our Transcultural Leadership Continuum project demonstrated that even in the presence of considerable ethnic cultural differences in faculty-student groups, over time, faculty insight increases and professional acculturation occurs in the student.

INNOCENT TUGBOATS

Knowing the desired destination is one thing, getting there safely is another matter entirely. As tugboats never know *exactly* how they will move a ship (there are tides, winds, currents, and water traffic), we also had a sense of having many unknown factors. There is an advantage to being innocent rather than "knowing it all." Innocence offers an openness and appreciation of variables, a certain wonderment at the multitudinous interactions that occur on so many levels when human beings come face to face. Problem solving becomes the routine and innovation becomes the norm because new paths are being sought.

SO WHAT HAS HAPPENED?

When a group of people achieves consensus regarding a perspective and acts from that perspective on a consistent basis that perspective (i.e., belief or philosophy) is described as having been "institutionalized." It becomes the standard way of thinking and behaving; it becomes part of the institutional culture.

Understanding Cultural Diversity is a demonstration of the institutionalization of the concept of culture as it exists now in our various organizations. We defined and experienced the lived definition of culture; we actualized the concept in our curriculum on all levels; and we have translated these beliefs into action in the communities that we serve.

Continued scholarliness demands that we document both the process and the product of our collective activities. In offering these anecdotes to our colleagues, we strive to stimulate serious discourse regarding this crucial topic. Certainly, understanding cultural differences might be *the* global imperative as we face the next century.

Trial and error learning is very inefficient. Our six-year qualitative and quantitative assessment of the impact of culture in health care education is offered to you, our colleagues, so that further growth can be achieved from where we stand now.

OK, NOW IT IS FULL SPEED AHEAD

Our recommendation as we complete this project is that you should enjoy the trip. Address *Culture* from a scholarly perspective. Scan all disciplines for varied perspectives. Use the literature of the academy, as well as from commerce. Always include philosophy: It is the history of human thought that scholars hang out in the library. Keep the literature close at hand.

Understand that the *Curriculum* is the vehicle (the ship as long as we are using a tugboat metaphor) which moves a person intellectually from here to there. If learning is a change in behavior more or less consistent over time, then change is impossible without education. Education addresses the human being in all domains: affective, cognitive, and psychomotor. Sufficient learning gives evidence of value complexes and skill competency.

The Ivory Towers is a symbol of an ancient time and it has no place in the new century. Scholarship and learning are best measured when acted out in all communities. *Community* describes culture in its broad definition and it exemplifies the beauty of diversity in its fullest measure.

Exploration, research, education, and practice matures the nurse and provides the community with a health planner who understands quality care, innovation, and diversity. Within our agencies, much learning has occurred and continues to occur. Changes in the norms and values have stirred up the waters and altered the form of the systems. Some days the change was very difficult. Most days, however, changes were growth producing and effective.

Change occurred—especially for the tugboats.